THE PAST IN QUESTION

THE PAST IN QUESTION

MODERN MACEDONIA AND THE
UNCERTAINTIES OF NATION

Keith Brown

PRINCETON UNIVERSITY PRESS   PRINCETON AND OXFORD

Library of Congress Cataloging-in-Publication Data

Brown, Keith, 1964–
The past in question : modern Macedonia and the uncertainties of
nation / Keith Brown.
p. cm.
Includes bibliographical references and index.
ISBN 0-691-09994-4 — ISBN 0-691-09995-2 (pbk.)
1. Macedonia—History—1878–1912. 2. Kruševo (Kruševo,
Macedonia)—History. 3. Macedonia—History—Uprising of
1903. 4. Nationalism—Macedonia—History. I. Title.

DR2214 .B76 2003
949.76′01—dc21
2002074873

British Library Cataloging-in-Publication Data is available

This book has been composed in Times Roman

Printed on acid-free paper. ∞

www.pupress.princeton.edu

Printed in the United States of America

1 3 5 7 9 10 8 6 4 2

TO THE MEMORY OF

C. M. Bennett and Chloe Brown

AND THEIR STORIES

Contents

List of Figures and Tables

Preface

I CAME TO THE MODERN Balkans by way of ancient Greece and Rome. As an undergraduate, I was offered the option of studying the golden age of Athens and the birth of the Roman Empire, but chose instead to focus on the murkier period in between. The sources were more fragmentary and the personalities less well scripted: Pericles and Julius Caesar were replaced by more elusive characters like Queen Teuta of Illyria and Blossius of Cumae, who operated between the worlds of declining Greece and ascendant Rome. Alexander of Macedon had created this Hellenistic world by defeating the city-states of Greece and then marching eastward with a significant proportion of his kingdom's adult male population, never to return. Scholarly debates over his intentions, desires, and his sense of self—as conqueror, liberator, or explorer, and as Greek, king, or god—constituted my initiation into historiography, where texts are not all that they seem.

When I first encountered the aphorism, "The Balkans produce more history than they can consume locally," I was curious to know who said it, when, and why. The British humorist H. H. Munro, or Saki, gave the world the phrase, which has been recycled, literally or metaphorically, by a good number of writers on southeast Europe. Yet two aspects have been lost. First, accuracy. Saki wrote, "The people of Crete unfortunately make more history than they can consume locally" (Davis 1977:239). Second, and perhaps more significantly, context. Saki put the phrase, ancestor of today's sound bites, in the mouth of a fictional politician, Arlington Stringham, whose penchant for such bad verbal jokes drives his wife to suicide (ibid.). Even if the character intended it as a last word, Saki did not. The short stories that he wrote from his experience in Ottoman Macedonia in the early 1900s are striking not so much for what they tell us about the region, as for the picture he paints of different European types and their reactions to events there. His characters include the vividly imagined armchair analyst, Luitpold Wolkenstein, struggling to come to terms with newspaper accounts of Ottoman defeat in the Balkan Wars of 1912–13; and the more stylized Wanderer and Merchant who discuss those same wars at cross-purposes, with the Wanderer lamenting what will be lost, as all that is "familiar and outlandish" in the region will lose its relevance and be consigned to "the cupboard of the yesterdays" (1919:597).

Stringham is another such figure, and his phrase—memorable although misremembered—conveyed his particular attitude, rather than a gnomic truth. But that is what happens with texts. All but the shortest and tautest— and perhaps even these—can be sliced and diced to serve their readers' pleasure or dissatisfaction. Contexts are ignored or suppressed and ironies lost or discovered, as throwaway lines are infused with deep significance and careful nuances overlooked. And when readers collate and relay what they have gleaned, they create new texts from the fragments of old, so that—as here—Saki's words may find themselves alongside references to the works of Arrian and Plutarch on the life of Alexander. If one accepts the scholarly extension of the concept of text to embrace anything that can be read for meaning—nods, winks, blinks, landscapes, dances, and rituals, to name but a few—then the weight of sources becomes at once immense and over-whelming, and the virtues of distillation compelling.

Texts about, from, and in Macedonia—whatever its extent—illustrate this phenomenon particularly well. I started reading them in earnest in 1990 when I was learning to be an anthropologist, and paid my first extended visit to what was then Yugoslavia. With Marko Živković, I traveled south from cosmopolitan Belgrade to Skopje by train, with his mother's admonitions to be careful "down there" ringing in my ears. After a short stay in remote, dreamy Ohrid, Marko returned home. I headed on to Thessaloniki, and en route I took my first trip to Kruševo, the town at the heart of this book, where in 1903 members of a revolutionary movement challenged the Otto-man Empire. The bus labored up the long, steep, twisting road and left me in an empty town square. My goal was to visit a monument I had seen in Yugoslav tourist brochures in Belgrade, and which I knew was on a hill above the town. But in the early afternoon heat there was no one to ask for directions, and from the empty square all roads and paths led upward. To locate my quarry, I reasoned, I needed first to find a point from which I could see it, and so I wandered through quiet, narrow cobbled paths flanked by houses of brick and stone, in search of a vantage point from which I could grasp the town's geography. Eventually I emerged into open space on a hillside and saw the monument on the horizon in a wholly different direc-tion from the square, separated from me by a sea of slate and tile roofs with no obvious direct route of access. I did eventually wend my way there, to find the doors locked and the site deserted. The only sign of recent human presence was a single plastic-wrapped wreath propped up in an odd, circular courtyard.

That was before the war, when it was still just possible, at least in Mac-edonia, to think of the "Yugoslav experiment" as a success story which had permitted a sense of national pride to flourish while putting an end to irre-dentist activism. Two years later, in April 1992, when Slovenia and Croatia were no longer part of Yugoslavia, I returned to Belgrade and thence to Skopje to undertake research on the role of history in identity formation. My companions this time, on a Yugoslav Airlines flight that no one could definitively classify as international or domestic, were Bosnians, and the old woman sitting next to me tried to convey to me some of her recent experiences, throwing her arms up and out to depict the explosions she had seen. Within a month Yugoslav Airlines had been grounded by international sanctions. As the crisis continued, violence in Bosnia escalated, driving hundreds of thousands of people into exile. The future of the Republic of Macedonia remained uncertain, under threat from the possible expansion of war and also from Greece's opposition to its statehood.

I lived in the Republic of Macedonia for eighteen months, spending most of my time in Skopje, Ohrid, and Kruševo, but also conducting some research in Greece. Whereas in Greece I was often treated with suspicion or distrust—Macedonian comes more readily to my tongue than Greek—I found in the Republic of Macedonia a broad interest in and enthusiasm for my project. I moved almost entirely in Macedonian and Vlah circles, and had little contact with members of the Albanian, Turkish, or Romani communities. In a country facing ongoing crisis and a society that had been part of Eastern Europe for fifty years, I argued and wrangled with people over their interpretations of the past. I challenged established historians and asked people of all ages to explain inconsistencies in the versions of history they told me. An overwhelming majority responded to this provocative attitude without rancor; some turned my questions deftly. I found myself trying to come to terms with the history of Northern Ireland, place of my birth, and that province's ongoing status as a historically contingent and "artificial" entity, site of a protracted "ethnic" struggle.

That extended residence in the region is at the heart of this book. Since then I have made further research visits to northern Greece and the Republic of Macedonia, returning in 1994, 1997, 1999, 2000, 2001, and 2002. I have also continued my anthropological education by teaching diverse groups of students in Britain and the United States, and supplemented it in working with archaeologists, historians, sociologists, and political scientists at four institutions. Through all this time I have continued to track down and read existing work on Macedonian history, much of it obscure or overlooked, and to try to monitor ongoing developments in the republic. As a result, this book has gone through several lives since I finished my doctorate in 1995. Those who read the dissertation will find echoes and resonances here, but only two chapters that they will immediately recognize.

In the course of this extended project I have incurred multiple and overlapping debts. Direct support for my graduate work was provided by the Fulbright Commission and by the Century Fund of the Division of the Social Sciences at the University of Chicago, which also provided support for archival research in 1994 through an Overseas Dissertation Research Fellowship. My primary fieldwork was funded by a Yugoslav Government Grant for Academic, Cultural and Scientific Co-operation and by the Social Science Research Council, which also provided write-up support. I have been able to continue to work on the project through support from other sources, including the Elisabeth Barker Fund of the British Academy, and two grants from East European Studies at the Woodrow Wilson International Center for Scholars in Washington, D.C. The four institutions where I have been based since 1995 have extended crucial assistance: Bowdoin College through its Faculty Research Fund, the Department of Anthropology at the University of Wales, Lampeter through travel funds and research leave, and the United States Institute of Peace and the Thomas J. Watson Institute through generous provision of research assistance.

In the Republic of Macedonia, I was based at the Institute for National History in Skopje. I could not have wished for a better mentor than Jovan Donev, and appreciated the welcome extended to me by others, especially Toše Čepreganov, Vasil Joteski, Stojan Kiselinovski, Marija Pandevska, and by Jana and Dimče at the library. The National Archives staff were helpful, especially Zoran Todorovski, Kire, and Tomo. I owe a substantial debt of gratitude to the individuals and families who helped make my Skopje neighborhood feel like a home away from home. Foremost among many are Peggy and Graham Reid; Biljana, Eli, and the extended Bejkov family, and Alex, Pero, and Kita Bicevski. Much of the comfort I felt I owed to my first Macedonian teacher, Evica Konečni.

In Kruševo, a host of people plied me with hospitality and stories of the town's past. Pačo and Sonja were ever-kind hosts, Duza a tireless guide, and *Paljoka*, under Gjoko's management, the only bar I have frequented where someone always knew my name. I learned the history of families with ancient names, including Kardula, Naḱa, Hasani, Hadži-Lega, Peti, Gabel, Telesku, and Topuza, and more recent arrivals, like Blagaduša and Soleski, from people too numerous to thank by name. Viktorija Peti, Jane Andreevski and Kočo "Brada" all offered vital perspectives and resources from their official positions. I owe a special debt to Hristu Hristoski, and hope that he sees here some traces of what he taught me. Others to whom I am especially grateful include, among the younger generation, Miki, Zoki, Nula, Zdravko, Saška, Kire, Snežana, Pandorče, Ljubica, Danica, and Joana. For their animated storytelling I will always remember Janko and Fanica Mele, Šula Gabel, Trifun Naḱa, Dico Stefanovski, Mira Angelkoska, Manu Kostoski, Ljuba Sekula, Domenika, and Pavlina Važarova.

My intellectual debts go back to college days, where I was lucky in my teachers. Nicholas Purcell was inspiring and relentless in his enthusiasm for new and creative approaches to ancient history, and when he farmed me out, it was to Simon Hornblower and Michael Whitby, equally engaging and demanding in their fields. Gordon Baker and Peter Hacker oversaw my mangling of themes Wittgensteinian with remarkable good humor, and would I hope do likewise here.

At the University of Chicago, the distinguished faculty of the Department of Anthropology treated me with unfailing civility. Again I was fortunate in my committee members. As chair, Marshall Sahlins was consistently supportive, and always saw the forest. George Stocking evoked Gertrude Stein's bon mot, "There is no there there," to challenge the notion of an ethnography of nationalism, while James Fernandez pressed the case for greater groundedness: both perspectives shaped the project significantly. John Comaroff, my advisor from day one, found time and energy to shape my course of study, respond immediately to every letter from the field, read every draft, and offer input that always made the written product better. Victor Friedman, encyclopedic and passionate on matters Macedonian, has remained closely engaged with the book's evolution. Raymond T. Smith, Nancy Munn, Michael Silverstein, Susan Gal, and Seteney Shami all influenced and encouraged me more than perhaps they realized. I also incurred debts outside the department, especially to Kostas Kazazis in matters Balkan and linguistic, and to Larry McEnerney for apprenticing me in the craft of academic writing.

If Marko Živković first introduced me to the idea that we were not simply graduate students, but already colleagues, others in my cohort helped him put the idea into practice. At various stages in writing up Barron Pineda, Shao Jing, Tom Lyon, Chris Oliver, Rob Albro, Tony Berkeley, and Margaret Bender provided support and reactions. As regional specializations took shape, Europeanists of West, East, and the spaces in between (or slightly awry) took over, including Daphne Berdahl, Dominic Boyer, Matti Bunzl, Eve Darian-Smith, Krisztina Fehervary, Janet Morford, Frank Romagosa, Paul Silverstein, and more than any, David Sutton. Other friends contributed energy, humor, and creative stimulus, especially Wilhelm Werthern, Meg Armstrong, Sarah Krive, Josh Marston, Paul Ryer, and Gabe Lyon.

Beyond Chicago, I was quickly made to feel a part of a community of scholars interested in the region. Michael Herzfeld and Anastasia Karakasidou at the outset extended their encouragement and support. So too did Loring Danforth, who has continued to advocate and demonstrate engaged humanism. I also thank Jane Cowan, Giorgos Agelopoulos, Vasilis Gounaris, Piero Vereni, Laurie Kain Hart, Rozita Dimova, Maria Todorova, Susan Woodward, Peter Loizos, Charles Stewart, David Rheubottom, Misha Glenny, Ilka Thiessen, Greg Mihailidis, Dimitris Theodossopoulos, David Sutton, Shelley Stephenson, Lina Sistani, and Savetka Pecevska for their various readings and reactions. I am grateful also to Mary Murrell and Sarah Green at Princeton University Press and Marg Sumner for their patience and hard work, and to the reviewers, anonymous and known.

Over the years I have presented pieces of this work at East European Studies at the Woodrow Wilson Center, St. Andrews, and Kings College London, and I am grateful to Kristin Hunter, Nigel Rapport, Mario Aguilar, and Philip Carabott for their invitations and their own responses to my work.

I thank also the staff of various libraries, especially the Library of Congress, the National Library of Wales in Aberystwyth, the John D. Rockefeller Library at Brown University, and the institution of inter-library lending. Joel Halpern was generous in sharing access to the photographs and fieldnotes of Joseph Obrebski, and the staff at special collections and archives in the W.E.B. DuBois Library at the University of Massachusetts Amherst were similarly accommodating.

I have also been lucky in the institutions where I have worked. At Bowdoin College, colleagues and students, especially Scott McEachern, Lelia DeAndrade, and Marianne Mahaffey, helped me work through particular issues. At the University of Wales I was fortunate in my department chair, Fiona Bowie, and the opportunity for interdisciplinary dialogue, in which Dimitris Theodossopoulos, Patrick Finney, Margaret Kenna, Yannis Hamilakis, and Ian Cook all contributed. At the United States Institute of Peace, Joseph Klaits and Sally Blair created space for me to work on this project, and Becky Kilhefner provided invaluable research assistance, while Tone Bringa and Burcu Akan offered inspiration and expertise on different aspects of the Yugoslav context. And at Brown, David Kertzer, David Abramson, Ana Devic, Dominique Arel, and Deborah Healey have made the Politics, Culture and Identity program a forum for the central issues of the book. Milena Ivanova, Jaideep Singh, Marta Radman Livaja, and Lindsay Richardson provided research assistance, and technical support from Amy Langlais and David Reville was invaluable.

Lastly, I thank my family. Shelley Stephenson has lived with this book as long as I have, and now, in the spirit of Raymond Chandler, I hope it may warm her hands. My parents have been relentlessly supportive of, if sometimes puzzled by, my life-choices. I dedicate this book to people they were lucky enough to know better than I did, C. M. Bennett and Chloe Brown— my mother's father and my father's mother, respectively. He was a headmaster and prolific author of textbooks, school stories, and pirate yarns conveying a certain set of attitudes to sportsmanship, pluck, and the white man's burden that could easily be stereotyped as British neo-colonial. She was born in the segregated American south to Russian parents, moved to England with her family, trained in music, and then became, in her description, a seaside landlady. In their lives and the stories they have left behind, they taught me to see nation, race, and ethnicity as anything but permanent.

Notes on Transliteration and Pronunciation

The main language of research for this book was Macedonian, a Slavic language that was codified only after 1944. Macedonian is normally written in the Macedonian Cyrillic script:

А, а	a			Н, н	n	
Б, б	b			Њ, њ	nj	(as in venue)
В, в	v			О, о	o	
Г, г	g			П, п	p	
Д, д	d			Р, р	r	
Ѓ, ѓ	ǵ, gj	gj (as in argue)		С, с	s	
Е, е	e			Т, т	t	
Ж, ж	ž	zh (as in measure)		Ќ, ќ	ḱ	(as in cute)
З, з	z			У, у	u	
Ѕ, ѕ	dz	(as in lids)		Ф, ф	f	
И, и	I			Х, х	h	(as in hello)
Ј, ј	j	y (as in year)		Ц, ц	c	ts (as in bits)
К, к	k			Ч, ч	č	ch (as in chat)
Л, л	l			Џ, џ	dž	(as in grudge)
Љ, љ	lj	(as in value)		Ш, ш	š	sh (as in shoe)
М, м	m					

Standard literary Macedonian is based on dialects spoken around Veles, Prilep, and Bitola. Standard Macedonian is spoken throughout the modern Republic of Macedonia, although different regions have their own specific dialects (one of the best known being the Strumica dialect). Kruševo's dialect has some distinctive lexical items from nonstandard Macedonian, Greek, and Serbian influences. Nonstandard Macedonian is also spoken in northwestern Greece, southeastern Bulgaria, and some villages in Albania and Kosovo.

Chapter 4 draws heavily on two Greek texts. The system of transliteration is based on that used by Charles Stewart in _Demons and the Devil_ (Princeton University Press 1991). The accent systems from the texts, polytonic or monotonic, are preserved:

Αα	a		Ββ	v	Γγ	g
Δδ	d		Εε	e	Ζζ	z
Ηη	i		Θθ	th	Ιι	I
Κκ	k		Λλ	l	Μμ	m
Νν	n		Ξξ	x	Οο	o

Ππ	p	Ρρ	r	Σσ	s
Ττ	t	Υυ	y	Φφ	ph
Χχ	h	Ψψ	ps	Ωω	o

Digraphs αι, ει, οι, ου are transliterated as ai, ei, oi, ou.

For the limited Bulgarian in this book, a similar system is used as for Macedonian.

In the one Vlah word, v′rg′ri, ′ stands for the mid-central vowel or schwa.

CHAPTER ONE

Introduction

THIS BOOK EXAMINES the relationship between national history, identity, and politics in the disputed territory of Macedonia. It focuses on events in a town in the modern Republic of Macedonia, and on the different ways in which, at different points of the twentieth century, different communities described or analyzed those events. The goal of this book is to uncover the processes whereby contrasting world views take shape and can be embraced or rejected, emplaced or overturned. The narratives woven around this particular town demonstrate in a variety of ways the importance of volition and contingency in the making of the present. At the same time, they rely upon idioms of the taken-for-granted—the things one cannot help—for explanatory efficacy. Benedict Anderson's bon mot regarding the magic of nationalism—that it turns chance into destiny (1991:12)—is thus a central concern of the book, which seeks to explain how that alchemy was wrought in a spatially circumscribed and culturally specific context.

The immediate setting for much of the book is the town of Kruševo, in the southwest of the Republic of Macedonia. For most of the year, Kruševo presents itself as a provincial backwater. High in the hills, away from the major transit routes, and boasting no great industrial or agricultural resources, it has a population of around three thousand, including the Republic's largest concentration of Vlahs, a Romance-speaking minority. Yet every year since 1944, at the beginning of August, the town has shaken off its sleepy aura as political élites of the Macedonian government have journeyed to the town to deliver tributes and speeches. They have brought in their wake a host of ordinary citizens and the gaze of the Republic. Some have left more permanent traces on the town's landscape including new roads, public buildings, and monuments. Begun when the Republic of Macedonia was part of new Federal Yugoslavia, the annual national pilgrimage to Kruševo continued after the country declared its sovereignty in 1991.

The yearly prominence of Kruševo stems from the enduring symbolic significance attached to events there at the beginning of the twentieth century, when Ottoman Turkish rule extended west to the Adriatic coast and north to the border of Montenegro. In the course of a widespread anti-Ottoman uprising on St. Elijah's Day, or Ilinden, on 2 August 1903, Kruševo was the largest urban center held by the revolutionary movement. After the creation of a federal Yugoslavia in 1944, Ilinden 1903 came to be established as a pivotal moment in Macedonian history, and celebrated as a holiday each year. Its enduring significance was affirmed through a broad variety of official commemorative practices, including pension schemes and the construction of memorials. The town of Kruševo came to be marked as the uprising's symbolic epicenter, and its residents took pride in national recognition of their town's distinctive heritage.

Kruševo's history thus constituted a key symbolic resource in the establishment of Macedonian national identity in the twentieth century. The salience of this one town's past was heightened by the doubts, debates, and disputes that swirled around so much else to do with Macedonian distinctiveness. Today's members of the Macedonian people, or *narod*, speak a Slavic language codified only after 1944 with fewer than 2 million native-speakers and a slender body of literature. Macedonians are, for the most part, members of an Orthodox Church whose authority was established by a socialist political régime in 1968. Their kin-terms, household structures, marriage practices, and vernacular culture all closely resemble those of neighboring groups. They are descended from people who were called, and at times called themselves, Serbs or Bulgarians. Those who challenge the authenticity of Macedonian national identity—and as this book will show, there are many—use these facts to assert that its components are all newly minted, forged, borrowed, or even stolen from the Republic's neighbors. In such a hostile climate, the idea of a local uprising in 1903 gave adherents of the new national cause a welcome sense of historical depth and popular unity.

Kruševo was additionally celebrated for the activities of its defenders during the Ilinden Uprising. After driving out the Turkish garrison, they set up a provisional government in which townspeople and village representatives were to participate, and distributed a written proclamation of their peaceful state-building intentions. This short period of self-government has come to be known as the Kruševo Republic and the document its leaders distributed as the Kruševo Manifesto. It has come to stand as a unique piece of constructive and indigenous political activism in modern Macedonian history, prior to 1944. Before that, the last period in which a régime had its capital within the borders of the modern republic was the eleventh century, when King Samuil reigned in the lakeside town of Ohrid.[1] Kruševo's self-government, though, was short-lived: within two weeks, Ottoman forces converged on the town. A few determined rebels tried to stage a defense, most famously on a hill outside the town named Mečkin Kamen (Bear's Rock), but they were quickly overwhelmed by superior numbers. Then came the reprisals against civilians. After an extended bombardment, regular and irregular troops sacked the town. Houses were burned and looted, women raped, and a number of townspeople arrested and later imprisoned for their alleged involvement.

These additional facets of Kruševo's role in the Ilinden Uprising of 1903 contribute further to a straightforward narrative, familiar from studies of modern nationalism. The town, which remained inhabited, stands as a vital link to a past time of collective liberation struggle, political vision, and self-sacrifice. It is a place where a glorious history is enshrined and where, now, the living descendants of those who fought, suffered, and died enjoy the redemption that is their legacy. It appears to constitute, then, a multi-faceted national "memory-space" of the generic type explored extensively in the volumes edited by Pierre Nora (Nora [ed.] 1997). For modern Macedonia, Kruševo 1903 combines something of the flavor of France's Bastille, England's Runnymede, and the United States' Alamo. Yet also important is the imperial reach of the enemy in the past, the image of glorious defeat still unavenged, and the continuing vulnerability of a small country in the present. In this regard, Macedonia's Kruševo, and especially the battle of Mečkin Kamen, can perhaps be yoked more closely to Greece's Messolonghi, Serbia's Kosovo field, or even Israel's Masada in its emotive power.[2]

For scholars of "straight" nationalism, then, Ilinden 1903 and Kruševo appear easy to read. But what I aim to do in this book is illuminate the twists in the tale as it has been told and re-told in the course of one hundred years since the Uprising, and to explore the other meanings and messages that Kruševo 1903 has been made to carry. Some of these fall easily into the discourse of competing nationalisms: in Bulgaria and Greece, for example, in part as a result of political interests, Kruševo's history not only differs from, but is fundamentally incompatible with, the core, national narrative outlined above. In both cases the alternative vision owes much to the influence of refugees or exiles from Kruševo, driven out at various points during the twentieth century and denied return by subsequent régimes. Historical accounts produced by displaced residents of the town have been mobilized as part of wider political disputes in the region, especially over borders and the existence of minority populations. They feed a zero-sum mentality with respect to historical interpretation, in which the truth-status of any one account is predicated on the falsehood of its rivals.

Attention to other readings of Kruševo's past, and the traces they have left, yields evidence of more complex interactions between different visions. From 1944 until 1991, for example, when the Republic of Macedonia was part of the Socialist Federal Republic of Yugoslavia (SFRY), events of the past were not only commemorated for their national quality, they also represented steps in a process that led toward a socialist present and future. Historians, politicians, and artists re-cast the heroes of Ilinden as forebears of the pan-Yugoslav Partisan movement of 1941–44: the Kruševo Republic was thus celebrated as not only Macedonian, but as socialist and Yugoslav; and the egalitarian ideals of its leaders were highlighted. One product of this synthetic process was the memorial built in the town in 1974 and depicted in

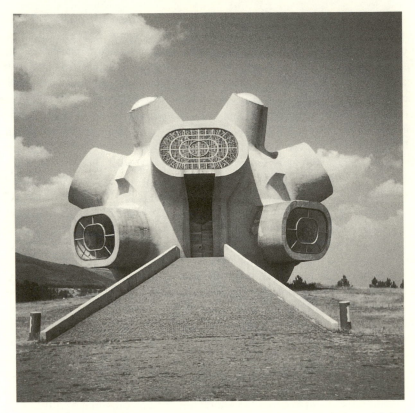

Figure 1: The Ilinden *Spomenik* in Kruševo, designed by Jordan and Iskra Grabul. Opened 1974.

figure 1. Designed by a husband and wife team who considered themselves socialist and humanist in outlook, its futuristic style aspired to validate an idea of the Macedonian past and present as a part of the new and forward-looking Yugoslavia.

At the local level, the narrative of Macedonian national activism is further complicated by the unique demographic composition of Kruševo. As noted earlier, the town is home to a sizeable community of Vlahs, a group distinguished primarily by their Romance language, known as Vlah or Arumanian, which is akin to Romanian. Among minority groups in the Republic of Macedonia as a whole, those identifying themselves as Vlahs are outnumbered by Serbs, Roms, Turks, and Albanians. Kruševo is known, first and foremost, as a Vlah town, as it has been since the peak of its prosperity in the nineteenth century. Even after the upheavals of 1903, the Balkan Wars of 1912–13, and the First World War, which displaced populations and redrew frontiers, Kruševo's community retained its distinctiveness. Unlike their rural Albanian- and Slav-speaking neighbors, who were generally agriculturalists or manual laborers, Vlah townspeople mostly earned their livelihood from commerce, stock-keeping, and artisan trades. Until the mid-twentieth century, they mostly married within their own community; it was only with the state's collectivization project and the confiscation of property from wealthier townsfolk that these patterns changed.

Even in the 1990s some older residents preferred to speak Vlah rather than Macedonian: most had grown up in households where Vlah was the first language. They and many others recalled the linguistic virtuosity of fathers and grandfathers who had known Turkish, Albanian, Arabic, and Greek, and spoke with nostalgia of ways of life swept away by the Yugoslav revolution. Across the generations, people often emphasized their families' mercantile activities and business connections, in which all these languages came into play. They also insisted that Kruševo's former wealth had worked against the town after World War II, when they had suffered disproportionately from the requisitions made by Tito's partisans in the alleged interest of "brotherhood and unity," and when some of the town's old mansions were bulldozed and replaced by ugly, functionalist modern buildings.

In the Yugoslav era, then, some segments of the town community could be taken as opponents—if not by passionate conviction then at least in their everyday practices—of the socialist ideals that were so insistently declared as motivating those who founded the Republic of Kruševo and proclaimed the Kruševo Manifesto in 1903. The oral record poses its own challenge to the simple linkage of the town's history with the forward march of the Macedonian nation or the Yugoslav project. A more tangible measure of civic dissatisfaction with the state-sponsored mode of historical recall was a construction project undertaken by townspeople and completed in 1983. In response to the abstract 1974 monument, they commissioned their own figurative memorial to speak more directly to events of 1903. The alternative memory-space thus produced on the battlefield of Mečkin Kamen has at its center a single bronze statue of a young man hurling a rock, depicted in figure 2.

These alternative tales of Kruševo's past might be labeled the "socialist" and the "localist" versions. They are of interest in themselves, but most compelling to me is the interaction that they have with one another, and with the nationalist narrative with which I began. Much of the literature on twentieth-century Macedonia emphasizes the adversarial mode in which its history is recounted, as Greek, Bulgarian, Serbian, and (more recently) Macedonian and Albanian perspectives on the Macedonian Question laid claim to exclusive authority. The disputes over the history of Macedonia in the nineteenth and twentieth centuries could be said to fit Deborah Tannen's model of an "argument culture," whereby it is taken for granted that attacking other

Figure 2: The memorial statue on Mečkin Kamen, designed by Dimo Todorovski. Unveiled 1983.

points of view—often after first simplifying them almost beyond recognition—is the best way to pursue truth (Tannen 1998). The overriding impression is of a chaotic and cacophonous mix of aggressive voices, each seeking to shout down its rivals, in the hope of having the last word.

Around 1903 Kruševo, though, that image does not do justice to the ways in which the story of the past has been told. A more apt parallel might be an ongoing conversation of the type described by Kenneth Burke (1957:55–56), and re-employed to illustrate processual analysis by Renato Rosaldo

(1993:104). Burke imagines a heated parlor conversation that has gone on longer than any of its individual participants. Newcomers try to grasp the general drift and then take up the debate: they might bring new insights, repeat points already familiar to some listeners, or revive arguments that appeared to have ended long ago. When they enter this conversation, perhaps, they may have strongly distinctive and individual voices, and insist on being heard at all times. Over time, though, participants may realize that there is greater texture and richness in reciprocal exchange than in dogged pursuit of individual agendas.

A Burkean conversation over events in Kruševo in 1903 has been going on for a century, with some additional features. In the weaving together of "nationalist," "socialist," and "localist" versions of the past exiles, residents, historians, ideologues, and creative artists have all played their part. They have not, though, entered the debate as equals. Some have worn badges of authority or brought with them intimidating entourages. Some have said their piece and left quickly, entertaining no reply; others have bided their time, waiting perhaps for a rival to leave before speaking. Some have listened intently to others, learning what is important to them and then using this knowledge to flatter, cajole, or persuade; others, so anxious not to forget their own points, or particularly struck by someone else's, have continuously repeated them under their breath, and thus missed much of the talk going on around them. Some have taken steps to make their contributions more enduring, by leaving behind texts or other objects, so that the room is now cluttered with them.

Taking this image as its starting point, this book attempts to analyze the nature of nationalism, socialism, and localism as they marched together, if not in step, through the twentieth-century history of Kruševo. It thus offers, at one level, a record of the conversation where alternative stories have been generated, and influenced one another. That record is, of course, partial. I have chosen to emphasize those moments and phases where apparent contradictions emerge, and the ways in which those contradictions are resolved so that the conversation can continue. Two such moments were the creation and the destruction of socialist Yugoslavia, in the 1940s and the 1990s respectively.

As citizens of the new People's Republic of Macedonia in 1944, Kruševo's Vlah residents, with their memories of wealth built on private enterprise, were neither straightforwardly "Macedonian" nor wholeheartedly "socialist." Yet their town steered its way to a central place in the new national history, as the Ilinden Uprising and the Kruševo Manifesto were invested with socialist and Yugoslav significance. In 1991, when the Republic of Macedonia declared its sovereignty and renounced the socialist and Yugoslav path, Kruševo maintained its leading role in the country's commemorative practices. The Kruševo Manifesto and the 1974 Kruševo monument, both crafted as repositories of socialist meaning, were swiftly re-branded as national treasures. At both moments, it appears that Kruševo's residents successfully jettisoned an inappropriate past, and renegotiated relationships between their town, Macedonia, Yugoslavia, and the wider world. How they did so, and how issues of memory, politics, and identity were implicated at each turn, are two questions driving this book's line of inquiry.

A final word should be added regarding the full implications of taking the discussion of Macedonia's past as a Burkean conversation. Not only have today's participants in the conversation forgotten when it began; they have no idea how it will end. And so attempts to stand outside the debate, trace its contours, and reach firm conclusions are exercises in futility. The conversation continues and, willy-nilly, the would-be overview is subsumed by it and transformed into nothing more or less than one more contribution. From that point, the fate of any contribution is uncertain.

The so-called Macedonian Question, discussed in chapter 2, is of long standing and has taken dramatic turns in recent years. In the 1990s, when a neighboring country used its political and economic weight against the new Republic, the question's Greek dimensions were prominent; in 2001, when the Republic was challenged by an armed insurgency on its territory, the issue of Albanian self-determination rose to the top of the agenda. Such rapid and substantial shifts in the topics of conversation, driven by the use of force in the world, would appear to make this study, focused on the Vlah town of Kruševo and its past, irrelevant. But one hundred years ago, Kruševo was in flames. Ten years later residents were still taking revenge against their neighbors, and ten years after that people were still fleeing to avoid state repression. Since then, the town's community has worked to make of a violent, fractious past a richly textured sense of historical identity. I offer this study, then, in the hope that in some conversation, somewhere, people may still care to see how it was done.

METHODS AND SOURCES: THE ETHNOGRAPHY OF HISTORY

The foregoing introduction makes clear, I hope, the agenda of this book. The focus on the conversation over the past represents an attempt to come to terms with the particular challenges posed by studying Kruševo. It is a Macedonian town and a Vlah town, but its present inhabitants do not necessarily agree on what those terms mean. It used to be a Greek town and a Bulgarian town, and the written traces left from that time indicate that those claims too were vigorously debated. In this regard, the town could be said to resemble many communities in the southern Balkans where broader disputes over territory and identity get translated into local idioms. While living in the town in 1993, I heard a Vlah in his thirties criticize "Vlah extremists" for creating potential friction by insisting on using Vlah in mixed company. An old man, sweeping cigarette butts in a church courtyard, blamed incomers from the villages—whom he called Macedonian, not Vlah—for polluting the town. Such comments, I am sure, are still being made today.

What further distinguishes Kruševo is the bewildering amount of attention its past has already received from people outside the town, especially since 1944. The events of 1903 in the town, in particular, have already generated millions of words, mostly in Macedonian and Bulgarian, but also in Ottoman and modern Turkish, Greek, Vlah, Romanian, Serbo-Croatian, French, German, Russian, and English. Some were written as events were in progress, others within days or months, others generations later. People wrote to try to evoke or to explain, to compare with other events or to correct misleading analogies, to inspire or to appease, to fulfill expectations or to gain advantage. Journalists, politicians, scholars, poets, playwrights, novelists, bureaucrats, pension-seekers, students, and schoolchildren at various distances from the town and the time have all told the story of Kruševo in 1903.

When I arrived in Skopje in April 1992 to undertake field research on Kruševo's place in Macedonian national history, I had little sense of the mass of words that had already accumulated. My hosts at the Institute for National History, professional historians all, sent me to the library, insisting that there was little point in visiting Kruševo itself until I had mastered the literature. Anxious to maintain rapport, I obeyed. Surely, I thought, knowledge of previous work will be invaluable, and for several months I spent my days filling index cards with references. Outside working hours I socialized with Macedonians my own age and dealt with the day-to-day business of living in a state of uncertainty regarding the future. Many of the people I met considered my interest in Kruševo absurd and antiquated, and urged me to devote my energy to investigating both the everyday life of Macedonians and the political games being played at the international level. The present, they said, was a time of historical significance.

Wading through the turgid prose of Yugoslav-trained historians, I began to see the merits of this suggestion. I was rescued by the intervention of a community with a different perspective on gaining access to the past: the archivists. I was already waiting for permission to access the papers of Jordan Grabul, the designer of the first Ilinden monument. Now a friendly archivist reminded my mentor of the existence of the Ilinden dossier, a fund of more than two thousand pension applications from a program implemented in the years between 1948 and 1953. Each folder included a short autobiography written by applicants to support their case. There, he said, rather than in the stale and ideologically inflected works of the socialist period, I would find the kind of local voices and unworked material that I could use. I was persuaded, and permission swiftly granted. For three months in 1993 and then during a shorter return visit in 2000, I entered a different world. In the dimly lit reading room, where my companions were often people looking for evidence to support their claims to property that was now to be restored to its pre-Yugoslav owners, I followed old men and women, most of whom had long since died, down the paths of memory to the Ottoman period.

Still, the voices of friends and acquaintances in Skopje nagged at me to pay attention to what was happening around me. One event that helped me to decide my direction was the establishment of a new Macedonian currency, the *denar*, and the issue of new temporary banknotes, or *bonovi*, on 27 April 1992. Kruševo's Ilinden monument was depicted on notes of every denomination, from ten *denari* up to ten thousand. When the bonovi were replaced by new notes in 1993, the monument's image was used for the watermark of authenticity, to distinguish real Macedonian banknotes from forgeries. In the crucial period of transition, a little piece of Kruševo was distributed throughout the Republic, passing through many hands every day within a newly circumscribed national territory. Surely, I thought, and said to those who scoffed at my interest in the town, this meant something?

Even as I felt comforted every time I paid for anything, I had the sense that back at the University of Chicago, my disciplinary elders would not consider an image on banknotes as sufficient evidence of the relevance of Kruševo's past in modern Macedonia. And so to the mild disapproval of historians, archivists, and friends in Skopje, I finally moved to Kruševo early in 1993. After some initial reserve—prompted in part by fears that I had adopted Skopjean ways and attitudes—I found my project embraced by a community with a strong sense of connection to the past and of the vagaries of history. I was taken by children and adults to meet parents and grandparents who remained close to their families, living or sometimes still working in neighborhoods they had known and played a part in maintaining over half a century or more. In small workshops around the town center and in a variety of homes, some small and simply furnished, others offering glimpses of faded grandeur, a generation of old men and women shared stories of their lives in Kruševo. They spoke of courtship and marriage, working conditions, leisure pursuits, and class and ethnic relations, and their different accounts painted an image of a community where the memory-traces of events of 1903 were far more diverse and divisive than any national narrative might suggest.

My stay in Kruševo culminated in my observation of and participation in preparations for the festivities of Ilinden 1993 when the Republic's President, Kiro Gligorov, made his way to the town to pay homage to the town's place in history. His speech, wide coverage in the Macedonian media, and an academic symposium added to the store of words on the events of Kruševo 1903. I made my own first contribution, in a co-authored paper that brashly treated the legacy of Ilinden as an example of the "invention of tradition" made famous by Hobsbawm and Ranger (1983). The paper was published in a weekly news magazine, and sparked angry or disappointed responses from professional historians and some residents of Kruševo. Gently or ungently, they suggested that I should undertake further research.

This book combines that research—historical, archival, and ethnographic—from before and after August 1993. As I have read, listened, and reflected further, I have grown less certain of the course and meaning of the events of 1903, and more aware of the great, unmasterable mountain of data that exists. Its contours change each day: even as another pensioner passes away in Kruševo, someone somewhere is adding another chapter to the town's history. The changing political and economic circumstances of the Republic of Macedonia only compound the problem, as concerns over the future drive people to trawl the past for proofs of status, or lessons that suit their needs in the present.

In this context, to attempt a single, synthetic narrative of what happened in Kruševo in 1903 would mislead the reader as to the book's agenda. I remain passionately interested in the details of town life in Ottoman Macedonia as the world of empires came to an end, and people learned to negotiate the demands of nation-states as best they could. I also find compelling the architecture and appeal of a revolutionary movement that inspired more than 20,000 men and women to work in concert for a cause. Writing an account of either, or ideally of both, remains a goal for the future, but one that I feel ill-prepared to undertake: I feel I don't know enough. This feeling leads me to try to learn more, by reading what others wrote at the time or have written since, and by trying to draw on whatever oral tradition remains. This in turn brings me up against broader questions about how individuals and communities create and communicate knowledge about the past. These are the broader questions that this book seeks to address.

By way of an introduction to events in Kruševo in 1903, then, I present here a sample of the sources on which the book draws. They provide three accounts of events in Kruševo written for different audiences, at different times, and uncovered in the course of different phases of research. I have selected these three for two principal reasons. First, they are products of three different "textual communities," as discussed in chapter 3. Each reveals something of the priorities that guided members of these communities in their writing, priorities that are explored more closely elsewhere in this book. Second, and more importantly, each account was produced wholly independently of the others. They therefore neither offer contradictory interpretations, as is the case where two interpretive communities are in close contact but disagree over key points of fact, nor are they simple repetitions of one another, as is the case where one community closely succeeds or overlaps with another. Instead they reveal different points of emphasis, and each adds something to the reader's understanding of events and their multiple meanings.

The first account is taken from a book published in 1906 by Frederick

Moore. Age twenty-nine in 1903, he was, as far as I know, the only European journalist to have visited Kruševo soon after the Uprising. His work and attitude are treated in chapter 3; the following description appears in chapter XIV of *The Balkan Trail*, entitled "On the Trail of the Turk" (1906:265–71):

This is the story of Krushevo:

Just after midnight on the morning of August 2, 1903 (this was the day that the general rising was proclaimed), a rattle of rifles and a prolonged hurrahing broke the quiet of the peaceful mountain town. Some three hundred insurgents under "Peto-the-Vlach" [Pitu Guli] and four other leaders had taken the town by surprise. In the little rock-built caserne were fifteen Turkish soldiers, and in the Konak [government building] and private houses were ten or twelve Turkish officials and their families and a few soldiers. The inhabitants of the town were Christians, Wallachians (or Vlachs) in the majority, and a colony of Bulgarians. The soldiers were able to grab their rifles and escape from the caserne, killing eight or more insurgents as they fled. The night was black, and a steep, rocky slope behind the building lent an easy exit. The Turkish telegraph clerk likewise escaped; but the Government officials who were in the town died to a man. The kaimakam [governor] was absent on a visit to Monastir [modern Bitola].

After surrounding the Government buildings to prevent the escape of the Turks, the insurgents broke into the shops and appropriated all the petroleum they could find. This they pumped on the Konak, the caserne, and the telegraph offices with the municipal fire-pump, and applied the torch. From fifteen to twenty Turkish soldiers and officials were shot down as they emerged from the flames; but the women and children were given safe escort to a Vlach house, with the exception of one woman and a girl who fell as they came out. Whether they were shot by accident or intention on the part of a committaji [member of revolutionary organization] is not known.

The flames spread, and a dozen private houses and stores were burned with the Turkish buildings. Some, I believe, were set afire to light the Konak and make certain the death of the Turks.

In the morning the insurgents placed red flags about the town and formed a provisional Government, appointing a commission of the inhabitants, consisting of two Bulgarians and three Wallachians, 'to provide for the needs of the day and current affairs.' Without instruction all the inhabitants discarded the fez.

Three chiefs of bands were appointed, a military commission, whose duties were drastic. Their first act was to condemn to death two ardent Patriarchists who had spied for the Turks on the organization and preparations of the local committee for insurrection in the district. The men were made prisoners, taken into the woods, and slain.

On the first day the insurgents made a house-to-house visitation and requested donations of food, and later required any lead that could be molded into rifle balls. More bands arrived and a number of Bulgarians and Wallachs of the town joined the insurgent ranks, altogether augmenting the number to over six hundred. They began at once to raise fortifications, and made two wooden cannon such as had been used in the Bulgarian revolt of the 'seventies. The cannon were worthless, and were left to the Turks, who brought one of them into Monastir.

On the second day the men of the town who possessed wealth were summoned to appear before the military commission. A list had been made (the information given by members of the organization whose homes were in Krushevo) of the standing and approximate wealth of each "notable" in the community. As these headmen appeared before the triumvirate a sum in proportion to his means was demanded from each. No protests and no pleading affected the commission, and in every instance the money was forthcoming within the time limit. More than 1,000 l. [lira, Turkish pounds] was collected in this way, and in exchange was given printed paper money, redeemable at the liberation of Macedonia.

On the following Sunday the priests of both the Greek and the Bulgarian churches were ordered to hold a requiem for the repose of the souls of the committajis who had fallen in the capture of Krushevo. Detachments of insurgents were present, in arms, and gave the service a strange military tone. Open-air meetings were held on the same day, and the people were addressed by the leaders of the bands.

During the ten days of the insurgent occupation sentinels and patrols saw to the order and tranquility of the town, and no cruelties were committed. Business, however, was paralyzed. The market place was closed and provisions diminished; and attempts to introduce flour failed, the emissaries to the neighboring village being stopped by Turkish soldiers and bashi-bazouks [irregular troops], who were gathering about the town.

The news of the capture of Krushevo reached Monastir August 3, but not until nine days later was an attempt made to retake the place. By that time three thousand soldiers, with eighteen cannon, had been assembled. About the town, also, were three or four thousand bashi-bazouks [irregulars or paramilitaries] from Turkish villages in the neighborhood.

When the guns were in position on favorable heights above town, Bakhtiar Pasha, the commander of the troops, sent down a written message asking the insurgents to surrender. The insurgents refused, and an artillery fire was begun. Most of the insurgents then escaped through a thick wood which appeared to have been left open for them, but some took up favorable positions on the mountain roads leading into the town, others occupied barricaded buildings in the outskirts, and resisted the Turks for a while. Two of the leaders, Peto and Ivanoff, died fighting.

Peto-the-Vlach was a picturesque character. He was thirty-five years of age, a native of Krushevo. He had been fighting the Turks for seventeen years. He was made prisoner in 1886 and exiled to Asia Minor. But benefiting by one of the frequent general amnesties he returned to Macedonia, rejoined the insurrectionary movement, and led the organization of Krushevo and the neighboring district.

At a conference of the leaders immediately prior to the Turkish attack, Peto declared that he would never surrender his town back to the oppressor; the others could escape if they would, the Turks could not again enter Krushevo except over his dead body. With eighteen men who elected to die with him, he took up a position by the main road and held it for five hours. It is said that he shot himself with his last cartridge, rather than fall into the hands of the Turks.

The natives put on their fezzes again, and a delegation of notables bearing a white flag went out to the camp of Bakhtiar Pasha to surrender the town. On their way they were stopped by the soldiers and bashi-bazouks and made to empty their pockets. Further on more Turks, whose rapacity had been less satisfied, demanded the clothes and shoes they wore. Arriving at headquarters of the general, situated on an eminence from which there was a full view of the proceedings, the representative citizens, left with barely cloth to cover their loins, offered a protest along with the surrender. Bakhtiar had their clothes returned to them, and told them he could do nothing with "those bashi-bazouks"—though beside him sat Adam Aga, a notorious scoundrel of Prelip [Prilep], who had brought up the largest detachment of bashi-bazouks, and with whom, subsequently, Bakhtiar is said to have shared the proceeds of the loot.

The Turks entered the town in droves ready for their work, rushing, shouting, and shooting. The bashi-bazouks knew the town, its richest stores and wealthiest houses; they had dealt with the Vlachs on the market day for years. They knew that the Patriarchist church was the richest in Macedonia. The carving on the altar was particularly costly, and there were rich silk vestments and robes, silver candlesticks and Communion service, and fine bronze crosses. They went to this church first. Its doors were battered down in a mad rush, and in a few minutes it was stripped by the frenzied creatures to the very crucifixes. Then a barrel of oil was emptied into it and squirted upon its walls; the torch was applied and the first flames in the sack of Krushevo burst forth.

The Greek church was on the market place among the shops. The Turks who were not fortunate enough to get into the church went to work on the stores. Door after door was cut through with adzes, the shops rifled of their contents, and then ignited as the church had been. 203 shops and 366 private houses were pillaged and burned, and 600 others were simply rifled—because the petroleum gave out.

Some of the inhabitants escaped from their homes and fled into the woods. Turks outside the town met them and took from them any money or valuables they had, and good clothes were taken from their backs. A few pretty girls are said to have been carried off to the camps of the soldiers. But the Turks were mostly bent on loot. The people who remained in their homes were threatened with death unless they revealed where they had hidden their treasure. Infants were snatched from their mothers' breasts, held at arms length, and threatened with the sword.

The second account is that of Donka Budžakoska, and was submitted on 11 February 1952 as part of her application for an Ilinden pension. Aged twenty-three at the time of the Uprising and seventy-two when she applied for the pension, she gave the following account of her experience before and during 1903. She uses the old Orthodox calendar, in which Ilinden falls on 20 July rather than 2 August. Her account was typewritten, and is preserved in the National Archives, the Ilinden dossier, Box 5-B, Folder 52. The data from accounts such as these are used throughout the book, and explored in particular in chapter 6:

At the beginning of 1901 I entered the ranks of the Macedonian Revolutionary Organization, which worked for the liberation of Macedonia and the Macedonian people from Turkish enslavement. I took the oath of loyalty before Kosta Škodra, the teacher, Tirču Kare, the standard bearer, and Tome Nikle, all of Kruševo, and at first I was enrolled as a courier, to carry messages and weapons. I held that responsibility until the siege of Rakitnica in 1902, which stood for the liberation of the enslaved Macedonian people from the Turkish Ottoman Empire and Janissary violence.[3] In that siege died twelve souls: the prominent were Velko Vojvod, a teacher, Tirču Kare, the standard bearer, and Dame Nonev, a teacher, along with nine others, whose names I do not recall.

After the siege of Rakitnica, I was given another duty; to gather together from the villages and the town of Kruševo cartridges, tin and lead, and metal containers, and collect them in my house. After a great quantity of material had been collected, it was decided by the headquarters of Pitu Gule, with Dimitrija the director from Ohrid, Metodija Stojčev, the painter, and others, to establish in my house a foundry for bullets, and to send the bullets out to the bands.

Early on 20 July, around 2 o'clock in the morning, the foundry in my house began to operate and produce bullets. This work was organized under Vele Kalinoski, the watchmaker, who also made the casts for the bullets, and I kept the list of the distribution of the munitions we made. Our work finished before noon on 31 July.

On the same day, in the afternoon, Todor the Officer of Veles came last of all to the house and gave me a bag full of books from the whole Revolutionary Organization, to hide somewhere in a safe place. I had just finished covering the foundry with earth, and he told me to take shelter as soon as possible, as the Turks had reached the town. I took the bag and buried it in a dung heap by the Proja fountain, and after ten days, when we'd all reassembled and returned home after the burning of Kruševo, I told Kosta Škodra, the teacher, about the bag and he went to get it, and I don't know what happened to it after that.

After the Kruševo Uprising I got married and wasn't able to work for the Organization, and later on I moved to Bitola.

From the very beginning of 1901 until 31 July 1903, I worked tirelessly for the Popular Revolutionary Organization for liberation from the heavy yoke of the Turkish agrarian oppression, under which Macedonia and the Macedonian people had groaned for centuries. For that reason it was with a happy heart that I took the oath of loyalty. In the course of my activity, I lived through the first People's Republic, the famous Ilinden Republic of the Macedonian people, and their anger against centuries of oppression.

The third description of Kruševo 1903 is taken from an article by Gligor Todorovski in *Nova Makedonija*, Macedonia's newspaper of record. It was published on page 6 of issue 16711 in year 49 of publication, dated 31 July, 1 and 2 August 1993, under the title "The Ilinden events in Kruševo." The same edition included the reprinted text of the Kruševo Manifesto, articles on the wooden cannon of the insurgents mentioned by Moore and the international legal status of the Uprising, and an editorial entitled "From one Ilinden to another (1903–1993)." It represents, in broad terms, the "authorized" version of events which came to be shared in the Republic of Macedonia but which, as chapters 8 and 9 demonstrate, is challenged by local knowledge in Kruševo:

On the day of Ilinden, 2 August 1903, early in the morning hours, villagers, men and women, old and young, headed for the mountains at the call of the Uprising's leadership. Food had been stockpiled for the insurgents and the population: bakeries and kitchens were set up, as well as workshops to make munitions, and health centers. After the first assaults of the Uprising had driven out the Turkish government in various places, villagers returned to their homes and lived freely.

Once the bands were assembled, the insurgents began their attacks on various small towns. Among the first to be captured was Smilevo, where on the night before Ilinden 150 insurgents attacked and destroyed a garrison of 100 Turkish soldiers, and freed the village. In Kruševo meanwhile, before the attack was launched, the head of the revolutionary district, Nikola Karev, sent a proclamation to his colleagues in other districts and to the people of the Kruševo organization.

Brothers!

We hasten to congratulate you. Today the entire district of Kruševo along with the whole of Macedonia has risen in revolt with the cry— "Down with tyranny! Long live freedom and brotherhood between the Macedonian nationalities! The church bells are ringing out everywhere, people have gathered under the banner of freedom with heady joy. Maidens and brides are garlanding the heads and rifles of our fighters. All the Turks found on the roads or the villages have been captured and are being held. Everywhere there is singing, joy and celebration. We are burning with impatience, waiting for nightfall so that we can capture Kruševo and then, together with the whole people, cry out a triumphant Macedonian hurrah! God and justice are with us! Long live Macedonia!

[Signed]
Nikola Karev
Tome Niklev
Todor Hristov

At the same time, the Kruševo headquarters gave orders to open fire as a sign that the battle had begun to free Kruševo, and to begin ringing the bells of the town churches. After these first steps were taken, the battle began to take Kruševo that same night, and it was achieved with good speed. The town of Kruševo found itself completely in the hands of the insurgents. Next day, August 4, the headquarters came into the town, eagerly welcomed by Kruševo's happy inhabitants. There Nikola Karev, the commander, gave a speech before the assembled people of Kruševo, and thus declared the Republic. A council was chosen and at the same time a temporary government was formed, with representatives of the nationalities that lived in the town—Macedonians, Vlahs and Albanians.[4]

The election of the government in Kruševo marked the great success of the Macedonian revolutionaries and insurgents, and the realization of the goals of the Macedonian revolution. It was the first Republican government in the history of the Balkan peninsula and demonstrated the democratic and participatory character of the movement. The government included individuals responsible for internal affairs, supplies, finance, building, health and so forth. Other special tasks included mobilizing and arming people for self-defense, digging trenches and preparing munitions.

With a mind now to protect the town from Turkish soldiers and from *bashibazouks*, and to neutralize and perhaps win over the Muslim population around the town, the well-known Kruševo manifesto was issued. This momentous act was another declaration of the revolutionary, democratic and republican ideals of brotherhood and unity between peoples. Again, it demonstrated the core logic and principles of the revolutionary struggle of Macedonian insurgents, in its call for a common struggle against tyranny.

The first impact of the insurgents' attacks had freed many mountain villages and small towns. The success was due to the element of surprise, and the high morale and daring of the insurgents, who numbered 20,000 against 150,000 Turkish troops. But the enemy was dispersed in small garrisons, which permitted the insurgents to mobilize people, especially in mountain villages, and then mount attacks on larger towns. There was a real possibility that they could have taken Bitola, the *vilayet* [province] capital, where only three battalions of troops were stationed. However the high command, because of its delaying tactics, lost the initiative and permitted the enemy to strike back. The Turks used the tactic of burning villages and destroying the harvest to demoralize the peasantry, who were the largest part of the insurgent force. This tactic was ultimately successful.

One of their first counter-attacks was against Kruševo, which was strategically significant because of its central location, and size. Under the command of Bahtiar Pasha, a Turkish army of 20,000 soldiers was thrown against the town. The valiant defense and death of the *voivod* [military chief] Pitu Guli at Mečkin Kamen with his heroes, and the fighters at Sliva, did not help to save Kruševo, for the Turkish forces were too strong. Turkish artillery indiscriminately bombarded the town, causing great destruction and fire. The high command ordered the greater part of the insurgent force to evacuate, and they left for the mountains, leaving ninety-one of their number dead. The shelling also killed twenty women and six children, and completely destroyed 159 houses. After the recapture of the town, the Turkish soldiers received license to plunder and do all that they desired.

The three accounts given here together make the perhaps self-evident point: that writers have access to different kinds of information and also have different interests in writing. Moore provides an overview which includes many of the details noted by eyewitnesses—the initial ruthlessness of the insurgents, their setting up a form of temporary government, the overwhelming military response from the Ottoman authorities, a last stand led by a man named Peto, and the brutal sack of the town. Donka Budžakoska, writing fifty years later, offers a more intimate level of detail, and provides a glimpse into the Revolutionary Organization of which she and so many others were a part, making reference to her oath-taking, chains of leadership, and the existence of written records. She also links her story of the past to the national present. The newspaper account from 1993 takes that impulse a step further, offering not just an account of events from the past but also an explanation of their historical significance. In putting the story of Kruševo into the broader national context, though, the author selects only those details that fit with the overall theme of the piece, and uses somewhat abstract language.

The different dimensions of these three accounts will be taken up again in the main body of the book, when the focus returns to Kruševo. Chapter 2, though, moves away from Kruševo to put the Macedonian Question in context, focusing especially on its renewed significance within the Republic of Macedonia as Yugoslavia broke apart in 1991–92. Chapter 3 maintains the focus on foreign interest in Macedonia, but looks primarily at international media and diplomatic sources from the beginning of the twentieth century that describe the turbulence within the Ottoman Empire. These accounts have retained their authority for subsequent foreign commentary on the Balkans, ostensibly constituting a disinterested, accurate record against which to measure the truth-value of local claims over territory and population. Closer examination reveals the difficulties and preconceptions under which Western observers operated at the time, which compromised their own quest for objective accuracy in ways that continue to influence representations of the region and its people.

Chapter 4 offers an analysis of three accounts of events in Kruševo during Ilinden 1903, all written by eyewitnesses resident in the town; two were written by self-identified Greeks, the third by a self-identified Bulgarian. They reveal different interpretations of actions and motivations, and different approaches to understanding historical change. Since 1944, one has been largely overlooked, one championed in the Republic of Macedonia as objective and accurate, and one reprinted in Greece as a response to supposedly false Yugoslavian propaganda. The chapter seeks to move beyond the argument that national identity determines perspective to examine how and why these accounts differed originally, and have been used differently in subsequent debates over the past.

Chapter 5 examines how those who remained in Kruševo after Ilinden concerned themselves with the business of living under the rule of the first Yugoslavia, between the two world wars. Drawing primarily on oral historical material, it portrays a period in which the legacy of 1903 was divisive, serving as the basis of powerful economic and spatial fault-lines in the town's social fabric. The past played a particular role in the present, even as some residents sought to overcome its weight through the exercise of their personal and political will. The chapter concludes with a discussion of how this period was interpreted in retrospect, especially in socialist Yugoslavia, which promoted such different values.

Chapter 6 explores how the place of the past was defined in different channels of communication between Yugoslav Macedonian citizens and their new government in the 1950s. Pensions were offered to Ilinden veterans, while at the same village level agricultural collectives, called *zadrugas*, were set up. Collectivization served to reduce the status and economic power of precisely those old men and women who were the targets of the pension plan, for whom it thus became crucial to describe their past lives in such a way as to deserve a pension. This apparently economic transaction between state and the older generation was thus also symbolic: in rural communities throughout Macedonia, it focused people's attention on the events of 1903, and ultimately compelled applicants to narrate those events in such a way as to cast themselves as contributors to a distinctively Macedonian history.

Chapter 7 traces the debates and dilemmas involved in the late 1960s planning and construction process of the Ilinden monument in Kruševo which opened in 1974. Designed by architects with a modernist agenda and an abstract vision, its construction was monitored by a committee whose members sought a far more figurative and specific reference to the Macedonian past. The narrative component of the monument, contained in a memorial crypt, reveals in its omissions and modifications the ongoing attempt to put the Macedonian character of Ilinden beyond question.

Chapter 8 examines reactions within Kruševo to this monument, given concrete form in the commission and erection by townspeople of the figurative statue in 1983. While some townspeople focus on the components of history that portray Pitu Guli and Nikola Karev, two leading figures in 1903, as rivals, others draw on the state-sponsored but locally inspired history of the Kruševo Manifesto to frame the events of 1903 as consistent with their own visions of Kruševo's present and future. Chapter 9 explores how similar sentiments shaped a broader reevaluation of the town's history in the immediate aftermath of Yugoslavia's breakup in 1992, while chapter 10 offers a conclusion to the argument.

As the above summary demonstrates, this book is concerned as much with the past as the present. The chapters are arranged in broadly chronological order to provide a history of the history of 1903 in Kruševo. But while the argument focuses on Kruševo, the book seeks to contribute more generally to discussions of national identity. Stories from a town where the meanings of Greek, Bulgarian, Vlah, Albanian, Turkish, Yugoslav, and Macedonian were all disputed in the course of the twentieth century can serve to remind us that history and ethnography are both genres that can be exploited in a struggle against nationalist thinking.

Each chapter mobilizes different sets of source materials to examine different modes of imagining Ilinden. But beyond the statement of the obvious, that different communities construct the past in different ways depending on their present, I hope that this exposition will demonstrate that these different imaginings do not exist in splendid isolation from one another, and that their form is not fixed. Each has its own constitutive logic, so that to argue that such "imaginings" can be contrasted with some "reality" is to miss the point. In each case, I have tied an imagining to a particular community at a particular conjuncture, on which the other imaginings may impinge, and I have tried to demonstrate their mutual implication.

The result may baffle the reader who wishes to know the answer to the question put baldly in the title of Hugh Poulton's 1995 book, *Who Are the Macedonians?* But I consider that question, ontologically loaded as it is, to be the wrong one. It is freighted with an implicit commitment to the zero-sum nature of historical interpretation mentioned earlier—not this, but that, is the case. It pushes the debate into a realm in which reality is contrasted with illusion, falsehood, or imagination. Framing the question in this way contributes to a misunderstanding of the concept of the "imagined community" introduced to the literature of national identity so fruitfully in the seminal work of Benedict Anderson (1983). Various scholars, Poulton among them, have distinguished real from imagined communities, but Anderson suggests in his introduction that this was not his intention. "In fact," he writes there, "all communities larger than primordial villages of face-to-face contact (and perhaps even these) are imagined. Communities are to be distinguished, not by their falsity/genuineness, but by the style in which they are imagined" (1991:6).

My book is intended as a cultural study of a national history, in which the "state" plays a dynamic but not determining role. In emphasizing one event in one town, and its successive evocations, as a nexus at which different "imagining communities" interact, I have tried to apply the methods of anthropology to a study of "nationalism" without privileging the role of any state—many were involved—and without seeing states as monolithic. Macedonian history, then, is not just a resource contested by nation and state, or by nation-states. It has been made and re-made in the course of extended interaction between individuals, institutions, ideologies, and ideas, in which none have so far secured the power to pronounce the conversation over.

CHAPTER TWO

A Double Legacy

MACEDONIA'S YUGOSLAV AND BALKAN HISTORIES

Between 1944 and 1991, maps of southeast Europe included a country named Yugoslavia. Covering almost 100,000 square miles, it was more than twice as large as Bulgaria, almost twice the size of Greece, and nine times larger than Albania. Constituted as a socialist federation of six republics, the country was home to a diverse population that in 1991 numbered more than 23 million. Between 1991 and 1995, four Yugoslav republics sought to become sovereign states. Simultaneously, groups united by national identity but separated by republican borders pursued agendas of self-determination. The result was a series of brutal wars pitting Serbs, Croats, and Bosnian Muslims against each other, and leaving the country divided.

Between 1870 and 1912, many maps of southeast Europe included an ill-defined region called Macedonia. With an area of around 25,000 square miles, it was slightly smaller than Bulgaria, the same size as Greece, and larger than Serbia. Under Ottoman rule, the region was home to a diverse population of around 2.5 million. The three new states of Bulgaria, Greece, and Serbia sought to establish claims over parts of the region in order to expand their territory. Simultaneously, different groups united by ethnic identity pursued liberation from Ottoman imperial rule. The result was a series of brutal wars that pitted the armies of Bulgaria, Serbia, and Greece against Ottoman Turkey, and then one another, leaving the region divided, but its borders still contested.

In two sets of wars in southeast Europe, waged eighty years apart by different sets of protagonists, many contemporary observers saw ethnic chauvinism at work. In Yugoslavia in the 1990s, it was argued, the idea of national belonging had retained a primordial power, transcending allegiance to a multicultural state and driving otherwise ordinary people to support dangerous ideologues and, in the last resort, to participate in acts of barbarism against their former fellow-citizens. In early twentieth-century Macedonia, ethnic antagonism was fanned by national governments, spurring on soldiers to slaughter civilians and torch their homes. In Serbian, Croatian, Greek, and Bulgarian variants, nationalism could be defined by an obsession with purity that was both pathological and destructive. People in the Balkans, it seemed, thought of themselves and their enemies first as members of ethnic or national groups, and much later, if at all, as citizens of the same country, or bearers of a common humanity.

The violent break-up of Yugoslavia in the 1990s thus came to appear as a case of Balkan history repeating itself. Apparently motivated by popular sentiments that could be observed in earlier periods, it acquired in retrospect a certain aura of inevitability. Even if the Socialist Federal Republic of Yugoslavia had once been a leading regional power and a significant player in the nonaligned world, its dramatic collapse suggested that it had never achieved true stability, but had survived only because of a temporary equilibrium between powerful contending forces. Its long-time leader, Josip Broz Tito, had played one bloc off against another, both in dealings with the superpowers and with the different constituencies within the country. By nurturing some national sentiments, and keeping others firmly in check, and by continuous refinement of the country's constitution, he crafted an illusory unity. The weakness of his successors, the country's economic crisis, and the end of the Cold War all eroded the delicate balance, historical antagonisms between peoples, suppressed but not erased by socialist rule, burst forth anew.

The weight of Balkan history, though, served not only to explain Yugoslavia's bloody demise, but also to predict an apocalyptic future for the wider region. The Balkan Wars of 1912–13 served double duty in this regard, providing precedent for the horrors of Vukovar, Sarajevo, and Srebrenica, as well as raising the prospect that nationalism could spread into old areas of dispute and rekindle past animosities in Yugoslavia's neighbors.[1] The Republic of Macedonia, in particular, was perceived by policy makers in Europe and the United States as having the potential to spark a wider war.[2] Macedonia's quest for independence posed a Yugoslav problem, threatening as it did the future status of ethnic groups with links to other republics, in particular Serbs and Albanians. It also provoked fierce political and popular reactions in neighboring Greece, spurring fears that the late twentieth century might see a replaying of old conflicts between countries now enmeshed in complex, yet fragile, security arrangements.

The burden of history posed different challenges for the different republics and peoples of the former Yugoslavia. The Republic of Macedonia and its 2 million citizens found itself confronting the same issues of political and economic transition that all the former republics did. At the same time, the demise of Yugoslavia prompted a reexamination of earlier periods of the twentieth century, when the ten thousand square miles of the Republic had been part of a larger Macedonia that had been a battleground for wider interests. Particular attention came to be focused on the status and scope of the national identity claimed by the majority population of the Republic, which appeared on close examination to have shallow historical provenance, and to harbor the seeds of future conflict. At stake in the so-called "Macedonian Question" of the 1990s, then, were theoretical categories and political agendas from past and present. This chapter seeks to trace the complex interplay of the different legacies left by socialist Yugoslavia and Ottoman Macedonia in the modern Republic of Macedonia, and their impact in the early years of sovereignty.

TITO'S YUGOSLAVIA AND THEORIES OF NATIONALISM

For scholars of nationalism in the 1980s, Federal Yugoslavia represented something of an anomaly. Classical work on nationalism relied upon a distinction between two ideal-types of solidarity and loyalty, generally referred to as "civic" and "ethnic." In the first, the social unit is defined by political boundaries, and interpersonal bonds are instrumental; in the second, cultural affinity and primordial ties are what hold people together (Gellner 1983; Smith 1979). One scholar, working in the context of the Balkans, redrew the distinction as Western-Eastern forms of nationalism (Plamenatz 1974). Significantly, among those who developed the categorical distinction were modernization theorists, who became involved in initiatives that used the analytical distinction as a prescriptive template. Former colonies reconstituted as "new nations," such as Indonesia, were tracked for their success in inculcating civic ties (Geertz 1973a; see also Shils 1957).[3]

Yugoslavia's approach, drawing on Soviet practice more than Western theory, was different from its post-colonial counterparts. In the first place, the country as a whole made no claims on history, instead making a virtue of novelty and nonconformity. A marker of this was its leading role in the nonaligned movement, by virtue of which Yugoslavia—a European country—was invited to participate in tricontinental conferences for countries of Latin America, Africa, and Asia, from which, for example, Israel and Japan were excluded (Wallerstein 1991:199). There was no rhetoric of an ancient Yugoslav past. To be sure, it was acknowledged that South Slavs were groups that had been in the Balkans since the sixth century, but there was no suggestion that there had ever been such a Yugoslavia before. The state of the same name which had existed on the same territory between 1929 and 1941 played no part in the new state's self-image. Instead, the post–World War II leadership constituted Yugoslavia along very different lines: as a federation of socialist republics. The slogan of "brotherhood and unity"—in Macedonian, *bratstvo i edinstvo*—evolved from a partisan movement which began its struggle only after the invasion of Russia by Germany. It had never aimed at the restoration of a pre-war nation, but rather, had striven to establish a post-war federation of the Yugoslav peoples.

The agency that had led to the state's establishment, then, was part of a recent past. The will of the citizens of Yugoslavia was at the forefront of the state's charter, which emphasized ties forged by struggle and common purpose, rather than assumed to derive from any prior history. In so far as Yugoslav nationalism existed, then, it did so in a form which drew attention to its own novelty and its own volition—in short, to its own constructedness, rather than its naturalness.

Yet this Yugoslav nationalism did not only link citizens together directly, as the classical theory of civic nationalism allows. Rather, it operated through an ethnic medium. Individuals were not simply Yugoslavs because they wanted to be. They were also Yugoslavs by being Macedonians, or Serbs or Croats, or Slovenians or Montenegrins. These were the *narodi*, or peoples, of Yugoslavia. Each was identified by a mixture of factors, including language, religion, history, and association with a particular territory, one of the country's republics. Individual membership in one of these collectivities simultaneously made one a member of the broader collectivity that the narod, as a whole, had joined. Whereas the category of Yugoslav thus operated to tie together narodi, membership of a narod tied together individual citizens.

In this vision, Yugoslavia drew its strength from the strength of its constituent peoples. For the classic scholarship on nationalism, this presumption defied logic in asserting that the inherent antagonism between civic and ethnic could be transformed into a symbiotic relationship. There seems little doubt, though, that Tito maintained faith in this formula. The 1974 federal constitution confirmed the Communist Party decision of 1968 that promoted Bosnia's Muslim population to the status of narod. The revised constitution also extended concessions to Kosovo's Albanians, which increased their autonomy by granting the province quasi-republican status. By instituting a system of intermediate stages of belonging, Federal Yugoslavia could be said to have represented an attempt by its leaders to think beyond the nation in ways that anticipated later scholarship urging theorists to do the same (Appadurai 1993:411).

The pattern of Yugoslavia's break-up served to restore faith in the old academic dichotomy. With the benefit of hindsight, it was possible to see that Federal Yugoslavia's unique qualities had served only to buttress the potentially destructive force of nationalism within. Holders of this view drew attention to the failure of the Yugoslav state to inculcate successfully a single mode of belonging to the state, and to the relatively small number of people defining themselves as "Yugoslavs" in censuses (Sekulic, Massey, and Hodson 1994). They also emphasized how Tito's maneuvers had played one ethnic group off against another, and permitted and authorized *cultural* differences—operating in several languages, tolerating the practice of different religions—even while insisting on *political* unity. In retrospect, these efforts that had seemed so successful in winning popular support were cast as increasingly desperate, ad hoc measures taken against a flood tide of history. Once heralded as a social and political engineer of rare skill, Tito has since 1992 come to resemble a figure like Canute, that King of England who commanded the waves to turn back from the shore. Tito's creation, a Federal Yugoslavia, now lies like Canute's throne, submerged by a remorseless, natural advance.

This, then, is the view of Yugoslavia's demise that a theory of nationalism provides. And with the end of Tito's engineering, the argument continues, the radical division between ethnic and civic forms of nationalism reasserted itself. The conflicts over succession were understood by some analysts as falling entirely within this straightforward conceptual framework, as constituent republics and peoples veered toward one pole or another. In Slovenia, the separatist government quickly established control over its territory and population, marking the triumph of a civic vision. In Bosnia-Hercegovina, a Muslim-led coalition sought to do the same, prioritizing a republican sense of belonging, but ran afoul of ethnic sentiments among Serbs and Croats who together constituted more than half of the population. Croatian nationalism featured both components at war with each other. Lingering commitment to federal principles among Serbs also had a strong civic dimension. Prioritizing nationalism as the main force at work led easily to the misleading comparative classification of its qualities in different regions.

The classificatory exercise also prompted further explanation as to the bases of the differences that were observed. Within Yugoslavia, republics and peoples had been formal and constitutional equals: why, then, were Slovenian or Bosnian nationalisms more civic than Serbian or Croatian? And why did Slovenian independence "take" when Bosnian did not? In this debate, a wider literature came to play a part, as the questions resonated closely with contemporary work by prominent political scientists, who saw long-term history and deep-rooted cultural patterns as vital determinants of present and future prospects (Putnam 1993; Huntington 1993, 1996). By this light, Slovenia's success could be seen as the product of civic traditions created under Hapsburg rule that tied the most northerly Republic to Western European norms, while the ongoing problems of Kosovo and Macedonia in the south reflected the persistence of ethnic ways of thinking shaped under Ottoman rule. This new "symbolic geography" (Bakic-Hayden and Hayden 1992) was promoted vigorously by champions of Croatian independence, who traced democratic credentials back to the age of Renaissance-era city-states like Ragusa (modern Dubrovnik), and cast Yugoslavia, in all of its incarnations, as the product of brute force and oppression, overseen by Serbs. The recipes for successful Slovenian and Croatian sovereignty, in this vision, had been scripted centuries earlier; Yugoslav rule had been merely an intermission.

This new form of historical determinism, understandably, appealed less to those concerned for the future of other parts of the federation. Objections were also raised by scholars concerned with the power politics of such broad classifications, who detected racism in them. Anthropologists and cultural historians in particular raised their voices against the casual use of a lexicon of tribal passions, ethnic violence, and primordial sentiments trumping civic loyalties south and east of the Slovenian frontier. They suggested that such language could be seen as demonstrating a brand of Orientalism, as defined by Edward Said (1978), or a linked phenomenon that Maria Todorova termed "Balkanism" (Todorova 1994, 1997).[4] They found allies in their revolt against over-simplification from the more materially minded field of political economy, in which analysts offered convincing alternative explanations for the different achievements of the successor states. Slovenia had been the wealthiest of the republics, with the strongest potential to enter other markets. It was also where the boundaries of Republic and narod were most closely mapped onto each other: more than 95 percent of its inhabitants were Slovenes (Woodward 1994:33). These contingent factors, political economists suggest, played a larger role in Slovenia's successful exit from Yugoslavia than the essential quality of Slovenian nationalism.

THE REPUBLIC OF MACEDONIA AND THE YUGOSLAV LEGACY

In 1990 elections across former Yugoslavia, national parties performed especially well in Croatia and in Bosnia-Hercegovina, but less well in Macedonia. Albanians did vote overwhelmingly for one party, the Party for Democratic Prosperity (PDP), which took 25 seats in the 120-seat parliament. A strongly anti-communist, Macedonian nationalist party, VMRO-DPMNE, emerged from the second round of voting as the largest party in Parliament with 37 seats.[5] But the federalist alliance of "forces of reform" set up by Ante Marković, the Yugoslav prime minister, also performed well, winning 17 seats and revealing enduring popular commitment in the Republic to the maintenance of some form of federation (Woodward 1994:129; Magaš 1993:241). A government composed of "experts" (rather than constructed on party lines) was formed to manage the initial period of transition until Spring 1992, when a coalition government took over, led by the Social Democratic Alliance of Macedonia, or SDSM. As the League of Communists, this party had won 31 seats in the 1990 elections. The new government included representation from Albanian parties; VMRO-DPMNE had refused the opportunity to form a coalition government and was excluded.

The Republic's first president, Kiro Gligorov, had been a major player in planned economic reforms of the Yugoslav state in the 1980s and 1990s, and as late as June 1991 was still, in association with the Bosnian President Alija

Figure 3: The Republic of Macedonia, 1991. Broken lines are provincial borders. Provincial names are italicized. The Republic of Macedonia is shaded.

Izetbegovic, trying to hold a loose federation together (Silber and Little 1996:148). Macedonian soldiers were still serving in the Yugoslav National Army, or JNA—indeed, one of the first victims of violence was a Macedonian soldier lynched by a civilian mob in Split on 6 May (Magaš 1993:294).[6] After Slovenia had gone its own way and fighting in Croatia began in earnest, the ideals that held the state together had clearly lost their unifying capacity, and Gligorov and the Macedonian government of experts faced the task of extricating Macedonia from a federation, which they saw clearly would be dominated by Serbia, to create a sovereign state (figure 3).

Their first success was in securing an overwhelmingly positive response to a referendum held in September 1991 on the question of sovereignty. Of 1,288,904 registered voters, 976,339 turned out, and 907,907, or 97.9 percent of those who turned out to vote, voted for sovereignty.[7] Gligorov's greatest coup was in achieving the peaceful departure of JNA from its Macedonian bases in April 1992. Later that month, when I arrived in Skopje, people vividly recalled the tumult of the night when the withdrawal took place, leaving Macedonia virtually defenseless. The Macedonian government played its hand well; it doubtless seemed to President Milošević of Serbia and the generals of JNA fighting to retain territory that they would be able to return if it should prove necessary. But once UN troops arrived in Macedonia in the summer of 1993, invited by Gligorov's government, that prospect became unlikely.[8]

THE EXPERIENCE OF TRANSITION

Any sense of exuberance or self-congratulation that Macedonians might have felt in the wake of these major achievements dissipated in the following years as the process of retooling the mechanisms of government continued. Although terminal authority was relocated from Belgrade to Skopje, the problem of reorienting a society and economy that had been wholly entwined with that of former fellow-republics was a daunting one that affected the lives of many people. One group especially hard hit were those with ties to the Yugoslav army, which had been one of the core institutions that held Yugoslavia together. The army's transformation under strong Serb and Montenegrin leadership into an instrument of Serbian foreign policy was both a death knell for, and a blow to, ideas of Yugoslav solidarity. Macedonians who had been part of the officer corps or who had married into military families faced particular crises, both down-to-earth and symbolic. Where should they live? If they chose Macedonia, then what would happen to their pensions? Where should loyalties ultimately lie? Other Macedonians were also confronted with situations in which the taken-for-granted processes, institutions, and practices of everyday life were thrown into question. New opportunities and obligations appeared frequently, administered through bureaucratic channels designed for a different system. People were often frustrated by a life that seemed to combine the worst of two worlds: the queues and confusions of a shortage economy, and the insecurity, risks, and competition of an unfettered market.

Many of the dimensions of the changes taking place can be traced in the property revolution of February 1993, when people in Skopje, the capital of the Republic, had the opportunity to purchase property that had previously been socially owned, including the apartments in which they lived. At the time I was living in Skopje and deep in my archival research on the Ilinden pension plan at the National Archives of Macedonia, which shared a building with the Institute for National History. Like their counterparts in the Institute, and in other workplaces I visited, the archivists were strict in their observance of the *pauza*, or coffee-break, and often insisted that I join them. On one occasion we were drinking hot chocolate while one of the archivists, Jana, regaled us with the trials she had faced in buying the apartment she had previously rented. She had set out with her *dogovor*, or contract, in triplicate, along with at least two other documents. She had gone to the bank to pay, but only after she had obtained from the post office some official stamps, as well as the statement of what she owed. She described fighting her way through the crowds of people at the bank, all buying and selling. To succeed, she said, she had to force her way into a closed office to get information, and she felt fortunate that she ran into a sympathetic male clerk at the post office. But now, she said, it's finished. And, she added, it's good to have your own apartment.

Privatization marked the final destruction of the complex concept of social ownership that had been so central to the Yugoslav experiment, and which gave workers a stake in their firms (Horvat 1976:169–71). The break-up of Yugoslavia brought other changes in the economic realm. The Republic of Macedonia had always been dependent on the Yugoslav internal market and much of its infrastructure was routed through Belgrade. The break with the "Rump" Yugoslavia (consisting of the Republics of Serbia and Montenegro) caused considerable hardship. In the first winter I lived in Skopje, in 1992–93, electricity and heating were restricted at times, and gas and oil supplies were limited. Inflation was also a problem. The new currency of denari that replaced the old Yugoslav *dinari* was not introduced until late in the process of establishing autonomy. Short of hard currency, the government was forced to restrict people's access to their savings, and to impose controls on the movement of money.

The crowds of people that Jana, the apartment buyer, encountered at the bank were a product of these controls. Bank accounts in hard currency (*devizi*) were frozen (*zarobeni*) and withdrawals not permitted. Through the initiative of account-holders and other citizens, a market sprang up whereby this "notional" money, in the bank but temporarily inaccessible, could be traded for "cash in hand"—the rate being, as far as I could tell, about two to one. But zarobeni devizi could be used, at full face value, to buy one of the few assets the government inherited from Yugoslavia: the housing stock.[9] Individuals thus faced a choice: they could supplement existing savings, buying other people's zarobeni devizi at a discount, in order to purchase real estate; or they could make inaccessible money immediately available, though at a loss. The net effect, as Thiessen (1999) describes, turned Skopje into a city of owner-occupiers and private renters, where it had previously been a place of public ownership.

Some people were undoubtedly forced to trade in their savings, as the value of wages dropped, when paid at all. How they were paid was at times mysterious. I occupied an anomalous position, as a recipient of a grant from the Yugoslav Government—a funding source surely bankrupt by early 1992. My stipend continued to arrive at the Institute of National History, where I was a guest; when I inquired where it came from, I was told just to count my blessings that it did. Many colleagues' pay was months in arrears, which posed additional pressures, even though Skopje did not experience the hyperinflation of Belgrade described by Lyon (1996) and Gordy (1999). Other elements of their description of Serbian lives in the years 1993–94 resonate with the Macedonian case. Although the new Macedonian currency was declared as the denar at the end of April 1992, the first notes issued were bonovi, or coupons; formally, they were nonconvertible. People operated mainly in German marks, as a stable currency. Although Swiss francs and American dollars could be changed on the black market, British pounds commanded no appeal. The difference between the official and black rates was enough to drive a flourishing trade on what was known as "Beat Street" in the old town. Often it was not necessary for someone with hard currency to resort to that, as friends and neighbors also changed, and people could find the official and the *crn*, or black, rates printed side by side in the daily newspaper.

People made extensive use of cheques from their denari accounts. Although it did not achieve the savings it might in the hyperinflating environment of Belgrade, it did make handling cashflow easier. People supplemented their incomes in a variety of ways, usually buying and selling for import and export. For food, they relied considerably on fresh seasonal produce; workers at the Institute for National History frequented the large open air market known as *Bit Pazar*, close at hand, where prices were low. Pickling seasonal food in various forms to make the preserved winter relishes known as *zimnica* was not a new phenomenon in the region (Smollett 1989), and flourished in the climate of uncertainty. In the late summer of 1993 my neighborhood was full of people boiling peppers on small outdoor stoves, preparing large batches of *ajvar*, a pepper-eggplant-and-oil combination. This followed the international imposition of strict sanctions against Rump Yugoslavia on 26 April 1993—an attempt at intervention that had a collateral effect in Macedonia, and undoubtedly boosted the growth of illegal and criminal operations. As in Belgrade, the shortage of fuel meant that there were fewer cars on the streets, and industry closed down. The air quality improved, and people took to fishing the River Vardar.

This economic hardship was contrasted by many with better times. This was especially apparent in circles of highly educated urban professionals whose families had invested so much in a Yugoslav future. In her doctoral work, Ilka Thiessen has documented the reactions to transition of a group of young professional women in Skopje (Thiessen 1999), mostly students at the engineering faculty. In the 1980s, engineering was one of the most prestigious fields for study, and places at the university in Skopje were objects of fierce competition. A diploma was a guarantee of a stable and lucrative future in management, as well as a marker of status. The young women whose experiences Thiessen describes looked forward to the security of a good career and a good marriage. Many saw their loss of certainty as bound up centrally with the activities of the wider world, and lamented what they saw as the deliberate destruction of Yugoslavia—the country which promised them so much—by internal and external enemies. Victimization of

Yugoslavia, and of Macedonia within and after Yugoslavia, was a dominant theme that ran through my interactions with a wide range of people in Skopje. Parallel to the realities of economic deprivation ran a strong sense of status loss and threat in a realm of ideas and beliefs. Colleagues expressed indignation at the way in which Macedonia was being treated: "No one asks," one woman at the Institute said bitterly, "We're just told to obey." She asked me whether people outside had any idea of the effect that the sanctions imposed against Milošević's Yugoslavia would have on Macedonia.

DOMESTIC ISSUES

A number of concerns coalesced around the issue of future intercommunal relations in the new, sovereign country. The 1991 census, published in November of that year, demonstrated the extent of the Republic's internal diversity (see table 1). As in every other Yugoslav Republic except Bosnia-Hercegovina, one narod, or people, constituted the clear majority in the Republic of the same name. Macedonians constituted around 65 percent of the Republic's 2,033,964 registered inhabitants. Members of other narodi also lived in Macedonia, most notably Serbs, who made up only 2.2 percent of the population, concentrated in Skopje and the mountainous region of Skopska Crna Gora north of the city. A large Romani, or Gypsy, community of more than 50,000 was counted, as well as a number of other ethnic groups, including Vlahs.[10] Far more numerous, though, were members of two groups defined in Yugoslavia as *narodnosti*, or nationalities—groups which did not have republican status in the federation but which had a kin-state outside it. Turks comprised approximately 4.7 percent, but most significantly, Albanians, numbering more than 400,000, accounted for close to 21 percent of the Republic's population, concentrated in the northwest of the country around Tetovo and in Skopje. This marked a substantial increase since 1953, when Albanians had constituted only 12 percent of Macedonian residents.[11]

Macedonians in the Republic watched with horror and bewilderment the outbreak of violence in Bosnia-Hercegovina in April 1992, and its continuation through that year and the next. Additionally, many thousands of refugees arrived from elsewhere in Yugoslavia, bringing eyewitness accounts of fighting between members of different communities. What Macedonians quickly grasped was that Serbs in Bosnia-Hercegovina had objected to sovereignty, which they feared would constrain their relations with Serbs in Croatia and Serbia and make them a "minority" in a Bosnian Muslim-led state. No one missed the potential parallels with Macedonia. In Kosovo and Southern Serbia live more than 1.5 million Albanians, with economic and family ties to Macedonia's Albanians. Albania, the "kin-state," had an ethnically homogeneous population of at least 3 million. Both within the bor-

TABLE 1
Population in Macedonia according to the censuses 1953–1994[a]

	1953	1961	1971	1981	1991	1994
Total	1,304,514	1,406,003	1,647,308	1,909,136	2,033,964	1,936,877
Macedonians	860,699	1,000,854	1,142,375	1,279,323	1,328,187	1,288,330
Albanians	162,524	183,108	279,871	377,208	441,987	442,914
Turks	203,938	131,481	108,552	86,591	77,080	77,252
Roms	20,462	20,606	24,505	43,125	52,103	43,732
Vlahs	8,668	8,046	7,190	6,384	7,764	8,467
Serbs	35,112	42,728	46,465	44,468	42,775	39,260
Other	13,111	19,180	38,350	72,037[b]	84,068[c]	36,922

[a]Figures taken from Friedman (1996:90).
[b]Includes 39,513 Muslims, 14,225 Yugoslavs.
[c]Includes 31,356 Muslims, 15,703 Yugoslavs.

ders of Federal Yugoslavia, though, and on the Balkan peninsula as a whole, the Albanian population outnumbered the Macedonian. The dissolution of Yugoslavia, within which ethnic Macedonians felt a certain sense of south-Slavic solidarity, brought into question the future of a mix of the external and internal borders that fragmented a potential Greater Albania.

It was in this climate that many Macedonians in Skopje increasingly expressed their fear and distrust of their Albanian fellow-citizens. In particular the Bit Pazar incident in November 1992, when police exchanged fire with Albanian protesters, created anxiety among Macedonians in Skopje. This operated on several levels. Albanians in Macedonia had largely boycotted the Republic's referendum on sovereignty in September 1991, and had held their own alternative referendum in January 1992. The result was overwhelming support for the creation of "Ilirida," an autonomous Albanian political entity. (Poulton 1995:136). Albanian political parties used this popular support to press for increased cultural and political rights for their constituency, which aroused Macedonian resentment. Macedonians were also fearful that Albanian militancy might provoke conflict of the kind witnessed in Croatia and Bosnia-Hercegovina, especially if neighboring Serbia used disorder in Macedonia as a pretext to intervene to protect its fellow nationals in the Republic. Especially galling to Macedonians, though, was the severe blow that Albanian activism dealt to the process of securing international recognition for the Republic. Participants in the Albanian protests against security forces were clearly aware of their capacity to influence decision making elsewhere. In an interview after the Bit Pazar incident on 6 November 1992, a Macedonian Albanian told a British journalist that foreign recognition of the new Republic of Macedonia would be seen as a provocation to his people, and that "We'll put up barricades just like the Serbs did in

Croatia; we're fed up with being cheated" (*Guardian*, 17 November 1992). Again, Macedonia found the legacy of Yugoslavia, as well as parallels with current war-zones, weighing on its future.[12]

Macedonians in Skopje were confronted with a range of challenges stemming from the Republic's former membership in Federal Yugoslavia. As time went on, this generated an increasing level of anger against the international community, stemming from a strong sense of injustice. As most Macedonians saw it, they had played fair by Yugoslavia to the end. Their elected government had worked hard to avert violence and create a constitutional state where all citizens had equal rights. They had made no hasty moves, petitioning for formal recognition from the European Community (EC) only on invitation. When the Badinter commission, set up to advise the EC on recognition issues, had recommended certain changes in the new constitution, the Macedonian government had complied without fuss or rancor, and welcomed the commission's judgment that, together with Slovenia, Macedonia met all the criteria for recognition, while Croatia and Bosnia did not (Weller 1992). The general mood in the country changed when the European Community ignored the commission's findings, and recognized Croatia and Slovenia on 15 January 1992, and Bosnia on 6–7 April 1992 (Woodward 1994:147). The Republic of Macedonia had to wait until late 1993 for EC recognition, and even then received it only from individual member-countries (Williams 2000:26). In this long waiting period, the initial enthusiasm of 1991 that had generated a massive Macedonian turnout for the September referendum turned sour. Economic conditions remained difficult and the increasing foreign diplomatic and military presence in Skopje signalled ongoing uncertainty. Growing resentment was expressed in different ways. Identified as English, I was the audience (and possibly the target) of edgy jokes when Britain implemented a restrictive policy toward Macedonian travelers. German initiatives to support the housing of war refugees in Macedonia were poorly received, as people suggested their country was viewed as a kind of *cordon sanitaire*. The arrival of UN troops in Skopje was followed by criticisms of their poor behavior. The most extreme of the charges against them, through widespread rumor, was that a group of Norwegian soldiers had gang-raped a young Macedonian girl.[13]

In their disgust with the workings of the wider world, Macedonians in Skopje expressed particular anger over the role played by Greece. From its position of relative stability and security, as a member both of the North Atlantic Treaty Organization (NATO) and the EC, Greece appeared determined to block the smooth political transition of its former Yugoslav neighbor. The Greek government, with strong domestic support, raised objections to European recognition of the Republic under its constitutional name, the Republic of Macedonia, asserting Greece's absolute sovereignty over the domain name of Macedonia and expressing outrage at the attempted "theft" of their history and heritage (Sutton 1997). The result was provisional recognition by the EC under the temporary name of The Former Yugoslav Republic of Macedonia, quickly abbreviated in Greece to FYROM. Greek-Macedonian confrontation leapt from the symbolic to the material realm when in the summer of 1994, goaded by continuing perceived provocations from Skopje, and perhaps playing for domestic political advantage, the Greek government imposed economic sanctions on its new neighbor.

GREECE, FYROMANIA, AND THE MACEDONIAN QUESTION

Seemingly irrational and implacable Greek resistance to the recognition of the Republic of Macedonia in the 1990s attracted considerable attention, and raised further questions about the relevance of the past in the present. To many, it appeared to many that the dispute was all about history. A major theme of the angry debates conducted in the Balkans, and in diaspora communities around the world, was the connection to ancient Macedon and its world-famous kings. The tension over ownership of the past was made manifest when the Republic's government replaced its socialist-era flag, which bore the five-pointed star shared by all the Republics, with a new flag that had deeper historical associations. The flag's sixteen-pointed device replicated a symbol associated with the ancient Macedonian royal dynasty and its two most prominent members, Philip II and his son Alexander the Great. In the 1980s, the Greek government had sponsored international exhibitions of archaeological finds from the tombs of Vergina where this device had been prominently displayed (Green 1989). The new Republic's use of what Greeks called the Star of Vergina became a major bone of contention between the two countries, ending only when the Republic changed its flag in 1995 (Brown 1994, 2000).

At the same time, other disputed histories prompted strong reactions in Greece. In 1993, Anastasia Karakasidou, then a doctoral student in the United States, published an article in the *Journal of Modern Greek Studies* dealing with political and ethnic identities in the Florina region of northwestern Greece. She documented the existence of a long-standing linguistic or cultural minority in Greece whose members called themselves Macedonians. Karakasidou's work sparked debates over the relative truth-status of ethnographic and archival data, and also triggered a series of personal and professional attacks (Karakasidou 1993, 1994). In an ugly climate of suspicion and fear in Greece that might be dubbed "FYROMania," the British publisher, Cambridge University Press, created a furor by withdrawing its plan to publish Karakasidou's book, citing fears for its employees in Greece. Free speech and open debate appeared under threat.[14]

From a realist perspective, it is possible to argue that these concerns over history merely concealed the material basis of Greek anxiety, which lay in contemporary geopolitics. Greek reactions to the Republic's claims on history, and to scholarly work on minority consciousness within Greece, could be seen as products of concern over possible threats to security. The logic of such a connection is relatively straightforward: If FYROM's claims to ancient Macedonia were successful, they would buttress the campaign to name the new state Macedonia. Its Slavic-speaking population would then be known as Macedonians. If there were Slavic-speakers in Greece who called themselves Macedonians, they might be mobilized by their new kin-state to seek recognition as an ethnic minority. Success would set a precedent for recognition of other groups. Greece would then confront a range of potential threats to sovereignty, ranging from groups such as these securing privileges at the expense of other citizens, to foreign powers exploiting the situation to intervene on a group's supposed behalf. None of these scenarios seemed particularly alarming for the Macedonian case; however, the existence of a large Turkish-speaking minority in Thrace, and historical tensions between Greece and Turkey, changed the equation.

Enticing in its reductive logic, such a reading grants supremacy to nationalist thinking, in two dimensions. As well as presuming that state and nation enjoy a symbiotic relationship—so that the destiny of ethnic "Turks" or "Macedonians" who are Greek citizens is always tied to that of their alleged kin-states—this reading also discounts historical contingency. Linking past symbols and present geopolitics to a crude model of instrumental interest neglects the complex process by which particular symbols gain or lose their significance and relevance. One hundred years ago, around 1900, Greece was reeling from a disastrous military defeat by the Ottoman Empire, and Greeks were defending the legacy of Alexander the Great against Bulgarian claims (Kofos 1993:308). Although an argument could almost certainly be made for an instrumental linkage in that period too, it would of necessity rely on a different logic in which the critical idea of minority would play no part.

As noted at the beginning of the chapter, much has been made of the potential parallels between the early twentieth-century Balkans and the 1990s, especially over the issue of Macedonia, which emerged as a central concern at both moments. Broad brush comparison, though, downplays the critical influence of almost a hundred years of intervening history. Although the Macedonian Question with its symbolic and geopolitical dimensions achieved salience in southeast Europe at both times, that question—or more precisely, the set of questions that the phrase carries—has a history of its own. In the course of the twentieth century, when the region experienced two world wars and a long ideological struggle, it was contested by different powers and peoples, and the relative weight of its component parts shifted. In the following section, I provide a simple outline of key twists and turns in the debate, which identifies the salient players and themes that have shaped its ongoing evolution.

DISTINCTIVELY INDISTINCT: THE MACEDONIAN QUESTION IN THE EARLY TWENTIETH CENTURY

Modern scholars specializing in the study of Macedonia in the 1900s and the 1990s have identified three core underlying realms of argument. In his pioneering study of early twentieth-century Macedonian revolutionary activism, Duncan Perry identified three linked elements: What was the exact extent of Macedonian territory? Which state had rightful claim to it? What was the nationality of its inhabitants? (Perry 1988:2) This tripartite division of the question analytically separated geographical, political, and ethnographic dimensions of the adjective "Macedonian." In a similar vein, through his even-handed scrutiny of Macedonia's many meanings in the 1990s, Loring Danforth draws a broad distinction between the word's regional, national, and ethnic senses. In the confusion between different uses of the word by different speakers describing different phenomena, he argues, much of the potential for conflict arises (Danforth 1993, 1995a).

In the latter part of the nineteenth century, much of that confusion lay in the future. General consensus had been reached in European circles on the location and extent of geographical Macedonia. At that time the Ottoman Empire still controlled a considerable part of southeast Europe, including much of modern northern Greece, all of Albania, Kosovo, and the modern Republic of Macedonia, and parts of southern Serbia and southwest Bulgaria (figure 4). The Ottoman authorities divided this territory into administrative provinces called *vilayets* and did not use the term "Macedonia" (Adanir 1984–85:43–44). From the mid-nineteenth century, though, most European sources had assigned the term to an area of around 25,000 square miles, including most of the three Ottoman vilayets of Uskub (Skopje), Monastir (Bitola), and Salonika (Thessaloniki).[15]

Greece, Bulgaria, and Serbia, all of which had become states only in the nineteenth century, advertised their claims on Ottoman Macedonia. All three countries were composed of land and people that had formerly been under Ottoman rule, and sought further enlargement at the expense of the retreating empire. Neighboring Macedonia was an obvious target for their expansionist ambitions. A significant proportion of its inhabitants were Orthodox Christians, and the primary aim of the new Balkan states was to establish rightful claim to territory by transforming these people into their conationals by any means possible. All the resources of the new states were put to work

Figure 4: Ottoman Macedonia 1903. Thinner lines mark provincial (vilayet) borders. Vilayet names are italicized. Thicker lines mark international frontiers. Town names are given in the common form of the period.

as priests, scholars, teachers, merchants, and soldiers enlisted in the service of their country, using religious conversion, academic argument, economic necessity, or in the last resort, brute force as tools in their campaigns to resolve the question of the nationality of Macedonia's Christians.[16]

A number of scholars have explored the campaigns launched by the Balkan states in the late nineteenth and early twentieth centuries, emphasizing their different orientations. In 1951, the British geographer Henry Wilkinson traced how Greek, Bulgarian, and Serbian cartographers drew maps that classified people by what they called racial criteria, including faith, language, or custom (Wilkinson 1951). In combination with a principle of self-determination, such maps made claims on territory. The compilation of statistics was a parallel exercise, as explored extensively as early as 1918 by French historian Jean Larmeroux (cited in Perry 1988:19) and outlined effectively by linguist Victor Friedman (1996:82–88), who shows how interests shaped the precise criteria used by rival head-counters. For those looking to demonstrate a high number of Greeks, for example, schooling and religion were prioritized; to locate Serbs, in Friedman's analysis, "specific isoglosses, that is, dialect boundaries based on individual linguistic features," were used to trump other means of measurement (Friedman 1996:84).

Such classificatory practices were the work of intellectuals in the new states. Increasingly, advocates of expansion concerned themselves not just with counting heads from a distance, but also with converting hearts and minds on the ground. Bulgarian claims were advanced by the Exarchate, a Christian Orthodox church granted recognition by the Ottoman Sultan in 1870. Using Church Slavonic in their services, and teaching literary Bulgarian in their associated schools, the clergy sought to establish themselves in Slavic-speaking villages across the whole of Macedonia. Their efforts were actively resisted by the Patriarchate, the more senior Orthodox Church that used Greek as its language of worship and sponsored its teaching as the language of enlightenment. The confrontation between the two churches is described from close at hand in Brailsford's study of Macedonia (Brailsford 1906), and is the subject of valuable work by Evangelos Kofos (1984, 1986b).

The question of religious belonging also had economic dimensions. Where the Exarchate, at least initially, sought to recruit members by appealing to their sense of shared cultural identity, claiming to offer worship and education to Macedonia's Christians through their "own" language, the Patriarchate relied more on its reservoirs of capital, both symbolic and material. Patriarchate clergy represented Greek as a sacred language, and the only medium through which prayers could reach God. Alternatives were pronounced heretical, and the Exarchate in particular was proclaimed schismatic. Also outlawed were attempts by Vlahs of Macedonia to use their language in church. Patriarchist congregations also recognized that Greek was a language of finance, trade, and upward social mobility. In his seminal article, Trajan Stoianovich identified the "Conquering Balkan Orthodox Merchant" as a key figure in the region's economic development in the eighteenth and nineteenth centuries, serving as middleman between European business and the resources of the Ottoman Empire (Stoianovich 1960). In the setting of a market town outside Thessaloniki, the intimate linkages between religion and commerce which shaped class and property relations are compellingly traced in Anastasia Karakasidou's award-winning book *Fields of Wheat, Hills of Blood* (1997a).

The various projects of the Balkan national states faced opposition on a number of levels. In the first case, because their claims overlapped, they fought one another. Conflict between Greek- and Bulgarian-sponsored bands reached its peak in the years 1904–1908, during the phase known in Greece as the Macedonian Struggle (Dakin 1993). Even before this, though, sections of Macedonia's population had organized to campaign for self-rule or autonomy. They formed a number of organizations, the best-documented of which was the Internal Macedonian Revolutionary Organization, or VMRO, among the Christian population. Its activities have been extensively documented by Bulgarian and Macedonian historians, who dispute the national orientation of its members, but generally agree that it fought not against Ottoman rule, but also the ambitions of the governments in Athens, Sofia, and Belgrade. Drawing on nationalist and socialist ideologies, VMRO leaders pursued whatever means they could to win support for their cause, at home and abroad. Their primary method, though, was terror, targeting civilians and property in Macedonia, both to hamper the advance of foreign state propaganda and to raise their own international profile (Fischer-Galati 1973; Perry 1988).[17]

Other Ottoman subjects in Macedonia organized to seek greater cultural and political freedoms in less violent ways that nonetheless undercut the claims of neighboring states. The Albanian-speaking population of the Balkans included Muslims and Christians. The former were viewed, especially by the Slav-speaking Christian peasantry, as the implementers of Ottoman rule; the latter by Greek propagandists as "theirs." They were united, though, in seeking education in their own language, denied to them in both faiths. By the early twentieth century, Albanians were organizing cultural associations to promote their language, and later they would rise against Ottoman rule (Skendi 1967). Vlah-speakers in Macedonia, meanwhile, scattered throughout the territory in commercial towns and cities, and villages with mountain pastures for stock, had long been counted as supporters of the Greek movement. Vlahs also campaigned for the right to worship in their own language, with support from Romania. Their efforts were rewarded in 1905, when the Sultan authorized the use of Vlah in church services. The threat to Hellenism provoked strong reprisals, and Greek militias killed many of the "renegades" to persuade others to return to the "true" faith.

In the critical period of the early twentieth century, then, the three components of the Macedonian Question were bound together by three states that laid claim to Macedonian territory by identifying its Christian population as their own. Within all three, public opinion was mobilized through media and political rhetoric, so that the salvation of unredeemed brethren, or the land they occupied, became a point of faith. This activism culminated in the Balkan Wars of 1912–13. Greece, Serbia, and Bulgaria, weary perhaps of the opposition they encountered from Vlahs, Albanians, and Macedonian revolutionaries, made common cause and attacked the Ottoman Empire. The ensuing conflict was marked by horrific crimes against civilian populations and large-scale displacement of people, documented by an international commission set up by the Carnegie Endowment (Kennan [ed.] 1993). The first Balkan War was quickly followed by a second, in which Bulgaria fought against its former allies to try and win a larger share of the spoils. In the First World War, Serbia and Greece fought on one side alongside France, Britain, and Russia, while Bulgaria and Turkey joined the Central Powers, Germany and Austria-Hungary.

When at last the Versailles Peace Conference drew the borders of the Balkan countries in 1919, they had changed radically from 1912 (see figure 5). Former Ottoman territory in Europe had been divided with Woodrow Wilson's principle of self-determination in mind, but also in a way that rewarded the victors. The existence of Albania was confirmed, but its bor-

Figure 5: "Divided Macedonia," 1919–41. Italicized names denote common terms for parts of a "Greater" Macedonia, whose extent is shaded. Town names are given in the official form of the period.

ders did not include all Albanians. A new Serbian-dominated Kingdom of the Serbs, Croats, and Slovenes, renamed Yugoslavia in 1929, controlled close to 40 percent of Ottoman Macedonia, including the cities of Skopje and Bitola, called by their Serbian names Skoplje and Bitolj. Greece acquired 50 percent of the territory, including the major commercial port of Thessaloniki, while Bulgaria, on the losing side again, retained only around 10 percent of the territory that it had aspired to control completely. The new international frontiers sliced through former Ottoman administrative units, most emphatically in the old vilayet of Monastir, which was divided among Greece, Albania, and Serbia. Bitola, or Monastir, the former vilayet capital and business and diplomatic center, found itself transformed into a provincial border town. The Macedonian autonomists, meanwhile, sent a delegation to Versailles, but were unable to get a hearing.

BETWEEN THE WARS: THE BIRTH OF THE MINORITY QUESTION

The new national frontiers after the First World War transformed the Macedonian Question; whereas in Bulgaria, "Macedonia" still referred to the larger area that had been divided, its geographically restricted meaning was reaffirmed in Greece, where "historical Macedonia" was envisaged as that part of the former Monastir and Salonika vilayets that Greece occupied (Christides 1949; Kofos 1993:314). The Ottoman territory taken by Serbia, meanwhile, was named "Southern Serbia" by its new rulers. Scholars writing of the area since the Balkan Wars have reached a new consensus on naming which dispels this ambiguity and evasion, by referring to three distinct Macedonias: Aegean Macedonia (in Greece); Pirin Macedonia (in Bulgaria) and Vardar Macedonia (the former Yugoslav Republic of Macedonia).[18]

In all three countries, the doctrine of national self-determination continued to be taken for granted, but had different consequences. In Aegean Macedonia, campaigns were waged to eradicate the use of local Slavic dialects and to convert people into Greek-speakers. Different régimes changed the names of villages, and imported teachers and other government officials into the region from the rest of Greece. The project to transform the so-called new territories was greatly assisted by population exchanges with Turkey and Bulgaria. By 1928 more than 600,000 Orthodox Christians from Asia Minor had been settled in the region (Voutira 1997:119), permanently transforming the demographic composition of the region and effectively ending the prospect that any kind of plebiscite in northern Greece would detach it from the rest of the country. Within Greece, at least, the Macedonian Question came to revolve around issues of national assimilation and the future of a small linguistic minority.[19]

Across the Yugoslav border, in Vardar Macedonia, the question of the identity of the local population remained a pressing issue. Although most of the residents with strong pro-Greek or pro-Bulgarian sentiments left for those countries, the less politicized majority that remained continued to speak Slavic dialects recognizably different from standard Serbian. Turkish, Albanian, and Vlah were also widespread. As in Greece, a firm language policy was adopted here as part of a campaign to "Serbianize" the region. In addition to teachers and administrators, many Serbian colonists, especially war veterans, were settled on agricultural land formerly held by Turkish landlords. The countryside was dotted with gendarmerie posts, and a defensive line of barbed wire and armed watchtowers was established along the frontier with Bulgaria. Vardar Macedonia at times appeared to exist in a state of virtual war between the population and the forces of government, which many civilians perceived as foreign. Against this backdrop violent clashes continued between armed bands and police, and assassins targeted Serbian officials, reinforcing the view that the Macedonian Question here remained unresolved and posed a vital threat to domestic order (Reiss 1924; Christowe 1935; Swire 1939).

In Bulgaria, organizations of Macedonian refugees played a vital role in keeping public attention focused on the historical injustice of Versailles, which they claimed had ignored the essential Bulgarian identity of Ottoman

Macedonia's entire Christian population. After 1919 political and intellectual cadres in Sofia included many members who traced descent to Macedonia. Research institutes in Sofia, staffed largely by émigrés, continued to amass materials to document what Macedonia had looked like before the Balkan Wars, a subject which was far less consuming in Greece and Serbia, newly committed to the status quo. Similar intellectual and heritage activities were pursued in the United States and Canada, where in 1921 a vocal diaspora created the Macedonian Political Organization, the MPO, to lobby on behalf of their kin in Vardar and Aegean Macedonia.[20] This cultural activism oversaw the production and publication of memoirs, photographic images, literary works, and statistical surveys of the period of Ilinden 1903.

VMRO, also active in exile, had changed considerably. The failure of the Ilinden Uprising prompted bitter internal recriminations, and the organization split into warring factions. By the 1920s two dominant groups had emerged. One was left-leaning, with strong ties to international communist and socialist organizations, and headquartered in Vienna. Among its more famous intellectual leaders was Dimo Hadži-Dimov, who wrote *The Macedonian National Question* (Hadži-Dimov 1986). He was assassinated by Vlado Černozemski, an agent of the other wing of VMRO which had its base in Pirin Macedonia in western Bulgaria and continued to pursue a more straightforward national vision. Where other organizations pursued diplomatic or political routes, the VMRO in Pirin continued to pursue the violent overthrow of Yugoslav rule in Vardar Macedonia, conducting raids and murders there to provoke a wider regional conflagration. The organization operated outside Bulgarian governmental control, playing a central role in the savage coup of 1923 and subsequently building a local fiefdom in the mountains of western Bulgaria financed by the profits of tobacco smuggling and protection rackets. Only in the mid-1930s, goaded by international sanctions, was the Bulgarian state able to uproot the organization, which by then had acquired a global reputation for ruthlessness and criminality. Its parting shots were fired in Marseille on 9 October 1934 when Hadži-Dimov's assassin struck again. Working with a Croatian fascist exile organization, the *Ustaše*, Černozemski killed King Alexander of Yugoslavia.

King Alexander's last words, reportedly, were these: "Preserve Yugoslavia." By 1941, though, his kingdom was in ruins, as Axis forces partitioned Yugoslavia, largely along ethnic lines, and the Macedonian Question shifted again. Germany retained direct control of the strategic rail and road corridor from Belgrade to Thessaloniki, and Italy controlled Albania, expanded to include areas where Albanians constituted the majority. Bulgaria was granted control over much of the territory of Ottoman-era Macedonia (figure 6). The interwar VMRO dream of a united Macedonia appeared to have been realized, under the administration of a kin-state that many in the Macedonian movement had viewed as an understanding and

Figure 6: The partition of Yugoslavia, 1941–43.

supportive ally. The new Bulgarian régime brought with it official recognition of the Macedonian struggle against Ottoman, Greek, and Serbian oppression. The legacy of Ilinden 1903 was granted a central place in history. Macedonian activists returned from exile to take up influential positions, and it appeared to many in the region that a resolution of old issues had been reached.

COMMUNISM AND NATIONAL MINORITIES

The sense of closure was short-lived. In Aegean and Vardar Macedonia, people recognized that Bulgaria sought not to support the creation of a new Macedonian state, but to annex territory. New legislation, including strict nationality and language policies, increasingly recalled the policies of interwar Greece and Yugoslavia. Many Macedonians saw clearly for the first time that they, their homeland, and its history were viewed and treated as subordinate parts of a Bulgarian national whole. Their frustration had no obvious nationalist avenue: VMRO was by this time closely tied to Bulgarian interests. Instead, they found new allies in the communist parties of Yugoslavia and Greece, both of which embraced a principle of self-determination for former subject peoples.

Many Macedonians enlisted in the broader anti-fascist struggle in both countries, confident that they would have a say in shaping the post-World War II boundaries of the region. By mid-1942, small groups with names derived from the Ilinden period of 1903 were conducting guerrilla warfare against the Bulgarian and German occupation forces, in what was called the National Liberation Struggle, or NOB. In November 1942, in the Bosnian town of Bihać, the Anti-Fascist Council for the National Liberation of Yugoslavia, or AVNOJ, was created, which located the struggle of the Macedonian people for autonomy within the wider Yugoslav struggle. Political preparations continued to be made for the post-war government of the country, and the defining moment of this state-making activity for Macedonians was the Anti-Fascist Assembly for the National Liberation of Macedonia, or ASNOM, which was held on 2 August 1944—the forty-first anniversary of Ilinden 1903. The meeting was held at the monastery of Prohor Pčinski, on the border with the Republic of Serbia. When communists came to power in Bulgaria in September 1944, the stage was set for a new round of negotiations and maneuvers over the future of Macedonia.

By the time of the defeat of the Axis Powers in 1945, Yugoslav partisans had all but eliminated their domestic opposition. The wartime leader, Josip Broz Tito, quickly consolidated control over the pre-war territory of Yugoslavia, creating the system of six republics which was to last until 1991. His immediate vision, though, was larger, and included communist Albania, Bulgaria, and, potentially at least, part of Greece in an expanded federation. With regard to the annexation of Albania, the province of Kosovo was the key bridge; with regard to Bulgaria and Greece, it was the new Republic of Macedonia. In early negotiations with Bulgaria, Tito won important symbolic victories over the question of Macedonian identity. Teachers of the newly codified Macedonian language were permitted to enter Pirin Macedonia, and materials on Macedonian history accumulated in Sofia were transferred to Skopje, all in apparent readiness for an enlargement of the Republic of Macedonia, and the inclusion of Bulgaria within an expanded federation.

In Greece, the situation was more complex. After 1946, communist forces were involved in an open power struggle with royalists, who enjoyed the support of Britain and, later, the United States, already eyeing Soviet Russia as an enemy. Across most of Greece, royalist government forces quickly defeated their communist enemies. However, northwestern Greece remained a communist stronghold, in part through the support of the local Slavic-speaking population, who responded to the communists' promise of greater political and cultural rights. Greek communist resistance in this mountainous territory also relied on Tito's assistance: hospitals and training camps were set up in Yugoslavia, and supplies and personnel could move easily across the borders. With these resources, the Greek partisans seemed set to retain control of what they called "Free Greece," that might formally join an enlarged Yugoslav federation.

Two political developments brought an end to the military stalemate in Greece—and to prospects for an enlarged Macedonia. The communist party of Greece recognized that its association with the Macedonian autonomist movement cost it domestic support, and reasserted its unwavering commitment to Greece's territorial integrity. In the same year, after criticism from Moscow, Tito broke with Stalin and Yugoslavia was expelled from the Cominform. This immediately changed the dynamics of negotiations between Yugoslavia, Albania, and Bulgaria, as well as between the Yugoslav and Greek communist parties. The vision of a wider federation led by Belgrade dropped out of any equation for the future. Kosovo and the Republic of Macedonia, formerly launch-points for the expansion of Yugoslavia, took on the appearance of enemy bridgeheads that threatened Yugoslavia's integrity. Macedonians suspected of autonomist sentiments suddenly found themselves viewed as potential national enemies of Yugoslavia, and many were jailed. Yugoslav cooperation with Bulgaria ceased abruptly. The border with Greece was closed, sealing the fate of the communist forces, but opening the possibility of Tito's repairing relations with the Greek government and its British and American allies.

As the geopolitical balance of power shifted, so, once again, the components of the Macedonian Question were rearranged. Throughout the life of socialist Yugoslavia, Greece and Bulgaria pursued policies of national assimilation toward parts of their population that identified themselves as Macedonian. The rationale of this policy was simple: Macedonian identity was a Titoist invention, and those who believed in it were either dupes or political agitators. In the Republic of Macedonia, by contrast, the Yugoslav frame of "brotherhood and unity" provided a backdrop for extensive government-sponsored research and writing that sought to demonstrate the deep historical roots of a distinctive Macedonian cultural identity. In line with Marxian concepts of ethnogenesis, Alexander the Great was less relevant than the nineteenth century roots of the popular liberation struggle. This served a domestic agenda of securing loyalty and support for the Yugoslav project, and every opportunity was taken to demonstrate the early expression of socialist or communist sentiments in Macedonia's past. Yugoslav Macedonian research into the history and current plight of the people of Aegean and Pirin Macedonia also constituted a claim to legitimate interest in those regions. Although the split with Stalin had reduced his options, Tito continued to show willingness to raise, when it seemed politically expedient, the issue of Greek and Bulgarian treatment of people that he referred to as members of the Macedonian narod.[21]

CONCLUSION: HISTORY REDUX

Proprietary rights over territory, people, and meaning were all at stake in the twentieth-century history of the Macedonian Question. At various points, people took action or raised their voices against its enduring capacity to do harm to the interests of states and the lives of their citizens. Thus in August 1950 a *New York Times* editorial reported international efforts to repair good relations between Greece and Yugoslavia, which at that time were jeopardized by Yugoslav complaints over Greece's treatment of the alleged Macedonian minority. The writer made clear that Yugoslavia was at fault, in stating magisterially, "The notion that a protected minority inside a state enjoys special privileges and status is not only alien to the West but is considered incompatible with statehood" (*New York Times*, 19 August 1950). In October, matters had escalated and, over the issue of Macedonia, Greece refused to allow American aid to reach Yugoslavia (*New York Times*, 18 October 1950). In early November, Tito affirmed Yugoslav concern for "Slavonic" minority rights in Greece, but renounced all territorial claims upon "Greek Macedonia" (*New York Times*, 7 November 1950). On 22 November Marshall Plan aid began flowing to Yugoslavia, and on the next day, a *New York Times* editorial celebrated the Yugoslav-Greek reconciliation, and offered a response to any who might say that Tito had been pressured by the United States:

> Marshal Tito feels free to act on his own just because the help the US is offering carries no conditions. The pressure that moves him is the pressure of logic and events and when we see where these forces inevitably lead those who are free to follow them we have ground for hope that the currents of life cannot finally be dammed up or turned backwards. (*New York Times*, 23 November 1950)

In 1991, forty-one years later, the currents of life had flowed on in southeast Europe. Minorities complained over their lack or loss of status and privileges, and their arguments often won greater favor from international audiences. People around the world, including scholars and journalists, would scoff at the idea that American foreign aid had no strings attached. And in the Republic of Macedonia, on the eve of the 8 September referendum on sovereignty, President Kiro Gligorov asked all Macedonia's citizens to heed the logic of pressure and events and think past the ethnic nation in responding positively to the referendum's motion. Toward the end of a presidential address circulated to all the Republic's media, he offered the following arguments:

> The vote "for" is a call for an end to the senseless, bloody war in Yugoslavia. We need no new human victims, new historical hatreds, nationalist passions and sick desires to carve out new borders and alliances. What we need is Yugoslavia as a modern association of sovereign states, built on principles of equality and tolerance that will provide a path for us to take our place where we rightly belong, in the European house of nations.
> The vote "for" is a vote for the twenty-first century, which definitively con-

signs to the past all the ghosts of the nineteenth-century Balkans—the divisions and hatreds, the enduring historical appetites for territorial expansion, the national negations, and the interethnic wars.[22]

Gligorov thus made a simple equation, which connected contemporary fighting in Croatia with past conflicts in the wider region. In this model the current violence was a product of aggressive attempts to redraw the existing boundaries of republics in order to unite people of the same ethnic identity in new nation-states. The pursuit of such policies would then re-open historical disputes over identity and territory. The Republic and its citizens, the president made clear, would be the losers in any such initiative. Now was a golden opportunity to exorcise the demons of the Balkan past and the Yugoslav present, and demonstrate a shared commitment to a bright European future. He addressed one passage specifically to "all citizen Albanians," assuring them that in the future the Republic would continue its own tradition of "coexistence, mutual respect, tolerance and full equality" and asking them to put aside whatever current dissatisfactions they might feel in the interests of the common good.

Gligorov's words reveal something of the tensions that the circumstances of 1991 created for the Republic of Macedonia, and the multiple constituencies whose interests had to be addressed. The referendum itself, if successful, would lead to the transformation of an internal and ill-defined demarcation between the Republic of Macedonia and the Republic of Serbia into an international frontier. Even as he spoke eloquently against the redrawing of borders, he was calling on Macedonia's citizens to authorize a process that would profoundly affect Yugoslavia's Albanian community, by dividing its members living in northwest Macedonia from those in Kosovo. Political leaders in Macedonia's Albanian community balked at this, and Gligorov's targeted appeal was a response to this resistance.

The pressure of logic and events demanded that the line be drawn quickly. If it were not, one scenario could unfold whereby Macedonia would remain mired in Yugoslavia. Slovenia had already left, and Croatia was seeking to do so. Without the contribution of these wealthier republics, those left behind would have little prospect of prosperity; they would also inhabit a federal country where one people, the Serbs, constituted a significant majority, and would likely dominate political life. Even if violence were avoided— and Kosovo, with its Albanian majority and a history of anti-government protest, would still be a part of this federation—Macedonians would be likely to find their quality of life substantially eroded.

A second scenario, should the drawing of the line not receive public support, would include proposals for different borders to be created in the future. The most likely and disturbing prospect for Macedonians was that Yugoslavia's Albanians, who had never had their own republic within Yugoslavia, and not been granted the status of narod, or people, might now unite to create their own sovereign state from the wreckage of Yugoslavia. Such a state would likely be centered on Kosovo, but if built on ethnic principles, it would include much of northwestern Macedonia. Doubts also hung over the regional aspirations of countries outside the former Yugoslavia. Albania, Greece, and Bulgaria had all in the past contested either the boundaries of the Republic of Macedonia or the legitimacy of the national identity claimed by its majority. Any sign of disunity within the Republic might encourage them to do so once again.

The political situation demanded that the referendum be an overwhelming success, and Gligorov therefore exerted special effort to reach Albanian voters. As well as evoking images of long-established harmony, at the end of the address, he offered a vision of a future in which borders would not matter. The Macedonian state would be a "bridge of stability" in a future "Balkans without borders" where the question of the rights of Macedonians in neighboring countries—and implicitly, those of all peoples divided by the frontiers of nation-states—would be resolved.

The speech also contained material for the core constituency, members of the Macedonian narod. Seeded through the visionary rhetoric were specific references to a particular part of the national past that worked to establish a point of origin for processes that the president projected into the future. In his closing sentence, Gligorov made the only reference to an individual in the entire speech: invoking "the spirit of Goce"—*Goceviot duh*—he relied on his listeners' knowledge of and investment in the life and work of Goce Delčev, inspirational leader of the Macedonian revolutionary movement until his death in 1903. Delčev, whose remains lie in Skopje, famously claimed to understand the world as an arena for cultural competition between its peoples. By framing a "For" vote in the referendum as a continuation of a hundred-year-old hero's work—for freedom, for peace, and for Macedonia as a state of all its citizens—President Gligorov embedded the past in the future and the future in the past, while seeking to transcend the threat of violence that lurked in both.

In an earlier section, the president similarly traced continuity back to two initiatives taken by a named community. Describing the historical struggles for statehood waged by Macedonian people and Macedonian citizens, President Gligorov acknowledged Macedonia's participation in the creation of Federal Yugoslavia in 1944 and the war of national liberation between 1941 and 1944, but gave first place to the formation of the Kruševo Republic in 1903. And in mapping the indigenous roots of interethnic cooperation, and of national and religious toleration and respect, he charted a similar path back to the spirit of the Kruševo Manifesto of the same year. In a speech otherwise dominated by an abstract language of ideals and challenges, the double mention of Kruševo evoked a time and place when ordinary people put into practice principles recognizably similar to those of the present.

As a whole the speech marked a bold attempt to put history to work for a progressive agenda, by casting long-dead Macedonians as virtual participants in a modern political process. It was the culmination of an extensive campaign by Macedonia's government to encourage participation, which led to a high turnout in all communities except those where Albanians constituted a local majority, and almost unanimous support for sovereignty from those who cast their ballots. Whether they were motivated more by rational calculations about future prosperity and present insecurity, or by sentiments regarding a treasured past, we cannot know. Nor can we definitively disentangle the reasons for the Albanian boycott. What is striking, though, is that support among Macedonians crossed the lines of generation, gender, region, and party affiliation. Whatever their disagreements—and there were many, especially over the Macedonian experience during the Yugoslav period—Macedonians could find common cause over the personality of Goce Delčev and the symbolism of events in Kruševo in 1903.

The processes that provided Gligorov and others with this usable past began in earnest in the 1940s, even as Tito entered the arena of cultural competition over Macedonia. It was then that first one state, and then another, set to work to locate the sources of present conditions in past activism by people they claimed as kindred spirits. They found in 1903 tangible signs of collective action, and in Kruševo in particular a community launched upon a project that they recognized as a forerunner of their own. Gligorov's speech represented an ambitious extension of this impulse, which traced the currents of life backward and forward: earlier manifestations of attempts to yoke past and future are examined chapter 6 and onward. Kruševo 1903, though, had a life before it became wrapped up in Yugoslavia and Macedonia after 1944, and the next three chapters focus on parts of the period between 1903 and 1944, when the direction of the current undammed by ten days in August 1903 was not yet certain.

CHAPTER THREE

"Crowded Out by a Plethora of Facts"

DISTANCE AND EXPERIENCE IN WESTERN
NARRATIVES OF KRUŠEVO

THE NUMBER OF Macedonians in the Republic of Macedonia grew in every census between 1948 and 1994. Those who classify themselves in this way have in common a strong sense of themselves as heirs to a distinctive Macedonian history. They may disagree on the details, especially regarding the impact of alliances made between Macedonian activists of the past with Bulgarian nationalists or Yugoslav socialists. Some believe firmly in their collective descent from Alexander the Great, and others find such claims absurd. Cultural figures like the ninth-century Christian saints Cyril and Methodius, the nineteenth-century dictionary compiler Ǵorǵi Pulevski, or the interwar poet Kočo Racin are all generally viewed as more or less significant. But certain historical events and personalities are revered as vital to Macedonian history, and especially prominent are those associated with the period between 1893 and 1903, culminating in the Ilinden Uprising of 1903 and acts of bravery and principle around the mountain town of Kruševo.

Initial glimpses of the small slice of Macedonia's history represented by events in Kruševo in August 1903 were provided in chapter 1. In this chapter, and those that follow, I explore the ways in which different communities have interpreted those events and their aftermath. I conceive of all these communities as "imagined," but I take seriously the caveat provided by Benedict Anderson (1983); that we should pay attention to different "styles of imagining" in the constitution and maintenance of communities. As well as nations, whether conceived as "daily plebiscites" or momentarily manifest in a high-profile referendum, the communities under examination include towns whose members are linked by their locality, refugees and survivors connected by their memory, and élites defined by their ideology. One useful way to think about these communities is provided by Joanne Rappaport, who in discussing the Paez of Colombia evokes the notion of the "textual community, comprised of a group of people whose activities revolved around the interpretation of key texts" (1990:183). She goes on to state:

> The textual community par excellence is comprised of the followers of a world religion, united in the interpretation of sacred writings, such as the Christian

gospels. . . . But the textual community could also take the form of a nation, whose means of social control are based on a series of interpretations of fundamental texts, such as a constitution."

Rappaport's discussion illuminates two points of particular relevance to the discussion of the Macedonian past in general, and the events of the Ilinden Uprising in particular. However we construe the imagined quality of communities that are built around interpretations of the past, the particular role of historical documents as reservoirs of knowledge highlights the central importance attached to establishing absolute and irrevocable truth. In two of the accounts in chapter 1, for example, written materials feature centrally. Donka Budžakoska recalls being charged with preventing a "bag of books"— almost certainly Organization records, referred to in other biographies in the Ilinden dossier as *arhivi*, or archives—from falling into enemy hands, while the 1993 newspaper article reproduces a circulated proclamation in full.

Although this concern with documentary evidence is most commented on for the sway it holds over people in southeastern Europe, they are not the only ones with a stake in understanding events in Kruševo in 1903 through their written traces. Already in the mid-nineteenth century, Ottoman Macedonia had increasingly attracted European visitors (Jelavich 1954–55), but their numbers swelled dramatically with the region's increasing unrest, and especially the dramatic events of 1903. Diplomats, merchants, journalists, travelers, humanitarian aid workers, and gendarmerie officers all wrote accounts of what they saw, experienced, and understood, as did a smattering of foreigners who joined one or another of the revolutionary bands. Their accounts have helped mold enduring ideas about the region and the issues at stake both then and subsequently. In this chapter, I trace a debate over modes of explanation in a textual community originating in early twentieth-century Ottoman Macedonia, and continuing to the present. In the textual community I imagine here I am, perforce, a candidate for membership. For those who police its boundaries, I offer what follows as my statement of intent.

THE MACEDONIAN QUESTION: A PHILOSOPHICAL PERSPECTIVE

I begin not in the 1900s, but in the 1930s with Rebecca West: not the first British traveler to the Balkans, but one of the best known. Her monumental book *Black Lamb, Gray Falcon* has been used as a source of color and anecdote, and reportedly as a virtual guidebook by Robert Kaplan, whose own *Balkan Ghosts* acquired such a high profile during the violent break-up of Yugoslavia. West acknowledged the work of her own predecessors in a wry commentary which labels them as "Balkan-fanciers," championing one another of the many national causes of the region, and engaging in passionate claims and counterclaims regarding events which would indicate the guilt or innocence of one side or another in violence. As vivid and satirical illustration of the depths plumbed by the disputants, she offers an account of a heated debate that took place in 1912 over "whether Mr. Prochaska, the Austrian Consul in a town named Prizren, had or had not been castrated by the Serbs" (1941:20).

In West's own work, subsequent authors have seen a pro-Serb orientation. Yet what distinguishes the book is the author's observations of minutiae, which then serve as the basis for rumination on wider themes and illuminate her approach to knowledge. This pattern is clear from the opening of the book, where she describes watching a newsreel of the assassination of King Alexander of Yugoslavia in Marseille in 1934. Even in the context of such a dramatic event, West inserts a paragraph sparked by the sight of the suspension bridge in the harbor of Marseille which, she writes, disturbs her because "it reminds me that in this mechanized age I am as little able to understand my environment as any primitive woman who thinks that a waterfall is inhabited by a spirit, and indeed less so, for her opinion from a poetical point of view might be correct" (1941:15). The passage reveals an identification with and sympathy toward "non-rational" points of view, as well as a recognition that such understandings are under threat in a modern world that makes them inappropriate.

West devotes two hundred pages to Yugoslav Macedonia, for which she claimed a particular affinity. Among the sites she visited was a mountain called Kajmakčalan on the Greek border, where in the First World War, after earlier retreat through Albania, the Serbian army returned through Greece to defeat Bulgarian forces on Yugoslav territory. In the description of the site, she reflects on the nature of explanation and the difficulties in communicating complicated histories to American and British readers:

> Of this battlefield, indeed, we need never think, for it is so far away. What is Kaimakshalan? [sic] A mountain in Macedonia, but where is Macedonia since the peace treaty? This part of it is called South Serbia. And where is that, in Czechoslovakia, or in Bulgaria? And what has happened there? The answer is too long, as long indeed, as this book, which hardly anyone will read by reason of its length. Here is the calamity of our modern life, we cannot know all the things which it is necessary for our survival that we could know. This battlefield is deprived of its essence in the minds of men, because of their fears and ignorances; it cannot even establish itself as a fact, because it is crowded out by a plethora of facts. (1941:773)

Here West demonstrates her acute sensibility to the interconnections between the local, the national, and the global. One way to explain the meaning of Kajmakčalan, a mountain whose name could be translated into English as Butterchurn, was to recount not only the alliances and strategies of the First World War, but a wider history of national rivalries and border changes. Since West's words were published the contingencies of history have continued to work, turning first South Serbia (in 1944) and then Czechoslovakia (in 1993) into names from a past political order, demanding additional historical qualification. To do justice to the battle of Kajmakčalan, or perhaps any other event in the region, thus appears to demand a continuously expanding set of definitions, taking one further and further away from the original object of inquiry. The passage betrays a certain sense of despair in the face of such self-defeating regression.

West's account of Kajmakčalan resonates with the spirit in which her book opens. Although generally regarded as a travelogue, *Black Lamb, Grey Falcon* opens as a murder mystery. In her account of watching the newsreel repeatedly, trying to divine its meaning "like an old woman reading the tea-leaves in her cup" (1941:15), she claims that she understood the forces that killed the king, but she did not know enough of the king himself (1941:19). It was to understand the culture from which he came that she undertook her journey to his kingdom, where she came to realize that certain forms of knowledge demand different forms of knowing. Over the arc of 1,158 pages, she traces the struggle between two kinds of human intelligence and endeavor. From the unintelligible bridge and its intolerance of poetry, the argument unfolds to a conclusion which suggests that fascism's rise in Europe was built upon the antipathy of modern, sterile rationalization for the richer, more sensual and grounded understandings of life she found in her travels.

In Macedonia in particular, and its products, the author sees in almost every incident the threat that European blinkeredness poses to Yugoslav vitality, and announces her sense of duty to resist it. Watching Gypsies dancing in Skopje, she responds to her German travel companion, who calls them dirty and stupid, by attributing to them "a kind of nervous integrity, of muscular wisdom" (1941:661). In Ohrid, at the church of Sveti Jovan Kaneo perched on the lakeshore, she observes, "The congregation had realized what people in the West usually do not know: that the state of mind suitable for conducting the practical affairs of daily life is not suitable for discovering the ultimate meaning of life" (1941:713). And in the introduction to the book, after describing the tragedy of the king's assassination, she offers a more domestic example of the loss that results when the two worlds clash, and the sense of responsibility. Her Austrian doctor had insisted that some dresses she had bought from villagers in Macedonia be disinfected, and a washerwoman put them in strong soak:

> They were ruined. Dyes that had been fixed for twenty years had run and now defiled the good grain of the stuff; stitches that had made a clean-cut austere design were now sordid smears. Even if I could have gone back immediately and bought new ones, which in my weakness I wanted to do, I would have it on my conscience that I had not properly protected the work of these women which

should have been kept as a testimony, which was part of what the King had known as he lay dying. (1941:22)

West's book was published when Britain was at war with Nazi Germany and the United States was still neutral, which lends its feverish tone a political dimension. The contrast that she makes, though, between intimate forms of experiential knowledge and their more abstract rivals, also anticipated certain recent trends in social scientific writing. In the section on Ohrid, for example, West recounts the familiar Balkan story of the missionary activities of Cyril and Methodius, who translated the gospels into Old Church Slavonic in the ninth century, and their successors Clement and Naum, who built a university in Ohrid. "That is what it says in the books," she reports, but then immediately asks, "But what does that mean? How did these events look and sound and smell?" (1941:710). The line of inquiry she counterposes with dry history is that of ethnography, concerned with the sights and scents of what, after Clifford Geertz's famous formulation, anthropologists call local knowledge (Geertz 1983).

Social and cultural anthropologists have always tried in their writing to conjure this sense of "being there" and tie it to larger processes. One marvelous example is that of Michael Herzfeld's opening to his story of histories in dispute in the Cretan town of Rethimno:

> Early in the morning, above the fading dankness of the night, the warm spiciness of baking bread announces a long-established local craft. Another craft answers as, with the shrilling of their equipment, the carpenters' sawdust adds a distinctive sharpness, . . .
>
> As the shadows shorten, toward late morning, the vacuous sweetness of warming olive oil, wafted from dark windows, draws rich savor from meat, tomato, garlic, onion—and the neighbors' alert noses judge the wealth and care that goes into each household's dining that day. Meanwhile, an exigent modernity encroaches. The narrow streets have begun to reverberate to the screech and roar of motorbikes and the impatient horns of trucks trying to squeeze a passage through. Finally, with the leisurely, strolling tourists comes the chemical scent of suntan oil from, especially, the foreign women now heading for the beach, intensifying the scented soap and aftershave that the more modish local men have already spread generously round . . . as others exude the sweat of backbreaking labor and a whiff of mutton fat emanates from some passing villagers' heavy, dark clothes. The hours of this "smellscape" reproduce the larger changes in the town's history in a sensual, embodied, social time that risks losing itself, finally, in the packaged pollutants of the newest comers. (1991:3–4)

Herzfeld thus pursues explanation through evocation. Such rich descriptions of sight, sound, smell, and texture lie at the heart of the interpretive anthropological project, which derives from the immediate and observable processes of life governing social principles and enduring cultural ideals. This method can be traced to classic studies by key figures in the British, French, and American traditions, including Gluckman (1958), Bourdieu (1973), and Geertz (1973b). Attention to the senses blossomed in the late 1980s in works by scholars like Paul Stoller and Nadia Seremetakis, who made it their agenda to understand the wider world in relation to embodied experience. "In Songhay," writes Stoller, "one can taste kinship, smell witches, and hear the ancestors" (1989:5). For Seremetakis, "The erasure of one Greek peach poses the question: at what experiential level are the economic and social transformations of the EEC [European Economic Community] being felt?" (1994:3).

Rebecca West would recognize such interests and methods as kindred to her own. Yet her work also prompts comparison with philosophical discussions of meaning. The despairing tone of her reflection of Kajmakčalan, where she laments the vain task of complete definition, recalls work pioneered by Ludwig Wittgenstein. In the comments collected in *Philosophical Investigations*, Wittgenstein's principal goal was to demystify language, and demonstrate how people—especially philosophers—can be bewitched into a misguided search for essence behind names. Some concepts, he argues, like "game," are hard to define by means of a closed set of logical propositions; nonetheless, the word is generally understood from context. He goes on to discuss the use of historical names, such as Moses. A person might use the name to refer to a historical personality, but not necessarily always believe a unique set of propositions that meticulously define that personality's qualities. And an attempt to frame a set of such propositions, he goes on, would lead further into confusion rather than adding clarity. He illustrated this point with the following hypothetical situation:

> Suppose I give this explanation: "I take 'Moses' to mean the man, if there was such a man, who led the Israelites out of Egypt, whatever he was called then, and whatever he may or may not have done besides." —But similar doubts to those about "Moses" are possible about the words of this explanation (what are you calling "Egypt," whom the "Israelites" etc.?). . . . "But then how does an explanation help me to understand, if after all it is not the final one? In that case the explanation is never completed; so I still don't understand what he means, and never shall!" (1958:§87)

Wittgenstein's remedy was simple: explain only as necessary, and do not try to preempt potential misunderstanding for you may merely increase it. His audience was linguistic philosophers, and his purpose not to solve the problems they found in language, but to dissolve them.

Wittgenstein's discussion of philosophical confusion offers the potential for rethinking the roots of the Macedonian Question as it resurfaced in the 1990s. Clearly, there have been deliberate attempts by generations of Greeks,

Serbians, Yugoslavs, Albanians, Bulgarians and Macedonians to promote their own answers and discredit those of their opponents, and these have contributed to the confusion over the meanings of words. Clearly, too, more is at stake in wars over the territory of Macedonia than in parlor debates over the identity of Moses. Although the salience and urgency of these manifestly political dimensions varied through the course of the twentieth century, they were consistently perceived as constituting the heart of a single enduring problem, which foreign diplomats, journalists, scholars, and policy makers had all tried to resolve. Wittgenstein's observations, though, and the reflections of Rebecca West offer an alternative and subversive genealogy of confusion, which would suggest that successive attempts to craft definitive answers to the so-called Macedonian Question in fact constituted the very problem they aimed to resolve.

TELLING TALES OF MACEDONIA

When foreign observers tried to understand the fierce debates over Macedonia in the 1990s, they turned to their own predecessors for guidance. As well as invoking Rebecca West on Macedonia—though not in the same spirit as I do—journalist Robert Kaplan turned to writings from earlier in the twentieth century, citing John Reed and A. G. Hales.[1] In 1993, when violence in Bosnia was still raging, the Carnegie Endowment republished its 1914 report on the Balkan Wars of 1912–13, with a new foreword by George Kennan. These sources constitute only a tiny fragment of the mass of material on Ottoman Macedonia compiled by scores of journalists and travelers from the 1850s onward. Bourchier opened his essay "The Final Settlement in the Balkans," first published in 1917, by detailing not only his own experience in the Balkans, but also a compendium of sources he had read. "Among these," he stated, "may be mentioned Leake, Poqueville, Ami Boué, Cyrien Robert, Lejean, Tozer, Cousinéry, Mackenzie and Irby, Hahn, Niderle, Jirecek, Louis Leger, Weigand, Victor Berard, Evans, Chirol, Leon Lamouche and Brailsford" (Bourchier 1926:267). This does not exhaust the ethnographic and analytical sources, omitting for example A.J.B. Wace and M. S. Thompson (1914), Edith Durham (1905), and from Serbia, Jovan Cvijić (1907). It also omits a slew of books published for the popular market as violence increased in the region, especially after the Ilinden Uprising of 1903. Travelers, war correspondents, and enterprising writers who had participated in fighting against Ottoman forces all authored works on Macedonia and its people. As well as Frederick Moore, whose account of Kruševo was cited in chapter 1, others included George Abbott (1903), Gaston Routier (1903), Maurice Gandolphe (1904), Reginald Wyon (1904), John Booth (1905), H. H. Munro, who published under the name Saki (1919), Sir

Thomas Comyn-Platt (1906), John Fraser (1906), A.D.H. Smith (1908), and Albert Sonnischen (1909).

Much of this literature exemplifies what Maria Todorova terms Balkanism (Todorova 1994, 1997). Todorova argues that in the late nineteenth century in particular, certain tropes acquired dominance in representations of south-eastern Europe, especially those areas most influenced by Ottoman rule. Westerners describing their travels were particularly struck by the diversity they confronted, especially in the cities of the region where they spent much of their time. They also saw that diversity as the root of conflict in the region, which pitted influences and populations against one another. And these writers represented their overall experience as a brush with a kind of fantasy world, where colors and smells come to life and the modern traveler is confronted with images that belong in fiction or in ancient history.

The sense of alienation, and of determination to convey a vivid sense of place and sensory overload, is evident in many descriptions of Ottoman Macedonia. George Abbott, for example, described a visit to Petritz, a market town in Pirin Macedonia, in the following terms:

> It was market day (Wednesday) and the dry gravelly water course, which here also forms the main thoroughfare, was alive with buyers and sellers; a motley assembly, presenting a highly-coloured panorama of national costumes and dialects, features and faiths. Besides the familiar Turkish official in threadbare uniform and the equally familiar figure of the Greek tradesman, there were Bulgarian rustics in shaggy goatskin caps and sheepskin jackets, rubbing shoulders with Wallachian shepherds in white kilts and long blue cloaks; Koniars in shabby brown breeches mixed with shabbier gypsies [sic] from a ragged encampment outside the town.
>
> ... [C]attle, fruit, fowls, vegetables, salted fish, and cheap jewellery were exhibited on every side. The babel of tongues was swelled by the inarticulate braying and bleating of hairy quadrupeds, the cackling and crowing of feathered bipeds, and by the din of bells and the clang of chains. As heterogeneous a conglomeration of sounds and scenes, colours and forms, as ever furnished the stuff for a maniac's dream. (1903:154)

Such descriptions foreshadow those of later travel writing and ethnography, like the excerpt of Michael Herzfeld's work. As Todorova indicates, though, in the Ottoman Macedonian context they do more than conjure a sense of place. They demonstrate a remarkable unity of effect, which contributes to a bank of stereotypes at the same time as drawing upon it. A vocabulary of disrepair and disorder dominates the passage—clothes are "shabby" or "threadbare," a settlement is "ragged," the market itself a "motley assembly." Communication, too, is broken down, conveyed first by allusion to the biblical tower of Babel and then by a suggestion that beasts and humans are parts of one great cacophony.

And yet through this fantasyland, the Western observer claims to see clearly enough to distinguish some of the distinct parts of which it is composed. For alongside the visual and aural adjectives are some which link this scene to a wider political context, as Abbott picks out Turks from Greeks, Bulgars from Wallachians, and Koniars from Gypsies. Abbott draws clear lines between these Balkan types, relying on stored-up knowledge of an apparent ethnic division of labor also manifest in other descriptions of the period. In Ottoman Macedonia, he suggests, Turk meant government official, Greek merchant, Bulgar peasant, and Wallachian shepherd.

Some of these equations had stronger hold than others. Stoianovich exhaustively explores the case of the Greek merchant (1960), while the connection of Wallachians, otherwise referred to as Vlahs, with pastoral livelihood is registered also in the etymology of the modern Greek term for shepherd, *vlahos* (Campbell 1964; Fermor 1966:28; Wace and Thompson 1914; Winnifrith 1987).[2] Stereotypes of this sort frequently had local roots, reported by commentators. Stoianovich, for example, notes that "Class-conscious Slavic peasants also applied the term 'Greek' to most merchants, particularly if they considered them rogues" (1960:311). In 1907 Jovan Cvijić described the usage of the term "Bulgar" among Macedonian peasants in the following terms:

> When the Macedonian peasants use the term Bulgar, they mean by it 1) people of a simple and hard-working life, 2) the bulk of simple labourers who speak Slavic, in contrast to the non-Slavs, the Greeks and the Turks, who are above this majority and consider them inferior. The first meaning is the main one: the word "Bulgar" denotes in the first case a simple mode of life, work and thought. (1907:21)

Cvijić goes on to give further examples of linguistic usages that lend the distinction a moral flavor: when something deteriorated it was said to *pobougari se*; spoiled flour was said to *izbougari se* (ibid.).

The status hierarchy in Ottoman Macedonia, especially noticeable between urban Greeks and rural Bulgars, was a product of history. From the middle of the eighteenth to the middle of the nineteenth century, Greeks, Bulgars, and Wallachians were, from the Turkish point of view, all members of a single religious community, the Orthodox Christian, or *Rum millet*. Overseen by the Patriarch, who had his seat in Constantinople, *Rumi* worshipped in Greek and organized much of their lives as members of congregations controlled by local notables. All these groups, however, spoke different languages within their homes. It was only later in that century that attempts were made, by indigenous and foreign actors, to institute or revive alternative languages of worship and education.[3]

In western Macedonia, as noted in the previous chapter, Albanian language activism was launched, but was impeded by both the Greek Orthodox and Turkish Muslim religious communities. By the end of the nineteenth century, Serbian and Vlah language activism were also under way in the region. The greatest challenge to Greek cultural dominance among the Orthodox Christian community, though, was spearheaded by the Bulgarian language revival, which enjoyed Russian backing. The first Bulgarian language periodical was produced in 1844 in Smyrna (Gewehr 1967:34), but activism was soon concentrated in Ottoman Europe, where Bulgarian challenged Greek as the language of literacy and worship among the Emperor's Orthodox Christian subjects there. The Bulgarian cause received a major fillip in 1870, when by imperial decree a new religious institution was created, called the Exarchate. This created a new millet under Ottoman rule. The core of the new millet's jurisdiction was made up of the dioceses which lie within modern Bulgaria, a largely rural Orthodox population that was almost exclusively Slavic-speaking. The bishoprics of this area were simply transferred from the authority of the existing Patriarchate to that of the new Exarchate, which also had its seat in Constantinople.

From the point of view of the Orthodox Patriarchate, this represented a blow to prestige, as well as a reduction in its revenues. What made the creation of the new millet still more threatening was a clause in the decree which permitted further expansion of the authority of the new Exarchate beyond these frontiers, and which recognized aggregate decision making as a determinant of religious affiliation. If two-thirds of a congregation outside the frontiers of these bishoprics wished to transfer their church from the jurisdiction of the Patriarch to that of the Exarch, they could do so. The natural target constituency for the new Exarchist movement were the Bulgars: Macedonia's Slavic-speaking, rural Christian population. The creation of the Bulgarian principality in 1878 added another new term to identity categories; now it became possible to talk not only of Bulgars, but also of Bulgarians.

The radical political changes of the late nineteenth century generated the grounds for considerable confusion between the meanings of words. This is made clear elsewhere in George Abbott's text, where he encounters greater trouble in carrying out his classification than he reported in the marketplace in Petritz. He gives the following account of an attempt to enlist local assistance in defining the local peasantry in Dojran, a town now in the Republic of Macedonia on the Greek border:

> To my queries concerning the nationality of these people I received two answers, contradictory in appearance, yet easily reconcilable by those who are familiar with Eastern ways of thought and expression. The Commissary, being a Turk, called them Greeks, or rather Romans, Roum. He was thinking of their religion. To him Christian and Greek were convertible terms. The engineer, being a European, called them Bulgars. He was thinking of their language. By a

simple algebraical operation one gets the nett [*sic*] result: "Christians speaking a Slavonic idiom." (1903:60)

Abbott's easy answer to the conundrum ignores or overlooks the increasing political dimensions of religious belonging and language choice or ability. Macedonia's rural population perhaps tried to do the same; they certainly appear to have evaded direct questioning by Abbott, who relied on intermediaries in his investigation. Here he satisfies himself with a reading that strips away the possible confusion generated by two words whose meanings bleed over into the realm of national identity; he confines the range of each within a distinct realm of objective fact—one either is Christian or not, and one speaks Bulgarian or not—and thereby makes them compatible. The algebraic work does nothing to capture or convey the sense that other sources give, that a bland answer of this kind was a luxury the peasants themselves could no longer afford, as armed men began to appear in their villages, forcing them to choose one national designation or another, and live or die by it.

Diplomatic personnel had to deal over a longer period with the definitional challenges that the new nationalisms posed. The sense of their recognition of complexity is apparent in the range of terms that they used in the years immediately before and after 1900 to try and describe what was happening in Ottoman Macedonia, and distinguish truth from propaganda. In British Foreign Office correspondence in 1898, for example, one author revealed his skepticism over whether Serbian schooling would achieve its goal, that children "forget that they are really Bulgarians." On 30 September 1903, the consul in Monastir described an individual as "a Greek who, notwithstanding his protests before the Inspector General, in my presence, has been made to pose as a Wallachian." On 31 October 1903, interviewing discharged members from revolutionary bands, he discovered "Serbs, Wallachs and Patriarchist Slavs calling themselves Greeks." On 26 January 1903, one consul describes as critical the difference between Exarchists and "the Orthodox, or Roum as they are officially termed, whether Greeks or Vlachs." In February 1904, a despatch uses the distinct categories Patriarchist Bulgars and Exarchist Bulgarians without comment. In April of the same year, the same author describes the concept of "Bulgarophone Hellenes," used by the Greek government, as "anomalous."[4] Even where the state sponsorship of identities played a lesser role, names did not have straightforward meaning. Albanians might be qualified as being Catholic, Christian, Gheg, or Tosk—the latter two terms highlighting some regional, and linguistic differences. Wallachians, or Vlahs, could feature in reports as Greco-Vlachs, bearers of "Kutso-Vlach nationality" or as "Wallachs of Roumanian tendencies."[5] A clerk sitting in London, charged with summarizing this material, might well think they had wandered into a "maniac's dream."

CATEGORIES IN COLLISION: RELOCATING CONFUSION

The struggles to establish political succession by different groups contributed considerably to the confused picture gained by European and American travelers. Also important, though, was their profound sense of alienation in dealing with more basic aspects of life in Ottoman Macedonia. They came from countries where time and space were counted and measured with precision, and where central states controlled monetary systems of exchange, and maintained records of their populations which distinguished individuals one from another as a matter of course. In the Ottoman Empire, they confronted different practices that challenged principles they took for granted.

The European Gregorian calendar was out of step with the Julian calendar used by Orthodox Christians in the Ottoman Empire, and both were different from that used by Muslims (Akan n.d.). Ilinden 1903 for European writers fell on 2 August, but for those who organized the Uprising, it was 20 July. Once grasped, it was easy for travelers to deal with this straightforward relationship, and they used the established convention of designating Julian dates as old style, or o.s. More exasperating to travelers was Turkish time-reckoning, which by their different accounts designated dusk, whenever it fell, as twelve midnight, or sunrise as twelve noon (Barkley 1877:181; Abbott 1903:90; Fraser 1906:119). Watches, however reliable, had to be reset every day, and Westerners thus found their ideas and practices of timekeeping inapplicable. One traveler saw this as a marker of the inversion of the order of things in the Empire, where a watch had to be adjusted at least twice a day. "It may be the best time-keeper in the world, but the more accurate it is the less does it keep proper time in Turkey. Indeed, a watch that is somewhat vagrant in its moods is more likely to be correct" (Fraser 1906:119). In a similar vein, the value of silver was never standardized in the Empire, so travelers found themselves in unfamiliar territory each time they went to a different market to buy local currency.

Determining the locations of events and personal identity also posed problems. An irreducible locality and impenetrability was noted with frustration by Abbott when seeking information about topographical features. "To a native, a river is 'the river,' a mountain 'the mountain,'" he wrote. "Beyond that he neither knows nor cares to know" (1903:152). Thomas Comyn-Platt observed more bluntly that all maps were wrong (1906:14). Certainly villages in different parts of Ottoman territory bore the same name: the context had never arisen in which they would need to be distinguished. Similarly, villagers did not have formalized surnames, the product of states concerned to make their subjects "legible" (Scott 1998:64–71). Male Slavic peasants generally bore as patronymic the name of their father, while women replaced their patronymic with their husband's given name at marriage. Knowledge of

descent and kinship, vital for the calculus of possible marriages, was preserved in the local community. Such features of life were seen by some
visitors as signs of backwardness or illogicality: their effect, though, was to
put the travelers at a disadvantage. In the vilayets of Turkey in Europe in
1903, where Western observers encountered an alienated population and an
administration uninterested in creating maps and records, "local knowledge"
ruled, and travelers could not always gain access to it.

Travelers and journalists struggled to make sense of a situation where
their notions of what counted as accurate information did not match local
categories. They also operated under a number of practical constraints. Very
few knew the languages of the area—Turkish, modern Greek, Albanian,
Vlah, and the various Balkan Slavic variants—and so most put themselves at
the mercy of local interpreters. Their problems in making themselves understood were compounded by the obstacles that the Ottoman authorities put in
the way of travelers seeking to get away from the major towns and thoroughfares, where their activities were monitored.[6]

Such problems only spurred the enthusiasm of a generation of young and
ambitious journalists and diplomats, who saw opportunities for advancement
in such hardship and adversity. The practical discomforts of travel in Ottoman Macedonia—unwholesome food, the prevalence of dirt and disease,
flea-ridden lodgings, bureaucratic obstructionism—are made abundantly
clear in the wealth of writings from this period, especially the travel narratives.[7] So, too, is the threat of violence against Europeans. The dangers of
traveling in the area were not new: Edward Lear had been stoned by Albanians in Elbasan for trying to draw them, and accused of being a Russian
enemy of the Sultan ([1851] 1988:55), and the Dilessi affair in Greece in the
1860s had left British subjects murdered (Jenkins 1961). But the frequency
and audacity of kidnapping by brigands had increased by the turn of the
century, the most famous instance being that of the American missionary
Miss Stone, who was held for ransom through a whole winter and released
unharmed in 1902 (Stone 1902). A British employee of the Tobacco Régie
kidnapped in July 1905 was less fortunate, and was released only after his
captors cut off one of his ears (Martin Willis 1906). Diplomatic status did
not guarantee protection. Two European consuls had been lynched by a mob
in Salonika in 1879, and Rostowski, the Russian consul in Monastir, was
shot by a Turkish soldier during the Ilinden uprising in August 1903.

Rostowski's fate in particular demonstrated that risk came not only from
brigands, but also from representatives of the Ottoman régime. Although his
killer was quickly tried and executed under Ottoman law, suspicion remained
strong among Muslims in Macedonia that Europeans were sympathetic to
revolutionary activities among the Christian population, and paid insufficient
respect to the Sultan. Various accounts describe confrontations caused by the
signals sent by their dress: Brailsford, for not wearing a fez, was threatened

by a sentry who thought he should (1906:78n), while Booth, who wore a Norfolk cap resembling the headgear of VMRO band members, encountered trouble on the Turkish-Bulgarian frontier as a consequence (1905:46). Walking the streets of Monastir after the Ilinden Uprising, Reginald Wyon felt conspicuous and vulnerable as the only person wearing European headwear (1904:78). Sartorial know-how, allegedly, saved Saki (H. H. Munro) and Frederick Moore from death when they were walking on the railway line outside Salonika after a terrorist cell had launched a bombing campaign in the city. In a letter, Saki described his own cleverness in turning up his white collar, which made it clear even to Turkish conscripts that he was a European and no slinking brigand (Langguth 1981:97–98). Saki and Moore might have been shot, but instead were merely arrested and detained on suspicion of dynamiting.[8]

Other Western visitors speak with pride of risk-taking, dealing with recalcitrant officials, hoodwinking local authorities, or tricking their escorts. In 1898 L. S. Amery insisted on approaching individual Albanians between Skopje and Prizren with questions like, "Are you Serbian?" and commands like, "Stop, let me take your photograph." He also, according to the local *Vali*'s or administrator's complaint to the British consul and his own account in his diary, broke an iron umbrella on the head of a police officer (Amery 1980:26; FO 195/2029/45). Abbott recounts the favorable impression that a "firm and manly attitude" made on Turks (1903:56). When Booth and Moore, traveling unaccompanied, encountered potential danger in the shape of a picket of Albanian troops, they opted to play it "high and haughty," and produce their British passports, which overawed the soldiers (Booth 1905:218). Reginald Wyon, determined to document Turkish atrocities, entitles one chapter "Bearding the Turk" and describes how he defied travel restrictions, going without an escort to photograph a burned Christian village. He got involved in a confrontation with an armed and angry soldier, incensed by Wyon's refusal to accompany him to see his lieutenant, and by his remark that "an Englishman was not at the beck and call of every petty Turkish officer" (1904:126).[9]

Although these individuals defied the imperial authorities, and in their accounts often took a mock-heroic stance in so doing, those who came after 1903 recognized that in Ottoman Macedonia citizenship of a great power did not confer immunity. Rostowski's murder, provoked by the Russian's insistence that an Ottoman soldier salute him in accordance with diplomatic etiquette, vividly showed the danger in playing the high-handed European. So too, as the comments above on dress indicate, travelers realized that a visit to Ottoman Macedonia was not just an opportunity to observe eccentric styles of dress; they too were observed, and their very lives might be at risk unless they made certain compromises. Abbott, for example, donned a fez as "a talisman to ward off the evil eye of brigands" (1903:88). Wyon and a companion tried to walk to the village of Armensko, but after defying authorities turned back when they came across an Albanian regiment, encamped on their route—for, he writes, "Both of us knew enough of the

Albanians" (1904:117). What almost all the journalists mention in particular is having to comply with Ottoman regulations which demanded that they carry a *teskere*, or Ottoman passport, and have it stamped by the local administrator, or Vali, with what Wyon calls a *visé* when they wished to visit a particular region (Wyon 1904:27).

MACEDONIA AS FUTURE

The Ottoman teskere represents a form of modern state surveillance that at the time was revolutionary. Where travelers frequently described conditions in Ottoman Macedonia as primitive or backward, with regard to the teskere, they were experiencing a part of the future. The passport, and the demand that the traveler be always ready to present it, was a device that, as Paul Fussell writes in *Abroad*, only became familiar to British travelers in the 1930s (1980:24–31; see also Torpey 2000). The reactions of George Abbott and John Booth to this state classification project foreshadow the account Fussell gives of Robert Byron's reaction to the Ottoman demand for "Distinguishing Characteristics." Both Abbott and Booth satirize the personal description. In one case, this is because it offers "a far more flattering portrait of my person than the one presented by my looking-glass. Among other things I am therein described as exceedingly tall, with light hair and eyes recalling the azure of the sky, whereas nature has blessed me with a medium height . . . black hair and dark eyes" (Abbott 1903:43). In the other account, the teskere reportedly takes detail to an absurd level, recording ". . . name, profession, age, size, colour of hair and eyes, shape of nose, mouth and chin, and detailed intentions . . ." (Booth 1905:167).

The power of the Ottoman state to classify its European visitors was a reminder that for all its apparent rack and ruin, Turkey was still a Great Power and was in the process of modernization.[10] New legislation introduced under the *Tanzimat* reforms of the mid-nineteenth century affected property law, permitting Christians to purchase land. Railways crisscrossed the Balkan peninsula in the course of the last two decades of the nineteenth century (Gounaris 1993). Telegraph wires became a part of the landscape in the same period, linking the Sultan in Constantinople to the various provincial headquarters. New communications brought a flood of manufactured goods from Europe into Ottoman Macedonia. Although many of the travelers focused on the archaic aspects of the landscape and social life, chance references let slip that they were in fact wandering in a world filled with signs of modernity. One seemingly omnipresent in the fabric of daily life was the petroleum tin, put to other uses. Western travelers showered under them, used them as seats and tables in cafés, and saw shacks and chimneys and market wares made from the recycled sheet metal (Moore 1906:79, 173, 197; Abbott 1903:123–4; Brailsford 1906:81; Walshe 1920:197). Booth goes so far as to say, "The petroleum tin holds Turkey together as the raw-hide reim does South Africa" (Booth 1905:227).

Elsewhere in the world, such technology and market penetration worked in parallel to assure the maintenance and reinforcement of colonial rule through the indirect exercise of power. Thus in British-controlled Alexandria, according to Timothy Mitchell, new means of communication allowed the production, circulation, and consumption of images which conjured what he called "the enormous truth of colonialism—both its description and its justification" (1991:168). In the Balkans, though, new national states promoted their own images of the Christian population as yearning to be free. European powers pursued their own economic and strategic interests, and exerted pressure on Turkey to introduce more radical reforms. Such initiatives from outside the borders served to inspire anti-Ottoman activism by armed extremists who hoped to trigger more decisive intervention. In this climate, the Ottoman state wielded the coercive power of modern technology more directly. With modern weapons and training supplied by Germany, the Turkish army had proved more than a match for Greece in the Greco-Turkish War of 1897–98, and in Macedonia it could draw on the technologies of railway, telegraph, and modern artillery to mount brutally effective counterinsurgency warfare.

Some travelers, especially those who were advocates of radical change, drew specific attention to the disastrous effects of modern technology. George Young, for example, claimed that in the service of the Ottoman Empire, ". . . the machinery of civilization . . . the railway, the telegraph, the police . . . were instruments for the destruction of all that makes for civilization" (1915:20–21). Brailsford, one of the more penetrating critics of all empires, claimed in his writing on Macedonia that "the telegraph has done more even than gunpowder to perpetuate despotism" (1906:4). He reiterated the claim later, and in an early argument for the underdevelopment that accompanies modernity, claimed from the vistas of ruined Vlah cultural centers that "despite railways and reforms, Macedonia has actually retrograded in civilization during the past century" (1906:178). For Brailsford, increasing state capacity only worsened the lot of many Christian subjects. Along with other supporters of the revolutionary cause, he saw the Ilinden Uprising of 1903 as a measure of the desperation that the peasantry felt, and the savage reprisals of the Ottoman state as tragic affirmation of the destructive capacity that modern technology provided.

KRUŠEVO 1903: THE FIRST ACCOUNTS

The events of August 1903 left around 1,000 revolutionaries and almost 6,000 civilians dead, 200 villages destroyed or sacked, and more than 70,000 people homeless (Kennan [ed.] 1993:34). The scale of the destruction attracted considerable international attention, manifested in the efforts of consuls and reporters to establish precisely what had happened and who was to blame, humanitarian organizations to alleviate human suffering, and governments to increase pressure for the implementation of reform. The occupation of the town of Kruševo, and its subsequent bombardment and sack, was a central concern in this investigative and practical activity. The situation in the town during the Uprising was a subject of daily report in London newspapers, and British diplomatic correspondence included eyewitness evidence from Kruševo refugees. The town was one of nine locations where the Anglo-American Macedonian Relief Committee set up depots. European journalists pressed the Ottoman governor in Monastir, Hilmi Pasha, to account for what had happened and take measures to prevent further suffering (Wyon 1904:39; Gandolphe 1904:58–63). Frederick Moore was able to visit the town to write the account given in chapter 1 (Moore 1906:262–76).[11]

Yet the whole truth of what had happened proved elusive, as those conducting the inquiry ran into the various obstacles to knowledge described earlier. For all the modern communications technology in Ottoman Macedonia, information was slow to emerge from Kruševo. Who were the insurgents, and what was their intention? Did they have the support of the local population? How long did they hold the town? And what happened when the town was recaptured by Ottoman forces? Such apparently fundamental questions lay at the heart of coverage in the British media, including the London *Times*, where the unfolding of the story can be traced in issues from 5 August to 19 August. Part of the time lag in reporting was the result of the activities of the insurgents, whose first actions included the destruction of the telegraph office in Kruševo and the cutting of wires all over the Monastir vilayet to impede Ottoman communications. As a result, it was not until three days after the Uprising of 2 August that the first reference to events in Kruševo appeared in the *Times*, which included a piece with the byline of Constantinople, 4 August, reading as follows:

> A dispatch from Hassan Hilmi Pasha reports that a Bulgarian band, about 150 strong, attacked and set fire to the Turkish villages of Dolindje and Ramna, in the Caza of Monastir. The band destroyed the Government konak [government building] and the telegraph office in the village of Korshovo by means of fire bombs. The revolutionists also set fire to all the granaries belonging to Turks and Greeks, and forced the Bulgarian population of the villages they traversed to join them on pain of death. The authorities, who foresaw the movement several days ago, had adopted military measures of precaution, and it is hoped that the bands may be suppressed in a few days.

Not only was the name of the town wrong: the event was considered as an act of brigandage, part of the ongoing low-intensity conflict waged by a handful of malcontents among the Christian population, without wider support. Only on the next day were more numerous events reported and granted coherence and method, as part of a general insurrection. This came about, in the first case, because it was recognized as such by Ottoman sources in Constantinople, and secondly, because the "Macedonian Organization" published a statement that "revolution" had been proclaimed in the vilayet of Monastir (ibid., 6 August 1903:3). The dateline for this statement was 5 August, Sofia, Bulgaria. In the next few days pieces on Macedonia were published from the *Times* correspondent in Vienna, who offered British readers stories from the German-language press. As time went on the newspaper's London staff received letters from Monastir, and included the information in their reports.

The first reports highlighted the massacre of fifty troops in the Ottoman garrison, and commentaries suggested that this represented the enactment of a deliberate policy to provoke reprisals. It was also reported, on 12 August, that "Greek and Kutzo-Wallach" bands had been formed against the insurgents, who were also referred to as *komitajis*. The 13 August issue included a letter from a Special Correspondent lately in Macedonia, who objected to the suggestion that the revolutionists were an isolated minority. On the authority of three months in the region, he asserted "they all seem to be revolutionists at heart—Bulgarian, Servian, Greek, Wallachian, Albanian— even the Turk himself if you get him out of range of a mosque or the government konak" (*Times*, 13 August 1903:6).

Further conflicting reports began to be printed not only regarding the loyalties and intentions of different groups, but also the course of events. The different rates at which news reached the *Times* from different locations served to heighten the sense of chronological uncertainty. On 15 August, a report dated 14 August from Constantinople was quoted stating that troops had reoccupied Kruševo; on 17 August, a telegram was received that there was no official confirmation of this fact. The paper's same issue carried a story that the insurgents had defended the town, and a number had taken refuge in the church. The military commandant had been ordered not to attack, but to ask the Bulgarian Exarch to intercede, to bring about their surrender. Then on 19 August, at least three days after the end of the insurgent occupation as described by all eyewitness accounts, three separate references to Kruševo appeared in the newspaper. The first bore the dateline Sofia 18 August and stated, "The report that Krushevo has surrendered to the Turkish troops is denied." The second was from the the the *Times*'s own correspondent in Vienna also dated 18 August, and carried the first hint of the tragedy that had befallen the town, alongside a report of the official version of events:

> Private telegrams from Constantinople to the Zeit state that the Turkish troops have burned Krushevo and have massacred the inhabitants . . . An official telegram from Constantinople speaks again of negotiations between the Turks and

the komitajis near Krushevo "in order to avoid bloodshed." Possibly the Turkish object is to gain time for the mobilization and concentration of troops.

The same page of the *Times* also carried a report with the dateline Constantinople 17 August, which read, "According to news from Monastir, dated yesterday evening, fighting at Krushevo continues, and the Greek Metropolitan has left Monastir for that place. Many refugees are at Monastir."

The British reader of the *Times* on 19 August 1903 was thus confronted with three accounts that disagreed on the most basic sequence of events and which hinted at a logic that was alien. Not only was the question of who controlled the town at that time unanswered; also unclear was the nature of the relationship between the parties. The forces of order were at one moment negotiating with brigands to save lives, and at the next, massacring civilians. The insurgents were either holding firm or had abandoned the town. A religious leader was going up to a town that had already been abandoned by at least some of its population. Some reports deny others. The sources stack up and disagree over what common sense would suggest should be clear-cut: a surrender either happens or it does not. Each time the "reportedness" of an account is emphasized its authority is diminished, and the reader is reminded of the gap between events and descriptions that newspapers, in general, seek to close.

In the second story, private reports are juxtaposed with state versions. The two conflict directly, and seem equally credible on their own terms. The fact of negotiations is accepted, but immediately serves as the basis for speculation concerning the possibility of double-dealing by the Turkish government. Here lurks a sense that the Ottoman Empire would never genuinely seek to negotiate with brigands nor to save life: their real agenda must lie elsewhere, within the stereotypes of Turkish rule. The third story, meanwhile, in its bland assertion that "fighting at Krushevo continues," leaves open the question of who was doing the fighting, whether townsfolk or insurgents, *bashibazouks* or Imperial troops, and whether it was a large-scale conflict or mopping-up operations—details that matter a great deal in making sense of the situation.

It is perhaps no wonder that the editorial column on that day opened by saying, "What has happened at Krushevo seems to be quite uncertain." But in homage to the journalistic ethos, the editorial writer nonetheless produced the following attempt at overview:

It was believed in Constantinople on Sunday [16 August] that fighting was still going on there, and it was stated that the Greek Metropolitan had left Monastir for that place. The object of his mission is not stated, but presumably it was to render assistance in some form to the Turks, in whose service the Greek ecclesiastics, as well as the Greek government and the Greek people, appear to be showing a zeal which must gratify, if it does not edify, their adversaries of a few years ago. The Hellenic Government have done their best to give Abdul Hamid practical help of real value by instructing their consuls in Macedonia to advise the Greek inhabitants of the province to denounce refugee Bulgarian insurgents to the Turkish authorities, and the Ecumenical Patriarch himself is busy pouring complaints into the willing ears of the Porte [the equivalent of a Prime Minister] of the outrages which the komitajis perpetrate upon the Greek peasants. So true is Mr. Balfour's reminder to the impetuous friends of the revolutionists that the Christian peoples of the Balkan States are by no means of one mind amongst themselves. The Turks appear to have given out that the reason why they have not completed the capture of Krushevo is their reluctance to spill more Christian blood than can be helped. The assertion has been received with some natural skepticism in Vienna, where it is suggested that they have opened a parley with the insurgents simply in order to gain time to bring up more men.

The language in this commentary is of political maneuvering: a renewed Greek-Turkish alliance, the cementing of Greek solidarity, anti-Bulgarian propagandizing, and veiled motives in Turkish negotiations with rebels. The writer offers an account that purports to cut through the surface noise and provide an objective assessment of the motives that underlie the behavior of leaders. It is deliberative, dry, and rational, and presumes that the task of explanation is to catalogue the existing interests of different agencies. In this way the approach accounts not only for people's actions, but also for the selective way in which they interpret events. Although it opens at the ground level, with "what has happened in Krushevo," it quickly moves outward and away from the uncertain fate of the population to pursue an orderly exposition of the logic behind the accounts and reactions of external constituencies. The paragraph conveys a lofty detachment, suggesting that the details, in the last resort, hardly matter: whatever happened in Kruševo was just part of a larger story of nations and empires at war.

Three days after this commentary appeared, on 22 August the *Times* published its first account of the bombardment and sack of Kruševo by Turkish forces. In measured tones, the article reported that 360 houses, all Greek and Wallach, 215 shops, and the Greek church and school were destroyed by shellfire on 12 and 13 August, while the Bulgarian quarter was untouched. On 14 August, "Turks" entered the town where they raped women, pillaged houses, and slaughtered "about 200 local Bulgarians and also 60 innocent Greeks and Wallachs." The material damage was extensive, reckoned at several million francs, and around 8,000 people made homeless (*Times*, 22 August 1903:3). The dateline for the story was Monastir, 20 August. A day earlier, the British representative in Monastir had reported in a telegram that the troops in fact had entered the town on 12 August, and directed all their attention to the "patriarchist quarter," where 366 houses, 203 shops, and churches were pillaged and torched by "troops and bashibazouks." Forty-one patriarchists were killed, two women violated, and only three Bulgarians killed. Regarding the escape of the Bulgarian quarter from damage and the low casualties among the Bulgarian population, he wrote that "bribery is suspected" (McGregor telegram, Monastir, 19 August 1903: FO 195/2157/312).

Clearly, the town's civilian population had been the target of a devastating assault, and Western journalists and consuls interviewed survivors to try to ascertain more details. All the eyewitnesses concurred that the havoc had been wreaked by Turkish forces. The looting had reportedly been led by bashi-bazouks from Albanian villages nearby, and there was general agreement that it had been conducted on a massive scale. Apart from money, jewelry, and small valuables, the heavy booty, including furniture, amounted to 2,000 cartloads (Chotziadis et al. 1993:61). Violence against women, by contrast, was said to have been mostly the work of *redifs*, or conscripts, from Prešovo (in the modern-day Republic of Serbia) or Ghilan (in Kosovo). On this issue estimates as to the number of victims varied, a fact attributed in part to the unwillingness of families to bring further dishonor on their female members by publicizing their misfortune. As to the numbers of houses and stores destroyed by fire, the number of 366 houses and 203 stores was generally agreed upon. All were in the lower part of the town.

Even as Western journalists and consuls expressed their outrage at the human tragedy, the sharp image of Kruševo's suffering began to lose its focus. Part of this was the product of deliberate artifice or misdirection. Whatever their loss of control or deliberate unleashing of violence, in Kruševo itself Ottoman authorities quickly revealed their mastery of information management and public relations. The insurgency provided them a perfect justification to further restrict the travel of foreign visitors, for security reasons, and they were thus able to limit the number of first-hand accounts and photographs of destruction that reached the outside world. When journalists came to interview Hilmi Pasha, he presented them with his own eyewitnesses and also commissioned efforts to generate signed statements from victims that would exonerate the Ottoman army. When forced to confront the fact of Kruševo's destruction, he either presented it as collateral damage, or assigned responsibility to renegade bashi-bazouks, who had defied their commander's efforts to protect the civilian population (Wyon 1904:39). He also provided sound-bite statistics on the Sultan's relief efforts. He depicted his own government and army as forces of order, in a conflict with retrograde elements. The implicit message was that the Ottoman authorities had the same progressive agenda as Europe, and should be assisted rather than condemned: the "balance of criminality," in a phrase used by Prime Minister Balfour in the British Parliament in discussions of Macedonia, lay with the rebels.

Western journalists nonetheless continued to speak of the "Kruševo massacre," referring to the activities of the Ottoman forces. However, the defensive campaign waged by Ottoman authorities over responsibility was soon boosted by the efforts of other parties to pursue their agendas over the town's ruins and corpses. The French consul in Salonika, on 25 August, reported reading a press source that the Greek government had communicated to the Great Powers "a note imputing the pillage and torching of Krouchovo to the Insurgents" (AMAE/NS Turquie-Macédoine, vol. 36, ff.108–10, No. 38). He rejected the imputation as pure fiction; however, it did reflect an important aspect of accounts of survivors from Kruševo's lower town. A British report dated 30 August 1903 stated that ". . . the Greco-Wallachs appear to be more exasperated against the Bulgarians for having escaped the ruin which they brought upon the rest of the Christian population than for any of their actions while in possession of the town" (Graves to O'Conor, Salonica, 30 August 1903: FO 195/2157/426). It was a small step to connect the negotiations between the insurgents and Ottoman forces with the sparing of the Bulgarian quarter, and argue that the Greco-Wallachs had been sold out. Such speculation weakened the status of the insurgents as representatives of an oppressed people, and cast them instead as opportunistic brigands, lacking principle. Kruševo, in this reading, was not a casualty in a broad-based struggle for freedom, but rather victim of Bulgarian national aggression against Hellenism.

Within a remarkably short time, the force of the immediate outraged reactions was dissipated by questions around the events. Like Kajmakčalan, as visited and described by Rebecca West thirty years later, Kruševo was "so far away" that people might well ask, "And what has happened here?" The answer might take the form of a proposition: There was fighting in Macedonia, and the Turks have burned a defenseless Christian town. One response to this would be to simply shrug and resort to stereotypes and received wisdoms. Of course, someone might say: That is what Macedonia is like, and that is what Turks do. "Violence was, indeed, all I knew of the Balkans," admitted Rebecca West (1941:21), reflecting on the English-language literature of the early twentieth century. Visiting a torched village and confronted with the bodies of children, Robert Kaplan's source, A. G. Hales, called the Turks "saliva-slobbering maniacs" (1918:215). Reginald Wyon wrote of the "bestial immorality" exhibited by irregular troops and the "inhuman barbarities" they practiced (1904:66).

But as West did on the battlefield of Kajmakčalan, it is possible to imagine a flurry of further questions in response to such an answer, seeking logic in the sequence of events and precision over the identity of the protagonists. Was the town really undefended? Could it have been destroyed by artillery or in hand-to-hand-combat? Would the army not have been right to fear an ambush? Were civilian casualties really only collateral damage—regrettable, but justifiable in a battle to restore governmental control? Or were they the work of rogue elements in the Turkish forces, understandably angry over the massacre of their fellow-soldiers? And if the town was undefended, why was that? What motive could those who started the fighting have, to capture a town and then abandon it? Were the Christians, perhaps, divided among themselves, and did they quarrel? Did one group betray another? Was the town wholly destroyed, or did some parts suffer more than others?

The search for a strand of cause and effect, as demonstrated earlier, led to speculation regarding hostility between Greco-Wallachs and Bulgarians, the indiscipline of Albanian reservists and irregulars, and shady dealings between insurgents and Ottoman commanders. But the profusion of answers and theories advanced by different parties in the event had a further effect, which also fed into familiar impressions of the region. As well as a place of violence in thrall to savage overlords, Macedonia was home to intense competition between factions, which they pursued in their recounting of recent events. So between the smooth media spinning of Ottoman officials, VMRO's overt attempts to enlist foreign support by amassing statistics of Turkish reprisals against villages, and the crude attempts by the Greek government and church to cast Bulgarians as the chief culprits, it was easy for an outsider to conclude that truth was the real victim of all had transpired. The tragedy of Kruševo, as well as that of other villages destroyed in the course of the Uprising, became part of the past, succeeded by a battle to shape its representation.

Something of the effect of this shift can be seen in the longer-term discussion of the events of 1903 in Western journalism. In 1991 Robert Kaplan described Macedonia as "History's Cauldron," the place that "offers a clearer window than any other region of the Balkans onto the sources of strife in the area" (1991:94). His article focused primarily on disagreements between spokespersons of Bulgaria, Greece, and the Republic of Macedonia over the past, and he records different sides of two core issues: the national identity of Goce Delčev, the hero invoked by Kiro Gligorov in 1991, and the naming of towns and villages in northern Greece. With regard to Kruševo 1903, he tells a more straightforward narrative, in a propositional mode:

> High in the mountains of Western Macedonia, 1,200 IMRO guerrillas proclaimed the Krusevo Republic. It lasted ten days, until 20,000 Turkish soldiers, supported by heavy artillery, overwhelmed the rebels in Krusevo. Forty of the rebels, rather than be taken alive, shot themselves in the mouth after kissing one another good-bye. Wild dogs and pigs devoured the corpses of townspeople killed by the Turks. (1991:100)

In *Balkan Ghosts*, published two years later, Kaplan offered a slightly expanded account, which included more graphic detail of atrocities and provided more numerical information. It also decimated the Turkish force, and renamed the town:

In the town of Krushovo, 4,000 feet up in the mountains of Western Macedonia,
IMRO proclaimed the "Krushovo Republic." It lasted ten days, until 2,000
Turkish troops, supported by artillery, overwhelmed 1,200 guerrillas in
Krushovo; forty of the guerrillas, rather than surrendering, shot themselves in
the mouth after kissing each other good-bye. The Turks reportedly raped 150
women and girls in Krushovo. Wild dogs and pigs devoured the naked corpses.
(1993:61)

Kaplan does not provide specific sources for either version. They both
include details given in other accounts, and therefore could be said to contain a kernel of truth. In both the article and the book, Kaplan follows this
account of one particular act of resistance and its aftermath with a statistical
snapshot of the wider picture: 5,000 civilian and 1,000 insurgent deaths,
widespread rape, and international intervention.

In each case Kaplan puts the example of Kruševo to work in a wider
frame. At the beginning of the article, he poses two guiding questions that
reveal his overarching agenda: "Why are peoples pitted so relentlessly one
against another? Why do hatreds run so deep?" (1991:94) Within this broad
framework, the fate of Kruševo is presented not as a subject for disagreement over history, but rather as an example of the struggle between an
empire and its subjects. Ilinden is presented as a liberation movement against
the Ottoman Empire, and in Kruševo all the core elements were represented
in more or less specific form: a bold declaration of freedom (the Republic), a
battle against overwhelming odds, self-sacrifice and loyalty to comrades
(those dying kisses), then atrocities by the enemies and no rest for the dead.
It is, in short, a large tale writ small.

Perhaps because it is such a large tale, the attempt to inject vivid detail
rings slightly false. Even at this small scale, the numbers are all round, and
the gestures bold and unambiguous, as if all the actors and victims were
aware they were playing before a large audience. In this respect, these two
accounts of Kruševo in 1903 seem to miss the mark that Kaplan, quoting
from Paul Fussell, set himself in the preface to *Balkan Ghosts*: "to make
essayistic points seem to emerge empirically from material data intimately
experienced" (1991:ix). Here it seems that the reverse process has occurred,
and a sequence of points about the Uprising and its place in Macedonian
history have shaped a description that reads as if written without the local
knowledge on which travel writing and ethnography rely. Writing from a
distance of ninety years and ninety miles—for he did not venture out of
Skopje on his visit to the Republic—Kaplan was also betrayed by his trusty
handful of sources. None of his guiding lights—Reed, Hales, Sciaky, even
West—ever reached Kruševo.[12]

In the epilogue to *Black Lamb, Gray Falcon*, Rebecca West wrote that she
found "a coincidence between the natural forms and colours of the western

and southern parts of Yugoslavia and the innate forms and colours of my imagination" (1941:1088). But for Kaplan, the story of Kruševo held no such fascination. Even if West encountered nothing but fragments of a story, she might have asked questions of the kind she posed either in Ohrid about the smells of the Byzantine age, or on Kajmakčalan to try to capture the Serbian sense of the place. But for Kaplan, the episode constitutes a self-contained module that can serve double duty: to encapsulate a set of adversarial attitudes and to deliver some kind of ersatz intimacy. In a section on gendered attitudes to knowledge, West writes that "a fact does not begin to be for a man until he has calculated its probable usefulness to him" (1941: 678). Kaplan's treatment of Kruševo, molding the events to fit into a larger picture and giving the story a light dusting of dramatic color, might have served her as an example.

Yet Kruševo can serve as the core of a different kind of inquiry. The question "what has happened here?" leads one way into disputes over the definitions of words and the timing of events. This is especially the case where the response to the question is an attempt at a brief, magisterial overview. To take Kaplan's two short descriptions as a starting point, one might ask: What is the difference between a guerrilla and a rebel? What does it mean to be taken alive, as opposed to surrendering? Who stripped the corpses of the townspeople, and when? In that direction, as the examples of early media and consular accounts show, lies the possibility of long, wearying regress. This form of "truth-deferral" presents itself as interested only in greater clarity, but can in fact increase rather than reduce confusion. As such, it can serve a particular agenda, in obscuring issues of responsibility.

Asking the question What happened? can open another line of inquiry, where the first response is not an overview, but a self-consciously partial response. This approach begins by recognizing that the question's brevity is deceptive and that any answer will necessarily be long. Such an inquiry in Kruševo might begin with an account of individual experiences of the Uprising, told with no pretensions to exemplary status. The narratives in British consular reports and in Frederick Moore's description are condensed and summarized by writers trying to see the big picture, and were in most cases told by people with legitimate grievances. Archival research in Skopje and oral historical research in Kruševo itself revealed the existence, even ninety years after the Ilinden Uprising, of resources that show more vividly what happened there not to rebels, guerrillas, women, or townsfolk, but to individuals with specific names, friends, families, and plans.

Vele Sekula and his wife, for example, were citizens of Kruševo caught up in the events of 1903 and their aftermath. According to their granddaughter, with whom I spoke in May 1993 when she was in her seventies, Vele and his sons had assisted in preparations for the Uprising. When the insurgents left the town and other townspeople also fled, Vele and his wife—*dedo* (grand-

Figure 7: Cobbled path, house, and courtyard in Kruševo.

father) and *baba* (grandmother)—had barricaded themselves in their house. Like others in the town, it was sturdily constructed with a few small windows at ground level facing the street (figure 7). "The Turks" came in over the courtyard wall at the back. They were locals from the surrounding villages, and they knew the Sekulas had gold buried in the yard. After forcing dedo to dig it up and once convinced he had given them all he had, the Turks took them both into the downstairs hallway of the house, stood them against a wall, and shot them, dedo first, then baba. Then the Tursk ransacked the house, looking for more valuables. In the process they covered the bodies with all sorts of linens pulled from cupboards and other things they didn't want. And then they left. Later, a long while later, baba revived; she was only wounded. Vele was dead. Slowly, painfully, she fought her way out from underneath the layers of fabrics covering her. She was thirsty and dragged herself upstairs to where the family kept a big vat of milk. As she was drinking and drinking, she felt a pain in her ears, where she had been wearing heavy gold earrings. She reached up a hand, and found they had been torn off. Then she dimly remembered that moment, but nothing else of the time she had lain in the hallway, next to her dead husband.

She lived another fifteen years, but this was not the end of her misfortunes. Her oldest son, Stavre, had worked with his father on preparations for the Uprising, and as a result, he was later shot and wounded in the courtyard by Greeks in the town. He recovered, but then fell into a quarrel with a local Revolutionary Organization leader and his faction, and was sentenced to death. Baba created a hiding-place for him upstairs in the house where he could conceal himself day or night if they came looking for him. But one day he was careless, and even though she warned him ahead, and they found him hiding under a coverlet. They stabbed him through it, took away his body, and buried it up in the forests around the town. Baba could not endure that his body was in unhallowed ground, away from his family, and she spent long hours wandering in the mountains trying to find his grave. She searched through the winter months, and she would come home with the edges of her long skirts stiff with ice. In the end, her youngest son returned from America and paid fifty gold sovereigns to learn where the body was hidden. They brought back Stavre's remains, and laid them to rest in the town's main graveyard.

These stories were told to me as the house where the family had lived was being pulled down by its current owner, one of Vele Sekula's great grandchildren. They detail one family's complicated relationship with history, and the house served as the locus for the stories of Vele and Stavre's deaths. From Ilinden itself, there is no recollection of stirring declarations of purpose, or noble self-sacrifice. The enemies then were not alien monsters but came from surrounding villages; similarly, Stavre was killed by former friends turned foes, with whom his brother was later able to negotiate. There is no explicit mention of rape, though the claims of forgetting and unconsciousness by baba might conceal unspoken outrages. The story does not end happily, but the family did, through considerable efforts, regain control over Stavre's body and, thus, achieve a form of closure.

These stories, and the others I was able to find in the Ilinden dossier, in manuscript form in the National Archives, and in fragments of oral memory in Kruševo, do not aggregate to yield a straightforward narrative. They lie beyond the purview of many members of the textual community that I invoked at the beginning of this chapter, composed of foreign observers seeking to explain what happened in 1903 by reference to its documentary traces. In the first place, so far as I know, the story of the Sekula family at the beginning of the twentieth century has not previously been written down, at least in English. But even if it had, it would not offer much purchase to those concerned to demarcate clearly lines of identity, and to trace neat, clear histories of enduring hatred and vengeance, illustrated most explicitly in Robert Kaplan's two questions: "Why are peoples pitted so relentlessly one against another? Why do hatreds run so deep?" (1991:94).

Vele and Stavre Sekula bore a name that was clearly Vlah, were members of a wealthy family of the type often referred to as Greek, and contributed to a cause generally identified as either Bulgarian or Macedonian. Their relatives and descendants continued to live in the town, where for over ninety years they preserved stories that vividly evoke fear, thirst, anger, pain, cold, and grief, and the dramatic swings whereby one sensation replaces another. Stories such as this, therefore, urge a recognition of more elementary concerns, which may weigh more on the hearts and minds of those caught up in events than analysts might allow. For in the face of dramatic events and reversals for fortune, Kruševo has endured. Like baba Sekula, combing the mountains around the town for the body of her son, with the ice forming on her skirts, the town's residents have not turned to violence to avenge their wrongs, but have struggled to endure and deal with the world as they find it.

CHAPTER FOUR

Tipping Points

THE TRANSFORMATION OF IDENTITIES IN KRUŠEVO

As KRUŠEVO's inhabitants struggled with the immediate after-effects of Ilinden 1903, international media and diplomatic attention quickly moved on.
Some European observers did try to probe a little deeper into the riddles
posed by the town's fate—especially the vexed question of the exact relationship between insurgents, townspeople, and Ottoman government—but
by the time the Uprising wound down in mid-September, the drama of Kruševo had been superseded by other events. When violence began to escalate
again the region in the following year, VMRO was internally divided over
its future agenda, and the Balkan states were pursuing more aggressive measures to claim territory. Kruševo was strongly garrisoned by Ottoman troops.
The symbolism of its capture and subsequent sack was no longer a part of
the wider story of the struggle for Macedonia, in which rival Christian bands
threatened, tortured, and killed rural villagers in the name of one or another
new nation.

In Kruševo itself, as one might expect, the events of 1903 prompted
greater ongoing interest and concern among people who had been through a
traumatic experience, and in many cases had suddenly lost family, friends, or
property. European consuls found refugees willing to recount their experiences, and the town's inhabitants communicated to relatives abroad what had
happened. But also among Kruševo's population, reckoned at over fifteen
thousand in 1903, were individuals with the resources and the resolve to
establish their own enduring and ambitious historical records of their town's
fate. Three residents wrote and published monographs which drew on their
own first-hand knowledge of events and personalities, and on the accumulated knowledge of their fellow citizens regarding the origins, patterns of
livelihood, and status of people in the town.

These three accounts are the main subject of this chapter. Two were published in Greek and one in Bulgarian. All three seek to put the events of
1903 in context, either by tracing their roots in changing patterns of loyalty
and activism in the town through the course of the late nineteenth century or
by finding in them lessons for the future. These three authors present tensions between named ethnic, national, or religious groups as decisive factors
in Kruševo's past and present, and see human agency and chauvinistic

nationalism as critical components of history. They differ in their judgments of the moral standing and ordained quality of some historical transformations as opposed to others. Taken together, these vivid accounts of history illustrate what I call here the double standard of nationalist thought, by which some moments in history are classified as "ordained" while others, which may appear only superficially different, are an offense to the natural scheme of things. Two of the stories harness rationalist arguments to a deeply felt political agenda, and both have been mobilized by nation-states in subsequent debates over Ilinden between nation-states. The third story offers a vivid narrative of one man's attempt to deal with the crisis of 1903 by resisting the logic of nationalism, and an afterword in which he yields to the necessity of that logic. The story thus offers a unique presentation of Kruševo 1903 as what I term a tipping point, at which one world order came to an end and another was born.[1]

NIKOLA KIROV-MAJSKI AND THE QUEST FOR LIBERATION

In Kruševo, according to almost all the accounts from pension applicants, the years after the uprising constituted a lull in the activities of the revolutionary movement. Many of the more active revolutionaries had been killed, of whom Pitu Guli was perhaps the best known. Many more had gone into exile in Bulgaria, among them Nikola Karev. One VMRO member who returned to the town at this time, having been abroad during Ilinden, described in his autobiography what greeted him:

> I did not find the same Kruševo I had left before the rebellion. The city was half deserted. Every evening, when it was still early, we locked ourselves in the house and we didn't even dare go out into our own courtyard, because any exposure meant almost certain death. All my friends and acquaintances had fled somewhere else. The only ones left were the elderly and the women. The city was full of soldiers. They occupied all the larger houses and always kept an eye on what was going on. The authorities had organized a special detachment with the task of quietly and unobtrusively killing everyone who had been involved in organization activity before and during the rebellion. (Šapardan n.d.:27)

Šapardan fled the town after a short while to continue his involvement in the liberation struggle elsewhere. He returned only in 1909, when he took a leading role in a renewed cycle of violence between different factions. The pattern of continued activism that his case reveals was common to many former VMRO members, who had mostly renewed their oaths of loyalty to the cause before the end of the Uprising.[2] For those who had played a part in planning the assault on the Ottoman garrison and setting up a provisional government, 1903 had been a failure, but they continued to value the agenda and the sentiments it had represented. Some pursued the cause by taking up arms again to eliminate new enemies, especially those suspected of betraying or killing other members of the organization.

Other adherents of the Macedonian cause drew on their particular skills to carry on the struggle by chronicling the past and educating new generations of potential recruits. One who chose this route was Nikola Kirov-Majski, teacher and activist, and cousin of the local leader Nikola Karev. Twenty-three at the time of the Uprising, Kirov-Majski afterward continued to pursue a career as a teacher in Bulgarian schools in Ottoman Macedonia despite harassment from the authorities for his revolutionary background. In 1912 he made his way to Sofia, where he lived until his death in 1962 (Kirov-Majski 1994). There he turned to writing, working as a journalist as well as creating stage plays, of which the most famous was *Ilinden*, first produced in 1924. In 1935 his historical account of revolutionary activism in Kruševo, entitled *Krušovo and the Struggles for its Freedom*, was published in Sofia. As the title suggests, it depicted 1903 as a pinnacle of revolutionary achievement, a view summed up in the following statement from the book:

> It could be said that the Temporary Government was close to an ideal regime: no-one had anything to fear from it, nor could anyone compare it unfavorably to the Turkish authorities, and certainly not those five hundred citizens, mainly Grkomans and Vlahs, who were called to Bitola for questioning. On the contrary, even today, the different nationalities recall the regime of the Temporary Government as ideal. Krušovo's population then enjoyed a period of happiness and celebrations—there were no quarrels, no disturbances, nor one incident of theft, drunkenness or murder—all national antagonism was erased; everyone, in short, felt like brothers and sisters to the same parents. (Kirov-Majski 1935:54)

Although Yugoslav-era historians in the Republic of Macedonia objected to Kirov-Majski's classification of Macedonia's Slavic population as Bulgarian, they quickly embraced all else in his narrative of events and attitudes in 1903 as definitive. His work served as a key source for all subsequent work on Kruševo in Yugoslav Macedonia, including Zografski (1948), Matkovski (1978), and Pandevski (1978). Kirov-Majski's account was valued especially for two elements apparent in the short excerpt cited above: the image it conjured of "brotherhood and unity," and the author's categorization of the town's residents into linguistic and cultural groups, which he calls nationalities, or narodnosti. After stating that Kruševo was one of the few towns in European Turkey that were purely Christian, Kirov-Majski describes its population in the late nineteenth century as numbering 12,500, and composed of "Bulgars (*Brsjaci* and *Mijaci*), Vlahs, and Albanians" (1935:8). He goes on immediately to assert that there were only two families in the town that were purely or really Greek. The majority of the "Greeks" in the town, he asserts, were "Vlahs, Albanians and Bulgars, heavily influenced by the Greek propaganda" (1935:9). He expresses a similar view in a later discussion of the composition of the parliament of sixty members that he reports was set up by the temporary government of Kruševo in August 1903. He describes that body as composed of equal numbers of the three main narodnosti in the town, which now are named "Bulgars, Vlahs and *Grkomani* (Vlahs and Albanians)" (1935:49).

The Bulgarian and Macedonian term *Grkoman* is still in use today, and Danforth provides a set of glosses from Australia (1995a:221). It connotes devotion to the Greek cause, while simultaneously signaling that those who feel so passionate are themselves not "really" Greeks. The term thus reinforces Kirov-Majski's earlier distinction between Greek as a "propagandistic" identity in Kruševo, and other forms of belonging thereby cast as more "natural." The effect is to present the "Greeks" of Kruševo as bearers of an alien ideology, who engaged in a campaign of active conversion to their cause. This message is also carried in Kirov-Majski's assertion that the town was first settled by Bulgars, and later expanded when successive waves of Vlah refugees from the South and the West found refuge there. Although some Bulgars fell victim to the Greek propaganda, its most consistent carriers were Vlahs and Albanians, who were themselves of foreign origin.

In his 1935 book, Kirov-Majski says little about the subcategories of Bulgar identity, Brsjaci and Mijaci. He revealed more in later correspondence. In a letter dated 7 February 1957 to a regular correspondent in Kruševo, he reported that some scenes he had written were excluded from a cultural show due to in-fighting within the Macedonian community in Sofia. He had been told that the influential lobby from Galičnik had refused to allow his part of the performance to go ahead, once they learned that Kirov-Majski was a *Brsjak*.[3] In a letter dated 7 May 1957 to a different correspondent, he criticized Georgi Tomalevski's novel *Krušovskata Republika* (1968), which he felt did not do justice to the specific history of Kruševo's *Brsjaci*. "In the Ilinden Uprising in Krušovo," he wrote, "only one of the *Mijaci* took part—Veljo Pecan." These letters indicate Kirov-Majski's later emphasis on fault-lines within Krušovo's Bulgar population, and perhaps hint that *Mijaci* were more likely to be those influenced by Greek propaganda.[4]

With regard to the years leading up to 1903, though, Kirov-Majski emphasizes emergent Bulgar solidarity. Between the two sets of categories that Kirov-Majski uses to describe Kruševo's Christian population, changes in loyalties have occurred. Of the earlier period, he indicates that the "Greek propaganda" has influenced members from each of the three "natural" groups in the town. By 1903, Grkomani appear to include all the town's Albanians, but none of its Bulgars. In the course of the intervening years, then, in Kirov-Majski's vision, the power of the Greek movement among the Bulgar population has been utterly destroyed. With regard to the town's Vlahs, he alludes briefly to the influence of a teacher, Sterju Conesku, who led some of them in a struggle to establish their own church. This brought them into conflict with the Patriarchate, and into an alliance with the Exarchate—the two church organizations that were increasingly viewed as extensions of "Greek" and "Bulgarian" national activism, respectively. Kirov-Majski suggests that the campaign to use the Vlah language in church split the Vlah community, as some, the *Grkomani*, remained loyal to the Patriarchate. He thus represented Kruševo's Vlahs as torn between the appeals of a "natural" group identity that would be expressed through use of their own language, and an "artificial" identity based on fanatical obedience to an alien ideology.

Central in Kirov-Majski's vision of history, then, is the power of enduring national identity, realized in the idea of the unitary, language-based narod, to overcome other, less legitimate bases of solidarity. Hellenism, in his account, appears as a force carried by particular human agents with their own agenda, which historically aspired to modify other modes of belonging. Kirov-Majski assigns those other modes to the order of underlying reality: by 1903 the Bulgars of Kruševo (led, it appears, by the indigenous Brsjaci) had liberated themselves and reaffirmed their authentic roots, and under their influence the Vlahs were proceeding along the same course. The activism of VMRO, which culminated in the Uprising of 1903, aimed to accelerate that project and to restore national realities to their proper place at the center of history.

NIKOLAOS BALLAS AND THE MISSION OF CIVILIZATION

The view expressed by Kirov-Majski was not shared by all eyewitnesses of and participants in the events of Kruševo in 1903. Others in the town, especially those taken unawares by VMRO's coup and the Turkish reprisals, saw the Uprising and the blow that it dealt to the town's community as a monstrous offence to reason and order. For many, it marked the end of a golden age of Greek civilizing influence, in which the town had enjoyed growth and prosperity and Ottoman rule had lain lightly on its affluent population.

One spokesman for this view was Nikolaos Ballas, author of *History of Krousovo* (Ballas 1962). Ballas was thirty-two at the time of the Uprising: like Kirov-Majski, he was a teacher, but he taught and wrote in Greek. The following passage indicates clearly the author's general orientation toward what happened:

Conditions in Krousovo during the ten-day reign of the Organization were pitiable. Virtually everyone, from the very first days, was waiting for the appearance of the imperial army, and we were all at a loss and in despair, because it took the army so long to arrive. The isolation from the rest of the world because of the interruption of normal communications, the grim garrisons of the insurgents, which permitted no-one to leave Krousovo, and the panic which the event promoted, along with the high-handedness and tyrannical demeanor of the insurgents, all conspired to create a state of suspense, full of fear, because their rule was so precarious and their peace was likewise uncertain, and forebode dreadful disaster. (Ballas 1962:47)

As is the case with Kirov-Majski's text in the Republic of Macedonia, Ballas's account has enjoyed a prolonged life in a state that embraces its interpretation of the past. It was originally published in 1905, and its author died in 1932. The text was reissued in 1962 in Thessaloniki with a new foreword that explained its value in demonstrating Krousovo had been an "Acropolis of Hellenism" and a "heroic, martyr-town" for the Greek cause until overrun by the Slavic tide.[5] The foreword to the new edition was authored by Hristophoros A. Naltsas, who, in a near-contemporaneous work by historian Konstantine Vavouskos (1959), was described as being of a Krousovan family. Vavouskos himself was also from a Krousovo family, and offered his own short account of the occupation of Krousovo in an English-language history of the Greek struggle for Macedonia (Vavouskos 1973:30–31). He cited the personal memoirs of C. Lekas published in *Makedoniki Zoi* nos. 26 and 27, and stressed the Bulgarian character of the Uprising, the extraction of tribute from the townspeople, and the bribery of the Turks to attack only the Greek inhabitants.

Ballas's description of 1903 and the years that led to the catastrophe fit smoothly into this genre of research and writing, spearheaded by exiles and refugees from Kruševo and Bitola. He offers a rich account of events in the town during the reign of the insurgents, which has close correspondences with a memorandum in the British Foreign Office account (FO 195/2157/397, submitted in French on 24 August 1903). Ballas provides considerable detail regarding the membership of the committees set up by the insurgents for local government, and the conduct of a memorial service for the fallen insurgents which sought to bring the different religious communities together. On the facts, if not the interpretation, his account reveals broad agreement with Kirov-Majski's. With regard to events in the town after the departure of the insurgents and the arrival of Ottoman forces, his account resembles that given by George Ditsias, outlined more fully later in this chapter.

Ballas complements his account of 1903 with a description of the town's original settlement, and of changing relations between segments of the town's population in the late nineteenth century, more extensive than those offered by Kirov-Majski and Ditsias. The comparison with Ditsias's account will be made later. What is more striking, as one might expect, is the fundamental disagreement with the account given by Kirov-Majski, which holds such sway in the modern Republic of Macedonia. For Ballas paints Kruševo as a community of *Éllines*—Greeks—from its first settlement in the late eighteenth century, until 1903 and beyond. He paints Slavic-speakers as latecomers to the town and attributes their numbers in 1903 to the effects of Bulgarian propaganda. He similarly discounts the authenticity of Vlah language activism in the late nineteenth and early twentieth centuries, dubbing it the work of *Roumanisti*, or Romanianizers. Prior to their arrival, he asserts, the town was united by common *aísthima*, or sentiment (1962:35): it was wholly and indivisibly Greek. Processes set in train after 1870 upset this homogeneity, and Ballas traces the cause of these changes to the workings of malign human agency.

Where Kirov-Majski made bald assertions which juxtapose "natural" and "propagandistic" forms of loyalty, Ballas's line of explanation is more convoluted. He identifies four major subgroups with different geographical origins and professional characteristics: the *Nikolitsiánoi* (from around Naoussa in modern Greece), the *Grammostiãnoi* (from the Grammos range in Epirus), the *Mótslanoi* (from near Ioannina), and the *Voskopolĩtai* (from Voskopolis in modern Albania).[6] Ballas distinguishes in particular the first two groups. The Nikolitsiánoi, mostly merchants and craftsmen, possessed *politismòs*—civilization—whereas the Grammostiãnoi, who earned their livelihood by herding sheep and goats, had a rougher quality, being from the mountains.[7] These differences, according to Ballas, were smoothed away over time, as the Nikolitsiánoi—who in his narrative were the first group to settle in Krousovo—exerted a civilizing influence over the other groups that followed them to this new refuge. All, says Ballas, were from the same *phylí*—which can be glossed as race or tribe—of Vlah-speaking, or Vlahophone Éllines, but under the tutelage of the Nikolitsiánoi a single Greek community was formed (1962:18).

So much, then, for the "Vlahs" identified by Kirov-Majski. With regard to the "Albanian" population of the town, Ballas dates their arrival as subsequent to the Nikolitsiánoi, and dubs them *Alvanóphonoi Éllines*—Albanian-speaking Greeks. Over time, with communication and intermarriage with the wider Greek community, their linguistic distinctiveness disappeared, and they were recognized for what they were, Greeks (1962:19). The last group that Ballas identifies as having a long history in the town is the *Miákoi*—that is, Kirov-Majski's *Mijaci*. Ballas categorizes them as skilled masons who came from Lazaropole and settled in the northwestern quarter of Kruševo. He does not classify them as Slavs, or *Slavoũnoi*, as did Kirov-Majski and, in the same period, Jovan Cvijić (1907), but calls them instead Greek-speakers.

Ballas thus finds no faultlines in the town's past, which instead for him reveals Greek solidarity in religion and language. He entirely denies the historical presence of Slavic-speakers, and sees Vlah and Albanian as languages displaced by progress. The picture of hegemony that he presents relieves Ballas of the need to discuss the mechanisms of Greek cultural assimilation. The civilizational dominance that Ballas grants to the Nikolitsiánoi was exerted over coreligionists who were already Greek. In his model,

Hellenization did not make Greeks out of something else, but turned people who were already Greeks into better ones. The image he conjures is close to the example of the "typical" mountain community of the Orthodox Balkan merchant, which was "ethnically Vlach and culturally Greek" (Stoianovich 1960:276; see also Vermeulen 1984). Ballas mentions the opulence of the house of the Nitsóta family, elsewhere identified as being among the settlers from Nikolica (Popović 1937:292n.), and also describes in some detail the famous iconostasis of the Greek Orthodox cathedral of St. Nicholas, completed in 1832 (1962:22–24). Both these markers of prosperity were also mentioned in an early traveler's account from the 1850s by Austrian consul J. G. Hahn, which described Kruševo as a thriving commercial town (Trpkoski 1986:76) (figure 8).

All this, though, in Ballas's vision, was fatally disrupted by the establishment of the Exarchate in 1870. As noted earlier, the Sultan's recognition of the new church and authorization of its use of Church Slavonic, or the Bulgarian vernacular, in church services had heightened conflicts over congregational loyalty and church property across the vilayets of European Turkey. In Slavic-speaking villages in particular, the Patriarchate tried to maintain its ecclesiastical authority, while the new church offered converts the promise of priests who would be more responsive to their needs. For Ballas, the Exarchate was the spearhead of an unholy alliance which sought to bring Ottoman territory under Bulgarian and, ultimately, Russian rule. The struggle had already entered his town in the late 1860s, when a new church was under construction in Kruševo's upper town. Ballas called this the church of Panagia, and the first sign that things were set to go awry in his town came when it was "stolen" by the new Exarchist community for their use, and rededicated as the church of St. Mary the Virgin, or Sv. Bogorodica (1962:34).[8] He provides an account of a Roumanist assault on the sanctity of the cathedral of St. Nicholas in 1891, when a small group of men entered during a regular service and began to sing not in Greek, but in Vlah (1962:42–43).

Ballas attributes both of these assaults on community solidarity to outside forces that continued to work over the years leading up to 1903. Economic changes across the Balkans were affecting traditional ways of life, as mass-produced commodities and railway connections destroyed established trading circuits and threatened the economy built up around horse and mule transportation. Saddle- and bridle-makers, blacksmiths, hostlers, and caravaneers found their livelihoods at risk, as did innkeepers and merchants. Kruševo's population was hit hard, and the rate of economic out-migration increased, with direct and indirect effects on identities in the town. After the Russo-Turkish war of 1878, according to Ballas, demand boomed for skilled construction workers in the new Bulgarian capital Sofia. Kruševo's Miákoi, in the tradition of the town, had gone as temporary labor migrants, and when they returned, they brought the Bulgarian language home with them (Ballas

Figure 8: Kruševo before 1903, seen from the south. St. Nicholas is slightly right of center, and the Ničota house is just below it. The disputed church of Panagia/Sv. Bogorodica, with its two towers, is just below the skyline on the right of the picture, in the "upper" town next to the large Bulgarian school. The Greek school is visible to the left of the picture in the "lower" town. Image from *Album-Almanah Makedonia*, Sofia 1931. My thanks to Mark Garrison for this source.

1962:19). The impact of this was compounded by the in-migration of Slav-speakers from the countryside, whom he calls *Voúlgaroi*, who filled roles left vacant by the departure of so many Greek men, especially low-status manual labor (ibid.).

Rural-urban migration by Slav-speakers was not new to the region. A contemporary observer, Victor Bérard, wrote that "the Greek communities of Macedonia would soon dwindle away if they did not unceasingly recruit their bourgeois merchant class from among the enriched peasants from the Slavic mass which surrounds them (Bérard 1897:242). Bérard's comment does not distinguish gender dimensions of this trend. Stoianovich, in contrast, describing the situation of a century earlier, argued that males would generally be assimilated into the Hellenic community, while "women remained generally unilingual and thus preserved the ethnic individuality of the two national groups [Vlach and Orthodox Albanian]" (1960:290). Other analysts have accepted these assessments and describe Greekness as a category of public life, expressed and attained through membership of a religious congregation and, more centrally, by participation in commercial activity. Such an emphasis places a focus on male individuals. In this model of identity maintenance and transformation in Ottoman Macedonia, Greekness—at least in linguistic terms—had to be reinscribed on each generation of schoolboys. Ultimately, the central bearer of categories of identity was the individual, and a male individual at that. Inherent, then, in the very character of Hellenism in places like Krousovo, outside the Greek state was a stress on its transmission through the generations not by blood or descent—not, that is, by a set of "givens"—but instead by activism and initiative on the part of one segment of the population (Karakasidou 1997a:61–76).

According to Ballas, what happened in Kruševo in the years between 1870 and 1903 turned received wisdom on its head, and threw the Greek civilizing mission into reverse. His claim regarding language-change among the Miákoi cannot be taken seriously. Not only does it ignore an abundance of evidence that Mijaci were Slav-speakers, but in trying to construct an alternative narrative, it presumes language-change within a single generation. What it does suggest is that members of a community who had been willing and able to use Greek in business transactions, but who had spoken Slavic in their homes, now brought the latter language into new "high" contexts (Gellner 1983).

His discussion of the impact of new forms of in-migration presents another form of inversion along an axis of gender. Ballas saw Bulgarian men playing a role once reserved for their Greek counterparts, who had spread a worldview as they did business in coffeeshops, marketsquares, and guild meetings, and provided the primary interface by which this worldview traveled from the public world into the domestic realm. In Kruševo after 1870, reports Ballas, mixed marriages of Bulgarian (villager) father and Greek (urbanite) mother produced (male) offspring who "assert most fanatically of them-selves that they are truly Bulgarian—*kuriōs Voúlgaroi*" (1962:34). In the period of crisis of the late nineteenth century, he compared the Exarchist movement to "a hydra, nursed in our bosom" (1962:35).[9] Where the Greek assimilation of Bulgarian culture had been a civilizing mission, the reverse process constituted a monstrous threat to the taken-for-granted unity of the town.

The pattern of interpretation which emphasizes morally suspect human agency can also be seen in his treatment of the emergence of a Vlah-lan-guage movement in the period. The affray in the cathedral of St. Nicholas in 1891 clearly shocked Ballas and the Greek congregation, who reacted with force. The event could be seen as a demonstration of determination and commitment on the part of a body of people in the town to obtain the right to worship in their own language. Even Ballas acknowledged that people whose ancestors had been Vlah speakers constituted a major part of the Greek presence in the town. Rather than allowing any sentimental attach-ment to a traditional cultural form, though, he presented the Vlah language movement as the outcome of one man's unprincipled activism and a foreign state's intervention. He attributed responsibility to the same individual that Kirov-Majski called Sterju Conescu and Ballas calls Stérgios Tsionékos, who was schooled in the Romanian capital, Bucharest, and who returned to Kru-ševo loaded with threatening ideas and resources. The movement consisted of those who were attracted by the financial inducements that he was able to offer to those who converted. Ballas thus depicts the abandonment of the Greek church as an act motivated by personal greed or need, or in some cases by social obligations to families who had already converted; he asserts that not one household had converted out of aísthima, or sentiment (1962:35). In this way, Ballas characterizes the Romanianizers as an aggregation of money-grubbing individuals, and denies them collective status as a commu-nity. His stress on financial transactions as the basis for its foundation marks it as a movement without genuine roots in the community. Membership was a matter of money, and was not transmitted by blood or conviction.

Nikolaos Ballas portrays the period between 1870 and 1903 as one in which external, male aggressors menaced Kruševo. In his vision, growing tensions had no historical roots within the town, but were a product of alien plots against a once-united Greek population. In presenting Hellenic culture as threatened while continuing to emphasize its moral superiority, Ballas uncouples the associations of religious faith and secular success that had underpinned Greek hegemony. He does so by presenting Krousovo's Greek character, ordained by its glorious past, as hapless victim of a monstrous, shallowly rooted, external assault. The villagers from outside the town and the Vlah speakers within were in turn backed by the foreign powers of Bul-garia and Romania. At the highest level stands the ogre of panslavism, a conspiracy led by Russia, whose involvement Ballas asserts in his account of events in 1903 (1962:46).

Such attributions of malign agency and responsibility are driven by Ballas's desire to construct a coherent narrative which can make sense of the changes of the late nineteenth century. Too conscientious a historian to omit documentary data, he gives the Ottoman census figures for 1905, when the town population was 8,927. Of these, 5,395 were classified as Greeks, 2,664 as Bulgarian Exarchists, 650 as Romanianizers, and 218 as Serb Slavophones (1962:20). Each of these four communities had its own church; besides St. Nicholas and Sv. Bogorodica, there was the Vlah church of St. John and the Serbian church of the Holy Trinity, or Sv. Trojca. Ballas sought to explain the forces that had sundered the unity he claimed for the past, pinpointing 1870 as the key point of rupture for the town when contingency, in the form of a variety of political interests, began to interfere with the ordained passage of the town's history. The occupation of Kruševo in 1903 by Bulgarian armed bands represented the logical and literal extension of activity that had begun in the late nineteenth century, when foreign propaganda, carried by unprincipled men with evil intentions, intervened in historical processes and interrupted the order of things.

THE COMMON GROUND OF NATIONALISM

Kirov-Majski and Ballas reached radically different conclusions on the causes and significance of what happened in Kruševo in 1903. Their methods, though, were fundamentally alike. In particular, they shared a focus on the transformation of the dividing lines of community in the town as pivotal to understanding what brought about the crisis point of 1903. They also agreed on a rough historical periodization in which 1870 represented a turning point. Both were concerned with the dynamics of change whereby a town whose inhabitants had thought of themselves as members of one set of named groups, whether constituted by religion, place of origin, language, or other factor, by the end of that century saw in their town new categories of belonging, and increased stakes. In confronting this problem—of how past has become present—their focus was fixed on the town of their own birth and residence, where they had grown up hearing stories of the past, and in which they were surrounded by social memory. They did not rely on the work of scholars; both were primary source investigators, who drew on the weight of the recollections, family histories of origin, and oral tradition around them.

Both authors tackle questions that remain fundamental to social science: How exactly are social groups constituted? Under what pressures or circumstances do they or can they change? They interpret different transformations in different terms. Concepts like hegemony, assimilation, acculturation, political mobilization, and national awakening can be read into these works, although their language is more commonsensical and nontechnical. What emerges is a strong sense of a marked distinction between those changes viewed as necessary, or inevitable, driven by some principle at work in human history which I will call here *ordained*, and those which are viewed as the product of deliberate action in defiance of such principles which I will here call *unnatural*. In each case different elements of the town's population are seen as the agents of history, itself seen as a process with its own inertia. The realm of the ordained in each case carries a positive moral weight, such that those who oppose its force are condemned. Although their rhetorics are not identical—politismòs has a different set of resonances to narodnost, as used by Kirov-Majski—each author distinguishes the historical development of their own cause from willed human intervention represented by their foes. They mark social groups accordingly. Genuine collectivities are given by history, products of processes beyond human agency. False collectivities are those held together by fear, coercion, or manipulation.

Each historian marks 1870 to 1903 as a period in which a different historical process was at work. In Ballas's formulation, it was a period of Bulgarian propagandizing that ruined the town; in Kirov-Majski's account, it marked a period of awakening and national self-assertion against a former "forced" status quo. Each identifies different processes at work in Kruševo, and use a model of the unnatural, or the contingent, to attack the legitimacy of activism and interpretation different from their own. In the process, both authors encounter paradox. Although politismòs had stood for ordained expansion of Greek influence, Ballas finds himself resisting what looks like a Bulgarian form of the same phenomenon, and recasting the destiny of the town, the population, and a once-dominant patriarchal order in a different, gendered mode. Kirov-Majski acknowledges the significance of language and self-designation in mobilizing Bulgarians against Greek propaganda, but cannot accept that Greek-speaking, self-styled Greeks are not "really" something else.

Their terminology reflects the dilemma they face. Kirov-Majski's use of the term Grkoman rather than Greek to describe some townspeople stresses the role of propaganda and emotion in constituting this group, which resisted the struggles of Bulgarians to claim their true status as a sovereign people. Conversely, Ballas describes the insurgents who challenged the Ottoman government not as rebels, or *andartes*, but by the compound word *listandartes*, or robber-rebels, whose agenda was to despoil the true Hellenic community of the town. He thus uses language to undermine their legitimacy.

Their accounts reveal the seductive power of the double standard in nationalist logic, wherein truth-value is a central concern in the investigation of the past. Nationalists seek to demonstrate the enduring quality of some claims to solidarity and the named collectivities they produce, while denying the validity of others. The extent to which the texts by Ballas and Kirov-Majski demonstrate this quality, insisting on the ordained quality of some parts of history, denying it to others, and brooking no possible confusion between the two, is remarkable, and perhaps explains the extended lives that both texts have enjoyed. Kirov-Majski sought to document the Ilinden Uprising as the outcome of careful preparation by an organized liberation movement, while Ballas wrote to demonstrate both his personal and the town's dissociation from the rebels, as well as to rally civilized Greek opinion against what he depicted as a bestial threat. Though both authors fall into confused logic, they share the trappings of objectivity, delving into historical explanation and providing origins, dates, categorical frameworks, and magisterial overviews. They thus provide easy purchase for subsequent historians consumed with the same struggle over the meaning of events and eager to write Kruševo into wider national histories, incompatible as they may be.

GEORGE DITSIAS AND THE MANY STRANDS OF HISTORY

The Catastrophe of Krousovo: Outrages of Bulgarians and Ottomans against the Greeks (Ditsias 1904) is clearly identified by its author as a narrative of disaster and atrocities. It was written in Greek and published in Athens. Ditsias's approach is less analytical and fact-oriented that those of Ballas and Kirov-Majski, and more literary. Ditsias seeks to evoke the horror of what happened, and his own experiences in that dreadful August. Although his title implies stark divisions between members of clearly defined communities, his narrative reveals the fluidity of his own use of language and concepts as he confronts individuals who blur the distinction. His tone, however, changes dramatically in the afterword, which stands outside the action of 1903 and reveals a keen sense of the changes it portended.

Ditsias's story of Kruševo, far richer in experiential detail than those of Kirov-Majski and Ballas, has not been taken up by subsequent historians in the region. Where Kirov-Majski and Ballas adopted the stance of rigorous and rational analysts, Ditsias portrays himself as more intimately embedded in the circumstances of his time, giving the names of the people caught up in catastrophe, rather than those who controlled the fate of others. The narrative constitutes a personal recollection rather than a systematic account. In his afterword, Ditsias speaks from this experience and makes clear that he sees the new form of solidarity which circumstances demand as wholly unconnected to the sense of self and community with which he grew up. He does not embrace one vision as ordained and its rivals as threats that can and will be overcome: rather he presents a gloomy prognosis of the consequences for civilized humanity of making that distinction.

The bulk of Ditsias's book offers a vivid, blow-by-blow account of the author's personal movements and actions in August 1903. It opens with a short introduction to the earlier history of the town. In Ditsias's version, Kruševo was founded in 1720, and for at least a century its community had known no dissension. Its solidarity had been expressed primarily in the small, original church of St. Nicholas, where "they worshipped God in common brotherhood" (1904:8). By the beginning of the nineteenth century, the town's population had reportedly reached sixteen thousand. Already people began to seek their fortunes by traveling abroad, and many were successful, which resulted in wealth brought back to the town. Some stayed abroad, so that the population at the end of the nineteenth century was twelve thousand, whose members Ditsias describes as falling into three categories—Slavoũnoi, Vlákhoi, and Éllines (1904:5).

Ditsias's explanation of how the religious unity of 1800 was transformed into the ethno-religious diversity of 1900 is straightforward. He divides early nineteenth-century population into three *ethnikótites*: Éllines, Slavoũnoi, and *Alvanoí*, which will here be glossed as Greeks, Slavs, and Albanians (1904:9). The term *ethnikótita* as used by Ditsias does not have an exact semantic equivalent in English. Language played a part in distinguishing these communities, but so did neighborhood and marriage patterns. Albanian distinctiveness lasted only as long as their insistence on endogamy, which Ditsias suggests became unsustainable in so small a community, concentrated in the southwest quarter of the town. Once they begin intermarrying with the Greek community, they became Greek-speaking and, by the end of the nineteenth century, indistinguishable from other Éllines.

By contrast, Ditsias makes no reference to intermarriage between Slavs and Greeks. He calls the Slavs descendants of the Tatars, the same epithet he uses once in his account of the Uprising, but divides them between "old Slavs" and "new Slavs." The former he gives the name Miákoi, and the latter he calls Voúlgaroi, or Bulgars. Ditsias presents both groups as Slavic speaking, at least from the time at which the town was founded, and says that they always lived in the upper, northwestern part of the town. They were all, he says, "simple country-folk, skilled in farming and masonry" (1904:10). Ditsias thus describes the Slavic presence in Kruševo, through the existence of the Miákoi, as having deep historical roots. The new Slavs, most likely immigrants from nearby villages, settled in the same part of the town. Ditsias gives no hint of friction in relations between the two groups, or between them and others in the town. He divides the largest of the founding ethnikótites of Kruševo, the Greeks, along the same lines as Ballas in terms of their places of settlement before coming to the town. Ditsias acknowledges the same four distinct groups: the Nikolitsiãnoi, the Grammostiãnoi, the Mótslanoi, and the Voskopolĩtai. He also concurs with Ballas on the principal differences among these groups, describing the Nikolitsiãnoi as being the most numerous and most civilized—that is, possessing the greatest polit-ismòs—while the Grammostiãnoi were "a nomadic and simple people, but the most righteous—*dikaiótatos laòs*." The Voskopolītai, who spoke Vlah, he calls "the old *Romaîoi*" (1904:9–10). It is this latter group, in Ditsias's account, that in the late nineteenth century fell under the influence of "Vlah propaganda" and thus constituted a countable Vlah minority where none had existed before (1904:11).

Ditsias depicts the continuous existence of a core Greek community in Kruševo throughout the nineteenth century, united primarily by religious sen-timent. Language-use, regional origin, area of residence in the town, marriage patterns, and professional occupation could potentially mark distinctions, but did not do so in any perfectly consistent way. Two groups underwent change in the nineteenth century, as the formerly distinct Albanians became Greeks, and the Voskopolītai, formerly Greeks, came to be counted as Vlahs. The Alba-nian shift Ditsias attributes to demographic pressure, and that of the Vosko-polītai to a propaganda movement that capitalized on an existing linguistic marker of difference. Ditsias devotes no energy to making strong contrast between these historical changes. Overall, his account of history until 1903 portrays stable, enduring oppositions and distinctions rather than their dis-appearance, development, or invention. The town was home to different groups, each with long-established residence, most of which endured un-altered, but all of which enjoyed peaceful relations that permitted, in some cases, assimilation.

CATEGORIES IN ACTION

Where Ballas and Kirov-Majski see the action of 1903 as the inevitable outcome of building tensions, Ditsias presents it as unexpected catastrophe. Accordingly, his main narrative opens with people going about their normal lives. Eight weddings were to be celebrated on Sunday, 20 July, and towns-people had been visiting the families of the brides and grooms in the course of the week before, as was the town custom.[10] George Ditsias is relaxing at home after enjoying the gentle breeze and late summer sun in a walk on the hills, when the idyll is shattered, first by news that a small fire had broken out in the town and then, at midnight, by gunshots (1904:15–20).[11] This pitches the narrator into the first round of action, which he titles *katálipsis*, or occupation. Ditsias goes out and almost immediately runs across some insurgents on the verge of killing the wife and child of an Ottoman official stationed in the town. He intervenes, and is taken to the insurgent headquar-ters to account for his interference. After this brush with the Uprising's leaders, who included other townspeople, he is released. Ditsias then briefly describes the conduct of the insurgents during the next few days, who rob the Éllines, or Greeks, force them to obey their orders, show disrespect to women and to the church, and demonstrate little order or unity. He refers to them at various points as the spawn of the ancient Tatars (1904:52) and later as *Várvaroi*, or barbarians (1904:57, 59). Their lack of discipline and inability to agree drives him to compare them to the builders of the tower of Babel (1904:59).

Even as the community anticipates release when the Ottoman army returns, their hopes are shattered by a new round of outrages which Ditsias describes under the heading *i katastrophí*—the catastrophe. He describes the town filled with screams, groans, and fire, as the Ottoman troops, whom he also calls várvaroi, enter to threaten and rob his community and lust after the women. After getting his family into hiding in the woods, Ditsias returns to hear more tales of slaughter. He goes as part of a delegation to the Ottoman leader, Bahtiar Pasha, to plead the townspeople's innocence of involvement in the Uprising. Their initial appeal is unsuccessful, and he encounters more violent scenes, including the mutilated body of a friend who had also tried to help care for the Ottoman women, before orders come from the Sultan to stop the sack of the town. Ditsias's breathless narrative includes a mixture of classical allusions and graphic descriptions of murder. By using a great deal of reported speech and transliterating statements in other languages, including the local Slavic dialect and Albanian, rather than translating them, the author strives to convey the immediacy of his experience. Whatever his aims, the encounters and actions that he describes present a vivid and convincing picture of a man caught up in events that he does not fully comprehend.

Two decisive actions which put Ditsias at personal risk stand out. In the first case, he sought to protect the wife of a Turkish official from the insurgents, who seemed bent on killing anyone with the slightest association with the Ottoman regime. As a result of this principled act, he was arrested and taken before one of the leaders of the insurgents, Givanof.[12] In the second case, after the Turkish forces had entered the town, he became part of a delegation that went to Bahtiar Pasha to implore him to call off the irregular troops from their orgy of violence against an innocent Greek population. Each encounter gives him the opportunity to reflect on loyalties and affiliations not in the abstract schemas of the historian, as Ballas and Kirov-Majski seek to do, but in their direct relationship to social action.

When Ditsias is taken to the headquarters of the insurgents, they are at first too busy with the siege of the barracks, which poses problems that are ultimately solved by an insurgent leader he calls Dimitrios Gouli, and who in the modern Republic of Macedonia is better known as Pitu Guli. Ditsias describes him as *"omogenís sympatriótis mou"*—a compatriot of mine, of shared descent (1904:37). Even though Guli had fallen under the spell of Bulgarian propaganda, which had turned him into a "lost sheep," his previous devotion to the Orthodox faith showed him to be by sentiment—aísthima—more Greek than Bulgarian (Ditsias 1904:38).

When Ditsias finally converses with Guli, he appeals to him as a Greek, asserting again that they are of the same descent (1904:44). After securing his attention, Ditsias goes on to say, "Even though you are implicated with this Bulgarian organization I still can't call you Bulgarian, as you are Orthodox and Hellene to your marrow" (ibid.). He urges Guli to help the Greek population. Guli responds by saying that "circumstances beyond my will compel me to be a part of this illiterate propaganda," but he promises to do what he can (1904:46). He crops up again and again in the story as trying to soften the demands made on the Greek population, and opposing the more extreme demands of the occupiers.

These demands, according to Ditsias, are made not by the *komĩtai*, the armed bands, for which he seems to have grudging respect, but by those he calls *sympatriõtai Voúlgaroi propagandistaí*—Bulgarian propagandists who are natives of Kruševo (1904:59). These are the men he singles out as the real villains of the piece, and among them in particular he heaps abuse on one named Athanasios Naskos, from the house of Bastavella, whom he also sees at the headquarters of Givanof (1904:41–42).[13] This man he describes as having been brought up in the Greek community, but as turning to people from other wretched races—*heterogenon faulon*—when he found himself ostracized by other Greeks (1904:42). It is implied that this ostracism came about when Greeks recognized his moral shortcomings, and would have no truck with him.

Ditsias thus passes explicit moral judgments on two men, both of whom participated in the Ilinden Uprising, and both of whom had once been "Greek." Yet Ditsias differentiates them; he excuses the one who played a prominent role in the occupation of the town, while the less well known he abuses. Ditsias appears to recognize Guli as still Greek because of his moderate conduct during the occupation. Naskos, by contrast, motivated by envy, tries to have Ditsias shot, and toadies to the Bulgarians. His actions confirm his mean-mindedness and wretchedness, and deny him any continued recognition as Greek. The juxtaposition of Guli and Naskos, both active in the Revolutionary Organization, but contrasted in their style of interaction with fellow townspeople, demonstrates Ditsias's continuing attachment to the notion that Greekness is a synonym for civilized humanity.

ONE MAN'S TIPPING POINT

We have already seen how, in the settlement of the town, Ditsias acknowledged the presence of other groups on ethnic grounds. For him, the way in which the Albanians became members of the wider Greek community was a result of the continuous interaction between them; the Slavs, conversely, he recognizes as always having been separate, even when they came to live in the town. He recognizes, also, in the growth of the Romanianizing movement its basis in the language-use of some of the Greek community, and does not react to the movement with the same venom as Ballas. Where Ballas and Kirov-Majski both drew a sharp line between "ordained" affiliations and their "artificial" rivals, Ditsias, less rigorous in his thought, does not. He records Guli as calling the Bulgarian movement "propaganda," but his own account of the town's history reveals that he recognizes that Greekness, too, can be acquired. For him, unlike either of the two other authors, a change in affiliation is not by definition problematic. What distinguishes the changes experienced by the Albanian-speakers of the early period, and those of the Bulgarian-sympathizers among the Greeks, is the moral quality of the transition.

Toward the end of the book, Ditsias recounts his participation in a delegation of townspeople to the Ottoman leader, Bahtiar Pasha. In the course of the conversation, when they are accused of complicity with the brigands, one of the other delegates expresses outrage, exclaiming that "Greek and Bulgar are opposite poles" (1904:83). At first sight, this would appear to indicate a nationalist view of the type expressed by Ballas and Kirov-Majski. But in practice, as set out in Ditsias's encounters with others in the course of Kruševo's occupation and catastrophe, it demonstrates a different kind of contrast. To be a Bulgar is to be narrow-minded and petty, as is Naskos; to be a Greek is to observe certain principles of enlightened and universalizable behavior, as does Guli.

Such a picture clearly recalls the formulations of Stoianovich (1960), and can be traced through Ditsias's narrative of events. At one point in the midst of tragedy he makes his family laugh by comparing simple Slavic names like Velko, Trajko, and Zdrave with Greek names redolent of classical antiquity—Militiades, Achilles, and their like (1904:52). He invokes this treasured heritage almost as a talisman against the insurgents who he describes as lacking in common decency in their behavior toward the town and their Turkish prisoners. He invites his audience to view these villagers as bumpkins without wit or a shared vision of a glorious past; they bear the names of their own equally limited fathers and grandfathers, not those of great figures of history. Elsewhere, urban and cosmopolitan Greeks reportedly described rural Bulgars as *hondrokephali*—blockheads (Stoianovich 1960:304). Even in the face of disaster, Ditsias clings to this image.

At the end of the work, however, the author appends an afterword which takes a different tone, and expresses recognition that in the new world of aggressive nationalisms, narrow-mindedness may be essential for survival. In the main narrative, there are frequent hints that the Hellenic community had previously delegated its defense to the Ottoman state. In all their exchanges with Ottoman authorities, Ditsias and his fellow ambassadors emphasize their loyalty, referring to themselves as "faithful children of the Sultan" (1904:57, 81). Both Ditsias and Ballas record appeals from the town to the government before the Uprising, asking for an increase in the garrison. With their own young men gone abroad in pursuit of wealth, Greeks in Kruševo assumed that their obedience to the laws and their payment of taxes would guarantee them protection from harm.

In his afterword, Ditsias takes a very different tone. He points out that the Bulgarians have "unanimity of purpose, and brotherly co-operation" (1904:109). Their solidarity was rooted in the present and in collective action, rather than in the celebration of a distant past or the observance of laws. They were thus distinct from a Greek community that, priding itself on its culture and eschewing armed resistance, had lost its ability to act decisively as a unit. The very qualities that Ditsias praises in the main text and that had led to Hellenism's rise—toleration and certain standards of moderate behavior toward all—he questions in the afterword, in the face of a determined and extremist minority which recruited new members aggressively. It can thus be argued that George Ditsias took a new historical lesson from Kruševo's catastrophe, which he chooses to reveal at the last. Ditsias concludes his afterword by urging on his Greek readers the same attitude that Ballas displayed through his whole work. Greeks could no longer welcome others into their ranks; they would have to begin to think of themselves as a threatened community. Strength and survival would be assured by adopting the methods of their new national peers and rivals (1904:110).

THE CONSUMING LOGIC OF THE NATION

For the people of Kruševo, however they wrote the name of the town, 1903 was a turning point. Two of its residents, Nikola Kirov-Majski and Nikolaos Ballas, were able to explain the events of that year within wider frames of interpretation that reveal the logics of nationalism. Both were active players in campaigns of identity formation and maintenance underway in Kruševo in the late nineteenth century, and both mastered the particular form of tone-deafness that nationalism requires in its adherents. They are exemplary in that they reveal no difficulty, no lapse in sureness of thought in distinguishing the ordained processes of history, in which they and their allies are agents, from the artificial agendas pursued by their sworn enemies. These authors do not question themselves or reflect on the logical reversability of their judgments.

At first sight, George Ditsias appears more naive in his description of identity maintenance and change. However, as he draws the reader into the mêlée of Kruševo and reveals his bewilderment at the hardening lines of allegiance, his text works to disrupt the moral neatness of either of the other versions. More completely "inside" Kruševo, he appears to view the processes of nation-formation that drive events from "outside," unable—or unwilling—to think himself into a space where he can understand. The inter-actions he narrates, especially that with Pitu Guli, whom he calls Dimitrios Gouli, demonstrate his lack of certainty and his resistance to accepting that the people of his town and acquaintance should inhabit a world of absolute antipathies.

In his conclusion, or afterword, Ditsias faces squarely the demands that this new world imposes. His voice here is prophetic and melancholic, pre-dicting as it does the road along which the people of whom he considers himself a part will travel. Already in 1904, that change was underway in Ottoman Macedonia as antipathies hardened. Some observers had seen in the Ilinden Uprising the seeds of alliance between different Christian groups. One consul, for example, saw an answer to the riddle of Kruševo's occupa-tion in the new alliance, which Kirov-Majski had seen emerging between Bulgars and Vlahs:

> While the Greco-Wallachs side with the Greeks and so, in spite of ill-treatment at the hands of the troops and bashi-bazouks, maintain their loyalty to the Turk-ish government, those Wallachs who have been affected by the Roumanian pro-paganda in many cases show open sympathy with the Bulgarian bands, and it is even stated that it was on their invitation that the insurgents entered the Wal-lachian towns of Krushevo, Klissura and Neveska and Malovista. (Graves to O'Conor, Salonica, 16 September 1903: FO 195/2157/510)

Outrage at such defection from the Greek camp drove the force of Ballas's rhetoric, and soon had more deadly consquences. Greece had already spon-sored the deployment of bands of fighters from Crete in Ottoman Mac-edonia, where they had served as guides to Turkish troops and also fought against the insurgents during the Uprising (Dakin 1993:145). In 1904 the tempo of Greek activities increased, and a Greek army officer, Pavlos Melas, was sent into the vilayet of Monastir to organize the defense of Patriarchist villages against what Greece saw as Bulgarian-sponsored terrorism. Melas's death in October 1904 gave fresh impetus to the Greek cause, galvanizing public opinion in support of greater military and paramilitary movement in Ottoman Macedonia. Although Melas was killed by Ottoman troops, the new campaign of direct Greek action targeted the activism of the Macedonian Revolutionary Organization and the Exarchate and, with even greater feroc-ity, the Romanianizing movement which was gaining ground among Mac-edonia's Vlahs and which in 1905 achieved recognition from the Sultan.

The failure of the Ilinden Uprising of 1903 and the scale of the reprisals that ensued also had an impact on the Revolutionary Organization. A major-ity of its core personnel, the young men enrolled as *četnici* or *komitadžii* in the armed bands, had been killed or forced into exile, mostly in Bulgaria.[14] Of the survivors, some continued to pursue the old agenda of an autonomous Macedonia, while others elected to support Bulgarian expansion. They fought to control local networks in Ottoman Macedonia that had been severely damaged, as much of the Christian population found itself struggling to survive the destruction of homes and winter food supplies. Many civilians felt betrayed by the Organization and its leaders, who had made such grand statements, asked them for financial and personal contributions to the cause of freedom, and then left them to face the consequences. Those who remained loyal were the targets of an Ottoman government-sponsored campaign of terror, which continued despite the promises of amnesty. They also faced a choice over which wing of VMRO they should support.

The Ilinden Uprising of 1903 prompted further international intervention in the Ottoman provinces. The so-called Murzsteg program of reforms, spearheaded by Austria and Russia, was presented to the Sultan in October 1903 and accepted in November. As well as establishing an internationally led gendarmerie in which all segments of the population were to be represented, and calling for refugee return and aid to victims of army operations, the program included a clause which anticipated "a modification in the administrative division of the territory in view of a more regular grouping of different nationalities" (Lange-Akhund 1998:143). This clause, part of a package of measures intended to improve the security and stability of the region, in fact contributed to the deadly transformation of the situation on the ground:

> The programme of social and political revolution which had earlier been launched by the Internal Organization had by the end of 1904 disappeared as an immediate and practical objective; and the attention of the contending factions had become focused in the third point of the Murzsteg programme—on the need to demonstrate, in view of a possible re-arrangement of administrative areas according to "nationality," a national predominance in terms of churches. (Dakin 1993:161)

With all these influences at work, consuls were quickly reporting the transformation of villages into battlegrounds, and the polarization of the population. In the process, people became martyrs of causes that they did not necessarily support, and victims of revenge for crimes with which they had no connection. Writing from Monastir on 12 October 1904, the British consul Shipley reported the murder of four people in the village of Brod: "the Bulgarian Patriarchist priest Stoyan and his wife with two headmen named Veljan and Kotcha" (FO 195/2183/284). Two weeks later, he described what he called "Greek retaliation" for the Brod murders: an attack by eight young Greeks on one Lazar Tsouneff, whom Shipley calls an "inoffensive professor" in the city of Monastir (Bitola) (FO 195/2183/329).

The spiraling violence relocated the dispute from a village to the capital of the vilayet. The first attack was in all probability carried out by a band from outside the village, the latter dispute involved people from the city, possibly even known to the victim. An "inoffensive" Bulgarian teacher was attacked to avenge the deaths of four "Bulgarian" Patriarchists. Religion alone marked them as "Greek"; language and profession alone marked him as "Bulgarian."[15] Yet it was the new sense of national or ethnic belonging nursed by their attackers that was involved in the calculation of revenge. This episode also demonstrated how the modus operandi of the two sides had come to resemble one another. The assault of the young "Greeks" on a Bulgarian professor owed more to the methods of their ethnic adversaries than to the ideas of Hellenic civility once espoused by Ditsias.

The presence of Ottoman troops and the flight of many activists from the town slowed the development of similar violence in Kruševo. After the Young Turk Revolution of 1908 and the general amnesty that followed, some of the activists returned. Among them was Tome Niklev, one of the high command, who reportedly intended to leave violence behind. The memoir of Šapardan records a different fate:

> Tome Niklev had come back from Sofia and had in mind to start working as a farmer. He had set aside some of his savings to buy cows, with which he was planning to work on his father's remaining fields. Together with Stajce Letnikot, he went to buy cows in Bitola. As soon as they left, the Greek committee in Kruševo notified its terrorist mercenaries that Tome and Letnikot were on the road and that they should be attacked, not near Kruševo however but further away so that people from Kruševo would not be suspected. . . . Four assassins from Prilep had set up an ambush by the bridge by Pevnica and as soon as Tome and Letnikot passed by on their way back to Kruševo leading two cows, they opened fire. Niklev fell dead after the first few shots. Wounded, Letnikot managed to run away for 200–300 meters and shoot several times at the killers. He soon succumbed to his wounds and could neither get up nor shoot. He stayed like this, neither dead nor alive, till the morning, when he died. (Šapardan n.d.:28)

Šapardan and his associates were soon striking back, although they still saw the Ottoman Empire as their principal foe. But in the killing of Niklev, the call of Ditsias's afterword had already been answered: Greeks had taken responsibility for their future by destroying that of their enemies. Further along the same path lay the Balkan Wars of 1912–13, when Greek soldiers would be reported as filling postbags with their accounts of laying waste to Bulgarian villages in the territory they would turn Greek. One such account was reportedly written by N. Zervas, from the old Bulgarian frontier, who wrote at the end of a letter to his brother, "We have turned out much crueller than the Bulgars—we violated every girl we met." Others wrote of killing prisoners and burning houses, all to try and "wipe out the race" (Kennan [ed.] 1993:311ff). Elsewhere, metaphorical language makes the butchery even more chilling: "Not a cat escapes us." "We shoot them like sparrows" (Wallis 1914:523).[16]

George Ditsias's hometown of Kruševo itself lay outside the territory reached by the Greek army; instead, it came under Serbian control. The Serbian army itself left on 30 June 1913 (17 June o.s.), leaving in control what the international observers of the Carnegie Commission, using the same categories as Nikola Kirov-Majski, called irregular "Vlach and Grkoman bands" recruited locally. These bands set to work, beating a Bulgarian merchant for having a sign in Bulgarian, and beating and imprisoning women for calling themselves Bulgarian. In their final flush of triumph, a Bulgarian "chieftan" was killed and his head carried around the town (Kennan [ed.] 1993:180). These were the acts, then, of the Greek community of which Ditsias had been a proud member in 1903, and whose future actions he foresaw so clearly.[17] The shift which turned Greek into a national category, level with its rivals, was in part a cognitive one, which demanded a view of the past suffused with moral certainty, which distinguished truth from falsehood. That certainty, though, drove present and future action, as its bearers sought to put right the wrongs of the unnatural past, and fulfill the demands of ordained history.

CHAPTER FIVE

Between the Revolutions

LIFE IN KRUŠEVO 1903–1944

AFTER WORLD WAR I, Serbia's spoils from the Balkan Wars were confirmed and expanded as a new South Slav state was formed. Kruševo became part of the new Kingdom of the Serbs, Croats, and Slovenes, which was renamed Yugoslavia in 1929. The new borders in the Balkans, which firmly located Kruševo outside the boundaries of Greece and Bulgaria, brought about demographic change, as the strongest adherents of both national movements left the town. Many of the more committed philhellenes in the community had never returned after 1903; more sold up and moved away after 1919. Political tensions between Yugoslavia, Greece, and Bulgaria simmered in the inter-war years, especially in regard to the treatment of minorities or potential minorities in their newly annexed territories in Macedonia (Finney 2003). Kruševo's Greek school had been burned by the Bulgarians in 1914–15, and the Yugoslav government exerted its own pressure on self-identified Greek communities in Bitola and Kruševo. Among other measures, the government reportedly made it difficult for families to baptize their children with names of their choice (Anonymous 1920). Former residents fled to Greece, where their numbers and nostalgia were sufficient to create an association in Thessaloniki still active seventy-five years later. In one new house in the northeast quarter of Kruševo, a neighborhood known still as Strunga, an old man told me that in the early 1970s, some visitors from Greece came to the gate and looked in. They said that they were descendants of one of the members of the temporary government in Kruševo in 1903, who had lived in a house on that site. Reportedly, they still considered the plot their property; at the time, though, they merely said they were content to see that someone had built a nice home there.[1]

Already after the Balkan Wars of 1912–13, a significant element of the more active VMRO supporters had left western Macedonia and found their way to Sofia. G. C. Loggio reported that even before the Balkan Wars Bulgaria housed 300,000 immigrants from Macedonia; after 1913, the total rose to 500,000 (Loggio 1919:341). When the Macedonian delegation to the Peace Conference at Versailles failed to get a hearing, their exile was confirmed. Arguing for the significance of this population in Bulgarian public life, Joseph Swire states that by 1930 it had supplied eight cabinet ministers, twenty diplomatic representatives, and more than 1,500 school teachers (Swire 1939:16). Among the organizations set up was a Kruševo benevolent brotherhood in Sofia, which operated from at least the mid-1920s to the mid-1930s. Its president in 1934 was the author and ideologue Nikola Kirov-Majski.

THE WORLD OF THE PAST REMEMBERED

In Kruševo, the departure of the more radical supporters of Greece and Bulgaria undoubtedly contributed to the lowering of tensions after the trauma of 1903. According to oral testimony, though, the scars of Ilinden remained. At the most banal level, they were evident in the town's landscape: the fires started by shelling and by pillaging soldiers consumed many public and private buildings in the lower town, and damaged others. In 1993 people still recalled the greatest symbol of private prosperity in the town from before 1903, the Ničota house, that had stood below the cathedral of St. Nicholas. Although destroyed in the conflagration, its chimneys survived, ghostly pillars that until finally razed after the Second World War, reminded people of former glories and their town's trial by fire. The house was reportedly designed according to plans drawn up in Vienna, with forty or fifty rooms, fine wooden balconies, marble interiors, and its own water supply. Even among the other spacious mansions of the lower town, the largest of which might accommodate four or five hundred revelers on a wedding day, the Ničota house was a unique marker of the private wealth of the town's longest-established families.[2]

The salience of private property and enterprise in the town's early twentieth century also emerged in my conversations with elderly men who had plied their trade for many years in the heart of the town. One of these old men was Šula Gabel. He has died since we spoke in May 1992, when he was still working as a shoemaker and told me about his life. He was born in 1912 of Vlah parents, whose families had come to Kruševo from Albania several generations before. He reported that the family spent two years, 1916–18, in the Greek village of Ajvat, where his father worked his trade as a tinsmith before they returned to Kruševo in 1918. Šula attended three years of Serbian school in Kruševo, but wasn't able to go on to study at high school, or gymnasium. In 1922 he began training in the craft, or *zanaet*, of weaving. His master, or *majstor*, was called Janako, from the Vlah village of Gopeš. A local Turk hired Janako to work in Prilep, but Šula did not go because his family considered that Prilep was no place for a young apprentice to live. He signed on with another majstor but they could not agree on terms, and so he went to work for his father's mother as a shoemaker. This was how he spent his adolescent years. In 1937 he went to work in the new Monopol tobacco-processing factory in Kruševo. For reasons of ill-health he was never called up during the Second World War. Afterward, he set up as a majstor in a store in the lower town which he initially held under lease; the owners were in Bulgaria. When Šula opened the store, he recalled, there were twenty-four shoemakers in the town, strung out along the main street among trade-shops that ran all the way from his corner up to the spring separating the down-town from the "upper" quarter. He paid rent to his absentee landlords until the 1960s when they decided at last to realize some capital on the store, whereupon he bought it from them. In 1992, he said, there were just three shoemakers' stores left in the town.

Šula Gabel's narrative points to the interconnection of private lives in Kruševo with larger patterns. The capture of Kruševo by Serbian and Vlah forces in 1913 had heralded attacks on pro-Bulgarian elements within the town. Bulgarian occupation in the First World War reversed the power rela-tions again. Some families, including Gabel's, spent these years away from the town and returned only when the town changed hands again. In the wake of the Second World War, those who had fled Kruševo for Bulgaria still hung on to property in the town, and exiles of longer standing also main-tained their ties with home. From the mid-1950s until his death in 1962, Nikola Kirov-Majski was a regular correspondent with various individuals in the town, including two directors of the town museum, Mihu Andre, and after 1958, Nikola Telesku.[3] On the fifty-fifth anniversary of Ilinden, in 1958, Kirov-Majski sent to the museum a photograph of four surviving insurgents who had taken part in the attack on the Ottoman garrison. The photograph was taken in Sofia, indicating the vitality of Kruševo's memory there.

Alongside all this interest elsewhere, Kruševo itself remained a viable community where livelihoods and stories from the past were handed down from one generation to the next. Ilinden was one key symbolic moment that carried ambivalent messages, but also important were everyday practices of sociability. In this regard, Šula Gabel's brief story of his life offers insights into the organization of the wider community. He was first apprenticed at age ten to learn a trade, or zanaet. His family thus represented one of the branches of Kruševo's Greco-Vlah population, as described by various observers at the start of the twentieth century and in a number of individual stories I was told. Gabel represents himself as scion of a group identified by profession, composed of skilled artisan families. In this case, young men's lives followed a particular pattern. They would be apprenticed to a majstor where they would learn the trade, first as a junior apprentice, or *čirak*, then as journeyman apprentice, or *kalfa*. Their ideal would be to achieve *majstor* status themselves with their own premises. Particular trades of this kind maintained guild organizations, or *esnafi*, to which practitioners belonged and which, like their counterparts in other societies, had both economic and social functions. Pathways through life similar to Gabel's were described to me by other old men in the town, like the retiree Trifun Naḱa, who was also a shoemaker. Born in 1916, he became majstor in 1946, having his own store for nine years after that. The tailoring trade in Kruševo had been important, as had metalworking; another service-oriented zanaet was barbering.[4]

Skilled artisan labor was one economic activity practiced by the Vlah population in Macedonia; others were stock-keeping and commerce. In this regard the twentieth-century Vlahs of Kruševo appear as professional descendants of the eighteenth century Greeks described by Stoianovich (1960). Their small-town, or *varoš*, values were also described by Filipović (1982). Although 1903 was a blow from which some never recovered, many of Kruševo's townsfolk rebuilt their fortunes in the course of the next four decades. They did so despite the insecurity created by the Macedonian Struggle from 1904 to 1908, the Balkan Wars of 1912–13, the First World War, and clashes between Yugoslav authorities and the still-active VMRO, whose main base of operations was now the Pirin region of Macedonia in western Bulgaria.[5] The tinsmiths, shoemakers, tailors, and other artisans continued their work, and so did the merchants. At the heart of Kruševo's economy, though, remained stock-keeping, made possible by the sweeping upland pastures to the north of the town.

People in Kruševo now recall the town herds and their Vlah ancestors' holdings in them as considerable. One young man told me his grandfather had 3,000 sheep as late as the 1940s. A retired shepherd told me that in the same period his *kum*—godfather or wedding sponsor—had 4,000 sheep and that the town as a whole had 60,000 sheep, 1,000 goats, and 240 cows. Others gave figures for the town as a whole of 80,000 or 50,000 sheep. Individual families might own 5 percent or more of the town's entire livestock, a statistic that would appear to reinforce the notion that there were distinct social classes in the population, which was less than 5,000 at the time. The shepherd's own holding before the war, he reported, was 150 sheep. In his recollection, a quarter of the town's population was then involved in the dairy industry, and the ready availability of milk and cheese was what kept people healthy back then. Another elderly man said that meat was cheap in the town, too, and a lamb which could yield around seven and a half kilos of meat would sell for thirty *dinars*—a little more than the price of two kilograms of sugar. By a different measure, provided by another elderly resident, a "he-goat was cheaper than a goatskin, there were so many in Kruševo."

Profits came from selling dairy and meat products elsewhere, where they could command higher prices. Kruševo's herds supplied many large markets with milk, cheese, leather, soap, and meat—including *pastrma*, the dried salami for which the town had already been famous in the nineteenth century. The people of Kruševo continued to undertake the task of bringing their own goods to market as they had earlier. The guild of caravaneers, or *kiradžija*, had been weakened by the advent of the railway, as Nikolaos Ballas described (1962:32–33). The trend of long absences continued, producing the effect noted by Lebrun in a visit before the First World War:

> There are few adult men in Krusevo. Almost all are away working, especially in the big cities of Eastern Europe, and also in Asia Minor, Egypt and even America. They rarely take their wives with them. We were told things that seemed very strange to us. Some young people marry and live together for some months, or often just a few weeks, in the family home. Then one day the young husband is taken to the "Rock of farewells" at the gates of the town. There they are parted, and those who stay behind often come to that spot, to dream of those who are absent, and wait for them. (Lebrun and Voinescu 1911:67)

The practice whereby men traveled broadly while women stayed behind in the town is also described in oral history. One elderly woman, for example, whom I shall call Ekaterina, related in 1992 how her father and his brothers spent significant periods of time based in a village outside Thessaloniki, where they took their livestock during the winter months to be close to the major market of that major cosmopolitan city. During the First World War they were trapped there by the fighting, or chose not to return to Bulgarian-occupied Kruševo. They were interned between 1916 and 1918.

NEGOTIATING THE 1930s

After World War I, economic diversification proceeded apace, though the venues shifted. Kruševo's diaspora was already spread wide, across former Ottoman business centers including Constantinople, Alexandria, and cities in Palestine, as well as European and North American cities. Ekaterina's great-uncles, for example, had property in Egypt. With the break-up of the Ottoman Empire after 1919, they and others liquidated such holdings to invest elsewhere, often closer to home. Kruševo's Vlah community bought agricultural land and shops and businesses, especially those vacated by Turks or Greeks leaving the new Yugoslavia. Trifun Naka, the retired shoemaker, described his father's investment during the 1930s of 700 napoleons in eighty hectares of farmland on the plain to the northeast of Kruševo, in the former *čiflik*, or Ottoman estate, of Tursko. Others bought houses in the newly significant regional capital, Skopje, or opened businesses in Belgrade, their new national capital.

For Kruševo's wealthier families, in contemporary memory, the interwar period was a time of opulence and openness to the wider world. This impression is buttressed by the artistic works of Nikola Martinovski, the Kruševo-born painter who studied in Bucharest and Paris before returning to Macedonia, and thus in his very biography, exemplifies the spirit of cosmopolitanism.

Figure 9: "Town wedding," painted by Nikola Martinovski.

Although his paintings of everyday life in Kruševo date mostly from the 1950s, they are taken to represent the social milieu of an earlier time, when the interiors of the three-storied, generously proportioned mansions, like the one which is now the Martinovski gallery, were filled with laughter, music, and color (figure 9). Such was the world that Janko Mele, a merchant's son and an active musician even in his eighties, recalls. An elderly woman in the old town also recalled outdoor dances that whole families would attend. She remembered in particular her father carrying a stick on such occasions, and buying doughnut-shaped sesame-covered rolls in bulk and threading them on his stick to offer his daughters and their friends.[6] She drew from this gesture of extravagant generosity a comparison with the present, when she said townspeople had become more *ograničani*—narrow-minded or selfishly oriented.

Such accounts seem to be at odds with the picture presented by economic historians, that the interwar period was a time of stagnation for towns like Kruševo. Cut off from market outlets and winter pastures in northern Greece by new national frontiers, formerly prosperous centers like Kruševo and

Bitola became marginal to the new state-oriented economic order. Other narratives of the interwar period, provided by people with less wealthy backgrounds, reinforce this image. Trifun Naka, despite the wealth he recalled his father accumulating abroad, remembered his own life in the 1930s in rather different terms. Serving his apprenticeship as a shoemaker, he received no pay and worked long hours into the night. He worked by gaslight, and going home late at night would hear the sounds of singing elsewhere in the town. Another elderly woman recalled growing up as one of six children in a poor Vlah household. Their house had a beaten earth floor, and when they sat down for supper they perched on three-legged stools, the only furniture, reaching with their spoons into a single stockpot. They had no electricity, and slept on beds made of gathered wood and branches.

Other people's accounts suggested that even merchants, generally thought of as wealthy, had to adapt their practices to this difficult climate. An elderly woman recalled that her father, a storekeeper, would open up even for the sale of a half-bottle of brandy or a pack of cigarettes, just so the customer wouldn't take business elsewhere. Those with fewer capital resources and without contacts abroad were even harder hit by the changed conditions. The flight of wealthier families that began after the Ilinden Uprising and continued through the turbulent years of the following two decades, undoubtedly had a trickle-down effect on the town's economy and status. By 1916, according to Bulgarian figures, the population of the town was down to 5,201 (Matkovski 1978:294), and for 1921, Golab gives a figure of 3,862 (1984:23). According to oral accounts, the number was down to around 3,000 by the early 1930s. As the population fell, the less well-off who remained found their options diminished. With the departure of wealthy families and their capital, local employment opportunities dwindled. To be apprenticed to a trade was beyond the means of many families. Some could earn revenue from working the forests, making charcoal and selling it. Tobacco season provided others with labor, picking and stringing the leaves, as it still does for some families today. Others worked as sharecroppers in agriculture.

DIVIDING LINES TRANSFORMED

In these changed post-WWI circumstances, economic divisions in the town sharpened, and were mapped spatially and ethnically. The categories of differentiation, however, were no longer those that had characterized the late nineteenth century. As noted earlier, Kruševo's "Greeks" and "Bulgarians" had found refuge in the countries with which they identified. After 1919, according to one narrative, Greek was no longer used as a language of worship in St. Nicholas, the grand old cathedral built by the community, which switched to Serbian. Although various people acknowledge widespread knowledge of Greek in the past, few of those who remained in Kruševo referred to themselves in this way. After 1919 at least, the people of the southern and lower part of the town, or *dolni*, were increasingly referred to as Vlahs.[7]

The category of "Bulgarian" endured longer, and still carries a political charge in contemporary Macedonia. In interviews with elderly Vlah-speakers, I was told that their language has no way to distinguish "Macedonian" and "Bulgarian" as ethnic terms, using *v'rg'ri* to translate both.[8] The term has a clear etymological connection with Bulgar, and this upsets younger people who have grown up in Yugoslav or post-Yugoslav Macedonia, where the difference between Macdeonian and Bulgarian became a matter of concern. The importance of the distinction was perhaps less obvious to the Vlah inhabitants of Kruševo in the interwar period, when the Yugoslav state did not countenance Macedonian identity and took active measures against those suspected of affiliation with Bulgaria. In Macedonian, Bulgarian, or Serbian, Kruševo's lower-town residents would also refer to the mainly Slavic-speaking people who made their homes in the north and northwestern quarters simply as *gorni*, or "those up there."

The separation of dolni and gorni—the "lowers" and the "uppers"—was made again and again in oral narratives of the interwar period, emerging as more significant in the life of the town than the divisions among the professional segments of the Vlah population, or among Slavic-speakers of different origins. The line between the communities was asserted in various ways. Although all the churches were now generally known by their Slavic names, church-going was one practice which divided the town. Those in the upper town would most likely attend Sv. Bogorodica, while those in the lower would worship at Sv. Nikola, Sv. Jovan, or Sv. Trojca. The town's two graveyards segregated both the dead and the living members of the two communities, who undertook their rituals of remembrance in their own part of the town. Young men, in particular, were at risk from gangs of counterparts if they crossed the line into the other neighborhood. According to Trifun Naḱa, there were two football teams in those days, *Hajduk* from the lower town, and *Sloga* from the upper. It was rare, he said, that a game between them didn't spark a fight between rival supporters.

ENDURING DIFFERENCE: PATTERNS AND PRACTICES OF MARRIAGE

Attending different churches or supporting different football teams do not necessarily index enduring intercommunal antipathy. Yet, according to oral testimony from a range of interviews, the distinction between residents of the upper and lower town had cross-generational impact by shaping patterns of intermarriage. Trifun Naḱa stated that when he had married, it was taken for granted that he would marry a *Vlajinka*, a Vlah woman, and not someone from "up there." Strict familial and societal control over marriage was reported by most elderly people from the lower town with whom I spoke. Šula Gabel, for example, reported that the custom was for marriages to be arranged by match-makers, or *strojnici*: in his case, it was a cousin of his mother who made the initial approach. There was no question, he said, of a "love-match"; unmarried young men and women were strictly policed. There were elopements, when a couple formed an attachment that one or both of their families did not countenance; but in most cases and his own, he said, using a phrase that was commonplace in people's reminiscences of the time, there was no love—*nemaše ljubov*. At least he had seen his bride, who had worked at the Monopol factory, as he did; in earlier times, he recalled, young women in the town did not go out at all, day or night.

This impression was reaffirmed in other people's accounts of pre-WWII Kruševo. Ekaterina, the elderly woman mentioned earlier, was from a Vlah family, and described the extensive precautions that her family, especially her father, took to keep her from unsupervised contact with others outside the home. She was not allowed to attend school after the age of fourteen, and barely went out until she was seventeen, when she was apprenticed to a seamstress. She described how on one occasion she escaped with a cousin to go and view a new bride's trousseau, or *ruba*, as was the custom. Even this association with other women incensed her father, who threatened both her and her mother with his rifle when she finally returned. Šula Gabel recalled that parents also used psychological weapons to get the message across to daughters. Before they were married, his wife's mother told her daughters that being touched by a man could be enough to make them pregnant and thereby ruin them. With such an apparatus of control in place, it is hardly surprising that older people discount the significance of love in marriage. Janko Mele and his wife Fani described their own match as made by their parents without their agency, and that love came later. Ekaterina's marriage, too, in her own account, was orchestrated without her ever having talked to her husband. He took the initiative to pursue the suit, she said, when he was told that at a wedding she had not danced with the other young people, but sat demurely with her parents. Such impressions mattered. As in other cases in small communities described by anthropologists of the region, in 1930s Kruševo considerable attention was paid to reputation, or the public perception of a potential bride and her family. Her own personal characteristics, intellectual, emotional, or otherwise, were a lesser part of the equation.[9]

What also emerges from these narratives is a sense of courtship and marriage as an intricate system of signs and symbols. The descriptions given of wedding practices have elements that match those from other parts of the Balkans (Campbell 1964:132–38; Friedl 1962:556–58; Halpern 1958:191–98; Lodge 1934–35; Rheubottom 1980). In the long account given by Janko Mele and his wife, they described the schedule of the week before and after a wedding. Weddings were usually held on a Sunday. On the Tuesday before, the close families on both sides would meet for dinner at the groom's family's house; on Thursday, at the bride's family's house. On the morning of the wedding the groomsman, who might either be the groom's brother (*dever*) or a close friend (*pobratim*), would come to the bride's family's house with a group of friends.[10] The house would be barred against them. From inside, the bride's entourage would demand compensation for giving her up, and he would respond formulaically: For every girl a young man, for every young man a bride, and for both wealth. Once admitted, he would place a pair of shoes before the bride, facing away from her, for her to step into. She would turn them around and he would put money in them, and turn them back. They would repeat this three times, and then he would throw money into her entourage. As they picked it up he would make off with the bride. He would have still to run a ritualized gauntlet, in which the bride's supporters would beat him, and his friends fight back, before completing his task of escorting the bride—after confirming that she was the one betrothed, and not a substitute—to the church for the wedding.[11]

After the church service the groom's family would play host again, and the groom himself would be expected to lead the carousing. The married couple would not sleep together on the first night; instead the bride would pass the night with the husband's mother, or his brother's wife. The marriage was consummated only on Monday night, and people recalled the sheets being inspected for blood, as proof of the bride's virginity. In the following week, there would be one more dinner at the bride's family's house. At the end of the week the new bride would draw water for her new household from the town spring, and roll out dough to make *pita*, a large flat pie of cheese, vegetable, or meat. In the Meles' version, people would throw money into (or onto) the pita that she would pass on to her brothers.

All these are practices familiar from other accounts of ritual work undertaken where control over a woman's labor, reproductive and productive, changes hands from one family to another. Precise conduct and ascribed meanings sometimes vary. Lodge reports from Galičnik that the groom's father would provide clothes and shoes for the bride to wear at the wedding, while in a Greek example, Cowan describes the *koumbaros*, or wedding sponsor, providing shoes for the bride, which can be used to divine which of the bride's friends will marry next (Lodge 1934–35:659; Cowan 1990:95). Josif Obrebski described ritualized confrontation between wedding parties in 1930's Macedonia. Halpern describes the symbolic role of bread, the basic foodstuff, at a wedding party in Orasac, where a flat loaf is passed around and guests throw money onto it for the newlyweds (Halpern 1965:197). In Lodge's account of Galičnik weddings, the bridegroom's mother provides loaves with money baked into them for the celebrations (Lodge 1934–35:659). Bread also marks a transfer of responsibilities and fertility to the bride, as in

Galičnik the bride would roll dough when she entered her new home, and in rural Bosnia she would carry a loaf of bread, provided by her mother-in-law, across the new threshold (Lodge 1934–35:663; Bringa 1995:158; see also Sugarman 1997:245–48, 249). From northern Greece, Campbell reported that the first duty of a Sarakatsani bride once accepted into her husband's household was to draw water (Campbell 1964:63).

The intricacy and importance of symbolic practices of betrothal and marriage in Macedonia are most clearly set out in David Rheubottom's painstaking account (1980). What also emerged from stories told to me in Kruševo, however, was the development of a range of tactics designed to thwart or divert ritual restrictions. For example, people described some of the elaborate measures that suitors in the past took to try to communicate with the objects of their affection. One woman in her forties related how matchmakers arranged her paternal grandmother's marriage in the 1920s. Her grandmother, then a bride-to-be, came into the room when the negotiations were being concluded, to see two visitors, her groom-to-be and a friend he had brought with him, both in the uniforms of the Serbian gendarmerie. Both men were from Kruševo, but she had no idea which was to be her husband. One of the two lit a cigarette and slyly flicked it at her: this was enough to identify him. Others spoke of young lovers in the villages near Kruševo using mirrors to communicate from their respective homes. Šula Gabul recalled some young couples eloping. He also noted that a handsome young man, even if poor, might succeed in marrying into a wealthy family, showing that the system was not all-pervasive and that under some circumstances personal charms could work their magic. In her account of her wedding day, Ekaterina described her own exercise of agency. Apparently struck by the preponderance of rituals that seemed designed to reinforce her status as submissive chattel, she put into practice some symbolism of her own. Acting on advice from friends, she kicked her husband in the shins during the church service. He, apparently, was amused; the priest was angry.

Writing of marriage patterns cross-culturally, but making primary reference to France, Martine Segalen puts forward the hypothesis that a greater degree of choice is a function of greater egalitarianism (1986:130). She cites a study by Bourdieu of Béarn in southern France which suggests that in more hierarchical societies where marriage was seen as an economic transaction, "the family married and the individual married with it" (1986:123: citing Bourdieu 1962:33–34). Segalen invokes Van Gennep's work on folklore to suggest that courting in such circumstances is highly rule-bound. The lower town in Kruševo in the 1930s, as described by some who lived there, was a place where status and the protection of family interests mattered a great deal. Ultimately, it appears, the issue was the preservation of economic status. Despite the exceptions he noted, Šula Gabel made it clear that for the most part, the pattern was clear: "rich with rich, poor with poor."[12]

In inter-war Kruševo, and Macedonia more generally, a legal code based on the Serbian civil law of 1844 was in force (Kovačić 1947:44). Effectively, this invested all the property rights of a married woman in her husband. There were also restrictions on her ability to inherit property from her husband. Yet accounts of the 1920s and 1930s in Kruševo suggest that women were able to control financial assets. After the sale of a deceased brother's assets in Egypt, one elderly woman kept a share of the proceeds as cash, usually on her person. Formerly, when both her brothers had originally gone to work in Egypt, she had run the family's soap factory in Kruševo. According to a young man from a formerly wealthy Vlah family, his widowed grandmother took on the responsibilities of managing the workforce who looked after the family's extensive livestock.

Both these stories suggest that in practical terms, certain women could take on decision-making responsibilities and management roles. It can be argued that this possibility owed something to the characteristics of Kruševo described in the section cited from Lebrun and Voinescu earlier, whereby menfolk were abroad for extended periods. Kruševo's female population, though, did more than sit at home and mourn at the rock of farewells. It appears that, as in other cases investigated by anthropologists, the patterned absence of active men from the town thrust greater responsibilities onto women. Clearly they still had to maintain their reputation of irreproachable morality, which drove Lebrun to compare Kruševo to the kind of puritan North American community described by Nathaniel Hawthorne (Lebrun and Voinescu 1911:67). But Kruševo may have been a less clearly polarized and oppressive place to live than others. In her comparative study of life in Yugoslav villages between the wars, Erlich includes an analysis of a village in Macedonia's Prespa region where *pečalba*, or male labor migration, was a common pattern, suggesting that household relations were less characterized by violence and coercion than they were in other parts of the country (St. Erlich 1966:273; see also Vasiliadis 1989:152). One part of the explanation given is that women play a greater role in household management and therefore both husband and wife are more inclined to see marriage as a cooperative enterprise.[13] Kruševo's economic and social heritage seems to have created a greater role for married women than a strict reading of legal procedures might allow.

Before marriage the young women of Kruševo's wealthy families found themselves pawns in processes where too much was at stake to risk romance. The coexistence of ostentatious wealth and penury reported in the town provides a vital clue as to the basis of their particularly constrained lives. The opulent lifestyle recalled by some was founded on the expenditure of accumulated capital, or on the proceeds of business conducted elsewhere. As such, that lifestyle was under siege, and it might be argued that certain of the practices described from the period index an awareness of this fact. This seems particularly clear in the descriptions of the ways in which marriages were arranged and conducted. For a status-conscious family in Kruševo, the pool of marriage partners of suitable standing was in decline as a result of out-migration. In the nineteenth century, when Hellenism was still culturally dominant and Kruševo was economically prosperous and growing, individuals from upwardly mobile families could be recruited and absorbed. By the 1930s, the opposite was the case: intermarriage between different strata of the town's society was seen not as "leveling up" but as "leveling down." The cardinal rule forbidding intermarriage across the "upper-lower" divide appears to have had at least some economic basis; residents of the upper town were capital-poor, and as such, undesirable to families in the lower town anxious to avoid dilution of assets that had already begun to appear finite. The ongoing effect of such calculation was to further cement the boundary between north and south in the town. The boundary separated communities that worshipped in different churches, buried their dead in different parts of a graveyard, or a different graveyard altogether, used different languages in their homes, and seldom intermarried.

A further aspect of the upper-lower divide was political. As noted, some accounts of dolni and gorni distinguish them as adherents of two political parties, the Radicals and the Democrats. The Radical party dominated Yugoslav politics, reportedly via an efficient, Tammany Hall-type machine oiled by patronage (Stavrianos 1958:621). This machine was personified in Kruševo in the figure of Dušan Antonević, the Radical leader in the town, who campaigned in the elections of 1935 and 1938 on the promise of bringing employment opportunities to Kruševo for the less well-off who constituted the base of support for his party. He was elected, and he delivered: between 1937 and 1938 the Monopol tobacco factory was built in the lower town, on the site of the former Greek school which had been burned by Bulgarian forces in 1914–15. This not only provided employment for people already in the town, but in the course of its operation, attracted workers from outside the town. According to one account, three hundred people were employed there as soon as it opened, a substantial part of the town's working-age population. Others said that as many as a quarter of the working population was employed there; almost all the people from less well-off families with whom I spoke had put in some time as employees. According to one interviewee, though, upper-class Vlah families considered it shameful work for a woman. This was most likely because, as already noted, it was a place where men and women worked in close proximity. For this reason, as well as the economic and political rationale behind it, the factory appears to have been seen as a threat by the better-off families of the lower town. In their neighborhood, it represented an unwelcome intrusion, licensing dangerous or undesirable outsiders to breach an unwritten boundary between north/northwest, and south/southeast.

DEFYING STRUCTURE

Like any system, Kruševo's had its dissenters. Ekaterina, the woman who recalled disobeying her father's will and going out to examine a dowry and who kicked her husband at the altar, was one. Although her marriage was ultimately arranged, her narrative suggests that within the confined space allowed to her, she negotiated to exert some control over her destiny. The first instance came when her parents planned to apprentice her younger sister to a seamstress. Ekaterina argued that she herself should be allowed to go, warning her parents that if people saw an older daughter passed over for this, they would suspect there was something amiss with her.[14] Although committed to protecting their daughter from contact with schoolfriends whom they perceived as *rasipani*, or no longer respectable, the parents were trapped by their daughter's logic: if you go on hiding me, people may suspect your motives in so doing.

Ekaterina recalls being anxious to get out of Kruševo. Again, a story told in the present revolves around a text in the past, as she explained that her wish to see the world was spurred by pictures and accounts of cosmopolitan life in Zagreb depicted in an illustrated magazine. This served as background to her account of her second and more conclusive success in shaping her own course of action, which seems to have involved the complicity of several women. A friend of her father's in the guild of merchants wanted to marry his son to Ekaterina, and planned to open negotiations. At around the same time a Serbian military officer, an older cousin of some of her best friends, returned to Kruševo for his name day, or *imenden*, St. Nicholas' day, on 19 December.[15] Aged thirty-five, he was looking for a wife from his hometown. Two of Ekaterina's friends arranged for him to be able to see her—one invited her out to watch a wedding procession, while the other watched from a window with him, and pointed her out. He then undertook his own inquiries in Prilep, and received confirmation of her demure conduct. His aunt, Ekaterina's former teacher, took on the role of matchmaker, coming to visit Ekaterina's mother on Christmas Day. Ekaterina's mother consented, even though her husband, Ekaterina's father, was at that moment in negotiation with the other matchmaker. Afterward, his fellow guild member complained to him, outraged that he would give his daughter to an outsider, a Serb, even though he was from Kruševo.

A military officer with a government job and pension clearly seemed to Ekaterina's parents, especially her mother, to be a desirable son-in-law. It was, perhaps, recognition of the finite or dwindling prospects of prosperity for their daughter within Kruševo's shrinking world. After the fact, the match was approved by other matchmakers of the town; although Ekaterina had not married within the Vlah community, she had also not married across the upper-lower divide in the town. Her husband, identified as a Serb, occupied a separate category, and the couple would not live in Kruševo. Ekaterina recorded having misgivings when she realized she would be leaving friends behind. Her mother, to comfort her, took a calculating but presumably well-intentioned line. Her husband was older (twice her age, in fact) which might be hard at the beginning, but it also brought the prospect of a good pension and independent widowhood closer. The marriage took place within two weeks, and the couple left for his next station, presumably with the plan to return only for occasional visits.

A rather different register of opposition to the order of things is represented in an unpublished life history written by Kirče Risteski, whose descendants live in the town still, and who shared this autobiography with me (Risteski 1983). He was born on 2 July 1913 to what he describes as a poor town family: his father, Petre, had come from the village of Malo Ilino to Kruševo in the late nineteenth century with his brother, hoping to make a better life. They worked hard, bought some sheep, and thus his father became *svoj čovek*, or his own man, no longer forced into employment on someone else's terms. He died in 1919. Kirče's mother came from an artisan or *zanaetski* family: her father, Petre Kirkov, had been a barrelmaker (*bovčar*). Because her mother died when young, she was adopted by the Buklević family. Of the eleven children of the marriage, only Kirče and two sisters survived childhood: Kirče was born when his father was already fifty-four, and his mother forty-five. He went to school from 1920–24 and then, at age eleven, went to learn the zanaet of carpentry with his sister's husband, Miha Dimitrieski.

Risteski's own circle of friends from his teenage years reads like a roll call of key figures in Kruševo's communist history. He lists Miše Eftimov, the first leader of the Kruševo partisan detachment in the 1941–44 war of liberation; Vaso and Jani Tufa; and Tomo Kuturec, who after the war would serve on the council for the Ilinden pension program. Together, in 1927, in Risteski's account, they created an association named after Jovan Skerlić, which in the mid-1930s constituted the core of the fledgling communist organization in Kruševo.[16] Risteski became a member of the communist party in July 1937. One of their principal aims, he recalls, was to break down the differences that separated Vlahs from Macedonians, and to form "one united working class." The composition of the group was in keeping with such an ideal. The Kuturec family was among those that traced descent to settlers from Grammos, while the Tufas had come from Nikolica (Popović 1937:292n.). One side of Risteski's family were relative newcomers to the town from a Slavic-speaking mountain village to the west. Kruševo's early communists thus came from communities that in the nineteenth century had lived parallel but separate lives, yet they worked to create common purpose.

The difficulties of activism in heavily policed Yugoslav Macedonia quickly became apparent as the young men tried to communicate their message to others. Risteski heckled the Radical politician Dušan Antonević during the election campaign of 1935, for which Risteski was beaten and arrested. He and Jani Tufa were held by the gendarmerie in Dolenci for four hours when they were on a tour of villages spreading the communist message. In 1938 Risteski took a carpenter's job on the construction team of the Monopol factory, Antonević's pork-barrel project. Risteski attempted to organize a strike, which had limited success as there was still widespread unemployment. Jani Tufa and Miše Eftimov were questioned and beaten by police on 1 May 1939 when they held a meeting on Gumenja, the hill at the northwest edge of the town. On Ivanden, 7 July 1940, a week after Risteski became engaged to Niča Leonida Papakoča, the group painted slogans in red on various walls in Kruševo. A week later Risteski was arrested and taken to Prilep, where he was jailed and beaten again. He and Niča had a modest wedding ceremony in February 1941, but once the formalities were completed he resumed his political work. He was called to military service in the Yugoslav Army in March 1941.[17]

The stories of these two individuals—Ekaterina and Kirče Risteski—reveal something of the diversity of reactions to the established social and economic order of the town. Most crudely, they exemplify flight and fight. Ekaterina represents herself as defying expectations in a variety of ways. She chose her own friends and, despite the efforts of her parents to take her out her friends' company by stopping her attendance at school, she found a means to stay in touch with them. In her own recollection, she did nothing to disgrace the family's reputation, and could play the role of the model daughter in public settings. Nonetheless, she carved out for herself a space of freedom outside their supervision. One might argue that her mother's enthusiasm for the marriage, which did not break the rules of the town (though it did sidestep them), indicates her own awareness of the responsibilities and trials that awaited her daughter within the town community. In Ekaterina's narrative, a curious role is played by an illustrated magazine which offered a glimpse of fine living to a wide-eyed young girl, who perhaps read it in one of her favorite spots, tucked away in a corner of a downstairs store-room, while listening to her father berating her mother in the room above. In the way she frames such episodes, her choice was between escape and becoming part of a system in which she wanted no part.

Kirče Risteski's circumstances were different. In his narrative, family constraints played a much smaller role than did loyalties to friends made in school and retained through early adulthood. He gives no account of the origin of the ideals that he and his cohort embraced and tried to disseminate in the town and in nearby villages. At this juncture, communist party membership across Yugoslavia as a whole was at a low ebb, and so an external impetus seems unlikely—though it appears that their activism began in earnest after the murder of King Alexander in Marseille in October 1934, which brought an end to his de facto dictatorship.

The circumstances of life in a small town pressed in on them, too—although at times it worked to their advantage. When Kirče and Jani Tufa were arrested and held in Dolenci, it was because the gendarmes in the station there did not know who they were and considered them suspicious interlopers. VMRO bands were still active in Vardar Macedonia at this time from their bases in Bulgaria, and used violence against representatives of what they saw as Serbian occupation. In this case, Risteski and Tufa were released when Sotir Konjarec, who was the local representative for the Singer Sewing Machine Company, vouched for them.[18] However, more often life at close quarters, in which secrets were hard to keep, made work difficult. Risteski's arrest in July 1940 after the sloganeering of Ivanden came about because he had been betrayed to the police. The culprit identified in his account was a young woman from Novo Selo, a village south of Kruševo. She and her sister were among those who had come to Kruševo to work at the Monopol factory and were pro-Serbian; her father would later be a Serbian četnik during the Second World War. The two sisters boarded in the house of Petra Čučuk. When they returned to their village for Ivanden, Risteski's group used their room to conceal the paint they used. Someone must have been careless or perhaps the sisters overheard their hosts in conversation. At any rate, the young women went to the police, who tracked down Risteski. This was his last major action in the first Yugoslavia.[19] Like those who had resisted state authority in previous generations, family obligations intervened to shape the individual's life course: Kirče's marriage and the birth of his first son, Pero, pulled him in another direction.

THE RETURN OF WAR

In the first Yugoslavia Ekaterina and Kirče Risteski found themselves on opposite sides of Serbian rule. In 1941 Axis forces quickly overwhelmed the Yugoslav military, ordered to defend a fractious country which had never won the loyalty of many of its people and soldiers. This defeat led Ekaterina to experience a greater change than Kirče. She already had two children by this time in her new home—not Zagreb, where she had daydreamed of living, but Brod, then called Južna Brod, now Makedonski Brod, about ten miles north of Kruševo over the mountains. She lived close enough that her mother could take the oldest child back to Kruševo to look after for awhile. When Ekaterina was in Kruševo and preparing to return to Brod, in early April 1941, she heard that Belgrade had fallen. Her soldier husband fled over the mountains with a friend. Coming from the north, they came first to Gumenja where they found two townsmen on guard. Greeting them with the standard Serbian phrase, *Dobar dan*, they were told that they should now use *Zdravo*. This was their first encounter with the new, pro-Bulgarian sympathies in the town. They were taken to the new chief of police, who had participated in the Ilinden Uprising of 1903, but was also a friend of Ekaterina's husband. Although released, he and Ekaterina were marked as Serb-sympathizers, and once Bulgarian forces arrived they could not stay in Kruševo. After returning briefly to Brod and finding the former military base there deserted, Ekaterina and her husband spent most of the war in a village close to Kruševo. She recalled life as being hard in those years. They survived by her using her tailoring skills and by bartering for food until the partisan victory of 1944.

For Kirče Risteski, the Bulgarian occupation of Kruševo was a direct challenge. He deserted from the Yugoslav army in Kičevo on 14 April 1941 after the fall of Belgrade, and like Ekaterina's husband made his way back to Kruševo through the mountains. On his return, he found that people were anticipating the arrival of the Bulgarians, and had already set up what he called a kind of provisional, arbitrary authority—*nekakva improvizirana vlast* (1981:57). Its members, Risteski said, were the core of the traitors and collaborators who would hold power during this new occupation. He and his friends quickly undertook the same sort of work they had done under Yugoslav rule. They distributed leaflets and painted slogans against the occupation, and tried to rouse the national consciousness of the people. In July 1941 he personally put up posters around the town that challenged the forthcoming Bulgarian celebration plans that would attempt to claim the Ilinden tradition as their own.

The small group of activists continued for the next year to wage their campaign against the occupiers. They were financed by the activities of some members and allies who worked at the Monopol factory, taking tobacco and illicitly selling it in the villages or across the border between Bulgarian and Italian control, in Kičevo.[20] They disrupted the Bulgarian-sponsored celebration of Ilinden in 1942 by distributing flyers and painting slogans in the town and on the route to Mečkin Kamen, where the festivities were to be held. Their efforts within the town complemented those of the newly formed Kruševo partisan detachment bearing the name Pitu Guli, headed by Miše Eftimov, which on 6 August 1942 mounted an attack on the nearby village of Pribilci, burning government records, seizing weapons and ammunition, and making speeches to the villagers (Kudžulovska 1970:650).

At the end of 1942, disaster struck Kirče's circle. Already they had prepared hiding places in their homes, and had anticipated lives as fugitives, or *ilegalni*. On 16 November Miše Eftimov was betrayed, allegedly by Menda Mladenoska and her son, Metodija, who worked as a clerk at the police station. Miše was trapped; rather than surrender, he killed himself with a grenade. After that Mančo Matak, another activist from Kruševo, went into hiding in the Risteski home. A 24,000 Bulgarian *leva* reward was offered for information leading to his capture.

Again, neighbors betrayed the family's secret activities. During the construction of the hiding places, the Risteski family had been confronted with the problem of disposing of the earth they had removed. They put it in the yard, and covered it with new paving. A neighbor, Petra Pare, noticed the new construction, and reported it to a leader of the Bulgarian paramilitary forces in the town. The house was put under surveillance by townsfolk who supported the Bulgarian regime. Kirče's mother and wife were arrested and beaten, but did not reveal the location of the hiding place. Risteski and Matak escaped and made it into the hills. They went to Gostivar, in the Italian sector. Risteski told both Albanians and Italians there that he was a Vlah and had been persecuted by the Bulgarians because of his ethnicity. He stayed in Gostivar for more than a year, aware that he had to maintain that cover story; as a communist, he faced arrest in the Italian sector, too. He returned to Kruševo in August 1944, to find that he had been charged with deserting the Kruševo partisan detachment. Fortunately, enough of his close friends from before the war were still alive to vouch for his record of active involvement.[21]

Like Ekaterina, Kirče welcomed the end of Bulgarian occupation as liberation from oppression. Others in the town had fared better, surviving with families and lives intact after making whatever accommodations were necessary. Janku Mele recalled that people in the town lit candles for King Boris, who died in 1943. Several older men I spoke with had been conscripted into the Bulgarian army, and told stories of making their way back to Kruševo in 1944 similar to those of Ekaterina's husband and Kirče in 1941. People clearly recalled that some in the town had participated in Bulgarian-sponsored organizations and celebrations during the occupation, which they generally considered a form of "soft" collaboration. Compared with the fate of other towns and villages in Macedonia, Kruševo's mixed community was fortunate. In some towns Bulgarian forces mounted more sustained campaigns to root out communist opposition or forcibly dispossessed and displaced whole non-Bulgarian populations—the Jewish communities of Štip, Skopje, and Bitola being three of the most tragic examples.[22] In Kruševo, stockholding enterprises and the Monopol factory continued to operate much as before. Although the new Bulgarian régime siphoned off much of Macedonia's industrial product, Kruševo's consumer-focused economy appears to have been less vulnerable. The social division between the two communities of the town remained, but although the Bulgarian régime formally divided citizens into categories of Bulgarian and non-Bulgarian, and discriminated against the latter, these organized differences did not serve to channel widespread intercommunal violence, at least in Kruševo.

Those whose fortunes were tied up with the town's pastoral economy had faced privations during the Bulgarian occupation, as they were forced to supply the occupiers with dairy products and meat. They had also faced dangers from Yugoslav partisans who were not always scrupulous about what and from whom they stole to survive. If Kruševo's stockholders hoped that the end of conflict would permit them a return to better days, though, they quickly learned otherwise. Already in 1941, in the first "Partisan Republic" of Užice, the communists had shown the kind of ruthless intervention they planned. By sequestering private enterprises, craft shops, and smaller businesses, they seized the assets of potential leaders of opposition to their regime, thereby depriving them of the means by which to win support. The communists then used those assets to secure their own position by building a common fund and offering support to the poor (Bokovoy 1998:9).

ENCOUNTERING SOCIALISM: KRUŠEVO AFTER 1944

The same policy of seizing assets was followed on a wider scale after the victory of 1944–45. Ranko Brashich states that confiscation had already begun in November 1944, when the property of German citizens, people of German nationality or descent, and "collaborators," was transferred to government ownership. The process continued with laws passed in December 1946 and April 1948 whereby "the entire structure of commerce, industry, transportation, banking and insurance was transferred to state ownership" (Brashich 1954:46). Large estates, land owned by banks or corporations, and holdings above the legal limit set for peasants (twenty-five to thirty-five hectares) and nonpeasants (three to five hectares) were expropriated and a land fund created by the Law on Agrarian Reform and Colonization passed in August 1945 (Brashich 1954:47; Bokovoy 1998:38–39).[23]

In many cities and towns, one of the first victims was the Orthodox church which often owned commercial property. In cities like Skopje, Prilep, and Bitola, the state took possession of such premises as part of its project of collectivization. In Bitola, swathes of the old downtown area were reportedly flattened to make way for new construction. But in Kruševo, according to a churchwarden I interviewed in 1992, the state apparently contented itself initially with collecting the rental income from existing property owners, including the church. His account suggested that the state saw expropriation as not financially worthwhile at that point, but the threat of expropriation remained. It was only after 1954, when the collectivization experiment across Yugoslavia was abandoned in failure, that the church could feel secure in its ownership. Elsewhere, according to the churchwarden, those expropriations of the late 1940s had never been reversed, and many people with houses or stores in Skopje or elsewhere had never seen them returned. In that regard, the church in Kruševo had been lucky.

Wealthy families with large holdings in stock in the town herds were less fortunate. Significant portions of the town herd had been concentrated in the hands of relatively few families, giving them resources that might conceivably embolden them to challenge the new régime. The Partisans, reportedly, took no chances in Kruševo or elsewhere in Macedonia and quickly eliminated any possible threat. Between 1934 and 1938, the Vardar Banovina within the Kingdom of Yugoslavia was home to an annual average of 2,152,600 sheep and 667,400 goats. These figures represented, respectively, 22 percent and 35 percent of all Yugoslavia's holdings of these animals (Tomasevich 1955:518). In 1948 a special law was passed ordering the slaughter of goats, which reduced their number to 41,671 (Tomasevich 1955:530).[24] Sources like Tomasevich's support oral accounts from Kruševo in the early 1990s describing the communist program that destroyed the town's livestock. Landholdings and properties in Skopje and elsewhere purchased with the proceeds of business were reportedly confiscated. Stories were also told of cash being seized from houses.

The new Yugoslav régime oversaw a redistribution of capital assets that variously affected communities and families. In Kruševo, those who were hardest hit were the former élites whose wealth was built on stockholding and commerce, and who had made their living as rentiers or entrepreneurs. People in the town drew parallels between their fate and that of two other mountain communities, Galičnik and Sveti Nikole. In all three, resources built over generations on the profits from extensive pasturelands were taken from their owners. The effects extended beyond the "capitalists" stripped of their property; with the destruction of the town's herds, a whole section of the population whose livelihood had depended on the pastoral economy faced a major upheaval.

Yet despite the resentment still expressed by members of former stockholding families more than forty years later, other elements of Kruševo's population experienced less abrupt change. The Monopol factory, so central as an employer for a significant portion of the town's population since 1938, passed into state ownership and continued to operate as it had under the first Yugoslavia and, later, under Bulgarian occupation. Monopol employees had been drawn from the less well off in Kruševo. Work there now, in a less diverse economy where capital reserves had been wiped out, appealed to a broader section of the town's population. The state's untypical decision not to sequester and close all the small shops and industries in the town reduced the impact of the new régime on a longer-established socio-economic group in the town—those organized around crafts, or zanaeti. As Kirče Risteski's autobiography indicates, this group had provided the core personnel of communist activism in the town. Often educated beyond the level of their rural counterparts and committed to breaking down barriers of class and ethnicity, Kruševo's carpenters, coopers, shoemakers, clerks, and the like provided the backbone of the party. Kirče Risteski himself was elected secretary of the town council in 1948. Tomo Kuturec, one of Risteski's original group of friends, had been one of the town's representatives to ASNOM, the republic's founding assembly.

The shake-up of class relations in the town had an uneven impact on established ways of life. Reportedly, the most fervent communists in the town eschewed religious practices, including those central to social relations. However, most people seem to have reconciled the old and the new ways of life, which in many regards overlapped. The new doctrine of "brotherhood and unity," for example, with its basis in egalitarianism, could be seen as conterminous with ideas of mutual respect central to guild organization in the town. In this regard, the relative shift in status of different sections of the community, whereby the practitioners of zanaeti found their standing increased, served to accentuate continuity between past and present. Where the efforts of Kuturec, Risteski, and their associates to bring together different groups in the town had once been marginal and lacked support, they were now backed by the whole ideology of a country anxious to escape the potentially divisive effects of the past.

Other long-established town norms that had divided the community were also challenged in practice. In one of my interviews an old woman who had grown up in the south, Vlah quarter of Kruševo, described her 1952 marriage to a man from the north, Slav-speaking, quarter. Her own father had been a stockholder and during the war had found Yugoslav partisans stealing cheese from his sheepfold. He was denounced as a traitor and hanged. Her husband's father had been a policeman in the former Yugoslavia. At the time of their courtship, she and her husband recalled, the town's population was still divided into adversarial camps. When the matchmakers came, her brothers were angry, as they themselves were not yet married and she was only sixteen. But the lovers married anyway, despite objections but with the encouragement of friends, who pointed out to her that the prospective groom had only one brother and one sister, hence, they could expect economic security. They married without a big wedding, or *svadba*, and moved to his family's neighborhood, where they still live. Her family disowned her, but marriage across the old social dividing line became increasingly acceptable. It had been prevented or discouraged primarily by residents of the lower town conscious of their own community's longer history and better economic standing. After 1945 such views ran counter to both the economic order and the communal ideology of the new régime.

The accounts of Kruševo's twentieth-century past presented here, then, indicate dimensions of the town's past that would be downplayed in Yugoslav Macedonia. These accounts reveal that some who prospered under Ottoman rule were able to do so again in the laissez-faire economic system of the first Yugoslavia, and had even been able to protect their livelihood during the Bulgarian occupation. The initiatives taken in the first years of socialist rule changed the contours of town life, flattening out economic differences and substantially altering the choices available to subsequent generations. The intrusion of state power into this mountain community was unlike anything that had previously been experienced, heralding a legal and social revolution that sought to sweep away assembled precedent and knit this community with its own particular history into the fabric of a new national community. With the livestock decimated, land appropriated, access to foreign capital restricted, and hoarded cash seized, Kruševo's population found itself compelled to find new ways to live with a régime that appeared firmly entrenched, and set to exert more control than most of its predecessors.

CHAPTER SIX

Buying the Memories

COLLECTIVIZATION, THE PAST, AND NATIONAL IDENTITY

WHERE THE INITIAL advent of Yugoslav socialist authority in Kruševo worked to alter the material conditions that had so powerfully affected community life in the first half of the century, this was not the limit of the new régime's ambition. In this period, for the first time in history, a state acknowledged and indeed derived some of its legitimacy from the existence of a distinct Macedonian narod, or people. This represented a radical break with the ideologies of other claimants to the territory, especially those of the new Macedonian republic's southern and eastern neighbors. Apart from a brief period in the late 1940s when elements within each country recognized Macedonian nationhood, Greece and Bulgaria spent the rest of the twentieth century labeling it an artificial creation of Yugoslav politicians.

The fervor with which scholars and politicians in all three countries argued their case, for or against the reality of Macedonian identity, polarized the debate over the early post-war years. One side saw identity as primordial, the other as instrumental. Where one increasingly emphasized national continuity, the other called attention to state formation. Missing from both was an investigation of the ways in which existing conditions shaped the initiatives taken by privileged actors, and how these initiatives then affected the way in which those existing conditions were interpreted. In effect, both ignored the interconnection of the two perspectives that appear equally crucial in understanding a period when a régime sought legitimacy by granting a territory and some of its residents the same ancient name, rather than by incorporating either into an existing collectivity.

The experiment began in the late 1940s and early 1950s at a time when Yugoslav-backed Macedonia exerted sufficient power to convince individuals to cast their past behavior as steps in its own development. Among the traces left behind by this "persuasion offensive" is a set of records referred to as the Ilinden Dossier. These records document an ambitious bureaucratic initiative to identify individuals who had participated in the struggles of the last decade of the nineteenth century and the first decade of the twentieth, with the goal of rewarding them with state pensions. The pension program was put into practice at the same time as the new Yugoslav régime launched a broad collectivization program to industrialize rural production by creating village working cooperatives.

This chapter examines these initiatives as projects of semantic shift and social engineering. The first term—semantic shift—is taken from Liah Greenfeld's account of the emergence of national thinking (1992:5–9), but is extended to describe not only changes in the meanings of the terms narod and Macedonian but a number of other terms with popular currency that the régime sought to redefine. Over two words in particular—Ilinden and *zadruga*—people and state engaged in a dialogue that drew them closer together into a single shared discursive space, while simultaneously remaking the relations between them. Both words were symbolically powerful in the Macedonian past, and were harnessed by the new state in the creation of the pension program and the agricultural cooperatives. Both institutions were also programs of social engineering in that they sought to alter the contours of society and also the valency of the past. The argument advanced here is that they were bound together in their economic, social, and cultural logic. Although they were directed at different sectors of society and encountered various forms of resistance, their combined effect was to make socialism Macedonian and Macedonia socialist as state and individuals forged a new working relationship.

THEORETICAL APPROACHES TO NATIONAL CULTURE

The process by which the Macedonian narod came to be one of the initial five in the new Yugoslavia has been studied in great part by historians and political scientists whose primary concern is with international relations and who have less interest in the micropractices by which state-defined goals became a reality. Given the relative difficulty of access to the area and the political sensitivity of the topic of Macedonian nationalism for the last fifty years, such a perspective is hardly surprising. Unfortunately, the result has been an exclusive focus on the political stage as an autonomous sphere of action, with a corresponding disregard for other sites. This has contributed to the general acceptance of a narrowly defined "political" explanation of the phenomenon whereby, within a relatively short period, people turned from calling themselves Serbs or Bulgarians to calling themselves Macedonians. Thus, for example, Evangelos Kofos (1964, 1986a) lays stress on the central role of Tito's machinations and conflict with the Cominform in "creating" the Macedonian narod, and in tying it firmly to Yugoslavia. In these painstakingly researched and argued works, Kofos presents the people of the area and the international community at large as dupes of an unscrupulous and manipulative plot to hijack history in the service of politics. Less polemical, the excellent work of Shoup (1968), and studies by Troebst (1997), Palmer and King (1971), Barker (1950), and the U.S. Department of State (1954) confirm the importance of the shifting political terrain in creating a milieu whereby the communist parties of Yugoslavia, Bulgaria, and Greece all promoted the existence of a Macedonian people to serve their own ends.

Viewed as studies of nation-building, all of these works can be placed in what might be called the school of "social realism" in which states are presented as actors, and people as responders and mimics. Such an approach makes politics the realm of states, and reads history through that lens. Accordingly, it deploys history in a particular way and constructs its field of inquiry in such a way as to exclude as illegitimate or underage certain national movements. In such a frame, states or parties are the only actors, and it is historical coincidence that they seek legitimacy by enrolling their subjects in a single cultural group, or *ethnos*. It is only in a world of nation-states that these political actors rely upon bonds of identity, conceived in cultural terms, to construct a stable polity; and only in such a world that other states or actors, similarly, promote particular groupings in order to challenge a régime and destabilize it. Nationalism becomes an extension of politics; national problems are the result of agitation by external forces. Those who have espoused such a view include some of the most influential writers on the phenomenon of nationalism (Breuilly 1982; Gellner 1983; Smith 1979).

The very presentation of nation-creation in this way, however, displays some of the features of Orientalism as categorized by Said (1978). Scholars such as John Plamenatz (1974), for example, distinguished "Western" and "Eastern" nationalisms, presenting the latter as "culturally insecure." The potential ideological deployment of such divisions is apparent in the work of Franjo Tudjman and other Croatian ideologue-historians defining Croatian nationalism as conforming to some western European model, and contrasting it with the "Eastern" form in Serbia (Bakic-Hayden and Hayden 1992). The attention paid to the division between "ethnic" and "civic" nationalisms by scholars like Goulbourne (1991), Greenfeld (1992) and, in the Yugoslav case, Allcock (1992) marks a greater sensitivity to the possible implications of such classifications, as well as making the point that in such analyses what is under discussion is the state rather than the people who live in it. The persistence of the slippage by which, for example, Serbs in the period 1992–99 were collectively classed as degenerate because of the activities of their government is thus revealed as assuming that people from differently organized polities are, by dint of their ethnic affiliation to the régime, manipulated pawns, a political distinction which is then remobilized to cast them as primordially "other" and, usually, junior.

Once the inevitability and indissolubility of the link between state and individual are scrutinized, certain other assumptions come into question. The nation-state aspires to a flattening of other foci of social and economic relations; it is a truism that such an ideal has never been achieved, even by the most powerful central authorities (Corrigan and Sayer 1985). Yet in a region of transient régimes, what is emphasized about the inhabitants is their supposed willingness to adopt another national affiliation quickly. In parallel fashion, the new state is presumed to be ready and able to accept them as *tabulae rasae* and to inscribe national identity on them anew. Such a view at best credits the population with cynicism, a sort of post-modern shiftlessness; at worst, perceived from the stance of the nation-state, it presumes they have no notion of solidarity until given to them by a state (for, in this logic, only states make nations) and thereby makes them into ciphers. What one might term "experienced" history drops out of sight as the rhythm of every aspect of life is taken to be determined by the continuities or disjunctures in "top-down" history.

A rival position asserts that people's constructions of their social reality may escape the categories and plans of the centralizing state, and that the life of a small community may serve as a locus of continuity far more effectively than the often more fleeting existence that a territorially bound polity may enjoy. This approach is one in which the anthropological imagination is invoked in a consideration of what have variously been called the micropractices, cultural codes, or *habitus* of a society, which form continuities in individual and group life less visible in the national frame (Bourdieu 1977; Burke 1989; Comaroff and Comaroff 1992; Zonabend 1984).

While the people of Kruševo were pursuing their livelihoods in the ways described in the last chapter, their wider neighborhood changed hands repeatedly. Most of these transitions—the Young Turkish Revolution of 1908, the creation of the Kingdom of Serbs, Croats, and Slovenes in 1919 and its transformation into Yugoslavia in 1929—went unmarked in oral history. People instead recalled interventions that made a more immediate impact, such as the arrival of French troops handing out canned goods to children in 1917. They did not heed the fine distinctions of international relations, which indicate that Macedonia was never formally annexed by Bulgaria after 1941, but highlight instead their own experience of occupation. Similarly, their accounts do not register as significant the moment when the Republic's name was changed from People's Republic—*Narodna Republika*—to Socialist Republic—*Socialistička Republika*, and when talk of "autonomous Macedonia" was outlawed by Tito in the wake of Russian and Bulgarian assaults on the legitimacy of Yugoslavia's rule.

The emphases and omissions of local recall demonstrate the anthropological truism that meaning is a cultural artifact. Macedonians tended not to distinguish between "the Balkan Wars" of 1912–13 and "the First World War" of 1914–18. Many of the men who were drafted into the Serbian, Bulgarian, or Greek armies served continuously. Nor do people in Kruševo think of an event called the Second World War lasting from 1939 to 1945, but rather of an Anti-fascist Struggle for National Liberation running from 1941 to 1944. Lived experience and the verdicts of a national pedagogy both have an impact on the ways in which history is periodized and the ways particular events or structures are emphasized. Both shape the constitution and maintenance of collective memory and state legitimacy.

A focus on state efforts to fix identity overlooks the importance of such lived experience, and the multiple factors it introduces to the analysis. Attention to this multiplicity is central to the analysis, as without it the rejection of a state-centered focus harbors the concomitant risk of falling into romantic nationalism, whereby elements of village life, and institutions therein, are constructed as the "real" site of a unitary national identity. Rather than opposing state- and nation-derived identities, stress should be laid on the continuous negotiation of a whole spectrum of bonds of age, gender, locale, profession, and class; all of which may be eroded or transformed, highlighted or sidelined. In these respects this analysis seeks to engage critically with Geertz's work on identities within the new nations (1973b). It is influenced by the more recent work of Philip Corrigan and Derek Sayer on the formation of the English state (1985) and of Peter Sahlins on the crystallization of French and Spanish national identities in a border region (1989). In each case, a process of integration is demonstrated to have been simultaneously a project of disintegration. Such an approach appears particularly apt for the period under consideration, in which one régime built on the existing contours of society, even if opposed to the states in which that society took shape.[1]

THE ILINDEN *SPOMENICA*

In the National Archives of Macedonia in Skopje is a set of materials known as the Ilinden Dossier, forty-three boxes of documents containing the life-histories composed by some two and a half thousand individual Macedonians between 1948 and 1953. They were submitted to the state in support of applications for recognition of their authors' national revolutionary activity almost half a century earlier. These sources have not been extensively used by other Macedonian historians or by foreign researchers. Because of difficulties of access and limitations of time, I translated or made notes on nearly 350 of these applications, including all those from individuals from Kruševo or villages in the Kruševo district (a total of 76).[2]

With their requests for pensions, applicants were asked to attach a short autobiographical statement. These accounts, often written on the backs of documents that once served other purposes, are usually handwritten, more rarely typed. They range in length from a few terse lines to several closely covered pages. They have faded with time; the edges are often torn. Collec-

Figure 10: Ilinden spomenica, given to veterans of 1903. Photograph courtesy of Tomo Pavlovski.

tively, they conjure up two worlds that the régime of the time sought to draw together in a new vision of history: Ilinden 1903, and the new Yugoslav Republic of Macedonia, established in 1944 on Ilinden. Those whose applications were successful received two rewards: a monthly pension and formal recognition as *Ilindenci*, members of a select group of national heroes. As a tangible marker of this status they received a heavy metal badge about four inches square, depicting an armed individual backed by many others, encircled in a wreath of victory, and bearing the text "Ilinden 1903." This was the Ilinden commemorative medallion, or *spomenica* (figure 10), and the campaign to put it into the hands of men and women across the republic set in motion the large-scale production of texts recounting past and present.

The Ilinden spomenica plan was inaugurated in a decree passed on 12

January 1948. The conditions of the award were set out in the *Service News-paper of the Republic of Macedonia*, number 16, on 19 June 1950 as fol-lows:[3]

> The Ilinden *spomenica* has been established as a token of national recognition of individuals who served Macedonia and the Macedonian *narod* in the Ilinden Rising of 1903, in the national-revolutionary activities and in the struggle for the liberation of Macedonia and the Macedonian *narod* from Turkish slavery.
>
> The Ilinden *spomenica* is a national recognition of deserving participants, personally, and can be given only to those participants in the events listed in article 1 of this law, who remained loyal to the Macedonian *narod* and constant in its struggles for liberation. (Ilinden Dossier: Box 42)

These "deserving individuals" were then defined inclusively by the follow-ing categories:

> **a.** Those who in the national-revolutionary activities and struggles for the liberation of the Macedonian *narod* worked as organizers or leaders.
>
> **b.** Those who in that activity and struggle, took part with weapons in their hands, as fighters, first-hand, with the army, police, pursuers or other armed bands organized by the enemy with the aim of opposing the activity and struggle.
>
> **c.** Whoever at the command of organizers of leaders of the activity and struggle performed special tasks and actions for the benefit of the activity and struggle.
>
> **d.** Whoever in another way personally earned individual merit for activity and struggle or who achieved particular success in the activity and struggle for the liberation of the Macedonian *narod* (ibid.).

However, some were excluded from recognition by more recent activities:

> Those who are under prosecution in court of law for criminal activity under the law for criminal acts against the *narod* and the state do not have the right to an Ilinden *spomenica*. (ibid.)[4]

The term narod recurs in these texts and in the documentation of the pension plan more generally. As noted earlier, narod can be glossed as either nation or people and its adjectival form, *naroden*, as national or of the peo-ple. The noun is used here both on its own and in combination with the adjective "Macedonian" to designate a single collective operative in 1903 and in the 1940s, thus asserting continuity across that timespan. The adjec-tive features in the symbolically important phrase *narodna-osloboditelna borba (NOB)*, here translated as national-liberation struggle, but also carry-ing the implication of popular participation and support. *NOB* was in stan-dard use in Yugoslavia to describe the partisan struggles of 1941–44; its use here in reference to 1903, again, asserts continuity between the two periods.

That this policy was deliberate is revealed by a later description of the awards, given in a financial review of the pension program dating from 1956. It is described there as having been created:

> [W]ith an aim to note in this way too the historical unity and unity of purpose of the national-revolutionary struggles of the Macedonian *narod*, in the past against the Turkish enslavement, with their heroic struggles in the popular revolution against the German, Bulgarian and Italian occupiers and their homegrown servants (*domašni slugi*). (ibid.)

In this description, not part of the rubric that was distributed to a wider audience, the continuity is taken one step further. As the nation is written as existing from at least 1903 and its struggle made continuous, so here, by logical extension, its enemies all occupy the same ontological space with regard to it. Thus the Turkish enslavement is made the direct precursor of that practiced by the German, Bulgarian, and Italian occupiers and—in a formulation that is less than explicit—their "homegrown servants." All are put together into a group hostile to a nation which is engaged in purposive struggle.

SEMANTIC AND POLITICAL CONTEXTS

In this oppositional universe, the term "Yugoslav" does not appear. This post-war Yugoslav Macedonian vision thus marks 1903 and 1941–44 as significant, and demonizes the regimes against which Macedonian actions of those years were directed—the Ottoman Empire and the fascist, German-controlled Bulgaria. The texts of the Ilinden spomenica pass over in silence the period between these years, when Macedonia was first contested by Greek, Bulgarian, and Serbian movements, and later under Yugoslav rule. In that period the Macedonian language was not recognized, and many recall active efforts by the first Yugoslav régime to enforce the use of Serbian or Serbo-Croat. Large grants of land were given to colonists from Serbia, and teachers and policemen from Serbia proper were expected to perform a spell of duty in this "new territory" to assist in the process of assimilating the Slavic population (Apostolov 1962; Tomasevich 1958). The methods were often uncompromising, especially as violent resistance continued and Serbian officials fell victim to assassins armed with knives, guns, or bombs (Swire 1939; Christowe 1935). Contemporary observers noted the "ominous military stations" across the landscape (Alexander 1936:182); later accounts included reports of the gendarmerie's excesses, including the killing of ten protesters against Serb hegemony on Ilinden 1923, and the death in a Belgrade prison of eight Macedonian activists shortly afterward (U.S. Department of State 1954:11).

The Serbian occupation drove widespread resentment of interwar Yugoslavia in the region of Macedonia, voiced in complaints like those recorded by Rebecca West (1941:787). The enthusiasm she uncovered for Bulgaria was perhaps wider than she acknowledged. The goal of Macedonian autonomy was still pursued by various diasporic organizations, most of which were based in or had strong ties with Bulgaria, drawing manpower from native-born Macedonians in exile. Although Bulgarian political parties were prepared to jettison the Macedonian cause when expedient, as the Bulgarian government crackdown on VMRO's bases in Pirin Macedonia in 1934 demonstrated, Bulgaria was nonetheless widely perceived as the closest thing to a state-level sponsor and representative that Macedonians had. Certainly in terms of language, culture, and history, Bulgarian claims to connection had been made more unequivocally and for a longer period than any others.[5]

When Yugoslavia was invaded in April 1941 by Italian, German, and Bulgarian forces, the situation in Macedonia was thus substantially different from that in the other Republics. In Croatia, where Yugoslav rule had also been a source of resentment, German forces marched into Zagreb to a rousing welcome, and set up a puppet government under Ante Pavelić, who had coordinated the killing of King Alexander in 1934 (Glenny 1993; Kaplan 1993; Thompson 1992:265–67). The new régime was staffed by Croatians, and a set of new national insignia accompanied the new status of the former Yugoslav citizens.[6] In Macedonia, eyewitnesses recall and newsreel footage shows that the local Macedonian population went out to greet the Bulgarian troops who had helped remove the Yugoslav yoke, and that they waved Bulgarian flags. But instead of setting up a client state, the Bulgarians stayed, effectively annexing a large part of Vardar Macedonia.[7] A range of sources indicate that the Bulgarian representation of this as "liberation" rather than "occupation" was at first broadly accepted by Macedonia's indigenous Slavic Orthodox population, especially those from less well-off rural communities and from the lower socio-economic classes in towns.[8]

This Slavic-speaking underclass had also been the constituency that had given the Communist Party of Yugoslavia a substantial share of the popular vote as early as 1920 (Vucinich 1969:12; Burks 1961:78–80), and so would also appear to represent a natural power-base for Tito's pan-Yugoslav partisan resistance to the invaders.[9] But following the Bulgarian occupation Metodija Šatorov, or Šarlo, the chief of the Macedonian communist party, defected from the Communist Party of Yugoslavia (CPY) and transferred his allegiance to the Bulgarian Communist Party (BCP). The effect of this was to paralyze communications between the CPY and local communists, and to delay the commencement of armed action against the occupiers until 1943, when Tito finally sent effective lieutenants into the area to realign certain cells with his wider Partisan movement.[10]

By that stage, despite German refusal to permit formal annexation, the

Bulgarian kingdom had initiated a campaign of integration. By 1942 a nationality law had been passed, by the terms of which all inhabitants of the area were considered to be of Bulgarian nationality. They were permitted to declare themselves otherwise, but if they chose to do so they had to leave Bulgarian-controlled territory (U.S. Department of State 1954:41–42). The Bulgarians, by this measure, de-colonized the area, and probably won favor; most of the Serbs so resented by the local peasant population were driven back into Serbia and their land was generally taken over by locals.[11] Language laws were also passed whereby Bulgarian replaced Serbian as the official language. But the Bulgarian government took an initiative that the Serbian and Yugoslav had not, which was to make speaking Vlah in public illegal. Several people in Kruševo in 1993 still recalled paying fines for breaking this law, and noted that enforcement was carried out by locally-recruited policemen who were often former neighbors. By early 1942, the Bulgarian government was calling for still greater demonstrations of loyalty from its new Macedonian subjects, and the Macedonian committee of the communist party, under pro-Bulgarian leadership acceded to these fresh demands, authorizing the mobilization of Macedonians into the Bulgarian army. Coming at a time when the Soviet Union, the spiritual mentor of the communists, was fighting against Bulgaria's ally Germany, this seems a powerful representation of how thoroughly the Bulgarian occupiers had been able to capitalize on the unpopularity of the former régime. "National" rejection of Yugoslav rule had been affirmed as more important than any communist opposition to the old Yugoslav élites or to fascism more generally.

The delay of the Macedonian narod's armed participation in the national-liberation struggles discomfited post–World War II Yugoslav historians, who laid the blame at the door of the local élites. In a similar vein, the imposition of Bulgarian institutions was made into a site of heroic resistance by the Macedonian people, and instances of their apparent enthusiastic reception limited to the "home-grown servants" and dismissed as "opportunist" (Kulić 1970; Terzioski 1974). As a logical parallel with this, those practices that the Bulgarians introduced were termed "de-nationalizing" (Stojčev 1996). Such a definition presents the period as a deviation from the progress of Macedonian people to autonomous statehood. The Bulgarian occupation is thus described as an interruption of evolutionary history, which occurred only at the state level and was due to the tainted activities of individuals in pursuit of personal gain.

This interpretation of unpalatable periods of the past echoes the view of Ilinden 1903 advanced by Nikolaos Ballas, explored earlier. But just as Ballas's perception of Bulgarian activism provided him with a model for the creation of a new form of Greek solidarity, so Yugoslav-era criticism of Bulgarian strategies to create loyalty in Macedonia ran parallel to the adoption of similar strategies. Nowhere was this more apparent than in the two régimes' relationship with the Ilinden Uprising. In inter-war Serb-dominated Yugoslavia, the local celebration of Ilinden had been passively ignored or actively repressed by government officials. From its outset in 1941, the Bulgarian régime claimed the Ilinden legacy as its own, and organized commemorative events for 2 August. An Ilinden society, or *Ilindensko Društvo*, in Bulgaria sent two thousand copies of a book entitled *The Ilinden Rising* to Macedonia (Terzioski 1974:194). In 1943, they went further and inaugurated a plan to grant elderly citizens in the new territories a "national pension—*narodna penzija*—for special service in the struggles for liberation."

This was the logical extension of the Bulgarian cultural offensive to win the hearts and minds of the Macedonian population. Ilinden had been preserved in local memory in Macedonia; it had also been a major object of study in Sofia, where the initial work of collecting life-histories and archival materials from the period had been conducted, largely by Macedonian émigrés. Just as Bulgarian officials consistently referred to their 1941 entry into Yugoslav Macedonia as a liberation, so the rubric of the new pension plan did the same, asserting a historical link between the two years, 1903 and 1941, and celebrating the defeat of two forms of alien occupation: Ottoman Turkish and Yugoslav Serbian.

The 1943 Bulgarian pension program thus prefigured the post-war Yugoslav plan, taking the Ilinden legacy beyond yearly ceremonies into the realm of everyday life. Ilinden veterans were granted a visible social identity that persisted year-round. The terms under which they received this recognition dictated that they could not engage in "anti-Bulgarian or anti-state expression or activity." The narod, or people, were thus granted equal significance to the régime: the pension recipient must honor both. Although described by post-war Yugoslav scholars as *de*-nationalizing, such legislation indicates the Bulgarian régime's self-image as *re*-nationalizing. In the years 1941–44, it promoted a sense of identity, rooted in the past, that fit more closely the social and linguistic characteristics of the majority of the inhabitants of the area than any other state had done before.[12]

FROM BULGARIAN PAST TO MACEDONIAN PRESENT

The extent to which Macedonians were aware of the two-fold nature of the Bulgarian occupation, the ambiguities of their own past, and the undefined status of the new Yugoslavia is visible in the pension records of the post-war Yugoslav Ilinden plan. It is here, in an archive built with the goal of documenting Macedonian distinctiveness, that proof can be found of a Bulgarian pension plan, and the occupation-era Ilindensko Društvo. While the Macedonian historians Terzioski, Kulić, and Stojčev barely mention its existence, concentrating instead on other practices of alleged Bulgarian indoctrination,

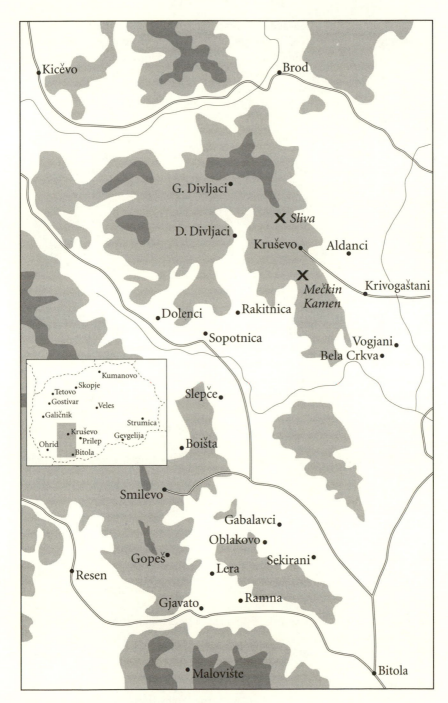

Figure 11: Kruševo and its surroundings.

assiduous archivists catalogued pension requests which present a range of accounts of the initiative. Their writers' diverse references to Bulgaria's treatment of Ilinden demonstrate how much more complicated were the relationships between people and government in the late 1940s.

The following examples are taken from villages in the Kruševo, Bitola, and Prilep regions in the heartland of the Ilinden uprising of 1903 (figure 11). Todor Burjanovski, of the village of Sopotnica, provides a good example of how people dealt with the switch from Bulgarian to Yugoslav Macedonian government. In his pension application, catalogued as 5-B-51, he submitted no autobiography, made no argument in his own words, and offered no account of present hardship, as so many others did. He merely sent in his old Bulgarian pension book. The implicit statement seems to be that this should serve as proof of his Ilinden activity, and that the new state should therefore similarly reward it. It is an application from which, superficially, politics and ideological readings are absent. It rests on a belief in historical facts and a belief, apparently, that the pension is a reward for historical acts.

Others followed similar strategies. A. Stefan Dimitrijevski, of Boišta, also included his Bulgarian pension book, which was numbered 1836. He stated in his autobiography, dated 22 April 1950 that he received a Bulgarian pension of 1500 leva monthly (10-D-9). Kote Stavrev Joševski, from the same village, reported the same size Bulgarian pension (15-J-42). I. Dimko Ačkovski of Prilep concluded his autobiography by saying straightforwardly, "In the time of the Occupation my participation as an *Ilindenec* was recognized and they gave me 3000 leva a month" (2-A-69). Another applicant, who claimed to have been a member of the force that occupied Kruševo on 1903, recorded the total amount given to him by the Bulgarian government, and followed this with the simple statement, "Then they went away and I didn't receive it any more" (15-J-44). Ilija Vasileski, from the Bitola village of Kočista, stated he had received 500 leva (6-V-11), while Dime Todorov Georgioski, from the Prilep village of Obrišani, reported his monthly pension of 600 leva (7-G-38).

In different ways, these individuals expected the new state to offer continuity with the previous regime. In Burjanovski's case, this wish appears to have been realized; he received a pension immediately, without submitting further documentation. Once awarded, his pension was regularly upgraded, in line with the standard rates. In his case there was no disjuncture between life under the Bulgarian and the Yugoslav Macedonian program. The entire individual-government interaction, across an administration change and major shift in national terms, is in its impersonality and smoothness reminiscent of a bank customer being issued with a new checkbook.

The impression that the pension was about physical activity in the past and not political stance since then is further reinforced in cases where the initial application was refused, on the grounds of "insufficient activity." Applicants frequently contested such judgments and provided further proof of involvement, as in the case of M. Risto Bojčevski of Crničani, near Bitola (5-B-5). He finally received a pension after submitting a complaint, or *žalba*, in August 1954, in which he provided more details of his Ilinden-related activism.

The success of Burjanovski's minimalist application contrasts with Bojčevski's case. Resolution could also take much more effort, as was the case for I. Dimko Ačkovski, mentioned earlier, who relied on his recognition by the Bulgarian régime as part of his argument (2-A-69). He did finally receive a pension in 1956, but only after a testily worded complaint in response to a challenge over the size of the armed band, or *četa*, that he had asserted. In a second autobiographical statement, he wrote that his memory now for "exact figures" was not good. This, again, reveals that he continued to work on the assumption that the whole question of his award depended on his activity at the turn of the century, and that his own more recent past had no impact. It also confirms the impression left by the underlinings and pencil notes on the scripts, that some of these scripts were read critically for their truth-value.

In other cases, applicants appeared to act on the assumption that more recent history *was* important, and that the relationship between 1903 activity and a Yugoslav pension would not necessarily be straightforwardly mediated by receipt of a Bulgarian pension. In the sample of the nearly 350 accounts that I transcribed, roughly as many applicants expressly asserted that they had *not* received a Bulgarian pension as acknowledged that they *had*. In addition, many laid stress in their applications on their more or less active support of the communist partisans of the period 1942–44, either by giving bread—as did Kosta Dabiža (9-D-1) and Petar Naumov Damčeski (9-D-17), both of Kruševo—or by losing a member of their family, usually a son, fighting in the partisans, as was the experience of Vasil Vasileski of Dunja, near Prilep (6-V-8).

In such cases, *non*receipt of the Bulgarian pension is written as an act of will. This is the narrative presentation even in one case where, by the terms of the Bulgarian award, the applicant M. Tase Bočvarski of Lopatica in the Bitola region would have been too young to receive a pension in any case (5-B-22). To state nonreceipt of funds from the Bulgarian régime in such a case is a statement of fact, but one which omits one part of the truth. Its inclusion strongly suggests an assumption on the writer's part that non-receipt would be positively valorized.

This judgment was shared by some who had been awarded a Bulgarian pension. Acknowledging that they received such a pension, they stressed that it proved they did something for the cause in 1903, but not that they were Bulgarian sympathizers. A phrase such applicants often used was that they "stayed home and weren't involved in politics." This is used elsewhere, too, to describe individual behavior during the Balkan Wars and the pre-war Yugoslav period, as well as the Bulgarian Occupation.[13] What this statement asserts is nonactivity. Its frequent recurrence, not just among Bulgarian pension-recipients, but also among nonrecipients and those who make no other statement about more recent history than that, suggests a broad consensus of opinion on dealing with the state. While activity in the 1890–1910 period can be presented as an asset in the present, the revelation of more recent activity may be dangerous. If in doubt, it suggests, then it is best to disclaim knowledge of or involvement with organizations or initiatives of which the new state might disapprove.

LOSING OUT TO THE NEW HISTORY

The perils of activism and how to circumvent them can be traced in the fate of three applicants whose involvement with the Bulgarian régime's project of nationalization became known. The first, Dame Hristov Adžikočoski of Prilep, submitted on 17 December 1948 a life history that was neatly typed and well written, that concerned his activity in the Ilinden period (2-A-72). The narrative it presents is clear, detailed, and consistent. He took the oath of loyalty, served as what he called a *terorist*, hosted the legendary leader Goce Delčev, and became a local leader. Then in 1902 he was arrested and jailed when an organizational archive was captured by Ottoman authorities. Two years later he led a group that tunneled its way to freedom, after which he again served as leader of local revolutionary activity. His application was originally approved, but the decision was overturned in August 1949. He was informed that new testimony had come to light which indicated that in the Bulgarian Occupation he had "worked and spoken against the partisans and *NOB* [the national liberation struggle]"; his pension was cut off. In a complaint dated 7 November 1949 Adžikočoski made it clear that he considered himself unjustly denounced by jealous rivals in his town who sought, in his words, "to make capital for themselves from me"—*da si pravat so mene kapital*.

Another applicant whose involvement with the Bulgarian occupation told against him was Mate Petrov Boškovski of Kruševo, who first applied in February 1952 and included a typed account of his activities (5-B-27). He described his role in securing arms for the organization, buying rifles and ammunition from Turks in Tetovo and Kičevo, and bringing them to Kruševo. Vančo Andreski and Petra Pare served as witnesses for his application. Boškovski found his pension denied on the grounds of insufficient Ilinden activity, and submitted a lengthy complaint where he provided greater detail on the contribution he had made in 1903, and how much he had suffered. In an internal memo of May 1954, preserved in his file in the archive, a functionary reveals the basis for the rejection. Boškovski had been a rich man and pro-Serbian in the time of the former Yugoslavia, when he was called *golemo Srbin*, and then had turned to be a Bulgarian sympathizer during the occupation when his son was a prominent member of *Branik*, the youth organization. His property had been confiscated in 1948, and he was considered to view the current régime with hostility. All this, the functionary concluded, made Boškovski an unsuitable recipient. It was only in 1955 that he finally did receive a pension for his Ilinden activities.[14]

In contrast to these two applicants, who concealed their involvement with the occupation until it was uncovered, Veljan Andreev Gurdževski of Bitola admitted that he had served as cashier and secretary of the Ilindensko Društvo during the Bulgarian Occupation (8-G). However, he claimed that he used his position to protect other people of his community, including recipients of the Bulgarian pension. In 1941 instructions came that people were to be fined for helping the partisans; he claimed in his pension request that he forewarned those targeted to hide their money. Later he was instructed to deliver a list of Ilindenci who had sons serving with the partisans, and stop their pensions. He did neither; as a result, he claimed, he actually paid some people's pensions from his own pocket.

Gurdževski's application to the Yugoslav Macedonian scheme was successful, and he continued to receive a pension, as he had done under Bulgarian rule. In retrospect (and conceivably, at the time) he laid claim to links with the partisan organization, such that he was able to present his membership of the Bulgarian Organization as an opportunity to take action contributory to the goals of the post-war Yugoslavia.[15]

THE VIRTUES OF OBSCURITY

These responses demonstrate different outcomes, but a common view of the play of past and present. Activism in 1903 is always considered by individuals a virtue: thus even the fairly numerous applicants who had not taken oaths of loyalty and who appeared ignorant of the Organization until the Uprising itself made much of what they did and did not do in obedience to the orders of leaders, or vojvodi. J. Stojan Jančevski, from the Bitola village of Gabolavci, represents such a case. In an autobiography submitted in May 1950, he described himself as working with livestock and the land until 1903, when Gjorǵi Sugarev came to the village and ordered the men to follow him to Oblakovo. Jančevski reported that he had no rifle, but joined a band there. They awaited orders for three days, and then followed a trail of arson through Dragožani and Sekirani to Gabolavci, in each of which they burned Turkish houses. They were then summoned to Gjavato, where Gjorǵi Sugarev was under siege by Ottoman forces, and on the way encountered

Turkish forces in the village of Lera. After taking part in an attack to allow Sugarev to escape, Jančevski's group went to Gopeš for four days, then to Smilevo, where they dispersed. He claimed no prior connection with the organization, and never reported carrying a gun—two of the straightforward conditions for receiving a pension. But it appears that as far as the pension administration was concerned, waiting for orders in a village, burning Turkish houses, or cutting telegraph wires all became activities undertaken for the liberation of the Macedonian people: they were submitted as such by individuals, and recognized as such by a state.

In so valorizing unsung heroes, the new state went some way to creating a new nationalism which behind its rhetoric of recognizing heroic activism in fact rewarded inactivity. As noted earlier, much of the previous history of Ilinden had been produced in Bulgaria, and had traced the roles of committed vojvodi, četnici, and komitadžii, many of whom were ex-Bulgarian army officers (Perry 1988). By encouraging the rank and file to come forward, the new Yugoslav-backed régime undoubtedly contributed to an inflation of claims of participation, and provided support and recognition to some who had been caught up by events in 1903, rather than being initiators themselves. The effect, though, was to help transform the image of Ilinden into that of a mass national movement.

Rediscovered activism as part of a collectivity in 1903 formed only one part of most applications. It was generally combined with an assertion of individuality in the more recent past, and of nonintegration into any wider politically charged grouping which had a Bulgarian tinge. In certain cases, either when an action seemed likely to be viewed favorably (like giving bread to partisans) or where it demanded justification (like being an official in a Bulgarian organization), a petitioner would admit to more recent engagement beyond the family. However, it was almost always individual initiative, rather than action taken at the orders of another, that applicants stressed during the troubled 1940s. In general, describing the recent past, they reported their noncompliance with the agendas of others rather than their participation in any collective enterprise. Macedonian nationality in the most recent past was thus expressed through inaction, as an aggregate of individual nonresponses.

AGRICULTURAL BACKGROUND AND SOCIALIST POLICY

The Ilinden pension program offered to elder members of society financial recompense for past activity. By this means, people in villages and towns throughout Macedonia, and especially those around Smilevo and Kruševo, were brought into direct relationship with central authorities. In this regard it resembled a range of new initiatives in the new socialist society, designed to establish contacts between people and state. Similar processes were reported across the Balkans. In 1945, revisiting the Bulgarian village where he had conducted fieldwork before the Second World War, Irwin Sanders reported that before the communist régime, "[t]he Dragalevtsy peasant had not yet become a joiner. He gained his social status by the position his family held rather than by the numbers and types of organizations to which he, as an individual, was elected" (Sanders 1948:194). Sanders also traveled in Yugoslavia in the 1940s, and drew similar conclusions concerning the rural population there. But by 1959, according to Palmer and King, the Macedonian premier, Lazar Koliševski, was able to report in a speech that "122,000 citizens in Macedonia, or one-sixth of the population over fourteen years of age, were involved in the various committees, councils and 'social' government bodies of the Republic" (Palmer and King 1973:141).

How, though, was this transition wrought? To assume that people gratefully and immediately embraced the opportunity to tell their stories of national struggle to the new state would be to fall into a variant of romantic nationalism. Individuals or families do not simply preserve "truth" at home—nor do they rush to hand it over to authorities at the first opportunity. The new régime had to battle legacies of mistrust created by its predecessors, which had fostered in the people of the region a certain reluctance to have much to do with their rulers. Beyond that, it was part of a new Yugoslavia that claimed to be different from and better than the old, but had not yet persuaded its residents of that. Although Macedonian national identity was being promoted within the new Yugoslavia, putting one's name into an official state record as a participant in an uprising whose national character was still disputed might have appeared dangerous.[16]

The prospect of societal recognition for past glories may nonetheless have played a part. What was probably decisive in many cases, though, was the financial incentive offered by the new state. Yet this, too, demands further investigation. There were strict property limits that petitioners could not exceed if they were to qualify for an Ilinden pension. As well as asserting their political quietism, many of the applicants also laid out their material circumstances for consideration by the awarding committee. In so doing, they left traces of a parallel project of socio-economic engineering undertaken by the Yugoslav Macedonian state in this period, the impact of which dovetailed with the goals of the pension plan to gain control over the past. This parallel project was the attempted collectivization of agricultural production.

Until 1944, Macedonia was predominantly rural. Before the Axis invasion, more than 70 percent of Yugoslavia's population derived its income from agricultural labor and lived in small rural communities (Tomasevich 1969:62). The area that was to become the People's Republic of Macedonia was among the least industrialized in Yugoslavia. The initial five-year plans of the new Yugoslav state targeted Macedonia for fast-track development. After Tito's break with Stalin, however, Yugoslavia experienced economic sanctions from the Eastern bloc and could not maintain its projected pace. Additionally, subsequent preoccupation with security meant locating what industry there was in less-threatened parts of the new country—notably Bosnia. As a result, the modernization plans for Macedonia were not met. Only after the Skopje earthquake of 1963, that city's subsequent rebuilding and population explosion, and Tito's success in attracting loans from the Western countries did the pattern of Macedonian production shift dramatically.

Turning farmers into workers did not necessitate taking them off the land. Following the offensive against property-owners in towns and cities, described in the previous chapter, the new régime carried its reforms into the countryside. Post-war Macedonia, and the rest of Yugoslavia, saw the institution of the village work cooperative—the *Selska Rabotnička Zadruga*, or SRZ. The SRZ aimed to improve agricultural productivity by collectivizing land and equipment, thereby introducing economies of scale. It has been described in the literature on the economics of post-war Eastern Europe: In Yugoslavia there were four types of zadruga, which varied according to the legal status of the property (Tomasevich 1958; Sokolovsky 1990; Bokovoy 1998). They remained as voluntary associations until 1949, when membership was made compulsory for rural communities where such zadrugas existed. By the end of 1949, 6,626 collectives were operating in Yugoslavia as a whole, with 1,707,073 individual members. Macedonia had 833 collectives, with 53,740 households and 339,014 members (Bokovoy 1998:121). Two years later, by mid-1951, membership peaked at just over 2 million in Yugoslavia as a whole. Macedonia then had 947 SRZs, comprising 70,381 households, or 439,177 individual members (Bokovoy 1998:147; Tomasevich 1966:173). In numbers of members, Macedonia was second only to the much larger Republic of Serbia: nearly one in three of the Republic's population was a member of one of the new collectives. When people were allowed in 1953 to leave the collectives, they demonstrated the unpopularity of the system by doing so en masse. The policy was discontinued as a result. Since then the agricultural sector has been largely private.[17]

THE ZADRUGA OF THE PAST

The term *zadruga* as appropriated by the socialist program had another meaning: it described the large, collective household supposed by some to be typical of the Balkans in its pre-industrial period. A zadruga in this context is defined as "a household composed of two or more biological small-families, closely related by blood or adoption, owning its means of production communally, producing and consuming the means of its livelihood jointly, and regulating the control of its property, labor and livelihood communally" (Mosley 1976:79). Mosley took the term from observers like Irby and Mackenzie, who used it to describe a family association they visited near Prilep where five brothers with their wives and children ate together and shared a common courtyard surrounded by high walls (Irby and Mackenzie 1877: 129ff.). Mosley drew on their suggestions that the zadruga was a defensive and conservative institution, and argued that industrialization would transform labor opportunities, making the zadruga obsolete. This analysis has been disputed. Halpern, for example (1958:146n), noted that new patterns of wage-labor had not had the effect claimed by Mosley in his field area, while Hammel (1972) and Rheubottom (1976b) have both argued that the zadruga was never a static form in decay, but was always flexible and adaptable to seasonal, generational, and other cycles.

Use of the term zadruga has been challenged by Maria Todorova, who argues that the southeast European household structure thus described is not unique to the region and therefore demands no special nomenclature (Todorova 1993). The term has nonetheless played a key role in discussion of social life of the region, especially as an ideal-type which serves as a prominent symbol of a traditional patriarchal society. According to some scholars, it had served in Serbia as the principal locus of national identity under the Turkish occupation, providing a system within which "Little Tradition" as identified by Redfield (1960) was protected.[18] Indeed, in local anecdotes the zadruga takes on attributes of statehood; both Mosley and Sicard record that they encountered households where the male head, or *domaćin*, was referred to as the "minister for foreign affairs" (Sicard 1976:79, 258).[19] This was, of course, intended humorously, but the functional and organizational analogy could be further extended between the large household (Mosley reported one with seventy-five members) and the modern state. It served as a frame within which the division of labor was organized for greater economic efficiency, making it possible, for example, for the workforce to expand and contract seasonally as needed. It provided systems of infant care, social control of youth, responsible and growth-centered administration of property, and a stable frame to accommodate the needs and earnings introduced by patterns of migrant labor. Operating within a central régime viewed as alien, the zadruga provided a locus of loyalty and activity, and directed its members' lives more than the distant state apparatus.[20]

Although large zadrugas were reportedly more easily located in the nineteenth century, they did persist into the twentieth century. Edith Durham reported finding a family of sixty-three in the Prespa region, under a head named Miloš (1905:150). According to St. Erlich's study in the 1930s, they proved particularly resilient in Macedonia, where break-up occurred after 1913 among Christians, and not until the depression of the 1930s in Muslim Albanian districts (St. Erlich 1966:46). She traces the reasons to economic exigencies: prior to the 1940s, no state had sought to regulate patterns of communal agricultural production that owed much to customary practice. Although successive régimes made great and various demands upon the population—to provide soldiers, food and wage-labor—they left in place the social system which produced those surpluses.

The Ilinden pension plan autobiographies reveal how the post-war communist system changed this. Individuals frequently set out the details of their enforced membership of the new-style zadruga, and of what they and their families had given up in order to join. Blaže Bošev Damčeski, for example, of the Prilep village of Zagorani, reported his pre-SRZ holdings as ten hectares, sixteen sheep, and four cattle or horses. With the expropriation of their land, their eight-person household had only two members in paid work, and his material circumstances were sufficiently reduced to qualify him for a pension (9-D-18). Risto Josifov Jurukoski, from the Prilep village of Galičani, had had twenty hectares, all of which were incorporated into the SRZ. Of the family's thirteen members, three had paid work (15-J-55). Nedelko Stojčev Bezovski, of the Prilep village Bela Crkva, had had thirty-five *dekari*, or dekares (one-tenth of a hectare) twenty-seven sheep, and two draught animals: now, in his family of twelve, four had work (4-B-52).[21]

Common to these accounts, then, is a statement of household size and the number that "have work." This new categorization of individuals altered the internal dynamics of families. None of those who count heads in this way distinguish male from female members of the new SRZ, suggesting that gender no longer divided labor and earning power as firmly as it had.[22] In combination with the collectivization of land, it also changed the relative socio-economic status of different families. Whereas large families with considerable holdings would formerly have relied on everyone's labor, especially in harvest season, and would also have developed relations with other households to exchange labor at critical periods in the agricultural year, the expropriation of land and the introduction of waged positions changed the basis of prosperity and could even threaten subsistence. The three applicants described briefly above had all been relatively prosperous, and headed households that most likely included three generations. Now they applied for financial assistance from the government, buttressing their claims of past activism in the Macedonian cause with accounts of their straitened circumstances.

From various villages in the heartland of the Ilinden Uprising, biographies told similar stories. In Žvan, about twenty-five kilometers southwest of Kruševo, G. Tale Grozdanoski (8-G-27) and Pejko Jankulovski (14-J-31) both described their participation in the attack on the Turkish village of Pribilci during Ilinden 1903. Both also described their recent loss of land and impoverished conditions. Grozdanovski had handed over four hectares, retained only four dekari, and two family members out of seven worked. Jankulovski's one and half hectares had been reduced also to four dekari, and four of the nine-member household worked, bringing in a total of 19,000 dinari a year. In the same village, Nikola Stojanov Kalapovski reported that his two hectares had been cut to three dekari. They still owned one cow and one calf, but the nine-member household relied mostly on the four in wage-work, one as a baker and three in the new agricultural collective (16-K-11). In Sveti Mitrani, in the lowlands about twelve kilometers south-southeast of the town, similar accounts came from Cvetan Angelev, whose family of ten now relied on the wages of two SRZ employees (4-B-29); and Dimitrija Murgov Georgioski, whose family of fifteen had turned over their "medium-sized" holdings to the SRZ, where six now worked for wages (7-G-39).

Perhaps the most detailed and most poignant account of the impact of state legislation on private life was given by Taše Gegoski, of the mountain village of Slepče in the Demir Hisar region. In his application for recognition as an Ilindenec, he gave no information about his activities in the 1903 Uprising: instead, his autobiography recounts what had happened to one old man, the former head of a none-too-prosperous household:

> In the former Yugoslavia, until 1946, I had a total property of six *dekari*, all of that in poor areas. I had no fruit gardens. On the official census I was listed with one horse, a cart, two oxen, a plough and fifteen to twenty sheep. From this, and from work ploughing other people's land for a share of the produce, I fed my family. In 1946, with the formation of the SRZ, I was one of the first twenty members; in 1949 the whole village was incorporated into the SRZ. I have three sons: one is fifty, with five children, the next forty, with three, and the youngest thirty-five, with two. Until 1948 we lived together; then they split into three households. I lived at first with the youngest, and then with the eldest. (7-G-18)

In this case (where a pension was awarded), the new zadruga directly succeeded the old as the basic labor organization to which this man and his three sons belong. But the relations between them had been wholly altered. In this regard, the SRZ struck at the principles of the old *zadruga* precisely where scholars have perceived the greatest pressures at work in modern history. That tensions existed in the old, large households is graphically demonstrated in life histories collected by Halpern (1958:214–20), and is convincingly argued by Rheubottom (1976b). These tensions had in general stemmed from younger people wishing, but unable, to set up house for themselves, wholly dependent for their livelihood on their elders, and resenting an oppressive or out-of-date household head, or domaćin. Often the reason for breakdown is assigned to conflict between young brides and their mothers-in-law, or over the distribution of money earned in wage-labor outside the zadruga.

In the post-war period, these same sources of tension arose on a more widespread scale under the increasing impingement on village life of the frontiers of the new state. The introduction of cash wages to the younger generations, coming at the same time as the state's expropriation of long-held capital, turned the previous economic relations upside-down: both

between families, where pre-war wealth often resulted in treatment as bourgeois enemies of the revolution and a loss in prestige, and within families,
where the traditional distribution of property down through the generations
was interrupted. Similarly, the new freedoms accorded to young women,
who might as teenagers travel away from home to spend work-vacations
alongside boys in the new socialist youth organization, the Pioneers, surely
reduced their willingness to return to what by all accounts constituted a
married life especially subject to social control.[23]

THE ZADRUGA AND SOCIALISM

Most writers on the traditional zadruga are careful to provide a note that it
was entirely different from the SRZ, and apparently see no connection between the two. Yet despite their silence on this issue, the existence of the
zadruga in the past has served to sustain an argument that communism
spread as successfully as it did into southeastern European Slavic cultures
because they are inherently communistic. Writing of the 1930s, for example,
Olive Lodge stated that:

> The *zadruga* works out a kind of family communism. Individual development is
> encouraged, and assisted from the common fund: in return each member does
> his best for the *zadruga*. He knows his place in the family-group, and the degree
> of deference due from him to the other members of it, and would not think of
> departing from its powerful tradition. (Lodge 1941:110–11)

That communalism underpinned the old zadruga had been preached by
Svetozar Markovic in the 1870s (McClellan 1964:212–52), and even after
the Second World War, before mass collectivization, by Radin (1946:14–15).
The denial of continuity has come largely from writers in the West who were
in one sense or another politically involved in their work: either from
a ground-level perspective, in close contact with local communities that
resisted the socialist government pressure, as in the cases of Halpern and
Sanders, or in their association with U.S. government-funded research projects, as in the case of Mosley. None dwell on the fact that the definition of
the old-style zadruga which they accept could be extended to fit the new one.[24]
An examination of the reclassifications that such a reading would entail
offers one way to glimpse how through the institution of the SRZ the state
could claim to be grounding its policies in local reality, even as it transformed the economic and social relationships that constituted that reality.

The old zadruga organized authority and affiliation on inherited, primordial bases. Secular authority resided in control of property and resources,
which in a patriarchal, virilocal setting was held by senior males. Affiliation
was organized by kinship; as Lodge's brief description suggests, different
members were ranked with respect to one another. Although the gradation

did not necessarily follow biological seniority (the older son did not necessarily become the next domaćin) it was nonetheless assumed that he would.[25]
The old zadruga represented what was, in Geertz's terms, the "terminal"
organization of these principles (1973a:257ff.). It was never integrated
within a state system or a capital economy, but rather coexisted with such a
set-up as an independent realm. It was self-reproducing, as younger males
increased in stature as they grew older, either to leave and set up their own
household, or to stay and succeed to the position of domaćin.

The new SRZ depended for its survival upon a system of authority and
affiliation, but it drew upon that provided by wider terminal organizations.
For the space of the domaćin was filled ostensibly by a committee of members acting together, and in fact by those who had become members of the
communist party (Halpern 1958:267). In place of the status system based on
familial ties and identified by Sanders, organizational memberships became
important, and through parties and committees the state apparatus thus constituted authority. Parallel to this, within the larger SRZ, kinship could no
longer serve formally as even the idiom of solidarity. In its place the
Yugoslav project sought to impose the notion of the *rabotnički narod* or
"working people," a collective which again was presumed to exist at a wider
level than that of the rural community. Ties formerly constituted as partic-
ularistic by idioms of blood and marriage came to rely on a new uniform and
omni-directional identity in which class and nation were blurred through the
invocation of the narod.

This implication of the SRZ with the wider world was designed to make
the institution serve the purposes of the modernizing, centralizing state.
Paradoxically, though, with the ideas on which its survival depended came
others that, in combination with locally expressed resistance, were to cause
its demise. As older farmers objected to the state appropriating land and
seeking to organize the way in which it was worked, so younger generations
confronted the reality that they might not inherit their parents' property.
Where work in the city had once represented for young men a chance to earn
money to invest in the village, it now became an option for a more permanent life of a higher standard. Instead of depending upon familial ties in a
small community, they sought to make wider networks of connections—
vrski—in an urban context, and to leave the SRZ permanently (Denich
1970; Ford 1982). Introduced as a part of modern socialism, the SRZ was
soon tagged as backward by all generations. The modern socialist solidarity
that it had sought to create came to be demonstrated and voiced against it.

FROM MEMORY TO HISTORY

As stated, the Ilinden spomenica program operated alongside the imposition
of the new zadruga system. At the same time, among the Orthodox Chris-

tians of Macedonia, the patriarchal domaćin passed into history.[26] Taše Gegoski was just one victim of this change: he had made a living by working land that he still controlled as head of household, drawing on the labor of his sons and their families. But with the introduction of the SRZ his household split up and he lived with one or another of his sons. Disinherited in turn by the state, they were unable to provide for him.

As a result, Gegoski approached the state as a single unproductive individual, to be rewarded on the basis of the activities of his past. He sought, and was given, a pension from the state that had taken away his property, making it impossible for his own family to provide for him. The tone of his exchange, and that of many others, suggests that this was how the petitioners saw the situation. For the most part they did not write as cowed suppliants. More often their letters expressed a sense of entitlement, on the basis of their youthful activism or more recent suffering. Even people accused of having contacts with the Bulgarian occupiers responded forcefully and aggressively; those whose pensions were refused gave more data or submitted complaints that were often successful in obtaining a pension.

For all their belligerence, the fact remained that in the retelling of their pasts to the state they were in some sense commodifying their lives under the pressure of collectivization. Under the terms of the Ilinden pension program, the state purported to offer a recognition of these senior males' part in the history of the Macedonian nation. But in terms of the present, the pension represented compensation for that generation's loss of economic and social primacy within their local communities. In this respect, the condition which specified that the pensions were not transferable or inheritable became significant; the award was an individual asset, rather than belonging to any familial group. Doubtless informal economic interaction between members of families continued, but a situation had come about where they could, in theory, lead lives as separate economic actors. In some sense, then, in the language of communalism, everyone became the employee of a single domaćin-state, which controlled resources.[27]

Two further institutions, compulsory military service and education, completed the state's penetration of local Macedonian lives. Service in the Yugoslav National Army for one or two years by all young men brought them into contact with a broader set of acquaintances and experiences. Universal schooling was enforced for a minimum of eight years, or until the age of sixteen. Halpern and Kerewsky-Halpern (1972) state that the typical experience of the pre-war generation had been less than four years of education: they also report the growing belief among the newly educated youth that they knew more than their elders.[28] Pension applicants often spoke of their own lack of education, which was a result of poverty: most of those from villages had started work before the age of ten. Even when the SRZ system was discontinued, the gap between the generations and their experiences continued to widen.

CONCLUSION

The Ilinden spomenica program and the SRZ system were interconnected in the politics and economics of their present. Both served to create continuity between the present and the past, in order to add legitimacy to the Yugoslav Macedonian régime. Where they differed was in the nature of the past they evoked, and the success of their implementation. The SRZ appears to have been intended to recall the zadruga of an ideal past. The success with which it did so led to its rejection by a rural population among whom such a system had never matched the ideal that its socialist admirers depicted. It had been the result of specific historical circumstances which were quite different from those of the new Yugoslavia. Its evocation may have been intended to point to the deep roots of "socialist" practices in the area, but it only showed that such systems of living were the result of pressures in the absence if which they were discontinued.

The Macedonian Ilinden pension plan, by contrast, sought to demonstrate continuity in national terms with a specific historical event. It was implemented at the same time as a general redefinition of the area's past as "Macedonian" where it had once been "Bulgarian." This was carried out at a state level, with the moving of historical archives from Sofia to Skopje and the creation of the Institute for National History and the National Archive of Macedonia in the capital. The dissemination of this view was undertaken at the national level: monuments were constructed, the daily newspapers *Nova Makedonija* and *Večer* were filled with life-histories and accounts of the past, and Macedonian history was taught throughout the school system.[29]

But alongside this production of history, the state was consuming memories. While in Kruševo, I was told more than once that old family documents had been taken by "historians from Skopje" in the years immediately after the war. I found the requisitioned account books of a Greek-speaking merchant in the National Archives; but not the diaries written by another prominent Greek-speaking burgher, which I was told had also been taken from Kruševo by the authorities. This requisitioning of materials took place in the same period that property was being confiscated from the better-off in the town, as described in the previous chapter. Although some small craft workshops survived, the social importance of the property-owning élites and of the esnafi, or trade guilds, which they often controlled was reduced.

The Ilinden pension plan served as a mechanism by which individual descriptions of the past came into the possession of a central state bureaucracy. They were transformed from individual memories into collective history. Thus appropriated, they were readministered to their narrators and subsequent generations by the state, acting through the agency of scientific and educational institutions and media channels. But the national history thus created was grounded in local accounts: it was not mere state invention. Those accounts had been preserved within local communities, outside the authorized history of the ruling régime until 1941, and acknowledged first in the Bulgarian Occupation. After 1945 local memories and national history were thoroughly integrated as they had never been before.

In the institution of the Ilinden pension plan and the materials generated by individuals in contact with a state bureaucracy we can read much of the conditions under which the apparently brand-new Macedonian national identity was "created." In fact, as Hobsbawm and Ranger (1983), and others, have suggested, this process represented less a creation than a reshaping and retexturing of society, conditioned by the multiple possibilities available to create continuities in individual, institutional, and national lives. While seeking to remake society, actors with principles and plans were constrained by the principles and plans of actors before them. Reacting to initiatives taken by a prior rival—the Bulgarian state—and to hostilities created by a prior namesake—the former Yugoslavia—the makers of the new Macedonia sought to enlist the legacy of grassroots organization to promote the country's legitimacy. Macedonian national identity in its modern Yugoslav form thus sprang from an exchange between state and people dominated by the resonances of a universe of old words with new meanings, and was fixed in the processes by which the glorious past and the mundane present were collectivized.

CHAPTER SEVEN

History Stated

THE MAKING OF A MONUMENT

THE ILINDEN spomenica program which recognized the contribution of elderly individuals to the struggles of 1903 wound down during the 1950s, as its beneficiaries aged and died. The national past became the domain of a new professional cohort of historians, and this chapter examines the role of their scholarship in making the Ilinden legacy more permanent. Its focus is the planning and construction of the Ilinden monument, or *Spomenik*, that stands in Kruševo today. In this process, which stretched from 1968 when the competition for designs opened until 1974 when the memorial complex was finally opened, different members of the Macedonian intelligentsia—historians, creative artists, bureaucrats, and politicians—worked together to make a monument worthy of Macedonian history. The records of their fractious cooperation and the contrasting representational styles in their creation reveal some of the turbulence that arises when different views of truth and representation meet in an ostensibly singular national project.

AFFAIRS OF STATE, 1953–74

In the course of the 1950s and early 1960s, Yugoslavia's relations with Greece and Bulgaria steadily improved, as it became clear that the frontiers set at the end of the war would remain in place. This stability contrasted with the maneuvers around the Macedonian issue during the Greek Civil War and in the immediate aftermath of the Tito-Stalin split.[1] Nonetheless, scholars of the three countries remained at loggerheads, producing accounts of the past that rested on different assumptions about identities and purposes claimed by historical actors. Although during the brief period of Yugoslav-Bulgarian cooperation the Institute of Macedonian Studies in Bulgaria had closed and its archives were relocated to Skopje, historians based in Sofia had quickly begun again to stress the Bulgarian identity of the actors of the Ilinden period.[2] In Greece, a set of institutions based in Thessaloniki produced works which stressed the Greek character of a movement known as the *Makedonikòn Agòn*, or Macedonian Struggle, between 1904 and 1908, as well as emphasizing the Greek history of towns in Yugoslavia like Bitola and Kruševo.[3]

In Yugoslav Macedonia, the historical profession was still taking shape. In the interwar period, higher education in Skopje had been conducted under the aegis of the University in Belgrade, and the number of Macedonians with higher degrees was limited. With the establishment of a university in Skopje and the creation of the Institute of National History in 1948, scholars began to write in a language that had not been used before, and to write a version of past events that had not been recorded (Shoup 1968:172). Some of the work produced had an obvious ideological purpose—work on Aegean Macedonia, for example, was a major component of the Institute's research activities and was often conducted by political refugees from Greece—but the new cadres of history also established criteria of evidence and professional standards in writing the history of revolutionary organizations in early twentieth-century Macedonia.

Greek, Bulgarian, and Macedonian historians had little direct contact: researchers from one country visiting another were in the best case treated with considerable suspicion.[4] The lack of cooperation between the different professional bodies did not prevent them from responding to one another. Although few scholars from any of the three sets of institutes contributed regularly to journals outside their own discipline or country, most were aware of the political implications of their work. Thus in the new preface to the 1962 Greek reprinting of Nikolaos Ballas's account of the events of 1903 in Kruševo (or, as he called it, Krousovo) written in 1905, the editor reported that current attempts to dupe the public demanded the book's reissue. Oddly, the accounts to which it responded were mostly in Macedonian: the debate was thus a virtual one, conducted between professionals with different audiences for their work.[5] The debate between Greece and Yugoslavia focused on the region known in Ottoman times as the Monastir vilayet, which straddled the post-1919 border between Greece and what would become Yugoslavia, and within which the modern towns of Bitola (Monastir) and Florina (Lerin) lie. Here the later immigration of Asia Minor Greeks was less intensive, and a high concentration of Macedonian-speakers still live on the Greek side of the border (Karakasidou 1993; Vereni 1998; Cowan [ed.] 2000). Conversely, there are still people in Bitola who consider themselves and their children Greek.

With the coup of the colonels in Greece in April 1967, a mini-freeze set in again between Greece and Yugoslavia. Diplomatic exchanges took place between the governments concerning the Greek use of the term "Macedonian," and a new law on local traffic across the border, which had allowed locals to cross with relative ease, was rescinded. In the same period, Bulgarian-Yugoslav tensions also ran high. The long-running dispute over the status of the Macedonian language, not recognized by Bulgaria, reached the *New York Times* on 7 December 1966 when an article detailed how a Yugoslav delegation had walked out of a meeting with Bulgarian writers in Sofia in protest that a communiqué had been issued in Serbo-Croatian and Bulgarian, not Macedonian.

In the aftermath of Yugoslavia's break-up in the 1990s, the 1966 *Times* article's title, "Ethnic Disputes Erupt in Balkans," appears hyperbolic, but the incident indicates the continuous interconnection of culture and politics in Macedonia's history. New initiatives followed on the Yugoslav side. In 1967 the autocephaly of the Macedonian church was recognized by the Yugoslav government. Although the date marked 200 years from the abolition of the Ohrid Episcopate in 1767, the timing also coincided with provocations from the new Greek government.[6] In 1968 a competition was announced for designs for a new monument to the Ilinden Uprising of 1903, that a Skopje publishing house printed copies of the Kruševo Manifesto in Macedonian and English. The sixty-fifth anniversary of the Uprising was a major production, marked by publications and cultural events planned by a committee of forty political figures, intellectuals, workers, and pensioners (Arsov et al. [eds.] 1968). Yugoslav Macedonia thus declared its intentions to secure the legacy of Ilinden, still claimed by Bulgaria and denied by Greece, once and for all. In August 1969, as if to set the seal on the new (counter-) offensive, Tito made his first visit to Kruševo.

Such governmental sanction and political motivation in the presentation of materials from the past did nothing to counteract the central argument that Greek and Bulgarian officials and historians made then, as now—that the Macedonian people and their revolutionary history were "invented" by Tito for political purposes. Such a view casts Tito as an arch-nationalist for promoting a national unity, a formulation that sits uneasily with the evidence amassed by Ramet (1984) which demonstrates the tight rein that Tito kept on national movements in Croatia and Serbia. Certainly, in the new openness that followed the break-up of Yugoslavia in 1991, many Macedonians discovered the extent to which a movement for greater Macedonian autonomy immediately after the Second World War was suppressed by Tito's partisans.[7]

Yet although Tito's state apparatus was constantly alert to attempts by different republics to exercise greater control or exhibit greater continuity with their exclusive pre-Yugoslav past, Macedonia occupied a peculiar place in the constitution of the Federal Yugoslavia. Certainly Yugoslav military and ideological support had made possible the setting up of the Macedonian Republic. But the foot-soldiers of this initiative had been Macedonians who were often imbued with the ideal of Macedonia in a non-Yugoslav sense.[8] And logically, the Yugoslav state was dependent on the theoretical idea that a Macedonian collectivity had existed before 1944. The core premise of the federal system was that Yugoslav unity was created when consenting collectivities voluntarily surrendered certain aspects of statehood to come together. The Greek argument collapsed this position by making the creation of Macedonia contemporaneous with the creation of Yugoslavia. The Greek assault on Macedonian history, then, put at risk the broader vision of Yugoslavia as "willed" collectivity.[9]

Uniquely threatened, the pre-Yugoslav history of the Macedonian nation was of more concern to authorities than that of others within the federation. In the late 1960s the Yugoslav attitude to Macedonian historiography seems to have taken a decisive turn, as it became not merely possible, but even necessary, for scholarly attention to focus on and celebrate pre-Yugoslav Macedonian history. A shift took place from accounts and celebrations that focused on socialist, Yugoslav, and recent history to versions that were more Macedonian. It can be argued that this developed in response to a new and overtly nationalistic Greek government, which ultimately forced Tito's hand. His visit to Macedonia and to Kruševo for the Ilinden celebrations in August 1969 was a part of the wider process of this confirmation of Macedonian identity.[10]

RIVAL HOSTS TO HISTORY

At the end of the 1960s, Kruševo was still a backwater. It lay at the end of a treacherous road up from Prilep: described in old sources as a nine-hour mule-ride, this road of switchbacks is still visible in places from the new, asphalt road which was built in the early 1970s. The town lacked amenities and resources. One issue of some political significance throughout this period was its erratic water supply which was seen as an obstacle to further development of the town as a resort site. It was the center of a municipality, or *opština*, but the region had few natural resources and was thinly populated. The confiscations of the immediate post-war period and the collectivization program that followed had hit Kruševo and the surrounding countryside especially hard. The destruction of the resources for stock-keeping and commerce, and the ill-fated attempt to rationalize farming—all had contributed to underdevelopment. Large numbers of the population had sought their livelihood in Skopje, especially after the capital city's earthquake of 1963, which attracted Yugoslav and international capital to the city for rebuilding efforts.

It was not until the construction of the asphalt road from Prilep in the early 1970s that Kruševo's population stopped declining in number. According to local accounts, the 1970s saw more new homes constructed in Kruševo than in any other comparable period since 1944. The local mythology of the road is that, perhaps aptly for anything in Macedonia, it was built because of Tito. His 1969 visit came on 3 August—the day after the Ilinden celebration, which he had spent in Skopje. His visit to Kruševo was followed by an intensification in the development of tourist resources as well as industrial capacity. The legend goes that when he was leaving the people called out, in a formulaic Macedonian farewell, "Come again, Tito!" Tito, jolted around in the potholes and perhaps even perturbed by the hairpin bends, reportedly replied, "When you build a better road."[11]

Besides sending a signal to Yugoslavia's neighbors regarding his régime's commitment to Macedonia's identity and heritage, Tito's visit to the southernmost republic also came at a time when memories of Ilinden were fading. In an exchange in 1983, the leading Macedonian historian Ljuben Lape commented in response to the work of one historian regarding the Ilinden Uprising that considerable care was necessary in methodology, as the descendants of participants might not necessarily remember accurately or correctly (1983:357). The article he was responding to was based on twenty years of oral historical work in the Kruševo region (Trajanovski 1983). Lape's was in some sense a very traditional historiographical objection, expressing the conviction that oral sources at second- or third-hand are not reliable.

The deaths in the late 1960s of the generation that had participated directly in the Uprising thus marked a critical point when aggregate memories demanded conversion into collective representation. Correspondence in the Ilinden Dossier regarding pension payments to Ilindenci indicates that their ranks had been considerably thinned by the late 1960s, and among the forty members of the committee for the celebration of the anniversary in 1968 were just three surviving participants. The construction of a new monument, then, served a domestic as well as an international agenda, in communicating the significance of the past to a new generation of citizens.

The first question that had to be resolved was that of the most appropriate location for such a monument. Today's inhabitants of Kruševo remember having to contest, with Bitola, the right to host the project. Recollecting this dispute triggered various responses: one such was, "In Bitola they danced with the consuls, while Kruševo burned." Although today it is something of a backwater, since the main rail and road routes directly link Skopje and Thessaloniki, Bitola was certainly a cosmopolitan city in 1903. As the capital of an Ottoman province it was a major commercial center and housed missions from most of the great powers. In the 1960s, its inhabitants may have lobbied hard for recognition of Bitola's former importance as the center for the regional uprising, seeing in the monument a way to restore some of their city's lost status.

How Kruševo won the dispute is not clear from the record. Tomo Kuturec, the long-serving Kruševo communist who had served as secretary for the Ilinden pension plan, and who was a member of the 1968 committee for the Ilinden celebrations, could have exerted critical influence in the decision-making process. Veterans from Prilep were also prominent in the corridors of power, and the historical antipathy between Prilep and Bitola may have swayed their judgment. Perhaps the single most important factor, though, was Kruševo's powerful claim to martyrdom. Bitola had not been a scene of fighting or planning during the Uprising. Some villages near the town had risen and been burned, and consular sources indicated that residents had gone out to join the četas before the Uprising; but in the town itself the strong Turkish garrison made activity impossible. By contrast, and as its youngest inhabitants quickly learn and tell their visitors, Kruševo burned and many of its finest houses were put to the sack.

COMPETITION, CRITERIA, AND PROCESS

In 1968, architects and sculptors were invited to submit designs for the monument that would be built in Kruševo. An initial shortlist of eight proposals was announced, which was then whittled down to three. The final decision was between *Vatra*, or *Blaze*, by Fega Kosir, an engineer-architect from Ljubljana, in Slovenia; a project which had only the code name *10123*, by Tihomir Arsovski, Boro Mitricevski, and Kire Receski from Skopje; and *Makedonium*, by husband-wife team of Jordan Grabul, a sculptor, and Iskra Grabul, an architect, both of Prilep. Initially, it was announced that no first prize had been awarded, and that *Vatra* and *Makedonium* were to share the second prize, while *10123* was given the third prize. Following this, the decision was taken in the Parliamentary Assembly of the Republic of Macedonia on 6 May 1970 to go ahead with the *Makedonium*, which was shortly thereafter renamed the Ilinden Monument. The project featured a central cupola in white concrete, set in what its creators called a "memorial space" composed of several sections and sculptures.[12]

As one might expect, the winning design was credited with greater artistic merit than the others. Jordan Grabul, who was also sometimes referred to as Grabulski, also had unimpeachable political credentials. Born in Prilep in 1927, he participated as a teenager in the War of National Liberation (1941–44). He and Iskra were thus indisputably Macedonian. Although the competition for the monument had been opened to contestants from throughout Yugoslavia, it would have been surprising for a Macedonian national monument to have been designed and built by a Slovenian. Grabul had already proved his status as an artist with other monuments, notably one at Gevgelija, the border town on the main Skopje-Thessaloniki road and rail route, which bore the name *Sloboda*, or *Freedom*. Jordan Grabul thus combined in one individual a suitable political record, an artistic reputation, and local roots.

These three elements met again in the make-up of the nine-member committee that was to oversee the production process. All were male, and either Macedonian or Vlah; the two largest Muslim minorities of Macedonia, Albanians and Turks, were not represented. The names and official positions of the committee were as follows:

Name	Occupation/Title
Boško Stankovski	Professional politician[13]
Antonie Nikolovski	Art historian
Vangel Mandilovski	President of Kruševo opština
Dimče Todorovski	Sculptor
Dragi Tozija	Professional politician[14]
Nikola Mitevski (Zuzu)	Member of the Council of Veterans
Ljuben Lape	Historian
Slavko Brezovski	Architect
Spase Kinovski	Painter

The committee constituted a cross-section of representatives of interested parties. Their number was composed of a member of the political organs of the Republic (Stankovski); one from the *sobranie*, or assembly (Tozija); two from the selection committee which had judged the entries, the *izvršniot sovet* (Brezovski and Todorovski); one from the Macedonian Academy of Arts and Sciences, or MANU (Lape); two from the Institute of Fine Arts (Nikolovski and Kinovski); and two from the Kruševo community (Mandilovski and Mitevski).[15] This combination—professional artists, professional politicians, and "professional citizens"—made the job of pleasing all nine members difficult, particularly when there were clashes of outlook and personality of the kind recorded in the minutes of committee meetings preserved in the archives. Part of the problem stemmed also from the challenging brief of the commission, which was to ensure that the project had both artistic merit and social meaning—*umetnička vrednost i opštestveno značenje*.

REPRESENTATION IN QUESTION

Construction took place over the years 1970 to 1974, and several changes were introduced to the design. These were mostly compelled by financial stringencies, especially when the project headed over-budget and beyond its scheduled opening. Originally intended for the seventieth anniversary of Ilinden in 1973, the opening was delayed a year to 1974: and the monument's form, according to Iskra Grabul in an interview in Skopje in May 1993, differed from what its designers had conceived. The most striking element of the finished product was the cupola, a massive structure of white concrete, inside which are abstract reliefs and an eternal flame. Light pours in through four stained glass windows. Visitors enter from a circular courtyard surrounded by brightly colored mosaics, climbing an entrance ramp to double doors more than twelve feet high (see figure 1).

The minutes of meetings preserved in Grabul's archive reveal how late in the production process agreement on this form was reached. The Grabuls appear to have won the commission on the strength of descriptions rather than blueprints, not until 1972 was even a scale model available. Thus on the eve of the laying of the foundation stone of the cupola, which was to take place on 13 July of that year, the meeting was acrimonious. Boško Stankovski, the head of the commission, expressed his concern by saying, "I want to point out that people with whom I've had contact are amazed, and ask how is it possible to proceed to the laying of the foundation stone, when we don't have a notion of how the monument will appear." Vladimir Haralampiev, a visitor present at the meeting, added fuel to the fire against Grabul by asserting that:

> Grabul has used almost two years to resolve these problems, and he still hasn't resolved them. Here we have no power. Grabul even now hasn't stated clearly and openly that the monument will be ready on August 2, 1973. Grabul holds the key to everything.[16]

The committee thus expressed its concern at the slow pace of preparations. On their side, it appears that the Grabuls were worn down by the constant bickering over the size of their honorarium for the project, which appears to have been a constant fixture on meeting agendas. It was soon after the beginning of their work that the committee insisted that Iskra Grabul be demoted from co-director of the project to associate. Iskra herself believed that this was a recognition of the fact that Jordan was impractical with respect to money, whereas she was fiercely insistent that he receive his due reward. She continued to accompany him to the meetings with the commission, and to play a large part in the negotiations, as well as in the completion of parts of the project.

The argument between the artists and the commission went further than the issues of money and of concern over the project's completion. It became even more shrill when the artists did reveal their vision of the project. At stake were issues of representation that capture a tension in Macedonian intellectual circles at this time and later. Where the Grabuls were socialists and left-wingers in a cosmopolitan sense, whose understanding of socialist humanism encompassed notions of universalism and looked to the future, they were faced with a group of people with a local and arguably more reactionary viewpoint who looked to this project to represent the particular, unique past of the Macedonian narod.

Iskra Grabul, in retrospect, saw the disputes as a sign of how ignorant the members of the commission were with regard to the principles of art. She and Jordan, as she recalled the period, thought of the monument as looking to the future. They saw it as representing a break with—or an escape from— the clutches of the past. For that reason, she said, they shied away from specific, figurative references to the past. With some humor, she recalled that Boško Stankovski, the president, would ask, "What does this bit mean? And that part, what about that?" She would write him two or three pages as an answer and his response would then be, "Is this all? Is this all the meaning it has?"

One of her written answers from the period, which survives in Jordan Grabul's archive, is an outline of her own and Jordan's objections to the inclusion of an eternal commemorative flame in the main building of the memorial complex. They argued that to include a flame was to reveal that there was no autochthonous or modern symbol more suitable to the purpose. It would thus represent, for them, "an admission of artistic failure." Their account consisted of two pages, and drew on complicated and technical terminology from the world of art. On this point, they lost: an eternal flame was a part of the monument when it finally opened in 1974.

The disagreements at times grew more personal and direct. In the early spring of 1973 the commission was still concerned over money, and in particular over the expenditure on the abstract reliefs inside the monument. These were Grabul's own pet project: the time sheets of the construction project show that he devoted most of his time to them between February and September 1972. Here again, a stand-off occurred between the committee's demands for clarity and Grabul's own quest to give some universally accessible representation of each of four themes: *Prerodba* (Revival); *Ilindenskoto Vostanie* (The Ilinden Uprising [1903]); *NOB* (The National-Liberation Struggle [1941–44]); and, finally, *Sloboda* (Freedom). Although these reliefs were intended to be read in this order, thus set up to tell a story of development toward a final goal, they are all, in the words of Iskra Grabul, "Formless, shifting, abstract." Far from including some figurative content, they again try to encapsulate the universal values that the experience of the Macedonian people represents.

On 8 March 1973, after Grabul had spent considerable time on the reliefs, the commission saw them, apparently for the first time. Dragi Tozija, in particular, was not happy, and the following exchange is recorded in the minutes from the meeting of that date:

> **Tozija:** The author told us that the reliefs would be figurative: those that we've been shown now are abstract. Personally, I will not withdraw the request that the reliefs should be treatments that are figurative and clear. It is not my job to say how they should be done: that is the work of the artist.
> **Grabul:** You are interfering in my artistic work.
> **Tozija:** Grabul, with this you want to mock the Commission.

Such heated debate in the construction and reception of national monuments is not unique to the Macedonian case. Maya Lin's Vietnam Veterans' Memorial in Washington, D.C., for example, prompted extreme reactions:

some called it a "ditch of shame." Partly under the pressure of such views, a set of three figures was added to the memorial complex. Many visitors have found that this addition subtracts from the overall effect, in part because it leaves a sense of partial representation, which the wall does not. It also set a precedent: the three figures were soon considered insufficiently representative of all those who played a role, and so a further group of figures, representing female nurses tending wounded men was added (Wagner-Pacifici and Schwartz 1991; Berdahl 1994). The idea that figurative representation is more meaningful than abstraction was also embraced by the sculptor Nathan Rappoport, who designed a monument to the Warsaw Ghetto Rising, unveiled in that city in 1948. Reportedly, he posed the rhetorical question, "Could I have created a stone with a hole in it and said '*Voilà*, the glory of the Jewish people'?" In line with the belief that he could not, he made one part of his monument a frieze depicting individual figures (Young 1989:82).

Other monuments in Macedonia, especially those that commemorate the national liberation struggle of the 1940s, include comparable friezes. But in the Ilinden monument, the artists directly challenged such presumptions about the limitations of abstraction: metaphorically, what they did was put up a stone with several holes in it and say "*Voilà!*" Part of their rationale was that they were not creating a monument to the exclusive greatness of the Macedonian people, but, rather, to the ideal that those people were assumed to share and express. The truths that they tried to capture and represent were universal rather than particular.

In this respect the Grabuls aspired to the spirit of the architects of Brasilia (Holston 1989; see also Scott 1998) and also those of post-earthquake Skopje in 1963 whose agendas were at the level of humanity rather than any section thereof. Like those projects, their efforts proved in the long run unacceptable in their futurism and idealism. In Holston's description of Brasilia and in those of residents of Skopje's new districts, it is clear that people experience novelty in design as inimical to their own preferences. Kruševo's cupola, now, is often viewed by Macedonians as a piece of bombast, of unnecessary symbolism that the Republic cannot afford. Whatever truth-value it once had has been largely eroded; its integrity has been compromised by internal re-engineering.[17] As a place of memory, then, it could be argued that it has failed.

THE MODULAR PAST

The cupola was envisaged as the crowning apex of a memorial complex, to be reached by visitors only after passing through two other components. The first of these was referred to as the "first platform" and is a large asphalt-covered space approximately 120 yards in width (figure 12). From this area,

Figure 12: Ilinden Memorial complex: first platform and spomenik.

which can serve as a parking lot or as a venue for cultural performances, a twisting path leads in the direction of the cupola, about 200 yards away. On either side of the path entrance are sculptures entitled *Broken Fetters*, which represent the first steps of the Macedonian people toward their freedom. The path covers around 90 yards before reaching the second major part of the complex, the crypt, where the influence of the cosmopolitan artists dropped to almost zero. At first sight it too relies on abstraction. Simple in form, it comprises a circular space approximately 12 yards in diameter sunk into the ground. Its walls rise from 6 feet high at the entrance from the first platform of the memorial to 10 feet high at the exit toward the cupola. The walls are studded with projecting cylinders, each of which bears a name, and some of which also bear dates (figure 13).

Wagner-Pacifici and Schwartz argue that the Vietnam Veterans' Memorial in Washington, D.C., represents an inversion of the characteristics of more traditional war memorials (1991:394–400). Certain of the distinctions they make are also apparent in Kruševo's crypt. It is "down" rather than "up," sunk into the ground; it appears at first sight to be a collection of names, rather than having any central figurative symbol; it is visually unimpressive, and does not include sharp contrasts in color or shade; and it diffuses a viewer's attention rather than presenting a single focus. As at the Vietnam Memorial, one has to enter a "sacred space" within the memorial in order to view it.

Although built at the same time as the large central cupola of the monument complex, the crypt does not make the same immediate visual impact. Nor does it lend itself to extraction from the whole in the way that the

Figure 13: Ilinden Memorial complex: crypt. The annual ceremonies on 2 August include the laying of wreaths in the crypt by organizations and individuals in the town.

cupola does, to be featured in television sequences or on bank notes as a free-standing symbol of Macedonia or of Kruševo within Macedonia. In the literature of the original project the crypt was described as a "place of meditation." Its scale is certainly more personal than the cupola's; at most, about two hundred people might be able to enter it at once. Perhaps most significant, it is, and always was, explicitly tied to the past. It was designed to encapsulate the struggle of the Macedonian people toward freedom, and it is for that reason that the crypt is construed not as an object but as a history lesson. Appropriately enough, this history lesson was orchestrated and carried out by professional Macedonian historians, from the Institute for National History in Skopje. The names in the crypt claim to represent a singular, true history of united struggle. Grabul's archive again reveals disputes, which demonstrate the existence of contrasting visions of Macedonia's progress toward nationhood.

The crypt contains fifty-eight names, written in Macedonian Cyrillic. They appear on circular metal plates, which cap the tapering concrete cylinders that project from the walls. There are twenty-nine names on each of two curved sidewalls; a row of fifteen about five feet above the ground, and a lower row of fourteen, each set between the two in the top row, but two feet closer to the ground. They are arranged in a broadly chronological order, running from earliest to latest, from the immediate right as one enters from the direction of the town around the sides, and finishing at one's immediate left. The order is top-bottom-top, and so on. The names as they appear are given in order below in Latin transliteration. The numbers are provided for ease of reference in this analysis; they do not appear in the crypt itself. (See table 2.)

The character of this list distinguishes the crypt clearly from the Vietnam Veterans' Monument. Maya Lin's memorial presents itself as a black slate on which names are engraved in approximate chronological order of their deaths. The names thus make up a population united by death in the course of a war that the wall asserts observed no distinctions. The memorial is inclusive; the only determining factor about whether a name should be included is whether its bearer died.[18] It draws on the tradition of village memorials or honor rolls in public schools in England, which list former members of the community who died in wars.[19]

The crypt of the Ilinden Monument, conceived and constructed many years before the Vietnam Memorial, presents a list of names that is very differently constituted. Individuals appear alongside places, names of organizations, and even a book title. Although composed in a time of socialism and purporting to celebrate a whole people's struggle, the list is exclusionary: an individual's appearance in it represents an honor. It is only the leaders from the annals of history who appear here, whose activities were in some way or another "significant" in the constitution and struggles for freedom of the Macedonian people. Their names are arranged not in order of their births or deaths, but in order of the date of their major contribution to the cause, alongside the organizations within which and the places where those contributions were made. It thus conceives of history as *res gestae*, offering a chronology of meaningful deeds. The individuals are there not because they died for the cause, but for what they achieved when they were alive.

THE FIRST DRAFT OF HISTORY

The list of names in the crypt, obviously, represents a selection from the whole arc of the disputed pre-Yugoslav history of Macedonia. Although it now has come to seem definitive, it was the result of an extended and contested decision-making process. Among the papers preserved in the Grabul Archive is a preliminary list of suitable subjects for inclusion provided by a committee from the Institute of National History, and a description of their priorities in making their recommendations. On the committee were two mid-career historians who made a specialty of the early twentieth century, Manol Pandevski and Krste Bitoski. Their first draft presented a somewhat

TABLE 2
The Names in the Crypt at the Ilinden Monument

Left Side	
(30) Ordan Piperkata	
	(31) Arseni Jovkov
(32) Lokvata i Vinjari 1903	
	(33) Gemidžiite 1903
(34) Smilevski Kongres 1903	
	(35) Ilinden 1903
(36) Kruševskata Republika 1903	
	(37) Dinu Vangel
(38) Klisura 1903	
	(39) Sliva 1903
(40) Smilevo 1903	
	(41) Kabrunica 1903
(42) Mečkin Kamen 1903	
	(43) Neveska 1903
(44) Armensko 1903	
	(45) Rašanec 1903
(46) Čaništa 1903	
	(47) Za Makedonckite Raboti 1903
(48) Vojdan Černodrinski	
	(49) Nikola Kirov-Majski
(50) Rilski Kongres 1905	
	(51) Taskata Serski
(52) Apostol Petkov	
	(53) Dimitar Vlahov
(54) Kašina 1905	
	(55) Nožot 1907
(56) NFP 1908–1910	
	(57) Dimitrija Čupovski
(58) MNLD-Petrovgrad 1904–1917	

different take on Macedonian history. It contained sixty names of individuals, events, and organizations, but only twenty-one of these appear among the fifty-eight included in the crypt. The differences between this first list and the final version illuminate some of the tensions inherent in the project of creating an authoritative script of the national past.

Where the final list began with a figure from the nineteenth century, the first list went back much further. The historians originally proposed Kliment Ohridski as the first name, to be followed by Tsar Samuil. Kliment was the patron saint of the Slavic Orthodox churches, active in the ninth century; Tsar Samuil was a tenth-century king who had one of his capitals in Ohrid.

Right Side	
	(29) Sava Mihajlov
(28) Radon Todev	
	(27) Ivan Anastasov-Grčeto
(26) Nikola Puškarov	
	(25) Mitre Pandžarov-Vlaot
(24) Pando Kljašev	
	(23) Pitu Guli
(22) Nikola Rusinski	
	(21) Vele Markov
(20) Ǵorǵi Sugarev	
	(19) Hristo Uzunov
(18) Lazar Poptrajkov	
	(17) Krste Misirkov
(16) Dimo Hadži-Dimov	
	(15) Nikola Karev
(14) Vasil Glavinov	
	(13) Petar Poparsov
(12) Jane Sandanski	
	(11) Pere Tošev
(10) Dame Gruev	
	(9) Ǵorče Petrov
(8) Goce Delčev	
	(7) Solunski Kongres 1896
(6) TMORO 1893–1908	
	(5) Teodosim-Mitropolit Skopski
(4) Kresna 1878	
	(3) Razlovci 1876
(2) Ǵorǵija Pulevski	
	(1) Iljo Maleševski

Next in this preliminary list was the Karpoš Uprising of 1689, followed by the Miladinov brothers, Dimitar and Konstantin, who lived and wrote in Struga, near Ohrid, in the mid-nineteenth century. All of these figures and events, undoubtedly prominent in the history of the Balkans, were excluded from the final version.

After evoking the distant past, the first list went on to include individuals and events from the principal period of revolutionary activism in the late nineteenth and early twentieth century. Most made it to the final list, though there were some changes in personnel, which will be discussed below. They were outnumbered by the names of individuals, organizations, and events from the period since the First World War, a period which provided thirty-two of the total sixty entries. After references to the early communist organizations in Yugoslavia, the bulk of these entries concerned the period of the partisan struggle of 1941–45 and its aftermath. Among these were the poet Kočo Racin, who died in 1941, and the battle of the Srem Front of 1945, where several thousand Macedonian soldiers died in Serbia fighting to push the German army off Yugoslav soil, long after the whole of Macedonia had been evacuated by Axis forces. Political organizations were included, with their dates, including ASNOM 1944, as well as cultural achievements, including the University of Kiril and Metodi, established in 1946. Also included were institutions and events from the Greek Civil War that emphasized its Macedonian dimension, including NOF 1948 (a military organization), and the battle of Vičo 1948, the significance of which will be discussed later. All but one of these entries—MNLD, the last in the crypt—were erased from the list that was translated into bronze and concrete reality.

How the first list was transformed into the final version is not indicated in the Grabul archive. It appears from the archival record that the artist did not interest himself to any great extent in the crypt. Iskra Grabul made no comment during interviews in 1992. Nor, when asked, did Krste Bitoski and Manol Pandevski, members of the advisory committee from the Institute for National History who by the 1990s were senior members of their profession. In a climate in which historical revisionism was rampant, both declined opportunities to reflect on the story of the two lists. Both have also continued to assert in newspapers and other forums that Macedonian historiography in the Yugoslav era was always independent and never explicitly influenced by political considerations (Brown 2000a). The mere fact of the existence of the two lists, though, would seem to challenge this and make the point that historians in Macedonia are sometimes unwilling to accept: that history does not write itself naturally, but is always written by historians in a particular time and place, who are inevitably subject, albeit unconsciously, to the spirit of their times (Butterfield 1931). Whatever their considerations in producing the first list, new influences clearly had an impact in the revised version. These may have been personal, professional, or political in origin; their combined effect was to create a very different narrative of national origin.

MARKING MACEDONIAN NATIONAL TIME

Accounts from the 1970s described the Kruševo monument as representing both the National Liberation Struggle (1941–44) and the Ilinden Uprising (1903). This reflected priorities in pan-Yugoslav modes of recall, which emphasized the participation of the constituent peoples, or narodi, in the country's liberation. Particularly salient was the "partisan myth" of widespread support and activism. The Ilinden monument's agenda thus perpetuated that of the Spomenica program, whereby activity in 1903 was cast as a prelude to the final act of the anti-fascist struggle of 1941 to 1944. Adherence to this connection appears to have motivated those who drew up the first list for the crypt's content, which included elements from both stages of modern Macedonian history, as well as a few from earlier periods.

Within the complex as a whole, the earlier period of Ottoman rule was commemorated in the lower platform, and the overview of national progress was represented in Grabul's unpopular, disputed reliefs inside the cupola. The crypt was to stand for liberation from servitude. A focus on the period from the mid-nineteenth century to the First World War, then, made more narrative sense than an attempt to encapsulate the whole sweep of the nation's progress.

After the rejection of the first list, the temporal frame of the crypt came to include a shorter period, from the 1860s to 1919. Maleševski, the first name, was an outlaw, imagined by Macedonian historians after Hobsbawm's ideal of the "social bandit" and active from around 1850 (Hobsbawm 1959). Maleševski reportedly took part in the Kresna Uprising (4) which, like the Razlovci Rising (3) and the attempt by Teodisim (5) to found an autocephalous Macedonian church in 1891, stands as a marker of Macedonian activism in pursuit of secular and spiritual autonomy (Apostolski et al [eds.] 1979:116, 123, 128–31, 142).

All this is prelude to the main temporal focus of the crypt on the year 1903. The date is given on fifteen of the fifty-eight plates, and twenty-four individual names appear between the dated entry for the Salonika Congress of 1896 (7) and the first of the explicit references to 1903 (32). Although the historians provided birth and death dates for everyone, they were not included on the plates and did not dictate the order of individual names. Framed by the events of 1903 are Goce Delčev (8), Pitu Guli (23), and Ordan Piperkata (30), who all died in that year, as well as Dame Gruev (10), Nikola Karev (15), and Dinu Vangel (37), who were key leaders in the Uprising, and whose deaths came later. Over one third of the items commemorated, then, depend for their place in the crypt on their link with 1903. Of the rest, only five are placed before 1893, and only four after 1905. A twelve-year period sets temporal parameters within which forty-nine of the fifty-eight names won their inclusion.

External political conditions at the time of the monument's construction perhaps contributed to this focus. The four early figures proposed in the first draft—Kliment, Samuil, and the Miladinov brothers—are all viewed as Bulgarian in modern Bulgaria. The same imperative to claim long historical continuity is exhibited in Greece, where Kliment is claimed as national forebear. For Macedonia to evoke the earlier period by naming Tsar Samuil would be to stake claims to a past that Macedonian historians had barely treated; it would also invite ridicule for a species of nationalistic bombast that the Republic had steadfastly avoided since 1944.[20] Explicit extensive reference to the post-war period, by contrast, would highlight the influence of the Yugoslav and socialist project in Macedonia. Part of the project of the Macedonian historical profession was to demonstrate that the Macedonian people had entered federal Yugoslavia with their own history, and that ASNOM in 1944 was the confirmation of a previously existing national reality, and not its creation. An account of Macedonia's past which spent more time on the socialist struggle since the 1930s than on all the preceding centuries would perhaps leave the impression that prior history was in short supply.

Some of the later references proposed in the first list raised more specific issues. Although the Srem Front stood as an epic engagement with retreating Germans and was part of the partisan myth-complex, it had also been a point of protest for many Macedonians. Accounts still circulated in Skopje in the 1990s that some soldiers had refused to march north and had instead called for the liberation of Thessaloniki, and that they were executed on and buried beneath Skopje's *Kale*.[21] They were just some among many Macedonians who had not necessarily distinguished the new Yugoslav project from the old, and offered various forms of resistance that led to imprisonment or death. In 1974 the year 1945 was still part of a living history, and the object of rumor. Enshrining a controversial event at a monument which was supposed to unite the Republic's people and express something of "their" history in such a context perhaps carried too much political charge.

The temporal frame selected in the final version excluded both Bulgarian-contested pre-history and Yugoslav-tainted recent events. It thus dispelled certain problems of inclusion raised in the first list. By laying out a forty-two-year period between 1875 and 1917 as central to the history of the Macedonian people, it staked a claim on a period on the cusp of living memory, into which most citizens of the new state could trace ancestry. Nowhere in the planning of the crypt did any of the historians or others involved suggest that Alexander the Great should come first, or Tito last. Although the narrative evokes national struggle, it does so by including specific, historical individuals at a particular juncture in historical time. Their efforts are presented as reaching a crescendo in 1903, the year of Ilinden.

CREATING MACEDONIAN SPACE

Of the fifty-eight plates in the crypt, nineteen include a specific reference to place. Of these, one is in Russia (58), while the other eighteen all lie within the borders of Ottoman Macedonia, as mapped in chapter 2. Twelve of these also carry the date 1903, already noted as central in the narrative. They serve, then, to territorialize that year in a set of names of places and battles. By their commemoration in the crypt, these places are elevated in importance beyond mere geographical points. In each case a specific moment of human agency is inscribed, thereby tying together these different localities to construct a particular vision of Macedonia that could not be realized elsewhere.

The greatest concentration of places associated with 1903 is in the Monastir vilayet, the Turkish administrative district that was the main site of the Ilinden Uprising. This vilayet was divided after the Balkan Wars between Greece, Serbia, and Albania, and the post-Yugoslav border between Greece and the Republic of Macedonia runs along the divide set in 1913.[22] The extension of space suggested by this set of sites in the crypt reaches into what is today Greece, most directly by the inclusion of the names Klisura (38) and Neveska (43). Like Kruševo, these two Vlah mountain towns were captured by insurgent forces in August 1903, and in both it is reported that provisional governments were created (Dakin 1993:101).[23] From a different former vilayet, the *Solunski Kongres* (Congress in Thessaloniki) of 1896 is also celebrated, as are the *Gemidžii*, or Boatmen, who planted bombs in the city in 1903 (33), emphasizing Salonica's central significance in the period of the struggles led by the organization called TMORO (6) and discussed later. Significantly, though, no other cities or prosperous towns feature. The emphasis is on poor, rural, and mountainous Macedonia, the heartland constituted of villages where the Organization had its strongest links and where the losses were most severe.

Both of Kruševo's battle sites, Mečkin Kamen (42) and Sliva (39), are included in the crypt. Neither was ever a site of settlement or constitutive action: they are hilltops distinguished from others only by their fierce defense during the last hours of Ottoman absence from Kruševo. On both hilltops, cairns bearing commemorative plaques were raised in the 1940s, to mark their significance. Their inclusion in the crypt thus denotes a form of double commemoration, whereby places already recognized have their importance asserted anew.

These two places also contribute their particular symbolic power to the crypt. According to popular memory within Kruševo, both Mečkin Kamen and Sliva were bloody defeats. At Mečkin Kamen, Pitu Guli (23) held out for several hours against an overwhelming force of Turkish troops marching on Kruševo before falling heroically. Accounts of the extent of the losses differ. Eyewitness accounts report twenty or thirty dead, and by their very existence suggest there were survivors; while more dramatic versions given by guides to the memorial complex now put the losses at over a hundred and claim that the rebels died to the last man.[24] Sliva, on the other side of the town, was where the četa of Todor Hristov, also referred to as Todor the

Officer, was wiped out by the Ottoman army. Whereas Pitu Guli's men were mostly villagers, Todor Hristov's četa was composed of townspeople. Additionally, some accounts report that in its ranks were several women, who died fighting. These two elements of the story combine to give Sliva particular prominence in Kruševo itself, even though the story of Mečkin Kamen is better known in the country at large.

Sliva and Mečkin Kamen are framed by other events from the same year, listed by place-name and date. Smilevo 1903, a spirited insurgent counterattack that enabled the high command to escape from the mountain village, comes between them (40). After Mečkin Kamen, though, the final three engagements included in the crypt from 1903 are Armensko, Rašanec and Čaništa (44–46). Armensko, now Alona, in modern Greece, was the site of a massacre of the entire village population; Rašanec, in the region of Ohrid, was a mountain retreat where women and children were discovered and killed by Ottoman forces; and Čaništa, in the Prilep region, was the site of a prolonged battle in which VMRO leaders finally broke through Ottoman lines to escape. The first two names convey horror and loss, foregrounding notions of endurance and suffering to create a sense of the Macedonian people as a community of victims. The third was a battle against the odds which ended not in victory, but escape to fight another day.[25] Together with other locations named, they emphasize the extent of the ground on which battles were fought and blood was shed for Macedonian freedom. The symbolic extension of this space across the post-Balkan War Greek frontier reaffirmed the assertion of a national territory centered in Kruševo, once a Greek town but now definitively Macedonian.

PEOPLING THE PAST

In the case of the individuals named in the crypt, the mode of recall shifts. Thirty-four out of fifty-eight plaques bear simply given and family names of figures from the Macedonian past. All those honored in this way are men, and all are celebrated for their purposive action. Almost all, additionally, are recognizably Macedonian names. The two most obvious exceptions, Pitu Guli (23) and Dinu Vangel (37), were both Vlahs from Kruševo. The commission had stated that one of its aims was to ensure the adequate representation of the narodnosti, or nationalities, of which the most significant in Macedonia were Albanians. However, this ambition was not realized. Non-Slavic participation is noted in the epithets "the Vlah" and "the Greek" in the names Mitre Pandžarov-Vlaot (25) and Ivan Anastasov-Grčeto (27), but no reference is made to Albanian or Turkish support for the cause. Given the troubled relationships of those communities with the Slav-speaking Christian population of Ottoman Macedonia and within Yugoslav Macedonia as described by Burcu Akan, this is perhaps hardly surprising (Akan 2000).

Included are several figures who through cultural initiatives promoted the existence of a distinct Macedonian people, especially by their own use of the term "Macedonian." Ǵorǵija Pulevski (2) compiled a multi-lingual dictionary in the late nineteenth century and called one of the languages he used Macedonian; Krste Misirkov (17) published *Za Makedonckite Raboti* (47), or *Of Macedonian Affairs*, in 1903; and Vojdan Černodrinski's (48) play *Bloody Macedonian Wedding* was first performed in Sofia in 1900. All three figures, then, served in the same mode as Teodisim and Iljo Maleševski, as resources against a view of history that pronounced Macedonian an invention of Tito.[26]

The majority of those named—twenty-four in total—were involved in establishing the revolutionary organization or in fighting for the cause in the period around 1903. This represented a major shift from the first draft submitted by the historians of the Institute for National History, which had included only nine such figures. These were the men who had already come to be central to the Macedonian pantheon of heroes: Goce Delčev, Gjorče Petrov, Dame Gruev, Jane Sandanski, Petar Poparsov, Nikola Karev, Lazo Poptrajkov, Hristo Uzunov, and Pitu Guli.[27] Those added represented a second league, in many cases having a substantial reputation in one region only. Gjorǵi Sugarev (20), Mitre Pandžarot-Vlaot (25), and Ordan Piperkata (30), for example, all added to the final list, were all četa leaders during the Ilinden Uprising. Vasil Glavinov (14), from Veles, played a key role in the development of socialist activism in Kruševo, while Vele Markov (21) was the first revolutionary leader there, killed along with many of his četa in the siege of Rakitnica in 1902, recalled in many pension autobiographies from the town, including that of Donka Budžakoska, related in chapter 1.

The inclusion of these figures, along with other region-specific figures, such as Sava Mihajlov (29) of the Gevgelija region, was perhaps intended to highlight the important role played by local as well as central leadership in the struggles of the period. The commission of historians stated explicitly that it had followed a policy of representing individuals above institutions, and the choice of people with specific local roots can be seen as representing a similar ethos of commemorating more tangible dimensions of the past.

Yet the recourse to such people simultaneously makes certain omissions all the more remarkable. A memorandum accompanying the second list indicated that three significant institutions or organizations were central to the conduct of the Ilinden Uprising; the High Command, the Military Headquarters in Kruševo, and the provisional Kruševo government. In line with the stated policy of preferring individuals for commemoration, the latter two are represented in the crypt by figures who played key roles. The Military Headquarters in Kruševo is represented by its chief, Nikola Karev, and the Kruševo government by its titular head, Dinu Vangel.

The High Command, however, was not so well served. According to both Bulgarian and Macedonian historians, it was based in Smilevo and had three members. One, Dame Gruev, appears in the crypt. However, in contrast to the tight chronology apparent in the location of the other two names that stand for institutions, Gruev's name does not appear to stand for the High Command. Instead, he is grouped with his colleagues who were the founders of the Secret Macedonian and Adrianople Revolutionary Organization (TMORO) organization in Thessaloniki in 1893.[28] Not only does the significance of the Smilevo base thus get transferred onto the shoulders of an individual, but it is also removed to second-hand: the highlight of Gruev's career, as presented in the crypt, is his association with TMORO in 1893 and not the far more central role that he played in the organization and conduct of the Ilinden Uprising.

Gruev's two colleagues in the Ilinden High Command, Atanas Lozančev and Boris Sarafov, were removed still further, appearing on neither the first nor the second list. Their exclusion from the roster of central participants in Ilinden 1903 carries its own message. In the case of Lozančev, the rationale appears straightforward. He was from Bitola, and never achieved the same status as Gruev. After the failure of the Uprising he fled to Bulgaria, where he continued to be involved in Macedonia's future. He was among the signatories of a petition dated 27 December 1917 that protested international support for Serbian claims on Macedonian territory (Bozhinov and Panayotov [eds.] 1978:662). Reportedly, he saw ASNOM as a tool of Serbian domination rather than Macedonian liberation. He died in 1944 in Sofia.

Boris Sarafov, by contrast, was one of the best-known revolutionary leaders. He died in 1907, when the dream of autonomous Macedonia had not yet been extinguished. As a representative of the movement for Macedonian liberation, he had traveled throughout Europe, and his appearance is recalled by journalists of the period in striking terms. John Booth, for example, met Sarafov in Bloomsbury and was impressed by his vitality (1905:22–23). His movements and rumors of his death were always the objects of attention for Western diplomats. But he was also well known in the field, mentioned even fifty years later in some of the pension requests described in the previous chapter.

Perhaps more than any other leader in the Uprising, Sarafov combined local and international appeal. Goce Delčev was well known in the region, and had won sufficient recognition by missionaries as "the most capable and most honest of the Komitadji" for his death in May 1903 to attract notice from the British consular staff (FO 195/2156/563–564; in Chotziadis et al. [eds.] 1993:60). Dr. Ivan Tatarčev in Sofia, by contrast, was a leading spokesman for the organization abroad. Sarafov, uniquely, won respect and notice as he shuttled between European drawing-room and Macedonian mountain village in the years leading up to 1903.

EDITING THE MIX

Seventy years later, Sarafov's name never appeared on a list of candidates for inclusion in the crypt. On the surface, the reason is straightforward: the Macedonian historical profession had passed judgment on Sarafov as a villain, on the basis of his actions after 1903. After the failure of the Uprising, the revolutionary organization split into rival factions. Sarafov still commanded personal loyalty from many in the organization, and according to contemporary accounts (Sonnischen 1909) and subsequent historical work on the period (Perry 1988), favored closer ties with the Court of Bulgaria. For this reason, he became a bitter opponent of the leftist wing that was especially opposed to Bulgarian aspirations to the territory of Macedonia. Given the particular position of the Macedonian state in the 1950s to 1970s, Sarafov's actions after 1903 appeared inimical to the interests of the Macedonian people.

The taint of close ties with Bulgaria affected other potential heroes too. At the engagement on Sliva, for example, the town četa was commanded by Todor Hristov, better known as Todor the Officer—*Todor Oficerot*. Pension requests from those involved in the major battle that was fought to break the encirclement of the General Headquarters in Smilevo unanimously attribute key leadership to Nikola Dečev, a vojvod who was also a military officer. Both Todor the Officer and Dečev, like Sarafov and others, served or had served in the Bulgarian army. In post-war Macedonia, where historians were eager to highlight the indigenous struggle for freedom, Bulgarian military officers' participation in Ilinden represented an alien element. As a result, despite their significant role and their presence in individuals' memories, such figures were seldom foregrounded in official accounts of the past.

Where many simply dropped out of view, Boris Sarafov did not go quietly. Although most accounts suggest his influence in Macedonia began to wane immediately after Ilinden, he continued to be commemorated in the Macedonian diaspora in the United States, where many activists fled. Even Macedonian historians acknowledged his pivotal organizational role in the years leading up to 1903, when he worked closely with Delčev, Gruev, and others in securing funds and munitions, and resisting Bulgarian attempts to usurp control of the revolutionary movement (Perry 1988; see also Misirkov 1974:119–30). He could not just be ignored; he had to be discredited. One example of attempts to achieve this goal can be found in Manol Pandevski's prize-winning work on the Ilinden Uprising, on the basis of which he was given status as an academician. In his book Pandevski describes Sarafov's actions during the Uprising as cowardly and motivated by self-preservation (1978:378). Pandevski provided neither documentation nor evidence for this assertion, which suggests that both he and his readership already knew what they thought about this particular individual.

Pandevski's position was foreshadowed in the first list of names proposed for inclusion in the crypt. After the nine fighters of the Ilinden period and before the cultural figures Dimitrija Čuposki and Dimo Hadži-Dimov from the period after 1910, the committee of historians of which Pandevski was a member suggested for inclusion only one individual, Todor Panica. Panica's lifespan was given as 1879–1925; his place on the first list came between *Nožot* 1907[29] and *Narodna federativna partija* (People's Federal Party) 1909, both of which were included in the final list. Applying the same principles that governed the selection of other individuals, it would appear that Panica was proposed on the basis of a significant action that he undertook between 1907 and 1909.

There seems little doubt that Todor Panica was recommended for inclusion by the commission for his killing of Boris Sarafov in Sofia on 10 December (o.s.) 1907. In the same attack, Panica also killed Ivan Garvanov, described by Duncan Perry as the "architect of Ilinden" (Perry 1986). Contemporary Western accounts of this action, produced by journalists who traveled in the area, reveal ambivalence; Sonnischen, who was more involved than most others, had spoken against the intrigues of Sarafov within the Organization (1909:104–10). For all that, the murder passed largely unremarked in the Western press, such violence in the Balkans already becoming something to be taken for granted.

The authorized Macedonian account of national history states that the left liquidated Sarafov and Garvanov "for the sake of Macedonia's integrity and the revolutionary movement's independence" (Apostolski et al. 1979:190). Panica acted on the orders of Jane Sandanski (12), the leftist leader who became an established member of the post-war Macedonian pantheon.[30] Panica obeyed instructions from the Organization, and struck down two men considered at the time and, later, in Yugoslav Macedonia as saboteurs of the Macedonian national movement. He also provided a temporal link between the Ilinden generation and the leftists of the inter-war period who laid the groundwork for ASNOM. To the historians who proposed his inclusion, he must have seemed a straightforward choice.

Yet Todor Panica's name was omitted from the final list. The details of the discussion that led to his disappearance are, as stated previously, not available. What seems clear is that the memorial complex was designed to tell a particular story. It was always a part of the monument's conception, in keeping with Yugoslav perspectives on art more generally, that it should have a didactic element, as well as a close relationship with ordinary people. Its designers and overseers projected that the monument would be thronged with visitors who would pass from the first platform, commemorating Macedonia's distant past of servitude, through the crypt and its tale of struggles for national liberation, to emerge at the cupola, the great heart of the Macedonian people, within which burned a constant flame. The whole was coordinated such that it could serve as a site at which the national past quite literally led to the socialist present and future. That story is still told—though with the socialism downplayed—by staff at the historical museum in Kruševo. In the mid-1990s, schoolchildren still visited the monument in large numbers from elsewhere in the Republic. The names in the crypt, as their compilers perhaps foresaw, continue to provide the framework for a historical narrative of struggle against external enemies and grievous suffering, eventually rewarded with ultimate victory.

Including Todor Panica in this narrative of continuous and united progress toward liberation introduces friction. Although Panica's act was undoubtedly in the interest of the Organization's left wing, it was prompted by disunity and generated further internecine violence. The war that was declared between Macedonian rightists and leftists after Ilinden 1903 claimed many lives and absorbed much of the energy of the movement, up to and beyond the 1930s.[31] Todor Panica was undoubtedly a key player in that struggle, in which bombs, revolvers, and knives were used against former allies, loyalties were bought and sold, and formerly proud autonomists sacrificed their ideals in exchange for assistance from foreign powers. The story of that struggle was neither straightforward, nor glorious.

More important still, one cannot commemorate an assassin without recalling his victim. Ilinden 1903 marked a watershed in the history of the Macedonian Revolutionary Organization. It was the culmination of a common project, and marked the end of a fragile unity. In state rhetoric, always careful to leave open the question of the deeper historical roots of the Macedonian people, the Ilinden Uprising and the Kruševo Republic symbolized "the struggle of the Macedonian people not only in what was then the Bitola Revolutionary District, but also in the Solun [Thessaloniki] area, and the Skopje, Serres and other regions. In short, everywhere in Macedonia" (from Boško Stankovski's speech on 2 August 1974 reported in *Nova Makedonija*, 3 August 1974). Boris Sarafov was a part of that unity. He led a substantial force to the battlefield, and took responsibility for the whole Uprising. He worked closely with Gruev as well as other leaders whose names appear in the crypt, including Delčev, the most celebrated of them all, who died between the agreement that an uprising should be held and the execution of that uprising.

The celebration of Sarafov's assassin in the crypt would require the story to be told of Sarafov's later fall from grace. In one way, then, it would draw attention away from Ilinden and toward its aftermath. At the same time, paradoxically, it would emphasize the importance of Sarafov as an individual so dangerous that he had to be liquidated. This in turn would lead to a discussion of his involvement in the planning and execution of the central event of Macedonian history, the emblematic status of which could therefore be compromised by association. By passing over Sarafov's assassin, such issues were not raised, and therefore needed no addressing. The picture of Ilinden-era Macedonian unity was thereby preserved, as plot elements which might have disrupted it were excluded from the zone of explicit recall.

In some regards, this representational tactic was close kin to the philosophy of the Ilinden pension plan discussed in chapter 6. There, activity or leadership during Ilinden or in the subsequent period carried its own dangers. Instead, the new Macedonian state rewarded inactivity and obedience as markers of patriotism and unquestioned loyalty. In excluding reference both to Sarafov's central role in 1903 and to his death as an anti-Macedonian villain in 1907, the committee sought to smooth the jagged edges of a turbulent history. By acknowledging neither peaks or troughs in a distinguished Macedonian's biography, they cut him down to size.

CONCLUSION

The role played by scholars in the creation of the space-time of the national past is often seen in relatively straightforward terms. Various studies have indicated the key roles assigned to archaeology, history, and ethnology in amassing material proof of a people's autochthony or at least longevity (Balakrishnan [ed.] 1996; Fox [ed.] 1990; Herzfeld 1986; Kohl and Fawcett [eds.] 1995; Meskell [ed.] 1998; Silberman 1989). Others have drawn attention to the significance of museums and monuments, as well as commemorative practices in providing the wider public with opportunities to participate in the affirmation of the sacred past (Mosse 1975; Gillis [ed.] 1994; Nora 1989, [ed.] 1997; Young 1989, 1993).

All memorials, though, have their own histories, and the Ilinden Spomenik in Kruševo is no exception. The documentary record reveals a variety of disagreements and revisions that arose in the protracted course of construction. In a socialist state coming to terms with a contested national past, a group of citizens and professionals wrangled over both form and content. That dispute appears to have carried through even into the grand opening. Thousands were present when Boško Stankovski spoke in August 1974, and as was the custom of the time, his words were reported in full in the following day's Skopje newspaper, *Nova Makedonija*. In the course of remarks that must have lasted at least fifteen minutes, there was not a single mention of the design of the monument. The artists, Jordan and Iskra Grabul, were not mentioned, and they played no significant part in the opening ceremonies.

Iskra Grabul, in 1993, clearly communicated a sense of frustration at the compromises she and Jordan had been forced to make. They had envisaged an underground screening room, where sound and light would be projected to bring history to vivid life, as well as floodlights to illuminate the cupola. She also described the purity and clarity of her late husband's artistic vision, which transcended national boundaries and won him appreciative reviews abroad. Speaking of more recent times, she expressed her distaste for the direction of historical discussion in Macedonia, criticizing especially those who lay claim to descent from Alexander the Great.

For the Grabuls, modern Macedonian identity was not about ancient roots. It was a dynamic and vital force that was the product of human endeavor. As exponents of socialist and internationalist humanism, they sought through abstract art to present a timeless and universal message of the struggle for freedom. Macedonians were the heroes of this process, but no specific enemy was designated. The victory was over historical circumstances, and did not constitute the defeat of some other named group. Macedonians thus stood for all peoples of similar aspirations.

The objections of Dragi Tozija and Boško Stankovski in the course of the monument's construction and the snub to the architects at the dedication highlight both sides' different priorities in commemorating the past. These critics advocated more easily decipherable representations, calling either for explicit figurative depictions of past events or for symbols whose previous use elsewhere made their intent clear, as was the case with the sacred flame.

In the crypt, the commission of historians initially proposed a vision of history stretching from the ninth century and the arrival of Slavic literacy to the middle of the twentieth century, in which the war of national liberation from 1941–44 was the single most important period. A process of revision shifted the focus to the period around 1903, and eliminated at least one figure whose inclusion could remind people of ideological disagreement and factionalism in the Macedonian past.

In the course of designing a monument to the Macedonian people and their historical development, artists, politicians, and historians all found themselves adapting their own visions and priorities to those of other segments of society. The traces left behind by their quarrels, debates, and compromises demonstrate clearly the inadequacy of an analysis that does not look beyond "nationalism" and "socialism" to understand processes of commemoration. Undoubtedly, Yugoslav ideology shaped people's initiatives and responses, but not everyone involved understood or enacted its strictures in the same way. For some, the Marxian march of history was a paramount concern, others were captivated by the lofty ideal of humanist universalism. Similarly, none of those involved put on record any doubts about the inspirational qualities of the Macedonian struggle for statehood. But they envisaged the duration of that struggle and the relative significance of particular moments in its course in different ways.

The different components of the memorial complex in Kruševo and the histories of their making that this chapter has laid out reveal conflicts and crises within Macedonia's intelligentsia about the past and the future, and the representation of both in the memorial architecture of the present. Outside observers, and especially Yugoslavia's neighbors, could trace in the cultural initiatives of the late 1960s and early 1970s a sinister and opportunistic manipulation of the Macedonian issue by Tito. But that is only one part of the story. As in the case of the Ilinden Spomenica plan, socialist and nationalist impulses did not so much collide as collude. The extreme approaches to history were represented most clearly in the first and last entries on the initial list of entries for the crypt provided by the Institute for National History. As noted earlier, it began with Kliment Ohridski, a figure claimed by Greece and Bulgaria. It ended with Vičo 1948, a battle between the Democratic Army of Greece and Greek government forces during the Greek Civil War. Vičo, or Vitsi in Greek, is a mountain between Florina and Kastoria; the battle in 1948 was considered by the left in Greece, Yugoslavia, and the Soviet Union as a communist victory against monarcho-fascism. Slavic-speaking Macedonians at that time were among the leaders of the Democratic Army, and provided nearly a third of its total strength (Kofos 1995: 301). While fighting was in progress, the Tito-Stalin split occurred, which led in due course to the purging of Slavo-Macedonian leadership in the Democratic Army and the severing of relations between the Democratic Army and Yugoslav Macedonia.[32]

The inclusion of Vičo 1948 in the first draft of the crypt's roll call of Macedonian history served as a tacit reminder of enduring Macedonian presence in the mountain villages of northwestern Greece. More significantly, though, it revealed a concern with the very recent past, commemorating an event when Macedonians contributed to the cause of communism as well as their own national struggle. Had the historians' initial proposals been accepted, then, the crypt would span eleven centuries, and run the gamut from a Byzantine priest nationalized for his religious and linguistic work to a mountain made into a communist icon by a local victory, won while the seeds of defeat were being sown in Moscow. In the process of revision, these incongruent imaginings were left in the background, displaced by a narrative of individual striving and collective suffering, rooted firmly in a smaller segment of space and time, thereby sacralized as the heart of Macedonia's national—and socialist—soul.

CHAPTER EIGHT

Local Truths

REREADING 1903 THE KRUŠEVO WAY

JORDAN GRABUL, the principal architect of the Ilinden monument in Kruševo, died in 1986, and the state that sponsored its creation, the Yugoslav
Republic of Macedonia, ceased to exist in 1991. The monument still stands.
The cupola is grimier now, and rendered less visible from below by the pine
trees that have grown up on the hill. The friezes in the open-air auditorium
show the effects of Kruševo's changeable weather, and have spent some time
wrapped under tarpaulins. But yearly commemoration activities have continued for Ilinden, and in 1990 acquired a new dimension when the remains of
Nikola Karev, the 1903 leader, were interred inside the cupola. In July 1993
workmen raced against time to complete renovations in time for the ninetieth
anniversary celebrations of the Kruševo Republic and the Ilinden Uprising,
whose historical importance continued to be recognized in the new, post-
Yugoslav independent Macedonia.

Since 1983, though, a second focal point for commemoration has gained
significance in Kruševo. Mečkin Kamen, a hill about five kilometers outside
the town, was already a site for outings for the town's residents, especially
groups of young people, who might hike out with a picnic. A new monument on the hill, depicted in figure 2, was unveiled in 1983. It commemo-
rates the battle fought there under the command of Pitu Guli. The monument
consists of a single statue and a simple text embedded in the ground, composed of three words and one date. In 1993 the figure and the text formed
the backdrop to the main events of the holiday itself, including a speech by
the country's president Kiro Gligorov, folkloric performances, and the laying
of wreaths. As well as the huge crowd watching, the images from Mečkin
Kamen were recorded by numerous cameras and broadcast to the rest of the
Republic's population on the evening news and in the next day's newspapers.

The two monuments, the sites at which they stand, and the personalities
they conjure represent two sides of the story of Kruševo's experience. This
chapter explores the dynamic relationship between the two, and the potential
for conflict between the communities that they separate. At stake are issues
of authority and authenticity similar to those encountered at other points in
this book. The focus in this chapter and the next is on the ways in which
people in present-day Kruševo defuse the tensions between the very different

narratives that lie behind these two monuments, in particular by appealing to the common ground represented by a less tangible but arguably more compelling evocation of 1903, the Kruševo Manifesto.

COMMEMORATION IN QUESTION

As described in the previous chapter, Kruševo's inhabitants recall having to fight rival claims on the past to have Grabul's monument built in their town. Yet soon after its opening, voices in the town began to question the value of their apparent victory. Unlike other towns of comparable size, Kruševo lacks an all-purpose community facility or cultural center where plays, movies, classes, and other activities might be held. Some people suggested this was because so much government money had been spent on the monument. While no one voiced regret that their town's historic significance had been affirmed, there was some feeling that this recognition had been purchased at the expense of more practical or banal forms of investment that would contribute to the town's ongoing social and cultural life.

More widespread were expressions of dissatisfaction with the abstract style of the monument. Grabul's hopes that the monument would stir feelings of common humanity and optimism for the future were seldom fulfilled, even by those who found clear meaning in the modern design. Some visitors, for example, assigned concrete historical reference to the "broken fetters" of the first platform. Playing host to a delegation of *Deca Begalci* (child-refugees) during the summer of 1988, local historian Krste Topuzoksi stated that each of the five represented one of the five centuries that the Macedonian people spent *pod tursko robstvo*—under Turkish slavery (Tanaskova et al. [eds.] 1993: 76–77).[1] The imposing bulk of the cupola itself was also subjected to figurative readings affirming connection to Macedonian history. It was described by some people as representing the head of a mace, which was the chosen weapon of the fifteenth-century national trickster-hero, Prince Marko.[2] At a higher level of abstraction, but still not that which Grabul set out to inspire, one historian in conversation explained that the four windows of the monument each looked out on one part of Macedonia, divided as it was still between Greece, Bulgaria, Albania, and the former Yugoslavia. Many more, though, were simply unable to find personal or national meaning in what they jokingly, sardonically, or sometimes angrily described as a sea-mine, spaceship, bomb, or simply a monstrosity.

What various people in Kruševo articulated more readily was appreciation of the significance of the monument's location. It stands at the northwest corner of the town on the hill known alternatively in Macedonian as *Gumenja* and in Greek as *Alonia*. One version, which official national sources

generally espoused, was that this was the site on which the Kruševo Republic was declared, and where the regional commander of the 1903 Uprising,
Nikola Karev, had his headquarters. Others in the town remembered different
elements of the history of the place. After Kruševo had been reoccupied by
Ottoman forces, Bahtiar Pasha had his camp there. It was to Gumenja that
George Ditsias and his fellow notables made their way to plead for the
town's survival, in the journey described in chapter 4. It was also where
some town residents were imprisoned and, according to some oral testi-
monies, hanged for their part in the Uprising. The location, therefore, has
associations with hostile outsiders and tragedy, as well as with revolutionary
activism.

Beyond the particular context of 1903, people had other memories of
Gumenja. Both its Macedonian and its Greek names reference the fact that in
more peaceful days the area was the threshing-floor of the town. Two middle-aged men recalled playing at this site as children, and recounted how the
wheat was threshed by a horse tied to a central pole. The horse circled the
pole, breaking the wheat with its hooves.[3] Gumenja was thus a practiced site
that carried in its periodic use for agricultural purposes a link between the
town of Kruševo and surrounding villages. In its more regular guise it was
the forum for maintaining social relations among townspeople. From the
1930s, at least, it was also where people from the upper part of the town
would take their *korzo*, or evening promenade, the very public exercise central to urban sociability. It was there that Serbian police found Kirče Risteski
out for a stroll, performing a korzo with his fiancée, when he was arrested in
1940. By such mundane means, the people of Kruševo had reclaimed the
space from its temporary service in 1903 as a place of terror, and domesti-
cated it.

The creation of the Ilinden monument was in turn an overwriting of this
history. It aspired to represent the struggle of the Macedonian people—the
makedonski narod—for their freedom and self-rule. Yet it did so by seeking
consciously to evoke the political project of the revolutionaries of 1903 and
shape it into an event coterminous with that of the post–World-War II Yugoslav state. In that process the specificity of Kruševo dropped out of sight.
Although the crypt includes the names of some of the Kruševo vojvods and
two of the engagements (Mečkin Kamen and Sliva), at the center of the
whole memorial complex is a generic flame and an empty space. The abstract sculptures and reliefs of the cupola and its immediate surroundings
make primary reference only to concepts, not events. Inside the monument
one could forget that one was in Kruševo. Just as the monument can hardly
be seen when one is in the lower town, so from the belly of the monument
the town is largely hidden by a fold in the ground.

RECLAIMING MEMORY

Dissatisfaction with the form of Grabul's monument appears to have provided the impetus for a project quickly undertaken by townspeople, and brought to fruition within a decade. A monument was commissioned for Mečkin Kamen, three miles outside the town to the southeast. The place already had a small memorial plaque, erected in 1948 to mark the site of the largest local armed engagement between insurgents and Ottoman forces. In 1983 the people of Kruševo gathered there to unveil their new memorial. Its most arresting component is a single figure cast in bronze around seven meters tall, depicting a young man straining with both hands above his head to hurl a large rock. He stands on a rocky outcrop with trees to both sides and behind him, and faces down across a grassy slope. At his feet, a series of letters spell out the slogan *sloboda ili smrt 1903*—freedom or death 1903. This was the slogan of the Ilinden Uprising and part of the oath that VMRO members swore (figure 14).

The sculpture was the work of Dimo Todorovski, a Skopje artist who was a member of the Macedonian Academy of Arts and Sciences (MANU). It was based on his own small bronze with the title "Mečkin Kamen" and dating from 1969 (Vishinski 1973:31). It seems clear that in that work, and the larger sculpture on Mečkin Kamen, Todorovski drew on a pictorial tradition of representations of the fighting around Kruševo. The figure of a young man holding a rock also appeared on a black and white poster which is reprinted in at least two places: an edited volume of papers on Nikola Karev (Tito [ed.] 1977) and in a short guidebook produced for visitors to Kruševo (Topuzoski 1986:17). In neither case is the provenance of the image given. The figure, though, closely resembles one from a frieze painted by Boris Lazeski, originally in a major building in Skopje. Depicting the struggle for Mečkin Kamen, Boris Lazeski focused on a young man with a bandaged left arm and shirt open to the waist, holding a rock aloft. He is poised dramatically, a straining point anchoring one flank of a row of defenders, with a sea of uniformed soldiers advancing toward him. The original frieze was destroyed in the Skopje earthquake of 1963, but subsequently recreated in Kruševo on the wall of the dining room in the Montana Hotel. In 1993, it was reproduced on a commemorative stamp issued by the Macedonian Postal Service (figure 15).

The original inspiration for the motif appears to have been a 1948 work entitled "Ilinden," which hangs in the Nikola Martinovski gallery in Kruševo. There, Martinovski, a Kruševo native, painted an image of struggle in which uniformed Turkish soldiers do battle with a collection of people resisting their advance, and the flames of the town light the sky red behind them. Center-stage is the flag-bearer of the group of defenders. The red flag

Figure 14: Mečkin Kamen memorial statue.

waves above his head even as he falls victim to attack from two sides, one soldier grabbing him around the neck from behind while another is running him through with a bayonet. Beside the flag-bearer stands another figure with a rock held aloft in both hands—the prototype of the monument.

Todorovski's sculpture does not simply replicate these predecessors. Where the larger pictures contain images of death and destruction, Todorovski selected one figure who epitomizes defiance. He has also stylized his subject's clothing; instead of Martinovski's uniform or Lazeski's simple bright white shirt and trousers, Todorovski's figure is stripped to the waist. He wears stiff trousers and, on his feet, representations of *opinci*, open-topped leather moccasins with pointed toes. In the smaller bronze cast in 1969, Todorovski emphasized the figure's connection to the ground by having his legs straddle an outcrop: in the monument on Mečkin Kamen, both feet are firmly planted. Todorovski increased the dynamic quality of the figure: from feet to upraised arms the figure curves at an anatomically improbable angle, the oversized boulder in its hands poised to be hurled forward with the force of every straining sinew. The statue is the result of an artist's selection and stylization of elements from a representational tradition.

Like Gumenja, Mečkin Kamen has its own historical resonances. Todorovski's composition explicitly points to one specific event and personality associated with the place by its inclusion of text and date. Pitu Guli, a

Figure 15: "Mečkin Kamen 1903." Commemorative postage stamp issued in 1993, based on Boris Lazeski's painting.

Kruševo native and insurgent leader, was reportedly wholly committed to the Ilinden ideal of "freedom or death" as the only thinkable outcomes. When Ottoman forces were approaching the town and the revolutionary leaders met to discuss what to do, his position was clear: the town should be defended at all costs. Mečkin Kamen was the site of his last stand, where he and his men upheld the oath they had sworn and were killed in fierce fighting. After the unequal battle, the Ottoman commander reportedly ordered his men to fire a volley over the bodies of the fallen defenders to honor them.

Kruševo's two principal monuments offer a stark contrast between abstract and figurative modes of commemoration, in part a function of their different commemorative objectives. Through the cupola, the crypt, and the first platform, Grabul and his team tried to tell the history of a people and their struggles toward independence. The Ilinden monument sought to conjure in one place the memory of different places, personalities, and events and to show their trajectory toward the socialist present and future. It seeks to offer an authoritative and coherent *synthesis* of a struggle over many years. Its imposing scale, elaborate layout, and lack of specific figurative elements are functions of this goal.

Todorovski's single figure, by contrast, evokes one specific event at the battle site, its date and context given in the simple text. It does not combine elements from the past, but creates a sense of unmediated access to one particular struggle. It therefore can be said to operate as an *analogue*. It does not seek to enhance the impact of its primary reference point, but marks it as fraught with its own significance. Stylistically, it highlights immediate, direct, and concrete human action.[4]

CONTINUITY IN DISPUTE

The obvious differences between the two monuments hint at deeper tensions inherent in the legacy of 1903 in Kruševo at the end of the twentieth century. Ilinden remained a public holiday in the post-Yugoslav Republic of Macedonia, celebrated as evidence of the historical unity of the Macedonian people and as a key event in their painful struggle to achieve statehood. For many of Kruševo's residents in 1903, though, it was a forcible reminder of civic disunity, and heralded their town's destruction by external forces. Despite considerable out-migration from the town since 1903, many families remained, so that a proportion of today's residents are direct descendants of those who actually experienced these events and who passed down their own accounts of what happened. For Kruševo's inhabitants, then, histories and memories of Ilinden overlap uneasily.

The commissioning of the Mečkin Kamen statue suggests that Grabul's monument did not do full justice to the past as some people in Kruševo saw it. Stories still circulate in the town which challenge the authoritative narrative of 1903, and cast doubt on the motives and actions of key personnel who played a central role; such stories are often recounted by people critical of successive governmental attempts to mobilize history for its own purposes. The Todorovski statue, for many townspeople, appears to transcend ideology and provide a more straightforward link with heroic history. But it too carries a message as to the relative historical significance of specific individuals and their commitments and actions, which prompts its own round of disputes and criticisms in the town.

Monuments constructed during the period of socialist rule elsewhere in Eastern Europe have come to be seen as memorials to bygone beliefs. Their various fates have served journalists and filmmakers as powerful images for broader societal changes—the cover of Misha Glenny's *The Rebirth of History* featured a Lenin bust on flat-bed truck (Glenny 1990), while in his 1995 film *Ulysses' Gaze* Theo Angelopoulos offered patient audiences several minutes of screentime showing a gigantic bust of Lenin being carried slowly on a river barge. In Kruševo, by contrast, monuments and the meanings they carry have not been so violently attacked or readily shunted aside. The town continues to be characterized as a *spomen grad* or monument-town, kindred to the British concept of a heritage site (Wright 1985), and Mečkin Kamen and Gumenja each continue to host parts of the annual commemoration practices of Ilinden. Beyond that, they serve to identify different ways in which Kruševo's inhabitants tie the past to the present. Critical in each case is the relationship conjured between the personalities and events of 1903 and sub-sequent developments in the history of the town.

Jordan Grabul's monument, as discussed in chapter 7, yoked together Ilinden 1903 and 1944. In so doing, it replicated a rhetoric of revolutionary continuity practiced in Yugoslav Macedonia from its origins after the Second World War. The insistence on the interconnectedness of the two dates acquired new urgency in 1948, when Stalin's split with Tito unleashed a wave of fear among Yugoslav leaders of a Bulgarian infiltration into Macedonia. In the same year, the politician Krste Crvenkovski gave a speech in Kruševo in which he reported that the Bulgarian communists were laying claim to one of Kruševo's own revolutionary figures from the past, Nikola Karev, and called upon his audience to resist this attempt to usurp a Macedonian hero (*Nova Makedonija*, 3 August 1948).

He did so, though, to a town population whose experiences of Bulgarian occupation and Yugoslav liberation were hardly uniform. Kruševo had its small group of committed communist activists, who had opposed Bulgarian rule from an early date and whose martyrs lay in the Partisan graveyard, which is located on Gumenja. But the violent confrontations between pro-Bulgarians and Communists that began in 1942 were preceded by Bulgarian state practices that appeared benign and that were built around the idea of reincorporation. The granting of pensions to Ilinden veterans was one Bulgarian initiative; another was recalled in an interview with an elderly woman born in 1923. In May 1941 she was one of ten young men and women who went from Macedonia to Bulgaria to take part in a parade of folk costumes from all the "Bulgarian lands." She was awarded a prize and shook hands with King Boris: the episode was recorded in a newspaper which has been kept, yellowed and faded, in the family. She wore Mijak costume, with the distinctive big-bossed belt, a patterned vest, and black shoes. Her granddaughters spoke of this part of their family's past with excitement and some pride. Afterward, this woman married a Bulgarian who came to Kruševo in 1941 to work at the Monopol factory, and has remained in Kruševo all her life.

Families such as this perhaps saw differently the association of 1903 with 1944, which post-war communist leaders and the Ilinden monument in 1974 sought to affirm. So too did others in Kruševo whose enthusiasm for Bulgarian occupation was hardly overwhelming, but whose experiences after the establishment of Yugoslav rule were negative, especially with regard to the new organization of economic life. Those who suffered directly, in the ways discussed in chapter 5, still show strong reactions. Speaking of Lazar Koliševski, the post-war party head in Macedonia, one man called down a curse: "May their bones not find rest, who have reduced me to poverty in my old age."[5] The memory of the impact of the expropriations has also been passed on to subsequent generations. In one household, a middle-aged woman keeps a shepherd's crook. It was, I was told, the only relic from her father-in-law's huge flock confiscated in 1945, and served as a reminder of what the social-ist government had taken away.

Such acts and artifacts of remembrance in the present challenge the con-certed Macedonian rhetoric in the former Yugoslavia, of which Grabul's vision was a part, that celebrated 1944 as the "second Ilinden." The meeting in that year of ASNOM was heralded as the realization of the ideals of 1903. But in Kruševo, this "second Ilinden" left for many a bad aftertaste of an illegitimate redistribution of wealth by force, which continues to influence social relations. More troubling for many is that the upheaval of the late 1940s fostered deep divisions between families in the town, still within memory. People recall that the period after the war was a time when denun-ciations flew thick and fast, and informers were active in the Kruševo com-munity. Their cooperation was, of course, central to the success of the state project of sequestering assets, for it was only neighbors and other townsfolk who could judge accurately whether the assets collected from a particular household matched their known worth, or whether some was held back. Denouncing others, as observed in exchanges between citizens and total-itarian régimes elsewhere, is also a strategy of self-rehabilitation (Fitzpatrick and Gellately 1996).

THE KAREV CONNECTION

In Kruševo, it is reported that former pro-Bulgarians were among the most enthusiastic and diligent supporters of the new post-war Yugoslavia régime. This represents a malign parallel of the cases described in chapter 6, where Ilinden pension-seekers were able to use as support for their applications to the Yugoslav government the fact of earlier recognition by the Bulgarian regime. As noted though, not all people made such an easy transition. One family whose history after the war encapsulates the problems posed by the Ilinden legacy is the Karev family. As the historical canon would have it, Nikola Karev was at the head of the Revolutionary Organization in the Kruševo region and in overall military command. He attended the Smilevo Conference where the Ilinden Uprising was planned, and, although report-edly one of those who opposed what he saw as its premature declaration, he honored the majority vote. Before the Uprising, between 1901 and 1902, he had worked as a teacher in the village of Gorno Divjaci (Matkovksi 1978: 177) and is described in various sources as making a greater contribution to the cause of freedom with his mind than his body. In 1903, Karev obeyed orders from Smilevo, the overall headquarters, to abandon Kruševo, took to the hills, and from there went into exile in Sofia.[6] He did not die until April 1905, when he was killed in a Turkish ambush in a village near Kočani, in

Eastern Macedonia, on his first return into Ottoman territory since 1903. He was at the time of his death twenty-eight years old.

What made Karev so valuable to the post-war Yugoslav Macedonian cause was evidence of his socialist ideals. Duncan Perry suggests that Karev's socialist ideas were not in line with those of most of the Organization's leadership, and that it was in part for this reason that he did not acquire more authority at the time (1988:172). After the Second World War, though, his previously low profile was a further attractive feature to Yugoslav Macedonian élites who discovered that most of the Ilinden leaders were already lionized in Bulgaria. The local significance of Nikola Karev was attested both by the published accounts of Ballas and Kirov-Majski, and in the narratives offered by various pension-seekers from the town and surrounding villages. Crvenkovski's call to defend Karev's legacy from Bulgarian appropriation was part of a wider campaign in which his socialistic and patriotic virtues were extolled: one enthusiastic account had him going into battle with his rifle in one hand and a copy of the Communist Manifesto in the other (Zografski 1948:16). Karev's socialist ideals appeared to offer a route by which to weave into Ilinden 1903 a continuity with the events of 1944 and the political program that followed. From the 1940s onward, he fit into a frame of remembrance that paid attention to political will and activism.[7]

Although nationally less well known than other leaders until the post-war period, Nikola Karev had hardly been forgotten in Kruševo. In the 1940s, two of his brothers still lived in the family home, in a street off the town's main thoroughfare. Along with Nikola and two paternal cousins, Tirču and Taško, both brothers had been involved in the struggles for Macedonia in the early part of the century.[8] Petruš, born in 1869 and thus older than Nikola, survived the Macedonian Struggle, the Balkan Wars, and the First and Second World Wars, and applied for an Ilinden Spomenica and pension on 13 September 1951. His one-page autobiography reported that he was a member of Vele Markov's socialist circle, and that they received two boxes of socialist literature from Vasil Glavinov of Veles, to help in their campaign to raise the consciousness of the town's youth. After taking part in the Uprising, he was entrusted with the local committee archive and organization funds, and fifteen months after the Uprising he took them to Sofia, at the command of his brother Nikola. Petruš's two witnesses to activism were Velko Koste Angeloski and Todor Borjaroski (Ilinden Archive 16-K-51). His request was initially refused, but after a complaint he was awarded a pension in January 1953, which continued until July 1956.

Nikola and Petruš's younger brother, Gjorǵi, was also involved in the Ilinden Uprising. He died before the pension plan went into effect, but it is unlikely that any application he made would have been successful. He was arrested in Bitola on 9 September 1944 in a Bulgarian uniform, and was put on trial for collaboration for the part he had played in Kruševo's occupation between 1941 and 1944. He was held responsible by some for the deaths of Miše Eftimov, the leader of the partisan band "Pitu Guli," and a number of other partisans, and for the internment of a large number of Kruševo's citizens. This is reported both in newspaper accounts and in a brief English-language guide to Kruševo, which denounces him as a traitor and suggests that the partisan band attacked his house during the occupation (Topuzoski 1986:26). Gjorǵi received a death sentence which was commuted to life imprisonment, and died in prison in 1949. In the 1990s, Gjorǵi's son Miše still lived in Kruševo in the old family house. Like his father, he served time in prison. In his case, it was an eighteen-month prison sentence after being arrested in 1959 for activities against "the people and the state"—*narodot i državata* (*Nova Makedonija* 10 April 1990).

Some of Nikola Karev's family, then, fell foul of the twists and turns of Macedonian politics after the Second World War. Their fate, as activists whose past worked against them, was not by any means unique. Venko Markovski, a member of ASNOM and of the first commission to codify the Macedonian language in 1944, was imprisoned between 1956 and 1961.[9] In his memoir of Goli Otok, Tito's prison island, Markovski records the sojourn there of others who had played an active role in Macedonia's past, including Pavel Šatev, one of the Solun boatmen, or gemidžii, of 1903 and Vasil Glavinov, the Veles socialist mentioned by Petruš Karev in his own pension request. Markovski perceived his own imprisonment as a result of his willingness to criticize Tito and what he saw as continuation of Serbian assimilation of Macedonia (Markovski 1984). In our conversation in 1993, Miše Karev explained his and his father's imprisonment as a result of their seeking a truly autonomous Macedonia, guaranteed not by Serb, Yugoslav, or communist control, but by some form of international protectorate.

The weapons that Tito's regime used against ideological enemies varied across Yugoslavia: one tactic was to label his enemies as doctrinaire Stalinists or cominternists, who were thereby opponents of his vision of Yugoslavism (Banac 1988). In Macedonia, resisters also found themselves under attack for pro-Bulgarianism—a rhetorical strategy that some Macedonian politicians continued to use even in the 1990s.[10] In 1993 Miše Karev suggested that this policy had been pursued against the dead, including Nikola Karev. The post-war pro-Yugoslav leadership in Macedonia, he said, and especially Lazar Koliševski, "wanted history to start with themselves," and they were jealous of the hold that Ilinden's leaders had on the imagination of the people. They sought to devalue that legacy by denouncing many of the personalities involved as Bulgarian.

Miše Karev's view reflects deep personal bitterness against a former régime. However, there does appear to be some truth in his judgment. In the early years after the war there were clear attempts to celebrate the Ilinden past. Nikola Karev was first commemorated in 1948, when a plaque on his house was unveiled on 2 August, and Dančo Zografski's account of the Republic was published (Zografski 1948). A statue of Karev, below Gumenja where the state monument now stands, was erected in 1952. As mentioned before, Goce Delčev's remains had been brought from Sofia to Skopje to be reburied in Sveti Spas. In a parallel initative Nikola Karev's remains were brought to Kruševo in 1953. Plans for their reinterment, though, were either shelved or never made, and the remains were put in storage in the basement of the town's historical museum. It appears that, despite their best efforts, the new régime had not quite made his legacy entirely their own, and Bulgarian claims on his legacy continued to be lodged.

The phenomenon noted by Miše Karev, that Nikola carried Bulgarian baggage at some points in Yugoslav history, is confirmed by others in the town. They do not, however, necessarily link the origin of this version of Nikola Karev's career to a policy of disinformation by Koliševski and his associates. Some people recall their grandparents' unshakable conviction that in 1903 Karev addressed himself to his "brother Bulgarians" as recorded in the account given by Nikolaos Ballas. Others in the town comment critically on Karev's decision to abandon the town before the Ottoman forces arrived. It seemed to fit with a template of action promoted by those Macedonian leaders who aimed to provoke Turkish outrages against the Christian population and thus compel foreign intervention, either from Bulgaria or from the Great Powers. The policy was explicitly endorsed by Boris Sarafov, who was consistently cast by Macedonian historiography as under the sway of the Bulgarian court, as described in the chapter 7. Karev's own close links to Sofia—he spent extended periods there before and after the Uprising—gave further grist to the rumor mill that associated him closely with pro-Bulgarian forces. Miše's commentary on Yugoslav suspicion of Karev therefore seems to have some basis, at least for the period of the 1950s.

By the late 1960s, in official discourse at least, Karev's place in a specifically Yugoslav Macedonian past had become firmly established. In 1969, during a visit to the town, Josip Broz Tito paid his respects at the statue of Nikola Karev in Kruševo, laying a wreath there. Slavko Dimevski published a narrative historical novel of Karev's life in 1971 (Dimevski 1971), and in an edited volume published in 1973 entitled *The Epic of Ilinden*, Karev was the subject of one chapter, where he was called the organizer of the Kruševo Republic (Ivanovski 1973). An edited volume on Karev's life and work appeared in 1977 with Tito listed as the editor, and with pictures of Tito's visit to Kruševo. The caption to the picture of Tito's wreath-laying calls Karev the president of the Kruševo Republic; the volume included a reprint of Ivanovski's 1973 essay, referring to Karev more cautiously as the Republic's organizer (Tito [ed.] 1977:8, 9). In a speech at the Ilinden monument in 1978, Blagoj Popov, president of the Executive Committee of the Assembly of the Socialist Republic of Macedonia, called Nikola Karev the socialist president of the Kruševo Republic (*Nova Makedonija* 3 August 1978). The 1980s account of the Battle of Mečkin Kamen mentioned earlier, which called Gjorǵi Karev a traitor, also called Nikola Karev the president of the Kruševo Republic, as did a published volume listing all the monuments in the Socialist Republic of Macedonia published in 1986 (Topuzoski 1986; Trajkovski 1986).

The culmination of Karev's re-elevation to a central place in Macedonian history was reached at the end of the 1980s, when journalists from the newspaper *Nova Makedonija* raised the issue of Nikola Karev's remains, still languishing in the basement of the town museum where they had been placed in 1953. A campaign was undertaken to redress this situation, which culminated in a solemn ceremony conducted in early April of 1990 and attended by representatives of the Macedonian government. Karev's remains were transferred from their basement storage to a new sarcophagus inside the Ilinden monument on Gumenja. The transfer preceded the commemorative activities planned for 28 April that year, which would mark the eighty-fifth anniversary of Nikola Karev's death. Present were three senior Skopje political figures—Tito Beličanec, Savo Klimovski, and Jovan Trepenovski—as well as the president of the Kruševo assembly, Vasko Pavlovski. *Nova Makedonija* carried the story of the reinterment on its front page, and claimed credit for its own investigative staff in bringing the event about.[11]

Also present were surviving members of the Karev family, including Miše Karev, Gjorǵi's son. He is quoted in the story as giving thanks that dignity had been restored to the president of the Kruševo Republic, and to the Karev family which had, in his words reported in the article, "for long years been victim to arbitrary and deliberate contempt, while their initiatives to resolve the problem of the mortal remains of Karev had been thwarted for many years" (*Nova Makedonija* 12 April 1990). Noted also was the presence of a new generation of Karevs: Nikola's *vnuci* Gligur, Ziska, and Danica.[12]

The socialism which had been so central a part of Nikola Karev's persona in Yugoslav recollection was absent in this ceremony. Its spirit, it could be argued, was driven out by the Orthodox rites with which Karev's remains were committed to their new resting place, conducted by a team of three priests. The new marble sarcophagus was designed by Iskra Grabul, who had collaborated with her husband Jordan in the original design of the monument. She told *Nova Makedonija* at the time that besides introducing a sacral element, the sarcophagus was carefully integrated into the broader artistic conception of the space. In an interview in 1992, she offered a rather fuller commentary. Nikola Karev for her remained an international figure, whose goal was to have all nationalities live together peacefully. The Christian reburial, in the context of the humanism represented both by her impression

Figure 16: Ilinden Memorial Complex: Inside the Spomenik, after 1990. Nikola Karev's final resting place.

of Karev and the monument she and her husband had created, struck her as faintly ridiculous. As in the initial design phase, she had found herself at loggerheads with others' opinions. They had wanted to put the sarcophagus in the center of the cupola, as if trying to recreate the layout of Tito's mausoleum. She had insisted that it stand to one side. She confirmed that the new square tombstone did work in the overall shape of the monument; she took a chip off one side, though, to give a dynamic twist (figure 16).

After presiding over the ceremony the senior priest, Boris Angelovski, reiterated Miše Karev's comment, that a way had been found to pay respect to Nikola Karev, whom he called "our first Macedonian President" (*Nova Makedonija* 12 April 1990). Little more, it seems, can be done to further bring together or synthesize the symbolic and material components of his legacy, which are now concentrated on Gumenja, and thereby reaffirm the centrality of that location in Macedonia's history. Ballas's account of 1903, as described in chapter 4, had Karev giving funeral orations for his fallen comrades in the different graveyards in town. Karev escaped Kruševo's destruction, and died fifteen months later trapped by Turkish forces in Eastern Macedonia. After an extended period of ambiguity induced by his historical ties to Bulgaria, Karev's life, work, and death have been brought together by an extended period of synthesis, and now all are commemorated on Gumenja.

THE GULI CONUNDRUM

The second most prominent figure from Kruševo 1903, Pitu Guli, has had a less turbulent afterlife. His history has been written in fairly straightforward manner: a Kruševo native, he had been imprisoned by the Turks in Asia Minor for many years. He had worked as a labor migrant, or pečalbar, an innkeeper and a stockman, and was thirty-eight at the time of the Uprising. He was the leader of a band, or četa, and it was his initiative that ended the stalemate at the Turkish barracks, when he orchestrated the use of petroleum to set fire to the building and force the garrison out into the open. His main activities during the next few days were military, but he also appears to have been involved in obtaining and transporting stores into the town from outside. Before the battle on Mečkin Kamen, he sent some of his followers away, and in various versions he encouraged others to make their escape once the outcome was set. He fought heroically, and many of the songs that record his last stand suggest that he followed the practice of other insurgents and saved his last bullet for himself.[13] By one means or another, according to local versions, his remains were brought back to the town by a female relative and buried.[14] They now lie in the Partisan graveyard on Gumenja, below the Ilinden monument. Guli's stand on Mečkin Kamen was quickly celebrated in folklore, and his local fame was sufficient that the first Partisan contingent formed in Kruševo in 1941 bore his name. Throughout the postwar Yugoslav period, he has been presented as a *junak*, perhaps best glossed as "champion." In 1948, a memorial plaque was put on his house and the first monument placed on Mečkin Kamen. His name appears in the national anthem of Macedonia, immediately after that of Goce Delčev. Firmly linked to the battle on Mečkin Kamen (though not physically buried there), his place in national commemoration at first sight appears stable and secure.

Closer examination, however, reveals a certain lack of definition even here. One property that has changed, for example, has been the spelling of his name. In different periods and in different sources he has been referred to as Pitu, Pito, or Dimitrios, and as Guli, Gule, or Gulev. The difference in name has connotations for his imagined national affiliation. George Ditsias, writing in 1905, presented him as Dimitrios Gouli: wholly and inescapably Hellenic. Pitu Guli is more often identified as Vlah. His mother's family, in the popular record, had come from Albania to Kruševo, and so he has been claimed as Albanian.[15] Calling him Gulev slavicizes him into a Bulgarian or (ethnic) Macedonian mold. The *-ev* version was used in some early post-war newspaper accounts and in some of the autobiographies submitted by applicants for Ilinden pensions.

The question of Pitu Guli's loyalties or affiliations has not been affected by the activities of his surviving relatives, in part because their own activities are less well documented. In folklore, Guli is commemorated for his alleged prioritization of the struggle over family ties. One story describes him as taking leave from his wife and four children by saying, "Woman, the mountain is our mother, my rifle my wife, and bullets my children!" (Vražinovski 1981:273).[16] The crucial activity of female kin in assuring his proper burial has already been noted. Of his two sons, one goes wholly undiscussed in Kruševo. Elsewhere, Nikola Guli is reported to have been an active member of the Internal Macedonian Revolutionary Organization (VMRO) in the years following the First World War. An account in a U.S.-based periodical stated that he fought in the Veles region, was captured by Serbian gendarmerie, and died in prison in Belgrade (Mihailov 1967:13).[17] The silence surrounding the inter-war activities of VMRO in the first Yugoslavia swallowed up Nikola altogether, erasing him from the record.

Pitu Guli's other son, Sterju, represents a different case, still recalled in Kruševo. He survived the first Yugoslavia and the Bulgarian occupation but was killed on the day of Kruševo's liberation in September 1944. According to oral testimony, he was a member of Kruševo's partisan detachment and armed with a British Sten submachine gun. Mass-produced, cheap, and angular, the Sten was notoriously unreliable, prone to jamming and misfiring. Two narratives placed Sterju in a café with his machine gun propped between his knees; it went off and he was shot through the heart. His body is buried with other partisan martyrs in the Gumenja graveyard (Trajkovski 1986:154).

The coincidence of an accidental death on the day that the town was liberated is striking. It becomes suspicious when reconsidered in the light of other oral and written sources indicating that, like Gjorǵi Karev, Sterju Guli worked for the Bulgarian occupation forces. One account in particular, Kirče Risteski's autobiography discussed in chapter 5, casts Guli as actively involved in the rooting out of communist activists in the town. One of the first activities of the "Pitu Guli" partisan detachment was an attack on the village of Pribilci on 6 August 1942 where they burned government records, seized weapons and ammunition, and held a meeting of villagers to advocate their cause (Kudžulovska 1970:650). At the end of the year, the Bulgarian authorities launched a strike against resistance in the town. As noted in chapter 5, Miše Eftimov was betrayed and, rather than surrender, he enacted Pitu Guli's slogan and killed himself with a grenade.[18]

Risteski and another activist from Kruševo, Manču Matak, went into hiding in the Risteski home, with a 24,000-leva reward for information leading to Risteski's capture. They were betrayed: Sterju Guli was part of the contingent that came to search the house, and he spoke to Risteski's mother in Vlah. If she revealed who was inside, he said, he would see that she was looked after; if she did not, the searchers would burn down the house. She refused to speak. Risteski managed to escape to Italian-occupied Kičevo. The next time he met Sterju was in August 1944, in Džer, when Sterju was a member of a partisan group. Risteski asked Guli what he was doing there, to which Sterju Guli reportedly replied, *"Pa znaeš kako e, site trgnale i red beše i jas da dojdam"*—"Well, you know how it is. Everybody had mobilized, so it was my turn to go, too." Sterju then went on to deny any involvement with the house search. When Risteski told him he had seen everything, Guli reportedly hung his head in shame and avoided Risteski from then on.

As Topuzoski denounced Gjorǵi Karev, so Risteski's account clearly reflected a deep personal animus against Sterju Guli, holding him to account for his willingness to work with the occupier and then switch sides as if nothing had happened. A different account is provided by others, who acknowledge Guli's official position with the Bulgarian occupation, but argue that he used that position to gain information and to warn people ahead of time that they were about to be arrested so they could make their escape. They suggest that members of the Guli family, like the Karevs, were actively recruited by the Bulgarian occupiers eager to lay claim to the legacy of Ilinden. As such, the Guli family was in a more difficult position than less well-known Ilindenci. Like Nikola Karev, Pitu Guli himself was the objective of Bulgarian claims in post-war history. According to one descendant, Pitu Guli's granddaughter in 1977–78 received from the Bulgarian government an offer to move to Bulgaria and live a life of ease there, if she would declare that Pitu Guli had been Bulgarian. The offer was not accepted.

Pitu Guli's inheritance, then, has some ambiguous and disputed components, some of which arise from his family connections. His own actions during the Uprising appear to offer little ground for reanalysis. He played a key role in the taking of the town and then died defending it. His death on Mečkin Kamen in particular has taken on mythic proportions, and remains the focus of remembrance. Its finality disables potential questions as to Guli's factional loyalties within the Revolutionary Organization, questions asked about others who survived longer. Guli's defiant stand also flatly denies any suggestion that he abandoned the town. Signaling refusal to compromise the ideals to which he had sworn loyalty, his death has proved more durable in popular memory than the lives of his progeny.

MEČKIN KAMEN IN QUESTION

Alternative accounts of events on Mečkin Kamen have been given, from the period immediately after Ilinden 1903 right up to the present. At the most basic level, the category of the confrontation that occurred proves to have been challenged. In contrast to Frederick Moore's account given in chapter 1, one report in the British consular archives gives the following version:

> [A] band of about 130 men, under one Pitou Ghoule, who had just succeeded in re-entering Kruševo with a quantity of flour from without, and had so lost touch with their comrades and were in such ignorance of the negotiations with Bakhtiar Pasha, were surrounded and cut up (Graves to O'Conor, Salonica 30 August 1903: FO 195/2157/422).

This contemporary account sketches the battle on Mečkin Kamen not as heroic defense, but as tragic blunder resulting from poor communication. Such an account robs Guli of agency, casting him and his followers as victims of a confrontation that they did not choose.

Uncertainty also surrounds the numbers given for those who died. Nikola Kirov-Majski reports that forty-eight died and six were wounded. These are only the victims he can name (1935:73). Biographies from the archives of the Ilinden Pension plan give numbers between twelve and eighty. Several pension-seekers claim that they were in Guli's četa to begin with and were able to slip away—a piece of information that, if true, should modify the image of a beleaguered band of brothers surrounded on a rocky outcrop.

In Kruševo today, most people agree that a battle took place in which Guli and members of his četa marched out from the town to oppose an advancing Turkish force, and they put the number of dead between fifty and eighty. However, the debate over the sequence of events which led to this battle is still very much alive. I heard at least four versions, each of which paints Guli in a different light. These four versions, and the representation of Guli they contain, can be summarized as follows:

1. Guli the (Macedonian) national patriot
Pitu Guli quarreled with Nikola Karev because the latter said they were fighting for Bulgaria while Pitu was fighting for Macedonia. Pitu declared that they had not begun the Uprising to leave the Macedonian population to face the consequences, and told the members of his četa that they could escape now, or follow him to Mečkin Kamen to die.

This was told by various people: a variant form substitutes "Kruševo" for "Macedonia." A descendant of Guli expanded the basic narrative, which casts Guli and Karev as adversaries, to assert that Guli was fed tales of Turkish savagery by Karev and this explains Guli's own ruthlessness in setting fire to the barracks and his unwillingness to compromise with them.

2. Guli the (Vlah) nationalist

Pitu Guli had resolved to die on Mečkin Kamen, fighting the Turks. However, he did not want other Vlahs to be killed, and so he sent the Vlahs in his četa home and took only Bulgarian villagers to their deaths on Mečkin Kamen.

I was told this version by a stalwart champion of Vlah heritage and identity. He believed that the Uprising in Kruševo was primarily Vlah in character. His version of events on Mečkin Kamen, accordingly, is partly driven by a need to explain why Kirov-Majski's list of the fallen included a majority of villagers with Slavic names and, other than Guli, no Vlahs from the town.

3. Guli the one responsible vojvod.

Guli went to Mečkin Kamen to hold off the enemy from the town. However, the other bands abandoned their posts making his position untenable.

This version complements the first narrative, emphasizing Guli's patriotism and loyalty to the cause. It also exists in a variant form which is less critical of the other bands, suggesting instead that they were ordered to make their escape, while Guli's band, as one of the better disciplined, was given the assignment of covering their retreat.

4. Guli the irresponsible bandit

Guli got drunk, had to be pulled out of a *kafeana* to attend the meeting of the vojvods, had a blazing row with Nikola Karev, and set out on his horse for Mečkin Kamen. A majority of his men deserted on the way, sensing that they were doomed, and so the number who died was comparatively small.

I was told this version by a Macedonian in the town. It provides a rationalization for the variation in the numbers of casualties, as people either give the number of people who left the town with Guli or the number who were still with him when he reached Mečkin Kamen.[19]

More people in Kruševo subscribe to versions 1 and 3 than to 2 and 4. All seem designed to deal with potential discrepancies in the historical record often left unexamined. The minimal explanation for Mečkin Kamen, mentioned earlier, is that it represents Guli's refusal to compromise his total committment to the slogan "freedom or death." This interpretation is offered in the scholarly volume *The Epic of Ilinden* (Vishinksi [ed.] 1973) and in the feature film *Republika na Plamen* (*Republic Ablaze*) made in 1969 by the state-sponsored production company, Vardar Film. In both, Guli presents to his fellow leaders a simple question: What is the point of making a Republic if we do not defend it? As part of a national mythology, taken in isolation, it is a compelling expression of principle. However, despite the folkloric and commemorative attempt to "zoom in" on the glory of his individual last stand, two potential questions arise when the lens widens. Pitu Guli was a heroic leader but a good leader always tries to save his followers by sacrificing himself. Why did so many die with him? Conversely, Pitu Guli was only one of several heroic leaders. Why did none of the others choose to sacrifice themselves?

The different stories outlined above answer these core questions with different readings of individual intentions and beliefs. In the first two, Guli chooses death for himself, but permits the survival of his *loyal* followers—in the first those who share his ideal, in the second those of his ethnicity. In the first, those who die with him have chosen to do so and thus are also heroes; in the second, they are mere walk-ons in his personal last stand, to whom he feels no special commitment. In the third account, Guli and his followers die because their own commitment to the ideals of the Uprising is greater than that of others. The first and third stories thus highlight the failure of the other leaders to live up to the standard set by Guli. In these accounts, the individual heroic status of Guli emerges from juxtaposition with others, notably Nikola Karev, whose reputations are tarnished.

The fourth story presents a radically different way of dealing with questions about Guli's status as hero, by simply dissolving them. Casting Guli as a clueless drunk flies in the face of the conventional narrative. Its particular appeal is that it permits a narrator to preserve the motif of the quarrel, and to accommodate both the different accounts of the size of Guli's band and the otherwise inconvenient survivor narratives, without diminishing the commitment of others involved in the Ilinden Uprising and Kruševo's temporary liberation. Nikola Karev in particular emerges from this story with moral rectitude and seriousness of purpose, while Guli's band appears as neither disloyal nor mindless, but rather heroes led by a buffoon.

Taken together, these stories demonstrate the greater knowledge of local history that people in Kruševo have. They are rooted in detail that has been marginalized in the official accounts of 1903, but has proved tenacious in the stories circulating in the town. Where the "national" version of events takes for granted the unity of the Ilinden Uprising, these local narratives record the debates over purpose and methods that were an integral part of it. In each case, then, the people who tell these tales reveal that they know more about the past than many of their fellow citizens in Macedonia.

Yet the stories simultaneously reveal that this superior knowledge has not been distilled into an authoritative and locally agreed-upon version. Although most people in Kruševo are certain that Guli was not Bulgarian or Greek, the question of what he definitively "was" in terms of *poteklo*, or descent, remains in dispute. At least one side of his family was Vlah, from territory now part of Albania. On the other side of the family, some assert that his ancestors may have been Albanian speaking. But this does not place him definitively; for in Kruševo, there are some people with Vlah poteklo who identify themselves as Macedonian, as well as people whose grand-parents spoke Albanian as their first language but consider themselves Vlah. Pitu Guli's absolute membership of a single ethnic group, then, if understood by a metaphor of "blood," remains elusive. Some people remain committed nonetheless to assigning him to one of these categories. This demonstrates a form of zero-sum reckoning with respect to the past, in which Guli's own identity must be fixed in terms of categories that have become distinct in the period since he lived and died.

This zero-sum reckoning is also evident in the way in which these stories reflect starkly adversarial evaluations of different personalities in the Ilinden Uprising in Kruševo. In the four stories laid out above, commemorative value appears to be measurable only in discrete quanta. If Guli's activities and attitudes deserve glory, then Karev's do not. Conversely, if greater honor is sought for Karev's legacy, then Guli's is questioned. As suggested earlier, this phenomenon appears to be a product of the desire to include detail in accounts of the events of 1903. By skating over the detail, the national narra-tive heaps honor on the memory of both men. Those who have more infor-mation at their disposal and feel a responsibility to incorporate it into their accounts of the past find it harder to do so.

RESOLVING DILEMMAS

Some people in Kruševo deal with awkward details of the past by choosing one heroic figure at the expense of another. Many in the town, though, de-plore this approach. Their reaction can be explained in part by the similarity that these partial accounts of 1903 bear to the denunciations that circulated after the Second World War. As in that period, these accounts are not com-plete fabrications, but arrange fact in a way that throws suspicion or doubt on the moral worth and activity of others who are thus cast as enemies of an imagined collectivity of "the people." The stories rely on discrediting others to increase the stature of the teller, who is in this scenario constructed as acting directly on behalf of the broader community. Such practice is in-herently divisive when critics and criticized, denouncer and denounced, or hero and villain are members of the same community. It is even more divi-sive when attempts to establish moral superiority by these means are traded back and forth between two or more sides of a shared story. It is for this reason that those people in Kruševo with a commitment to the town's unity in the present and the past strive to resynthesize the components of a fractious history. Their resolution of the problems posed by the resilient motifs of the relationship between Karev and Guli does not retreat from complexity. Rather, it relies on an encompassing symbol of principled practice in Kruševo in 1903 now known as the Kruševo Manifesto.

Nikola Karev's status in Macedonian national history is thoroughly interwoven with the provisional government in Kruševo that he is now considered to have led. One aspect of this government that received much emphasis in Yugoslav Macedonian historiography and commemorative practice was its multi-national nature. The committee of six townspeople that Macedonian historians identified as the executive council of the government is generally described as having two members from each of the three national groups in the town. The committee stood for a larger assembly of sixty people, which is recorded as including twenty people from each of the groups.

How those three groups can be labeled, of course, can be disputed, and depends largely on the ways in which "national group" is defined. If church categories of the time are used, then the three major groups were Patriarchists, Exarchists, and Romanianists—the first using Greek in church, the second Bulgarian or Church Slavonic, and the last the Vlah language. All were Orthodox, though the Greek church labeled its rivals, which recruited among its flock, as schismatic or heretical. If the "language of the home" rather than the "language of worship" is taken as determining identity, the groups might be classified as Vlah, Macedo-Bulgarian, and Albanian, with the footnote that the latter group had been largely assimilated by the first. The difference highlights the fact that in Kruševo in 1903, "Greek" was available as a category of "high" culture, and Albanian as a category of "low," while Macedo-Bulgarian-Slavonic and Roumano-Vlah were available as both.[20]

Yugoslav Macedonian historiography since the Second World War took the latter categories, used in the work of Nikola Kirov-Majski, and translated them. Where he had referred to Bulgarians, Vlahs, and Albanians, and asserted that the latter two groups included those he called Grkomans, historians and others spoke of Macedonians, Vlahs, and Orthodox Albanians. This demonstrated a concern to make the Republic intelligible to Macedonian readers in the present, and to fit it into Yugoslav and Macedonian history by dismissing the Greek cultural presence in the town as alien and colonial, by vehemently denying the suggestion of Bulgarian agency, and by asserting the participation of different groups in a spirit of brotherhood and unity. Some accounts went so far as to blur the line between the Christian Albanians of the town, a disappearing group in 1903, and the Muslim Albanians of nearby villages, asserting that the latter were also supporters of the Republic's ideals.[21]

The institutions of the Republic in Kruševo thus linked Macedonians of 1903 with Yugoslavs of 1944 and beyond. In the literature of Socialist

Yugoslavia, the ten days of August 1903 were connected with the Paris Commune in 1871 and thus cast as a period of world-historical significance, which simultaneously highlighted the endurance and the efficacy of the collective will of Macedonia's inhabitants. The existence of the Republic also transfigured Guli's last stand, making clear that this was not a mere fracas or product of braggadocio, but a conscious and principled defense of an ideal that had, albeit briefly, been realized.

The Republic of Kruševo has thus been an important resource for those anxious to find proof of Macedonian solidarity. Its commemoration nonetheless poses a particular challenge akin to that outlined by Benedict Anderson in *Imagined Communities* (1991). There he notes that whereas tombs of the unknown national soldier—the self-sacrificial hero—are commonplace, memorials to political ideals, whether liberalism or Marxism, are not so easily constructed. Mečkin Kamen quickly became the basis for folkloric recall, and appears to fit the template of last-ditch, desperate defense that inspires subsequent generations. Thermopylae, Masada, Kosovo field, the Alamo, and Verdun are just some of its kindred symbols, all identified by their association with a particular place.[22] Living by the sword and dying by the sword, in the masculinist mode of national memory, provide good purchase for commemoration—better, in general, than the constructive actions of others who make such direct action meaningful, by giving it a purpose.

HISTORY MADE MANIFEST

Where institution-building triggers its own mythology, it leaves tangible documentary traces. In the canons of English and U.S. history, the acts of signing the Magna Carta and the Declaration of Independence, respectively, are treasured moments. The transformation of ideals or principles into written form is arguably an even more effective way to exert influence over those yet to be born. In the case of Kruševo, the key source for the documentary traces of the Republic is the work of Nikola Kirov-Majski. He did not confine his efforts to the genres of history or autobiography, but also wrote dramatic works with historical themes.

One of the most famous of his theater plays, entitled *Ilinden*, was written in 1924, and purports to describe the activities of the revolutionary organization in Kruševo in 1903. In act 2, scene 2 a character called "the Teacher," generally considered to represent Kirov-Majski himself, reads to Nikola Karev a text which will be a proclamation to the "Turkish" people. At the end of the speech, Karev tells the teacher to translate the text into Turkish and lithograph it, and in the morning they will send it to the local villages (Kirov-Majski 1991:75). In his historical work, Kirov-Majski records the experience of one of the parliamentarians, Taško Hristov, who delivered a letter to the village of Aldanci, watched the Muslim villagers gather in the square to hear it read, and then received the answer (Kirov-Majski 1935:56–58). The letter written and read by the teacher in the play, and the answers transcribed by Kirov-Majski, are now key documentary sources for the Kruševo Republic's ideals, and its communications with others.[23]

The text that the teacher reads to Karev in the drama was republished in Skopje in 1968 in four languages—the original Macedonian, Serbo-Croatian, Russian, and English—as the Kruševo Manifesto (Apostolski et al. [eds.] 1968).[24] The text reads as follows:

Brothers, countrymen, dear neighbors!

We, ever your friends from beautiful Kruševo and its pleasant villages, and without regard for differences of religion, nationality, sex, and conviction, rise today to defend ourselves from our common enemies. We can endure no longer the tyranny of the *murtats*, thirsty for blood and hungry for human flesh, who seek to pit us all against one another, to make us beggars, and to make our dear, rich country Macedonia a desert, and so we rise today to set ourselves free.

You know very well that we are not evil, and you understand that it is suffering that makes us risk all, to live humanly or to die heroically. Because we have lived in this country like brothers since the time of our ancestors, we consider you as our brothers, and we wish to remain so forever. We have not taken up arms against you, for that would be shameful. We have no quarrel with the peaceful, industrious and honorable Turks who earn their livelihood as we do, through blood and sweat. Such men are our brothers, we have lived with them, and we say again, we seek only to live humanly or die heroically!

We have not risen to kill and to rob, to burn and to steal. We have had enough of monstrous crimes, committed by countless scavengers on our poor, bleeding Macedonia. We have not risen to convert people to Christianity, to dishonor your mothers and sisters, wives and daughters: you must know that your possessions, your life, your belief, your honor are for us as dear as our own. We have taken up arms only to safeguard our property, our lives, our beliefs and our honor. We are not disloyal to the country that gave us our life, we are not robbers and plunderers, but revolutionaries, sworn to die for rights and liberty. We rise against tyranny and slavery. We fight now, and we shall keep on fighting, against the exploiters, bandits, evil-doers, and plunderers, against the violence done to our honor and beliefs, and against those who are sucking our sweat and exploiting our work.

Do not fear us or our villages—we intend you no harm. For not only do we think of you as brothers, but we feel for you as brothers, for we know that you too are slaves as we are, slaves of the sultan and his pashas, slaves of the landed and the rich, slaves of the terrorists and evil-doers, who spread fire across the land and whose acts compel us to rise and to fight for rights and liberty, for life itself.

Join us in this fight! Join us, Muslim brothers, in order to attack our common enemies. Join us under the flag of "Autonomous Macedonia." Macedonia is our mother and calls for help. Join us to break the chains of the slavery, to put an end to suffering and pain, to stem the streams of blood and tears. Come to us, brothers, and we will unite our souls and hearts, and allow our descendants to work peacefully and to move forward together!

Our dear neighbours! We know that you, being Turks, Albanians and Muslims, might think that the empire is yours, and that you are not slaves, because there is no cross on the flag, but star and moon. The time will come when you realize that it is not so. But if that time has not yet come, and you will not join us and declare that you oppose the sultan's tyranny, we will not be angry, or hate you. You are still our brothers, in our homeland and its suffering. We shall still fight for you as well as for ourselves, and if we must, we will die under our flag for your liberty and ours, and for your rights and ours.

"Liberty or death" is written on our foreheads and on our bleeding flag. We have raised this flag, and there is no turning back. If you consider us your brothers and wish us well; if you think to live with us in the future, as you have lived up to now; if you are honorable and faithful sons of our dear mother Macedonia, then grant us this one great boon. Do not join the enemy. Do not take up arms against us. And do not terrorize Christian villages.

God bless our holy fight for rights and liberty!

Long live the fighters for liberty and all the brave sons of Macedonia!

Hurrah for Autonomous Macedonia![25]

In the 1968 edition of the Manifesto, accompanying notes provide an account of the provenance of the text that broadly follows that described by Kirov-Majski in the play. The Manifesto is described as being the text of a letter that the temporary government composed and sent to the neighboring Muslim Albanian villages, to try and gain the support of those villagers at best, and at least to secure their nonintervention in the confrontation between VMRO and the Ottoman government. It is recognized, then, as a document written for distribution to a specific audience, that of the non-Christian villages around Kruševo. It served, in other words, a particular and immediate function: to try and neutralize the population of those villages. Beyond seeking to impress upon that audience the grounds for solidarity—their limited rights in land and the onerous Ottoman government—it also sought to stress that the insurgents of Kruševo had no quarrel with their Muslim neighbors, but only with the Ottoman state. As such it could be said to represent the development of a strand in VMRO activism away from its ethnic origins, with a membership made up of people referred to at the time as Bulgars. The emphasis on peaceful relations with neighbors is also the theme of one of the few pieces of Ilinden folklore to feature Nikola Karev, who purportedly chastised a četa member for stealing sheep during the Uprising (Vražinovski

1981:265). It is notable also that Nikolaos Ballas, generally hostile toward the insurgents, nonetheless admits that after the initial fracas the town was governed in an orderly manner (1905:42–43). The Manifesto can be taken as demonstrating both the vision and the practical policy of a central authority. This quality made it a powerful component in the Yugoslav Macedonian imagination of the past.

What the 1968 edition of the Manifesto made clear was that the document as it exists now—in the Kruševo dialect of Macedonian—is a product of Kirov-Majski's creative labor in the 1920s. As Ljuben Lape, elder statesman of the Macedonian historical profession, pointed out in an early article which presented the text of the speech along with the Turkish answers, the originals have never been located (Lape 1953). What Kirov-Majski also suggests in the play, in some sense a forerunner of the genre of docudrama, is that the document only ever circulated in Turkish; the Macedonian version serves a dramatic function, and within the play is a template for a proclamation to people outside the boundaries of liberated Kruševo.

In contemporary Kruševo, though, the context of the document has been given a range of curious inflections. A common feature in narratives of Kruševo's period of liberation now is the reading by Nikola Karev of the Manifesto to the townspeople. This is considered variously to have taken place on Gumenja, where the insurgents had their military headquarters, or at the Greek school, now the site of the Monopol tobacco factory, where the government, with Dinu Vangel at its head, sat. These two sites were associated with the government of Kruševo in the period. A third site sometimes offered is the balcony of a house that overlooks the main road to Prilep. This balcony was the location used in the 1969 film *Republika na Plamen*, and reportedly, in a popular dramatized TV account of the Ilinden Uprising broadcast in the 1970s.

There is no evidence in the primary sources that any of these readings took place. Nikola Karev did address the people of Kruševo: in the accounts of both Ballas and Kirov-Majski, he presided over a funeral service held on 27 July o.s. (9 August) for insurgents who fell in the original taking of the town. Ballas, as noted in chapter 4, recorded the words of Karev's speech, which he saw as highlighting the Bulgarian quality of the Uprising. This documented event is not a feature of people's accounts of what occurred in 1903. What was, in contemporary accounts, a religious rite conducted before a part of the population to honor those killed in fighting has been transposed into a civic rite of solidarity, in which a set of shared ideals was articulated. In this move, the citizens of Kruševo in 1903 are retrospectively united as proto-Yugoslavs, as the differences which tore at their community at the time are deemphasized.

The other dimension of the rereading of 1903 is the close association made between Nikola Karev and the Manifesto. This has certainly been encouraged by the emphasis on his intellectual qualities and his pre-Uprising career as a teacher, and was carried to a logical conclusion in a Macedonian Radio broadcast on the anniversary of Karev's death in 1993, which referred to him as the Manifesto's author.[26] In Kruševo, most people discount this version, acknowledging Kirov-Majski as the author. They insist nonetheless that the Manifesto was first written in 1903, and take for granted that Karev did read the Manifesto to the townspeople. The effect of this association is to emphasize that Karev was not Bulgarian and that he did not address himself to Bulgarians. Rather, he was a spokesman for a vision of Macedonia which united its peoples, in the words of Kirov-Majski's document, "regardless of religion, nationality, sex, and conviction."

Such memories of Karev's speech, focused by the impact of dramatic works in which it has featured, have largely displaced rival versions in which he appears as narrowly pro-Bulgarian. In official speeches as early as 1948, the Republic was at the forefront of celebration, and Karev's place as president was noted. While his mortal remains lay unburied, Karev's histori- cal persona appears to have functioned in alchemical fashion: the undoubted fact of his existence gave substance to the less tangible Republic and Mani- festo which became so central a part of the proud legacy of Kruševo. It could be argued that the eventual interment of Karev's remains in 1990 served a similar purpose, invigorating a moribund monument by injecting personality into what had been abstract and anonymous. Alongside the press description of the 1990 ceremony, the Manifesto text was reprinted, reaffirm- ing its existence and its connection to Karev and to a particular time, place, and event—his reading it during August 1903 on Gumenja. Thus 1990 saw a meeting of individual and state, and of action and ideal, in which all the constituents gained status and legitimacy from their juxtaposition.[27]

Karev's reburial took place in a political climate satirized by Vladimir Čupeski in a polemical work on the ironies of Macedonian politics in the Yugoslav period (Čupeski 1993:125). One aspect he alludes to is "necro- philia" which led to an outbreak of what might be called "remains-fetish- ism." He draws attention in the book to the return of Dimitrija Čupovski's body from Russia and the interment of Nikola Karev's remains in the Ilinden monument as key moments in a move toward populism verging on fascism. A similar act of renewed veneration of prominent figures of the past is ele- gantly described by Susan Gal (1991) who pointed to the multiple valencies that Bartok had for Hungarians. Macedonia's crop of historical figures is less well known, but the goal of such rituals appears to have been similar: to raise people's consciousness of a national past.

A more significant strand of concern with the past in Macedonia is "docu- ment-fetishism." The term was applied to Turkey by Berktay and Faroqhi ([eds.] 1992:109), who applied it to a particular branch of the historical profession. It is the object of Andrew Lass's study of the importance of early manuscripts in nineteenth-century Czech nationalism, and the concept could also describe the methods of the "scissors-and-paste" historians criticized by R. G. Collingwood as long ago as 1946 (Lass 1988; Collingwood 1946). In Macedonia, it is exhibited by a larger cross-section of the population, especially in their attitude toward the Kruševo Manifesto, which has acquired a sort of hyper-reality. In arguments and discussions I had with people in Kruševo, it appears to occupy a privileged place in their understanding of the events of 1903.[28]

The importance of the Manifesto as a keystone can be seen when one considers the various versions of Karev's behavior and motivation, set out above. After 1944 two state-sponsored identities competed to claim him, both drawing together a fairly coherent set of characteristics: language, residence, profession, parentage, and self-ascription. Within Kruševo, straight-forward disagreement persisted on what people heard him say in 1903. In the disambiguation of Macedonian from Bulgarian in the person of Nikola Karev, the notion of an independent political movement toward autonomy was central. The set of ideals expressed in the Manifesto constituted one index of the existence of such a movement. And for the particular construction of Macedonian national identity fostered in Yugoslav Macedonia, which invoked the mantra of "brotherhood and unity," the Manifesto lent credibility to claims that the Uprising was inclusive or integrative, drawing together members of different religious and language communities in a movement against injustice and oppression.

FREEDOM, DEATH, AND OTHER OPTIONS

As suggested above, the Manifesto indirectly affirmed the significance of Pitu Guli's last stand on Mečkin Kamen. Without the Manifesto and the Republic, Guli's fate can be cut down to human proportions, a product of error, ignorance, quarreling, treachery, or even drunkenness. His defiance can be considered to have brought ruin on Kruševo by provoking the enemy's rage and giving them an excuse to treat a defenseless town as a defended fortress. The Manifesto demonstrates instead the principles for which Guli fought and died. Its language of cooperation among national groups serves as a rebuke to those who would read into Guli's decision making the expression of oppositional ethnic identity.

The Manifesto also bridges a contrast between clarity and uncertainty that can be perceived between the two men, Guli and Karev. Guli marched into Kruševo and burned the Ottoman garrison out of its barracks. He marched out to Mečkin Kamen and fought against Ottoman forces. Ilinden 1903 did not bring liberty, and Guli died, thus embodying the Uprising's slogan. Karev governed Kruševo but also obeyed higher authority located in Smilevo. He oversaw liberation from Ottoman oppression, and the collection of a tax imposed on Kruševo's residents. He made public statements recognizing self-sacrifice for Macedonia and espousing the ideal of mass uprising and defiance, and then escaped Kruševo when defeat seemed inevitable, to fight another day.

In all contemporary accounts, then, Guli is impetuous, direct, and uncomplicated, where Karev can be read as far-sighted, calculating, and nuanced. A further key contrast is that Guli acted alone, following some personal sense of mission and giving others the opportunity to follow. His idealization of Macedonia displaced all other social ties, and any connections that he had with the broader revolutionary movement were vestigial. Karev, by contrast, was integrated into a larger hierarchy of revolutionary activism. He was subject to instructions from outside Kruševo during the Uprising and was a member of a socialist political movement that spanned Eastern Europe. The Smilevo high command's strategy and the socialist literature Karev and his brother Petruš brought to Kruševo were both dimensions that shaped his capacity and disposition for action.

Consistent in Guli's activities was a refusal to compromise. He took up arms for a cause and he died for that cause without ever engaging in an attempt to play part in politics or defining himself by the categories of others. He was an implacable enemy of the Ottoman state; what all the histories agree on is that he also, in the last days of Kruševo, came to oppose the withdrawal from Kruševo that Nikola Karev undertook. Guli's champions see him refusing to renege on a principle that he had understood to be sacred—a revolution for "freedom or death." His critics present him as blind to reason and the good of others. Each reading also presumes a particular interpretation of Karev's actions, whereby he oversees either strategic withdrawal or plunder and abandonment. Karev can be seen as a pragmatist motivated by his close ties to other activists, and by an awareness of processes beyond Kruševo's present. He can also be seen as a betrayer of the ideal of Macedonia and the people of Kruševo.

The collection of facts, half-truths, and rumors that were generated by the events of Ilinden 1903 in Kruševo can contribute to either of these versions. The nature of the insurgent requisitions, the words used by Nikola Karev, the extent of armed participation of people from the different parts of the town, and then the course and objective of negotiations with Bahtiar Pasha and the uneven distribution of destruction within Kruševo all present puzzles that can be solved by simple recourse to one narrative or the other, in which Guli and Karev are opposed.

These narratives are buttressed by the spatial geography of the town, where historically different language communities inhabited different quarters. In this regard, the unveiling of the new statue in 1983 on Mečkin Kamen counterbalances the memorial complex on Gumenja. Each has its own set of associations in which location and style index a whole set of other oppositions, between provincial town and state capital, Vlah and Macedonian, specific and direct, abstract and diffuse. Both demonstrate the significance of location in a town where family memories are so powerful.

Although implicated with particular locations in memory, the Kruševo Manifesto nonetheless can be argued to keep its place above the fray. Whatever its historical status, the Manifesto represents a site of presumed consensus in 1903 in which both Karev and Guli can be argued to have participated. Karev, as author or declaimer, set out the ideals as a program. He features as a member of an organization which pursued those ideals and which deployed a range of political strategies to achieve them. Guli can be seen as expressing more directly, in both his own multi-ethnic identity and his actions, the ideals that the Manifesto declares. Any disagreement between the two men, then, is one of method rather than aim and can be cast as historically insignificant in comparison to their participation in this profoundly common project.

The town of Kruševo was under the pressure of different states throughout the twentieth century, and different generations of residents faced economic ruin for reasons beyond their control. As a result of these pressures, a strong sense of community has survived in the town, even as the personnel have changed. Although there remain divisions and distinctions within the town, a core group of self-identified *Kruševčani* nonetheless share a set of values and histories, of meanings and memories, whose construction they attribute to their own community and through which they resist easy assimilation into a larger collectivity. They consider themselves Macedonians—but they do so on their own terms rather than on the terms offered by external authorities. Central to their vision of their history, arching over the individual historical figures and events associated with each, is the integrative and synthetic image of the Kruševo Manifesto. What the accounts of history in Kruševo that have been generated in recent years demonstrate is a local determination to maintain control of their past, rather than allow the state's version to go unanswered. Stories of monuments, heroes, and a document of doubtful provenance, as told and retold in Kruševo, reflect the resistance to simpleminded renditions of complex truths that ties this community together.

CHAPTER NINE

On the Brink of a New, Old World

RECASTING SOLIDARITY AFTER YUGOSLAVIA

THE REBURIAL of Nikola Karev in 1990 described in the previous chapter and dubbed by one Macedonian writer of the time as "necrophilia" (Čupeski 1993) was one of a set of public memorial practices conducted in Macedonia in the last years of Yugoslavia. The subsequent dissolution of the country and emergence of new political parties defining themselves as anticommunist led to a further round of reengagement with the past. Critical attention has been paid, in particular, to events of the 1940s and 1950s when the new Macedonian state was constituted. The circumstances under which the first leader of the 1944 constitutive assembly of ASNOM, Metodija Andonov-Čento, was imprisoned, died, and was subsequently written out of history, were discussed, and ideological intent quickly uncovered. Čento's autonomist agenda had not fit smoothly into the federal imagination of Yugoslav Macedonia. With the passing of that order, he was soon rehabilitated. Conventional accounts of the "accidental" death of the famous Macedonian poet, Kočo Racin at the hands of partisans were loudly disputed in public meetings, and calls were made for a reexamination of the facts of the case. As noted in chapter 7, rumors circulated that Macedonian soldiers who had refused orders to travel north to fight the retreating Germans on the Srem front lay in unconsecrated mass graves underneath Skopje's ruined medieval fortress. Similar events elsewhere also re-emerged into public view. In June and July 1996, the bodies of fifty citizens executed in January 1945 were exhumed near the village of Letevci, close to Veles (MILS NEWS 06/18/96, 07/08/96).

Katherine Verdery has argued that dead bodies serve in various parts of the post-socialist world as "sites of political conflict related to the process of reordering the meaningful universe" (1999:36). Among other functions, she suggests that attention to the named and nameless victims of former régimes is part of broader efforts of symbolic revitalization of community and moral order often spearheaded by nationalist political parties. Elsewhere in the former Yugoslavia, the "return to the past" often seemed intimately connected with violence. As Bette Denich and Robert Hayden have described, counting and recounting the dead from the slaughters perpetuated by Ustaše, Četniks, and Partisans on communities in Bosnia, Croatia, and Serbia began as a war between scholars, but spilled over into a calculus of scores that demanded settling (Denich 1994; Hayden 1994). Jasenovac, the concentration camp where Ustaše killed Serbs as well as Jews and Gypsies, remained an irritant to ideals of brotherhood and unity despite the efforts of Tito's government to transform its meaning. It also provided a key resource for anti-Croatian rhetoric among Yugoslavia's Serbs. Specific knowledge of past betrayals and violence was also maintained at the local level. In Bosnian villages in the 1990s, even where neighbors got along, family lore still recorded the names of those killed and of those who did the killing in the war of national liberation (Sudetic 1998: Bringa, personal communication).

In Kruševo, people have a phrase to describe how such detailed, intimate knowledge of the past endures. It is passed, they say, *od koleno na koleno*— from knee to knee, on the laps of successive generations. Within the sturdy walls of houses where a family might have lived for a century or more, grandparents would regale their children's children with stories different from those they might read in their history textbooks or hear in the speeches on Ilinden. It was in recording such stories that much of my time in Kruševo was spent, as young and middle-aged residents of the town took me to sit and talk with their elderly relatives. Often the tales they told would be deeply nostalgic, recounting a world that they and their listeners had lost, in which lives were organized around work with the town livestock, wedding parties, and journeys to far-off places.

As illustrated in chapter 5, former prosperity and how it had been taken away was sometimes the focus, which in turn drove accounts of the treachery or the opportunism of others. A majority of narrators, though, continued to focus on their town's vital place in the national past, and on its state-sanctified tradition of solidary cooperation between different groups. They saw the town's history, and their own collective and intimate acquaintance with former generations, as a particular asset. This sentiment was made concrete in an initiative undertaken shortly before my arrival in Macedonia in the spring of 1992. At the very moment when Macedonia's independence was being codifed, Kruševo sought to redefine its relationship with the newly formed state, calling for a "re-establishment of the Kruševo Republic" as a tourist and financial center which would operate as a customs free-zone. The comparisons that were evoked in informally distributed documentation were with San Marino, Andorra, Hong Kong—then still a British territory—Monaco, and Liechtenstein.[1]

The proposal proceeded far enough to become a constitutional provision that was voted on by the Parliament in Skopje. It failed by a narrow margin. It marked nonetheless a locally driven attempt to manage a transition which in other parts of the former Yugoslavia was accompanied by horrific violence, as "brotherhood and unity" was rejected as ideological fiction. Individuals and communities fought in the symbolic and the literal realms over how the country the slogan had sustained should be divided. Divisive nationalist rhetoric and action, which claimed legitimacy via longevity and the commonsense blurring of culture and politics, proved decisive in shaping the future of people in Croatia and Bosnia. In Macedonia's capital city Skopje, home to a heterogeneous population of Macedonians, Albanians, Turks, Roma, Serbs, and Vlahs, the same tendencies were manifest. Tensions increased between the Macedonian majority and the large Albanian minority, in particular. As Macedonians celebrated the political autonomy that Yugoslavia's break-up promised, Albanians saw long-established ties with Kosovo threatened, and little prospect of improved status in an independent Republic of Macedonia. As Greece raised questions over the name and the flag of the new state, newspapers and television screens carried images of flag-waving, placard-brandishing crowds filling the main square in downtown Skopje. Some Macedonian politicians called for the reunification of the Macedonian people, or narod, which since 1913 had been divided between Albania, Greece, Bulgaria, and various incarnations of Yugoslavia. They sought popular advantage by urging a complete break with the Yugoslav past. Such rhetoric further blurred the distinction between "Macedonian" as a term of civic and of ethnic belonging, and further alienated ethnic Albanian support for the new order.

As elsewhere in the former Yugoslavia, people in Kruševo were keenly aware of the radical and frequently violent change their country was undergoing. They followed the news avidly as Slovenia and Croatia seceded and war ensued, and their horror grew when Bosnia's independence triggered further violence. They watched as a new Macedonian constitution was drafted and negotiations undertaken in a variety of international fora to smooth Macedonia's own contested passage to statehood. Their responses, especially in the proposed plan for Kruševo's future, represent clearly some of the paradoxes that confronted many Macedonians at the end of Yugoslavia. The symbolic universe of Macedonian nationhood and statehood assembled in the course of Yugoslav rule remained important, even as a new sense of distinctiveness or separateness from larger narratives was asserted. This chapter maps out the ways in which people in Kruševo in the mid-1990s reassessed the past in ways that distinguished them from other former Yugoslavs. Faced with uncertainty as to the future, they were also mindful of the divisive potential of attention to events in their town's history. While some of the stories that emerged in this context make truth-claims and aspire to amend the historical record, more salient were attempts to draw on Kruševo's unique heritage in order to think beyond the cycles of retributive history.

RECLAIMING ECOLOGY

Kruševo's modern inhabitants, by and large, are proud of their town's long history. This is especially true for those "old Kruševo families" that boast residential longevity. They sometimes contrast themselves with *novljaci*, or relative newcomers, to the town.[2] For the most part, the "old" inhabitants live in houses that they or previous Kruševčani have built. Houses and plots changed hands in the past—as noted earlier, there was an exodus of self-identified Greeks in the aftermath of the Balkan Wars and First World War, and fluctuations in fortune have also affected individual Vlah and Macedonian families—but in many cases, those who live in a particular neighborhood now are the direct descendants of previous inhabitants. Chapter 8 presented the example of Nikola Karev's family, still resident at his old town address, although the large house has been split into two separate households. Elsewhere, Ilinden's memory likewise resides in stones and slates. The family of the man who made the cherry-tree cannons that entered into the lore of the Uprising, Borjar, are still in the town, and his house is still in family possession. In another home, I was told how it had been saved from the flames that consumed the lower part of the town in 1903, by its occupants keeping the walls damp with water from the nearby spring. The current household head showed me a cunningly concealed hiding place for small valuables behind the stove in the back room, which was put in for his ancestors by masons at the end of the nineteenth century.

Apart from the great building project represented by the Ilinden monument, the Yugoslav period also lies lightly on the physical fabric of the town. There are few new buildings in the heart of Kruševo. Below the church of St. Nikola, rebuilt in 1905 after it was gutted by fire in 1903, the main square is flanked by the gray concrete of the post office, a bank building, the municipal offices, and the *gradska kafana*, an institutional and little-loved restaurant/bar. Up from the church on the main thoroughfare where the main market is held there are other boxlike structures: a general store and a small apartment block. Steps from the church in the other direction, though, is a small cobbled street with tiny workshops and stores on each side. Here in 1993 one could still visit the "Red Star" shoemaker's workshop or look at the examples of work in the tinsmith's store.

The physical quality of space in much of Kruševo still powerfully evokes the past. Despite the fire and sack of 1903, and other more localized acts of destruction in subsequent years, the town still boasts houses over a century old, and many of the newer residences have been built in styles that do not immediately jar. From many of the vantage points within and above the town, one still sees a landscape of roofs, now perhaps more tile than slate, and can still see the aptness of the descriptions of a hundred years ago, that there is often barely room for a laden horse to pass between the houses. Between the three roads that enter the town from west, east, and south and feed the single main curving asphalt road, the town's thoroughfares are roughly paved and often steep pathways. Few people drive in the town, and little traffic passes through.

For some in the town, this relative paucity of state investment is regretted, as they view it as a part of the process which has made Kruševo into a backwater. Young people in particular, and often their parents, lament the lack of opportunity to build a professional career in the town. At the time of my main residence there, between 1992 and 1993, there was still a fair-sized young adult population, who had various forms of employment. The economic fallout of Yugoslavia's break-up had not yet reached the town, and various state-run enterprises continued to operate, most notably a plastics factory on the road to Prilep. The tobacco factory in the town and a large agricultural combine still provided employment opportunities. The town was the administrative center for a municipality, hosting local government and ministry offices and a variety of service industries, publicly and privately owned. Thus, despite people's expressed concerns, for the last thirty years the population of the municipality and the town had remained stable. So too have residential patterns. Some Muslims reportedly moved into Krusevo in the early 1990s, but it remains a town with a population of a little more than 5,000, of which a majority consider themselves ethnic Macedonians, and around 20 percent identify themselves as Vlahs. (See table 3.)

Nonetheless, people in Krusevo do consider that the town is slowly dying. For those seeking higher education, Skopje has always been a first choice; increasingly, it seems, young people from Kruševo move away permanently. They return only at weekends during the ski season or in the summer to escape the high temperatures that the capital now routinely experiences. At such times, and especially during the ten days of Ilinden celebrations in early August, the cafés and restaurants are full and the town comes to life. In midweek in autumn or spring, when Kruševo's weather can be wet, cold, and miserable, pathways deserted, and doors firmly closed against the elements, the attractions of life here are less obvious and the flight of young people wholly comprehensible.

For key players in the town's leadership, though, the relative marginality of Kruševo in the latter years of Yugoslavia and the largely symbolic nature of the state's involvement in more recent years left the community uniquely positioned to take advantage of changed circumstances in the 1990s. The plan for the "re-establishment of the Kruševo Republic" envisaged a future of financial autonomy based on two parallel developments. First, in material terms, it was envisaged that Kruševo's pastures could still support substantial stock, which could provide the basis for cheese- and yogurt-making, crafts once practiced in the town. At its heart, the proposal anticipated the revival of economic activities similar to those conducted before the Second World War and the building of the Monopol factory. Second, the document called for a repositioning of what Kruševo became during the Yugoslav period, a specialized tourist destination. The advocates of the plan projected a vision that the downtown area, its historical architecture largely intact, again be

TABLE 3
Census figures for Kruševo opština[a]

Year	Total	Macedonian	Muslim	Albanian	Turkish	Vlah	Others
1971	12,990	8,303	66	158	2,756	877	830
1981	13,220	8,026	1,840	910	1,505	795	144
1991	12,620	7,291	—	961	1,615	—	2,640
1994	12,005	6,694	—	2,750	664	891	1,006

[a]Opština-municipality.
[b]The category of Others includes Roms and Serbs who were not recorded separately and, in some years, Vlahs or Muslims.

filled with a range of artisan workshops providing high-quality specialist products. The niche envisaged was "high-end" consumer products—health foods, metalware, leather goods—while maintaining winter tourism as an attraction. But beyond this, and beyond Kruševo's status as a *spomen grad*, or heritage site, the ambition embodied in the comparisons with a variety of European micro-states (Nairn 1997) was that more general and internationally oriented commercial activities would sustain the town.

The document's drafters, then, turned the previous nondevelopment of Kruševo, a source of grumbling for many in the town, into an asset. Unencumbered by links to the broader Macedonian economy and the Yugoslav economy beyond it, Kruševo could, as it were, be "extracted" from its immediate context and quickly integrated into a wider world of global commerce. Expanding the plan, its backers saw in this repositioning a return to Kruševo's historical roots. They drew, for example, on the description written by the Austrian consul, J. G. Hahn in 1858, to illustrate what had been and what might be again. Hahn wrote vividly of the town's wealth and industry; he was told by the town president that Kruševo had thirty-two *hans* (inns), ten smithies in which copper, tin, and iron were worked, eight workshops for tallow where 30,000 sheep and goats were slaughtered and processed each year, and three market days a week. The town sent its products to Constantinople, Salonica, Skopje, and Bitola (Hahn 1858, in Trposki 1986:76). In 1905, older men in Kruševo recalled a twice-yearly caravan to Vienna that brought back Western commodities (Brailsford 1906:177), and the town was still linked to commercial centers abroad in 1911 (Ballas 1905, Lebrun and Voinescu 1911). Even in the 1990s, elderly residents still recalled the town's cosmopolitanism in the 1930s, when the wealthiest families might shop in London or Paris, and have business connections with various transnational corporations. In the past, Kruševo's new dreamers could argue, the town had been tied more closely to world cities than to the rest of the country in which it was located. Could that not be the case again?

RITUALS OF SOLIDARITY AND RESPECT

In schematic outline at least, the proposal seemed plausible. Small shops are still open, and elderly men still employ their skilled trades, or zanaeti, that they learned as apprentices half a century ago. The term zanaet is also applied to more up-to-date professions, for example, radio and electronic repair, or mechanical knowledge. Those with mastery of any such skill are routinely called majstor.[3] Trades and stores have been handed down within a family: Šula Gabel's son-in-law now keeps his store, and Kruševo's barbershop is run by a descendant of the barber who contributed extensively to Golab's account of Kruševo's Vlah dialect (Golab 1984). As well as the large hotels on the edges of the town, several people let out rooms during the ski season. A framework of human and material resources has been maintained in the town on which a more ambitious body of cottage industries, retail outlets, and tourist facilities fuelled by the return to a pastoral economy might be built with new investment.

The proposal also highlights the persistence of a more generalized, positive orientation toward the "old ways." The particular skills involved in the practice of zanaeti continued to command admiration from younger generations. While in Kruševo, I assisted my landlady's nephew in the demolition of the old Sekula family house, described in chapter 3. He had worked an extended stint in construction in Switzerland to make money for this project, and planned the construction of a new, stylish chalet-type house.[4] He had always struck me as a pragmatic realist, seldom tempted by flamboyant gestures, and always attuned to finding the most rational approach to problems. Yet I learned from him that in the course of construction of the new house, an old ritual was carried out under the supervision of the old majstor he contracted to undertake the skilled work. A lamb was killed and its blood dripped at the four corners of the house; a container of oil was then buried at each of the four corners. The lamb's head was buried in the foundations.

Such a practice might seem easy confirmation of what some are always ready to label "Balkan primitivism," whether for good or ill. It certainly has precedents and parallels elsewhere in the Balkans, where ethnologists have traced stories of animals and humans being buried in the foundations of buildings and bridges to ensure success in construction, and long life for the structure (Dundes [ed.] 1996). But the ritual can also be interpreted as indexing respectful attitudes toward established ritual practices perceived as integral to craftsmanship. Residents identified a generalized orientation of this ilk when they described their town as a *zanaetski grad*, and thus distinguished Kruševo from other towns in the Republic of Macedonia. They often drew a particular pointed contrast with Skopje, the capital, where so many of Kruševo's younger generations lived and worked. A common criticism of the way in which business was conducted there, especially politics, was to refer to it as *improvizirana*, or improvised. The term rebukes those who undertake action that is ill-thought out, and for which they have no specialized training. In Kruševo, respect is given to those who do not rely on posturing to make their living, but draw instead on skills and knowledge accumulated through hard work.

This conservative cast also underlies the persistence of a variety of other rituals in Kruševo, many of which have a more explicitly Christian Orthodox basis. On the morning of the Saturday before Easter's Holy Week, young girls dressed in traditional costume go door to door in small groups, without adult supervision. They are known as the *Lazarki*, because this Saturday is St. Lazarus's Day. They sing two different songs, depending upon whether a child has been recently born in the house they are visiting: in each case, they express the wish for the house to enjoy the blessing of future children. They are given eggs and candies. Although not unique to Kruševo, to outsiders from the United States or even from bustling, sprawling Skopje, the strolling of the Lazarki seems like a custom from a time gone by, sustained against the odds in this place by the absence of vehicle traffic and the common perception that the town is a safe place for unaccompanied children.[5]

A greater cross-section of the town's population participates in another religious ritual on the Day of the Dead. The day itself is the first Sunday in June, and it marks the occasion for respects to be paid at the graveside of deceased family members. Similar rituals are practiced across the Orthodox Balkans, and figure 17 illustrates a ceremony of remembrance in Trebovle, a mountain village in Western Macedonia, from the 1930s.[6] Precise visiting patterns differ from place to place; in Prilep and Bitola, I was told, people go on the Saturday and the Sunday. In Kruševo, people go to the graveyard on Gumenja, just below the monument, on Friday afternoon between 2:00 and 5:00. There is widespread participation, so the cemetery is full. The celebrants are mostly women, especially older generations, but younger women also attend and participate fully. Family parties form around graves, and numerous dishes are produced and laid out, including most centrally *pčenica* or *koliva*, boiled barley or wheat, but also the Macedonian specialty *tavče gravče*, or oven-baked beans, and sweets of various kinds. No meat is consumed, and no alcohol. Neighboring grave-parties exchange food. When one receives food from another group, one says that one is eating "for the soul." A little barley is sprinkled at the head of the grave, and a plate is left behind. A priest moves between the parties, and is enlisted (and paid a small honorarium) to read from a book of the dead which each family keeps. I was told, in 1993, that the ritual was practised throughout the time of socialist Yugoslavia.

Such religiously based practices of solidarity have been reanimated elsewhere in Macedonia, as the Macedonian Orthodox Church has become an

Figure 17: Graveyard ritual of Remembering the Dead, Trebovle Macedonia, 1930s. At the six-month commemoration of her son's death, a mother distributes *pčenica*. Photograph from Joseph Obrebski Collection, Number 353. Reproduced courtesy of Special Collections and Archives, W.E.B. DuBois Library, University of Massachusetts Amherst.

important player in domestic politics. In Skopje for example, Easter and most other rituals had formerly been celebrated discreetly, outside the city center. One exception was St. George's Day (5 or 6 May) which was the occasion for highly visible festivities by Roms, both Christian and Muslim. In 1992 the Orthodox Easter ritual of bringing a flame from the sanctuary and lighting people's candles from it was conducted at the new cathedral downtown, and the surrounding streets were packed with people. January 1993 saw the reinstitution of the public ritual of *Vodici*, when a cross is cast into water and then retrieved. For the first time for many years, it was conducted in the heart of Skopje. The priest threw the cross into the River Vardar from the Old Stone Bridge by the city's central square, and young men dived in and competed to retrieve it.[7] Such public performances reestablish a central place for expressions of Christian solidarity in post-Yugoslav Macedonian identity, and follow established conventions.

In Kruševo, the Day of the Dead has the potential to highlight divisions within the town's Orthodox population. In previous chapters, the distinction was noted between a "Macedonian" northwest and a "Vlah" southeast part of the town. The distinction is reflected in the topography of Kruševo's burial places. As well as the graveyard on Gumenja above the northwest quarter of the town, there is another in the southern quarter. This was historically where the Albanian-speaking community had lived, before being assimilated in the nineteenth century. The graveyard on the south side of town is filled with tombstones bearing Vlah or Vlah-derived names. Some are inscribed in Greek. In both respects, it represents a contrast with the Gumenja graveyard, which includes some Vlah names and some older Greek inscriptions, but where there is a clear preponderance of Slavic lettering and Macedonian forms.

Viewed in static opposition, Kruševo's graveyards appear to signal the town's divided past. In 1903, Nikola Karev sought to overcome frictions by commemorating the fallen of the Uprising in both graveyards. But in the 1930s, as described in chapter 5, communities defined by linguistic as well as profound socio-economic differences were still spatially distinguished, and mixed little. Bulgarian occupation forces stoked tensions by outlawing the public speaking of the Vlah language in the town, and by enlisting local recruits to enforce the law. Several elderly residents recalled being fined by policemen whom they had previously known and trusted as neighbors. After the war Vlahs suggest that their community suffered further at the hands of the new régime, which was supported by other townsfolk.

One might imagine that the geography of the graveyards would reinforce a sense of two communities living parallel and separate lives. In the way in which the Day of the Dead is commemorated, though, the absolute distinction is blurred. While the Day of the Dead is marked on Gumenja on Friday afternoon, it is celebrated on Saturday in the other graveyard. Kruševo's population thus maintains a system which permits them to pay their respects at both sites. Although an individual can only be buried in one place and family precedent clearly influences where people are interred, members of families where intermarriage has occurred are not compelled, in this context at least, to choose one side over the other.

Movement between different parts of the town is also a central component of the ritual of which Kruševo's residents often speak most fondly, the celebration of name days. Acknowledging this as a widespread Orthodox practice, people reported their style of celebration as unique in the Republic of Macedonia, and distinct from the marking of birthdays which is increasingly commonplace. Although it takes place on saint's days, they distinguish it from the *slava*, a household or community feast, the celebration of which has in the past been taken as an index of Serb identity but is also practiced in Macedonia (Rheubottom 1976a).[8] The name day, or *imenden*, is celebrated in Kruševo by households where a male resident bears the saint's name for that day. On St. George's Day, or *Gjorgovden*, for example, on 6 May all households with a member named Gjoko or Gjorǵi celebrate; on Petrovden, or 12 July, those with anyone named Petre celebrate. The name-day is associated with the Orthodox calendar, and is celebrated in Kruševo by both Vlahs and Macedonians, with names derived from Slavic and Greek. Thus on *Krstovden* on 27 September, those with either a Krste or Stavre in the household celebrate the day, *krst* and *stavros*, respectively, being south Slavic and Greek words for cross. A household with more than one male member, then, will play host to a number of name-day celebrations in a single year.

Whereas elsewhere in Macedonia the name-day might be the occasion for a gathering of close friends, in Kruševo the celebration takes the form of an open house. Homes are thoroughly cleaned in preparation, and a variety of alcoholic drinks and sweets prepared or bought for the occasion. From early evening onward neighbors, friends, colleagues, and acquaintances will stop by, usually in groups rather than as individuals. They do not generally bring gifts, and accept either drink, sweet, or both. They stay only for a short while, usually refusing the offer of a further drink or sweet. Either when arriving, when making a toast, or when taking their leave, they will often use one of the two formulaic phrases for the celebration: *Za mnogu godini*, or Long life, if the celebrant is an adult, or *Da porasne golem*, May he grow up tall, if the celebrant is a child.

Why the celebration has taken this particular form in Kruševo cannot be conclusively known. Clearly Greek Orthodox influence in the town's history has played some part, though as is the case with Ilinden, St. Elijah's Day, the dates of name days in Kruševo are usually twelve days later than their equivalents in Greece.[9] Some speculate that name-days are celebrated in this style because of the high concentration of men and boys who carry the same name. Kočo, for example, is considered a distinctive Kruševo name; and I was told in 1992 that there were fifteen Kočos in the town just between the ages of twenty and thirty. In my own acquaintance, I knew at least two people each by of the names Gjoko, Krste, Jane, Pavle, Nikola, and Tome. The form of the short visit permits people to pay visits to multiple houses. On the evenings of name-days, then, the narrow streets are turned into relatively busy thoroughfares, as groups of relatives or friends criss-cross from one house to another. It is hard to ascertain priorities, though it appears in general that people are scrupulous in observing reciprocity. Not to put in an appearance at a neighbor, friend, or colleague's imenden would be a breach of etiquette; to ignore the ties of ritual godparenthood, or *kumstvo*, is unthinkable. There remains nonetheless a whiff of status competition: it redounds to an individual's credit if his house plays host to a constant stream of visitors. The generation of the named host can also affect the kinds of groups that will be assembled at any particular venue; an older host's house will likely be visited by contemporaries and by people with their families, while a high school- or college-age imenden would more likely be frequented by relatives and groups of friends.

The name-day in Kruševo has been actively and continuously maintained as a "living" holiday by the aggregate action of the town's residents. Although primarily associated with men's names, much of the labor of preparation and hosting is performed by women in the household. It is a celebration of Christian community, in which those who bear the same given name, no matter what their age and status, are treated as equals. Extended through the calendar year, the same treatment is given to all. Disagreements, frictions, or jealousies may be bubbling beneath the surface; but a name-day host cannot turn people away, and someone who might think about not paying a visit has to give some thought to the wider social ramifications that may ensue from such a visible snub. It can be thought of as a form of social glue, potentially regulating conflicts and providing a recurrent forum in which intermediaries can be found to patch up quarrels. It has also served as part of the process by which the old geographical distinctions have been eroded by the traffic of people between different quarters.

The name day celebration is not the only such practice that may serve reconciliation by bringing strangers or adversaries into contact under conditions where wider social and community pressures demand that they interact, albeit minimally. One can read the same effect as arising, for example, from the practice of celebrating multiple weddings on a single day. Some guests would remain involved in just one set of ceremonies, which extended over several days before and after the church ceremony. Many more would do what George Ditsias was doing on the eve of Ilinden in 1903, socializing with others who had spent the previous week doing the rounds. Writing from Galičnik in the 1930s, Olive Lodge paints a vivid picture of how social groups had fluid boundaries in such celebrations. As Lodge noted, there were eight weddings taking place on Petrovden. Each wedding party held a torch-lit procession on the eve of the ceremony, and Lodge writes how they get "entangled in all the other processions from the other houses where there are maidens to be married. All of them flame and wander along like a giant centipede, so that the little steep paths and the one road of the village are lighted up with dots and dashes of fire; and the air is filled with the aromatic scent of burning pine-wood" (Lodge 1934–35:656). The Morse code such processions send indexes amicable interaction, and in July 1903 the residents of Kruševo were perhaps gearing themselves up for the same kind of experience.

What they faced instead was a more deliberate and conscious effort to bring about a similar sense of unity in diversity. Several contemporary eye-witness accounts highlight Nikola Karev's presiding over rituals of remembrance for the fallen in the different town churchyards. By holding commemoration services in different languages at different locations, he sought to bring the people of the town together and perhaps break down some of the antagonisms between them. According to Kirov-Majski, Karev urged the priests to use the Easter liturgy, hoping to instill in listeners a sense of freedom from fear and oppression in which they could all share (Kirov-Majski 1935:42).

RELIGION AND IDENTITY IN QUESTION

The kind of solidarity that the proposal to "re-establish" the Kruševo Republic presumed, then, was buttressed by a number of established practices in the town. The fact that many had their basis in a Christian calendar shared by the town's inhabitants highlighted a further distinctive feature of Kruševo's history. Although the municipality includes Albanian and other Muslim villages, Kruševo itself has remained an exclusively Christian town from the time of its settlement to the present. Apart from the small Ottoman garrison, it has never been home to any Muslim community, and has never housed a mosque. In the course of various conversations in the town, I was told the fate of one Muslim who tried to open a sweetshop, or *slatkarnica*, in the town, only to find himself with little or no custom. Matkovski records the existence of another such economic boycott in the nineteenth century (1978:47). A Macedonian magazine editor in Skopje with whom I discussed my research project, spoke admiringly and enviously of the community spirit of Kruševo, where historically the population had always discouraged Muslims from buying property in the town.[10]

This feature of Kruševo distinguished it from most towns and cities in western Macedonia, which have some Turkish or Albanian residents. It also contributed to Kruševo's unusual position with regard to tensions between ethnic Macedonians and Albanians that were so much a feature of the early years of Macedonian independence. Quickly mobilizing around ethnic political parties, the Albanian population boycotted the 1991 Yugoslav census and Macedonian referendum on independence. Albanian politicians called for revisions in the constitution and greater cultural and linguistic rights, accusing the new Macedonian state of discrimination in state employment as well as other areas. Mindful of the destabilizing role played by newly constituted Serbian minorities in Croatia and in Bosnia, the Macedonian government tried to address their demands. Popular opinion among Macedonians, though, discounted the calls from Albanians for greater rights, and saw Albanian political activism as a sustained attempt to undermine or fragment the new Macedonian state. The violent clash in November 1992 between police and Albanians in Skopje's market, Bit Pazar, where four people were killed, was seen by many Macedonians as the shape of things to come. Subsequent confrontations between authorities and Albanians campaigning for greater rights in Tetovo in 1994 and Gostivar in 1997 further polarized society, as did the fighting between Macedonian security forces and Albanian paramilitaries in the northwest in 2001.

Members of Kruševo's Vlah population, in particular, have resisted such stark visions of interethnic relations. During the Second World War and in its immediate aftermath, many people reported spending time in Kičevo, which was part of the Italian zone until 1943 and a theater for operations against the Albanian nationalist forces known as the Ballists. Vlahs stressed the friendly relations they had enjoyed with individual Albanians, especially during the Second World War when Bulgarian occupation forces carried out repressive measures against both Vlah and Albanian populations. In the contemporary setting, reportedly, relations between Vlahs and Albanians remained cordial in the Kruševo region. So, more generally, do those between Kruševo's Christian population and the Muslim villagers in the municipality who come to the town to deal with administrative tasks and buy and sell on market days.

Macedonian visitors from Skopje, where intercommunal relations are charged, consider the more relaxed attitudes of Kruševo a product of its inhabitants' lack of experience. In late 1992, for example, a young Skopje-based engineer accused his Kruševo hosts of being detached from the political realities facing Macedonia, especially what he called the Albanian problem. As so often, his interlocutors turned to their town's history, and in particular to the ideals of the Kruševo Republic. They first pointed out that within Kruševo municipality as a whole, the proportion of Albanians and Turks to Macedonians and Vlahs was virtually the same as that throughout the Republic, around one to three. They thus rejected the accusation that Kruševo's bid to isolate itself from the rest of Macedonia, and its population's general unwillingness to take sides in contemporary ethnic confrontation, was a result of any privileged status or narrow-mindedness.

For evidence, they could draw on the government statistics cited in table 3, which told a relatively consistent story of the population of the municipality, or opština, since the 1970s. The category of "others" included figures for Roms and Serbs and, in some cases, for Vlahs or Muslims who were not always enumerated separately. The Vlah population was entirely concentrated in the town of Kruševo. In 1994 around two-thirds of the municipality's Macedonian population also claimed residence there, giving the town a total population of about 5,500.[11]

The so-called Albanian problem had as much potential foundation in population dynamics in Kruševo as it did anywhere in the country. One of the townspeople challenged by the visitor from Skopje went on to argue that if Kruševo was distinctive, it was not in its demographics, but rather in its history of cooperation between ethnic groups, as evinced in the Kruševo Republic. In a free use of historical argument, he stated that the Parliament of sixty deputies that was established in 1903 was made up of Macedonians, Vlahs, and Albanians in equal numbers. In so doing he imagined a new Republic with a scope beyond that reported for 1903. For Kirov-Majski the multi-nationalism of the Ilinden Uprising in Kruševo was first and foremost a response to tensions between different linguistic and cultural groups within the town—the Albanians he describes as participating were Christian residents of the town. In his 1978 account, though, Matkovski suggests that places were reserved on the council and in the parliament for representation from Turkish and other Muslim communities from neighboring villages. It was this broader vision of multi-national participation that enthusiasts for the town's plan shared (Matkovski 1978:205).[12]

DIVISIVE SENTIMENTS

In the course of the same conversation, the secretary of the municipality and a key player in the proposal stated that though he was a Macedonian by nationality (*nacionalnost*), he was a Kruševčanec by conviction (*ubeduvanje*). He thus articulated a more widely held and firmly expressed sense of urban solidarity that was grounded in a glorious history and in a set of symbolic practices maintained through the former Yugoslav era, and that trumped other loyalties that might undermine it. Kruševo, then, as such spokespeople present it, seems like an ideal community in which to live. Perhaps one of the closest parallels to this vision in anthropological literature is Robert Redfield's view of Tepotzlan, the rural Mexican community he studied in the 1920s. Redfield conjured an image of a "relatively homogeneous, isolated, smoothly functioning and well-integrated society made up of a contented and well-adjusted people" (Redfield [1956] 1960:134).

Seventeen years later Tepotzlan was the field-site for another young field-worker, Oscar Lewis, who famously added another side to the picture of life in the community. Aware of Redfield's work, Lewis radically disagreed with his senior colleague's findings, which he considered derived from over-reliance on a small number of informants, over-emphasized "formal" aspects of inter-personal relations, and misunderstood class dynamics. Lewis's own study drew on a wider range of interviews, and described the struggle waged by individual families to acquire and work land from the commons. His account of social and cultural life thus emphasized underlying individualism, lack of cooperation, tensions between villages, schisms within the village, and "the pervading quality of fear, envy and distrust in interpersonal relations" (Lewis 1953:38; cited in Redfield 1956:134).

If the municipality secretary has the Rousseau-derived view of Redfield, Lewis's Hobbesian take on life also has adherents in Kruševo. For all the utopian qualities that some people ascribed to life in the town, I heard an insistent backbeat of disillusion. One part of this is the familiar complaint of young people, and especially educated young women, whose ambitions are at odds with the expectations of their community. One young woman spoke of her horror at what had happened to classmates from school who had married young and lost all capacity for conversation. Another expressed how easy it is to be labeled as a "bad girl" and find marriage in the town impossible. Because reputation is undone by gossip and rumor, there is no way to respond and restore one's name. Especially among university students and graduates, who had often grown accustomed to the greater freedoms of Skopje, the prospect of living one's whole life in Kruševo was unappealing.

The concern is not just boredom but rather the strain of life in a small town where others observe and judge your every move. Although young women are its primary victims, the strain is felt more broadly. One young man put it simply and wearily: there is an art to living in the town. Another used a proverb to describe the norms by which people live: When you build a new well, you do not fill in the old one. Because gossip or rumor can spread so quickly and have so pernicious an effect, there is pressure to maintain cordial relations with everyone. A couple who had moved to the town from Prilep more than twenty years ago passed critical judgment on this quality of social relations in Kruševo, calling the townspeople *maskirani*, or duplicitous. Prilep folk, they said, are loyal friends, or *drugari*. If you are their enemy, they won't have a conversation with you. Kruševcani, by contrast, will put on a friendly face, even if they don't like you.

This quality of life observed by Kruševo residents has been described by many anthropologists of south and southeast Europe. One of the most extended accounts is that provided by Juliet Du Boulay, who persuasively argues the ties to issues of honor and shame (Du Boulay 1974). Parallels can also be found, though, in very different idiographic accounts of behavior in totalitarian régimes. In her detailed and riveting account of life in Moscow in the 1930s, Sheila Fitzpatrick cites a respondent in a research project as saying, "You should never step on anybody's toes. Even a minor incident may be fatal. Your wife has an argument with her neighbor and that neighbor will write an anonymous letter to the NKVD [Soviet secret police] and you will have no end of trouble" (Fitzpatrick 1999:208).

The particular form in which accounts of the past in Kruševo circulate, then, could be traced to different antecedents. As noted in chapter 8, the depredations of the communist régime still triggered strong reactions from older generations. The memory of the impact has also been passed on. In one household, I was told how they had kept until the 1940s a complete uniform in which a family member had fought for Macedonia's liberation in the early part of the century; it was stolen by a partisan from the town, and his family still had it. A younger woman I knew as friendly and outgoing was hostile toward one of her contemporaries. When I asked her why, she told me a story that went back to the 1940s. Her own family had owned property in Skopje then and had therefore been potentially suspect, and had it taken from them. The contemporary's family had been poorer and had better relations with the régime, and the property ended in their hands. Now, in the second generation, the young woman telling the story, living in Skopje, had to rent an apartment, while the other lived rent-free in the property in question.

These two stories highlight the particular opprobrium that was attached to acts by which people in the past enriched themselves by false presentation, robbery, or betrayal or denunciation of others. In one interview after I had turned off the cassette recorder that I seldom used, an old man mouthed the name of someone who had appeared on television to describe his Ilinden exploits, for which he had received a pension. The old man said the pensioner was lying—that he had hidden himself through the whole affair. Of the more recent past, I was told on several occasions that one respectable elder in the town who had flourished in Yugoslavia had previously been an enthusiastic member of the Bulgarian youth organization, Branik. It was often suggested that after 1944 Bulgarian sympathizers had become the biggest communists, and secured their survival by denouncing others. In one reported case, a family thought it had successfully protected some portion of its property from the confiscations after the Second World War by handing over the rest without major protest. Unfortunately a family member discussed what they had done with a friend or neighbor who betrayed the secret to the authorities.[13]

Frequently, then, these accounts not only recall loss of wealth but also pinpoint the beneficiary within the town community. The accounts often take the form of character assassinations. Striking in each of these cases, however, was people's insistence that I should use neither their names nor the names of those whose actions they described. The tellers of these stories clearly considered some venues appropriate for such stories, and others less so—in each case I was urged not to share the details with others. Passing judgment on those who had been granted recognition and status in the new Yugoslavia clearly carried certain risks, whatever the truth-value of their claims to that status. And so I was also told by younger members of families within which such dangerous information circulated that their grandparents had sometimes switched into a language from the town's past—Vlah in some households, Greek in others—when discussing such matters. By this means, they kept some details from their grandchildren, whose linguistic skills were usually more limited, until such a time as they could be trusted not to compromise the family by speaking out in contexts where such information might bring trouble.

The narrators' insistence on secrecy around these stories has two effects. First, it appears to demonstrate their recognition, conscious or otherwise, of a fundamental paradox that telling tales brings into being. Betrayal and denunciation by others are activities that the people telling these stories once feared and now condemn. Even as they tell these stories, though, they are effectively denouncing others. Their injunctions to their listeners not to propagate the information could be read as attempts to distinguish their own dissemination of information from the malicious slanders perpetrated by others. At the same time, they are a means to secure the authority of their spoken words. By categorizing their judgments as intimate revelations, they effectively deny the listener the opportunity to test their veracity. By contrasting them with the fictions created from self-interest, the narrators locate their words in a realm of truth. Their veracity resides in their autonomy with respect to other versions which are in public circulation and are therefore dismissed as subject to manipulation by those in power.

THE VALUE OF SECRECY

The ambiguous quality of the stories that I was told by people who urged me not to re-tell them, then, depends upon a distinction between what is publicly known or believed and an inner or deeper realm of knowledge. Secrecy, concealment of truth, and attention to maintaining a public face were all perceived as components of a well-lived life. Such phenomena have been observed in a variety of settings, especially in peasant societies where they are associated with ideas of "limited good" (Banfield 1958). Information and honor take on the attributes of resources to be hoarded and protected from others; exchanges of either are hedged in by social regulation. The prevalence of such worldviews in Kruševo is suggested in stories of the origin of the town's name and location. The main downtown area is invisible from the valley below, and was reportedly settled by people seeking to escape the surveillance and envy of others, whether authorities or bandits.

The importance of secrecy also informs a further cycle of stories which are not about more abstract and symbolic resources, but are built around the fate of hidden treasure. It appears in oral records that the practice of hiding gold was commonplace in Kruševo's past. Mention was made earlier of a concealed hiding place built into a house from that period; elsewhere people buried their valuables. During the sack of the town in 1903 by bashi-bazouks, people were threatened or tortured to reveal where their hiding places were, as was the case with the Sekula story told in chapter 3. According to one source from the time, the Macedonian Revolutionary Organization developed other methods of locating the wealth of those unwilling to contribute to the cause. Lucy Garnett describes how a band would kill the reluctant donor, make a candle from his fat, and carry it while searching his house. The candle was supposed to go out when they reached the hiding place (Garnett 1904:219).

Such stories were not only told of the distant past. In the present, however, what was hidden has now become lost. I was told of one old woman who owned two houses, and "knew" that gold was hidden in them somewhere. She didn't know where; her father, on his deathbed, could only make the money sign—the rubbing of thumb and forefinger together—but was unable to speak to say where it was. In another house, a man in his fifties remembered his paternal uncle would get drunk and then start digging in the pantry floor where he was convinced a previous generation had buried its gold.

In stories like these, family fortunes were hidden successfully beyond the reach of predatory enemies. By controlling the knowledge of their whereabouts, even from other family members, the original concealer also prevented betrayal by careless conversation or deliberate treachery. Both accounts can be taken as evidence of profound mistrust of others, and a corresponding reluctance to reveal information in anything but an indirect, allusive form. Besides resonating with accounts from small communities elsewhere in Macedonia and the world, this orientation can be attributed to the particular circumstances of Kruševo's history, especially in the early years of Yugoslav communism, but also at the beginning of the twentieth century when different revolutionary and national movements competed for people's loyalties and resources, and were ready to punish those who withheld either. Under such circumstances the actions of the members of former generations described in these stories make sense: by maintaining silence they preserved a patrimony for future generations of their family who might live in better times.

Yet the stories simultaneously recognize the paradox contained in the strategy. In order to preserve the family treasure from seizure or theft, the secret must be kept. But when the secret is kept too well, as it reportedly had in the last two stories, the treasure is lost or all but irretrievable. From the point of view of future generations, the material outcome is the same as if the gold had been taken by others. The stories indicate not only a climate of fear and suspicion, but also its far-reaching and malign impact on family fortunes.

THE MANIFESTO REVISITED

It is perhaps no coincidence that stories of lost wealth and of the glories of the 1930s should have circulated at the particular historical moment of 1992–93, the end of Yugoslav socialist rule. Like the proposal for Kruševo's customs-free zone, the stories expressed a hope for the possibility of restoration of former wealth and status. In addition, stories of lost treasure in particular speak to broader ideas about the location of historical truth which resonate with those discussed in chapter 8, in the context of the Kruševo Manifesto. This document sets out an agenda for cooperation between people in Macedonia, and enjoys a particular place in discussions of identity and history in Kruševo. It is a talisman of the town's significance in Yugoslav and Macedonian visions of the past.

The Manifesto remains a document with a disputed historical existence. The fact that its origins have thus far been traced only as far as Kirov-Majski's play in 1924 is acknowledged by most people in the town, and one means by which they bridge the two decades of missing provenance to 1903 is to lodge the memory of the text inside Kirov-Majski's head. The belief persists, though, that the document was written and distributed in 1903, as Kirov-Majski himself describes. With regard to the fate of the original, some in Kruševo advance the theory that it was taken by the Ottoman commander back to Constantinople. They point out that Kruševo was stripped of many different kinds of wealth at that time; cartloads of plunder were shipped out, an unknown number of women and girls raped or kidnapped, and more than one hundred prominent town citizens taken to Bitola in shackles. Other artifacts of the Uprising were taken, including one of the cherry-tree cannons which had so conspicuously failed. Some maintain that an original version of the Manifesto was also taken to the Sultan, and remains preserved in the Ottoman archives in Istanbul.

While this version of historical record-keeping might appear far-fetched, its logical coherence is remarkable. The fact that no record exists of this original manifesto is explained by the fact that the Turkish archives have never been fully catalogued. Although they have been visited by scholars from various countries, some of those scholars—in the Kruševo narrative—are deeply invested in the denial of autonomous Macedonian history, and therefore do not wish for documentary proof of Macedonian activism—like the Kruševo Manifesto—to be found. The hidden, inaccessible existence of the "original" Kruševo Manifesto is therefore indefinitely protected. Until such time as the archives are fully catalogued, the existence of the Manifesto cannot be definitively denied. If they are catalogued and the Manifesto's existence recorded, well and good; if the Manifesto is not found, it will be possible to claim that prior to cataloguing, it was destroyed by representatives of a foreign régime that sought to deny the historical roots of Macedonian national autonomy.[14]

The Kruševo Manifesto in the Turkish Archives thus occupies a curious existential position. A cognate image beloved of physicists illustrating indeterminacy at the sub-atomic level, is that of Schrödinger's cat, shut in a box with radioactive material the decay of which releases a poisonous gas. At any given time, without opening the box, we cannot definitively say whether the cat is alive or dead. The Manifesto in the Archives could be argued to enjoy a similar virtual existence, providing untestable and therefore irrefutable evidence of the town's early-twentieth-century commitment to principles of interethnic cooperation that drive its unique claims on the Yugoslav Macedonian state and its successor.

PROTECTING THE FUTURE FROM THE PAST

Gold once hidden, now lost, has certain qualities in common with the Manifesto. Families in various parts of southeastern Europe have traditionally hoarded gold and silver with the purpose of displaying it at certain significant times as an index of both moral and social standing. Marriage rituals offer one such challenge and opportunity for families to show, as it were, what they were made of. Single sovereigns were "pinned" to bride and groom at engagements in Vasilika (Friedl 1962:57). In a number of Orthodox villages in Macedonia, gifts of one or two ducats, or gold coins, were given to brides by their fiancés (St. Erlich 1966:196). Writing of Galičnik, a wealthy migrant village, or *pečalbarsko selo*, in western Macedonia, of a time when marriages were still arranged, Olive Lodge stated that the bridegroom's father passed one gold napoleon to the bride's father when a match was agreed (Lodge 1934–35:653). Lodge also describes young wives wearing heavy silver belts to which silver coins were attached, some dating back to the eighteenth century, and strings of gold coins around their necks (Lodge 1934–35:652). In seventeenth-century Macedonia, Edward Brown encountered women wearing coins around their heads (Brown 1673:42). In Krivogaštani, on the way to Kruševo in 1911, Lebrun met women wearing silver coins in their braided hair. Permitted to look more closely, he discovered Polish, Russian, and Austrian coins, as well as French coins from the reign of Henry III (1574–89) and Louis XIII (1610–42) (Lebrun and Voinescu 1911:60).

Describing the mountain community of Ambeli, Juliet Du Boulay wrote:

> Money was not, for former generations, a commodity to be parted with, it was to be kept in chests, given in dowries, it was to be used as an adornment, it was to be *worn*. It was an indication of the "strength" (δυναμη) of the house, and as such it was to be stored, not to say hoarded. The people did not live by money, but by the land. (Du Boulay 1974:37)

The lengths to which people in Kruševo would go to protect hidden wealth suggest that similar principles appear to have governed their views of accumulated capital. Preservation was valued over loss or expenditure, and ultimately, in the two stories given, became a permanent and unalterable condition. The ancestral wealth of the two families in question has attained a similar status of hyper-reality as that possessed by the Kruševo Manifesto. In each case a resource vulnerable to the vagaries of human emotion or attitude, and therefore contingent, has been elevated beyond human capacity to erode it.[15]

Perhaps most importantly, this transformation is wrought without stirring up the past in such a way as to foster resentments that might yield bitter fruit in the present. In his discussion of tales of discovered treasure in Mexico, George Foster argues that such stories index luck as the only socially approved explanation of individual economic gain, which would otherwise be viewed as obtained at the expense of others (Foster 1964). In Kruševo, the problem for members of a community proud of its wealthy past is to explain individual economic loss. While some blame opportunistic neighbors or a rapacious state, such accusations, made publicly, carry considerable risks. They also threaten to disrupt an illusion of community solidarity in which many people are invested, and which is valued even more in light of what has occurred elsewhere in former Yugoslavia where such solidarity has been shattered by violence.

By telling tales of lost treasure, present-day descendants mourn the inaccessibility of their family fortunes. Their only specific target for complaint, though, is an overly protective ancestor who lived in fear of violence, denunciation, or treachery. A climate of envy and distrust is thereby acknowledged only implicitly and at first remove, as existing only in the town's past. A lament of loss is thereby prevented from evolving into a statement of recrimination against other individuals or families in the community. Similarly, the Manifesto's presumed existence beyond debates over loyalties, motivations, and identities in 1903 makes it a shared symbol of solidarity, evoking the ideals of a community that survived the destruction of the town.

In 1992 people in Kruševo witnessed the effects of retribution-seeking else-where in Yugoslavia and could envisage a similar catastrophe in Macedonia. Their call for a resurrection of the Kruševo Manifesto, and the re-establish-ment of the fleeting Kruševo Republic with which it was associated, demon-strates an enduring faith that violence might be averted by adherence to a set of principles enshrined, though never enacted, in the past.

The foregoing account should not be taken as a roundabout way of assert-ing that people in Kruševo "find comfort" in a partial or distorted history, or that they are steeped in nostalgia. The salient aspect of the account is how townspeople balance different domains of truth, both in their everyday lives and in their accounts of the past. As the young man said, there is an art to living in the town. But there is also art in putting together the disparate components of the past into a coherent narrative. When television screens show pictures of former fellow citizens at war, and villages and towns much like one's own in flames, and when people remember the bitter divisions of their own community's past, mastery of that art becomes vital to ensure a future. Whereas in other parts of Eastern Europe people could more readily enthuse about the prospects of "living in truth," (Havel 1985) Kruševo's inhabitants revealed their more nuanced awareness of all the ills that such Manichean thinking could unleash and their own determination, through syn-thetic skills honed and refined over the past half-century, to defuse them.

CHAPTER TEN

Conclusion

SINCE 1992–93, when the bulk of the research for this book was completed, Kruševo has lost more residents. A number of the more adventurous or enterprising have made their way to Skopje for study and work, and have no plans to return. Most stress the greater professional opportunities that are available to them there. One young man, for example, studied telecommunications engineering at the university and graduated with high honors. If he returned to Kruševo to work in the post office, he would simply "count impulses" and calculate people's bills, whereas in Skopje, his skills were in demand for new, private Internet providers. The town's secretary who had enthusiastically promoted the plan to re-establish the Kruševo Republic moved to the capital and was for awhile an important figure in the Ministry of Justice. Some people have taken spouses from outside Kruševo's tightly knit community, and in at least one case, from outside Macedonia.

The town suffered further economic decline in the mid-1990s. Factories closed and state employees faced early retirement as the government sought to meet public employment expenditure targets set by international financial bodies. The drop in incomes and in traffic between Skopje and Kruševo also affected service industries. Cafés which had done such brisk trade in previous years were only slightly emptier, but their clientele was now teenagers rather than young professionals. Owners lamented that their new patrons would nurse a single soda all night, and were less willing or able to buy drinks for others, so takings were down. In a linked development, the old scheduled express bus service between Skopje and Kruševo became irregular, running only when demand was confirmed ahead by enough passengers to make the trip profitable. It has since been replaced by privately run minibus services that use twelve-seater *kombis* and are rarely stretched beyond their capacity.

Isolation increased for Macedonia as a whole in this period. In 1994 it was blockaded by its southern neighbor Greece, when tensions over the new state's name reached a head. The international embargo against rump Yugoslavia wounded the Macedonian economy, severing legitimate links with formerly vital markets and driving a considerable volume of trade onto the black or grey market. Although some private fortunes were made as a result, state revenues fell and a majority of Macedonia's inhabitants saw their standard of living drop. Efforts to reorient the economy toward more cooperative neighbors to the east and west were compromised by a lack of transport infrastructure. There was no rail link to match the Belgrade-Skopje-Thessaloniki line built at the end of the nineteenth century, and road routes to Albania and Bulgaria, former enemies of Yugoslavia, had not received investment.

As suggested in chapter 2, Macedonia's new place in the world created certain existential problems for its inhabitants. As economic restructuring forced people to plan in new ways for subsistence, retirement, and their children's futures, political changes compelled people to rethink their own loyalties and those of their former fellow-Yugoslavs. Fighting began in Bosnia in April 1992; by the summer of that year, Yugoslavia was a part of the past, and some people in Macedonia would point to the physical geography and the ethnography of the region to show that their newly defined country had no natural link with other republics. Symbolically charged moments might threaten their certainty. Speaking of Croatia's basketball battle with the U.S. "Dream Team" at the Barcelona Olympics, people might forget themselves and call the Croatian team *naši* (ours). But they would immediately provide a gloss on their own linguistic usage, saying that it was now "mistaken" to talk in that way, as it did not match the reality of the world.

While Yugoslavia existed, debates over Macedonian identity did not always affect individual citizen's lives. Although Greek and Bulgarian commentators had always denied the status of the Macedonian narod, and Macedonian historians had consistently documented its development through several centuries, their arguments were waged in a restricted realm. Yugoslavia had served simultaneously as guarantor of the existence of the Macedonian narod as one of the peoples of the federation, at the same time as it provided individuals with a state-based nationality which defined them differently when traveling abroad. In the summer of 1990, I witnessed how this double level of belonging played itself out. On the train from Skopje to Athens, a group of Macedonians were handed entry forms to fill out and submit at the Greek border. After some discussion, they addressed the Greek conductor: we are Macedonians and Yugoslavs, so what should we put as our nationality? He told them to put Yugoslav, thus making their entry unproblematic.[1]

With the passing of the federal state, the room for such amicable negotiation has been eroded. Macedonian nationality once enjoyed equal status with four (before 1968) and five (after 1968) other Yugoslav identities. Some, like Slovenian, have enjoyed successful careers, while others, most especially Serbian, have lost ground in the wider world. Macedonia has faced its own set of issues, as its close association with the Yugoslav experiment of which it was a part raises questions over its entitlement and capacity to retain its national meaning in the post-Yugoslav world.

AFTER THE FALL: MODELS OF TRANSITION

The problems of post-socialist transition and identity politics are not, of course, unique to Macedonia or to Yugoslavia. In the former Czechoslovakia, the Czech nation was perceived by its members, according to Ladislav Holy, "not as a collectivity of heterogenous individuals but as a supraindividual entity which exists in its own right" (1996:89). Czechs, in Holy's analysis, came to see their national identity as naturally given, enshrined in ideals of cultured, democratic individualism. Drawing primarily on her work in Romania, Katherine Verdery has argued that socialism is best understood as conjuring neither an ethnic nor a civic sense of "nation," but rather as creating quasi-familial ties of dependence between state and subjects. This she calls socialist paternalism, and suggests that it continues to shape transitional societies, in which majoritarian rule and state control continue to be fetishized, while the lines between "us" and "them" are redrawn along ethnic lines (Verdery 1992). Describing post-*perestroika* Sakhalin, Bruce Grant argues that indigenous Nivkhi on the Siberian island did not necessarily see the collapse of the Soviet Union as an end to alien rule that would usher in a return to their authentic ways. Many had seen themselves as Soviets first and Nivkhi second, or as Soviets only; their reactions were therefore more ambivalent and tinged with a sense of loss. Nivkh narratives, Grant reports, "were more about compromise and contradictory allegiances than revisionist heroics" (Grant 1995:158–59).

None of these groups, of course, were exact counterparts of Macedonians in Yugoslavia. Macedonians were thought of as less cultured and more "Balkan" by their Slovenian, Croatian, and even Serbian "older brothers" in the family of federal nations, and therefore, in Holy's model, more like Slovaks than Czechs (Holy 1996:104–8). Although Macedonians defend their constitutional status as a people, or narod, and many scapegoat ethnic Albanians for the difficulties of transition, they do not depict all minorities in the same stark, adversarial terms that Verdery describes. Other minorities, notably Roms, fare better in Macedonia than almost anywhere in the neighborhood. And as one of the constituent Slavic peoples of the federation, and the majority in a republic whose right to secede was internationally acknowledged in 1991, Macedonians occupied a less marginal position in Yugoslavia than Nivkhi in the Soviet Union, and a central one in "their" new state.

In some respects, though, all three descriptions resonate with some part of Macedonian experience since 1990, as the Yugoslav legacy created a bewildering set of relationships among citizens, communities, and authorities in the Republic. In Kruševo, some people saw themselves as distinct from the rest of the country, including the capital city Skopje, on the grounds of greater culturedness. This could take on an ethnic tinge, whereby Vlah heritage was valued above others. Macedonian solidarity nonetheless remained important for many; Kruševo's inhabitants embraced the repositioning of the town as symbolizing not socialist, but national revolutionary tradition. So too, the bid to reestablish the Kruševo Republic was first framed as an appeal to the central government for state subsidy. And Grant's description of the Nivkhi, whose circumstances are not only post-socialist but also post-colonial, captures aspects of Kruševo residents' responses to the new world in which they found themselves, haunted with nostalgia for a variety of pasts.

The contingency and contradictions of the town's experience were force-fully represented in individual family histories. One teenager, here called Irena, was able to name all her great-grandparents, narrate key aspects of their lives, and selectively go even further back in time. Her father's family came from the village of Vogjani, southeast of the town and close to the modern village of Bela Crkva. Their reputation was built on the activities of her great-great-grandfather, who had returned a rich and generous man from work in Chicago. His brother never came back; he served as an American soldier in the First World War, after which his Kruševo relatives lost touch with him. Irena's grandfather, son of the brother who returned, served as president of the council of Kruševo municipality in the Yugoslav period. He had married a woman from Bela Crkva whose own father had worked in America. Labor migration was the means by which both families acquired the wealth and status to move to the town and serve as community leaders.

On her mother's side, Irena's roots in the town ran deeper, as both her maternal grandparents were from long-established Kruševo families. She described her mother's father's father as a *Srbophil*, or pro-Serbian, though Macedonian; he had served as a Serb policeman between the wars. Her mother's mother's parents, by contrast, were both Vlahs; her great-grand-mother she called a "real European." She had been found alone and pre-sumed orphaned as a child in the turbulent years at the beginning of the twentieth century. In France and then England she learned both languages and worked as a governess before returning home, reunited with her parents through the activities of the Red Cross. Irena's great-grandfather was also Vlah, from Kruševo. He died during the Second World War, when he was denounced and hanged as a traitor by the partisans. His crime was to stumble upon partisans stealing cheese from his sheepfold and who were later be-trayed to the authorities.

Irena's mother's parents married in 1952, defying the strong pressure against Vlah-Macedonian marriages.[2] Cut off by the bride's relatives, and both from families that had hardly won the favor of the new régime, they were among the town's less well-off residents. When their daughter, Irena's mother, married the second son of the former council president, it repre-sented a further extension of the boundary crossing and blurring that others in the town had undertaken. In terms of *poteklo*, or descent, Irena can claim to be simultaneously Macedonian and Vlah. Among her forebears are people who found themselves on opposite sides of conflicts between pro-Serbs and pro-Bulgarians, communists and bourgeoisie, or the "upper" and "lower" parts of town. Her family tree includes people who refashioned themselves in the United States or in Western Europe. Some who did so never found their way home, while for others the town of Kruševo served as a magnet.

IMAGINATION AND ITS ALTERNATIVES

Irena's account offers a microcosm of broader experience in Kruševo, where people are constantly at work to reconcile the past with the present, and with itself. In this regard, they appear especially well positioned to appreciate the nuances of national belonging noted by some of the more insightful academic commentators on the subject. In particular, like other Macedonians, they are keenly attuned to the ideological quality of the way in which people—themselves included—mark divisions between the real and the artificial in their discussions of ethnic identity and history.

A key trope in this regard, famously introduced to the literature by Benedict Anderson in the early 1980s, is the imagination. But the idiom, of course, has a longer history than that. As Appadurai (1990:2) has made clear, the "imaginary" stems from Durkheim's work, as a site of study for phenomena that transcend the individual and contribute to the creation of links between people. Though Anderson does not emphasize his link with a disciplinary past, Durkheim's influence has been explicitly acknowledged in the work of anthropologists of the modern forms that nationalism may take, such as Kapferer (1988) and Herzfeld (1992). In a parallel vein, the centrality of "image" in the constitution of community has been emphasized by, among others, Fernandez (1986) in the context of a religious group. His apt phrase, the argument of images, was applied in a national context by Evans (1992).

The power of imagination is not limited to the realm of national or religious thought, appearing also as a component of various academic disciplines. As early as 1959, Wright Mills published *The Sociological Imagination*. Muriel Dimen-Schein's *The Anthropological Imagination* (1977) attracted less attention. Atkinson's account of the "ethnographic imagination" (1990) was closely followed by the inauguration of a series of publications of "Studies in the Ethnographic Imagination" which included a work that turns the metaphor once more: John and Jean Comaroff's *Ethnography and the Historical Imagination* (1992).

In each case, I would argue, the force of the term imagination is that the scholar or analyst makes sense of the object of analysis—a society which is separated from that in which the analyst lives—by *creating* links between fields and phenomena whose connection is not apparent. Wright Mills, indeed, considered it one of the key dimensions of the sociological imagination "to grasp history and biography and the relations between the two within society" (1959:6).

However—and this is a key distinction—the symbolic power of the term is different within a discourse about nations, rather than a discourse about history, or sociology, or even geography. For within scholarship, the term "imagination" conveys no commitment to a firm distinction between true and false. It is, instead, a tool to mediate between different understandings. To quote Wright Mills again, the sociological imagination is "the capacity to shift from one perspective to another" (1959:7). It should come as no surprise, accordingly, that it has surfaced most prominently in social scientific disciplines, and that the works alluded to above are all in some sense critical of a positivistic bent.

This key aspect of imagination—that it does not denote on the part of an author a hard distinction between the real and the false—was taken as self-evident by Benedict Anderson. In his introduction, he makes it clear that in his conception of the term, *contra* Gellner (1983), "all communities larger than primordial villages of face-to-face contact (and perhaps even these) are imagined" (Anderson 1991:9). What distinguishes them, then, in Anderson's vision, is the style in which they are imagined (ibid.). In making this argument, Anderson was using the term in a way that appears to have links with its use within the academy, and had been spelled out explicitly by Collingwood long ago in *The Idea of History* (1946:241):

> It may be thought that by imagining we can present to ourselves only what is imaginary in the sense of being fictitious or unreal. This prejudice need only be mentioned in order to be dispelled. If I imagine the friend who lately left my house now entering his own, the fact that I imagine this event gives me no reason to believe it unreal. . . . The imaginary, simply as such, is neither unreal nor real.

Yet despite such precedent and his own caveats in the introduction, Anderson has been criticized for naiveté in deploying a word so easily translated into invention. Given the readings of his work in subsequent years, the critique appears justified. Evangelos Kofos, the Greek scholar, cites Anderson as a source for his definition of the term imagined: "to define the subjective or visionary perception of groups or communities of their own national identity, heritage or 'mission'" (Kofos 1993:332). He then contrasts imagined with "real" in a number of contexts, referring to historical legacies, deeds, and historical titles as "real or imagined"—or, in one case, "real or 'imagined'" (Kofos 1993:320, 322, 326)—and to "an imagined world where anything *Macedonian* was automatically transformed in their ["the masses'"] minds to 'Macedonian' " (ibid.:320). His selective use of quotation marks, as Danforth indicates, suggests an "imagined" quality to Macedonian identity—based, for Kofos, on the work of historiographers who "labor with equal ease in the annals of history and the world of fantasies"—that contrasts with its more "real" Greek and Bulgarian elders (ibid.:318; c.f. Danforth 1995a: 33n.).[3] More recently, and less easily dismissed as the result of nationalist bias, journalists and scholars have taken Anderson to be indicating a strong distinction. Hugh Poulton, for example, states that Benedict Anderson contrasts the " 'real' community of family, village or city quarter with the 'imagined' which was the religious group" (1995:45). And in 1994 a trio of U.S.-based historians used Anderson in a discussion of immigrant consciousness:

> Shared information, shared stories, shared symbols invisibly pulled adult readers into new association dependent upon the mutual ties of language, commerce and governance. With these common reference points, people could form what Benedict Anderson has called an "imagined community" to take the place of the intensely real rural communities they left behind. (Appleby, Hunt, and Jacob 1994:101)

Anderson himself makes no such contrast. His "imagined community" is neutral in regard to its reality. In this regard, his vision of the "imagined" has close epistemological links to Clifford Geertz's "assumed." Geertz used the term assumed in seeking to further define what Edward Shils had already labeled "primordial" sentiments, in the following terms:

> By a primordial attachment is meant one that stems from the "givens"—or, more precisely, as culture is inevitably involved in such matters, the assumed "givens"—of social existence: immediate contiguity and kin connection mainly, but beyond them the givenness that stems from being born into a particular religious community, speaking a particular language, or even a dialect of a language, and following particular social practices. (1973a:259)

Like Geertz, Anderson was concerned with cases where human or state agency, or a political agenda *appear* absent. The importance of this inter-mediating layer of human interpretation runs through the phrases with which Anderson describes the processes at work. In keeping with his commitment to the "anthropological spirit" which he states at the opening of his work, he refers to the "idioms" by which "nation-ness is assimilated to skin-colour, gender, parentage and birth era—all those things one can not help" (Anderson 1991:143). It is these idioms, then, which give to nation-ness what he calls the "halo of disinterestedness" (ibid.).

This particular preoccupation, common to work on the topic by Anderson and Geertz, has attracted criticism from scholars who accuse them of over-emphasizing consensus and disregarding political process. Partha Chatterjee, for example, argues that Anderson's work eliminates agency and the potential for dispute, and that "instead of pursuing the varied, and often contradictory, political possibilities inherent in this process, Anderson seals up his theme with a sociological determinism" (Chatterjee 1986:21). Geertz has been read as suggesting that primordial sentiments are ineffable and unmalleable, and thus that their position outside the realm of debate and action is itself "natural" (Eller and Coughlan 1993).

Both Geertz and Anderson do place the basis of nationalism's appeal beyond the work of individual actors, and in a period other than the present. But nowhere does either deny that "givens" must, at some point or another, be assumed or that individual reflective people can "imagine" for themselves. If there is a criticism to be made, it is that both shy away from the questions of power and contestation that go into making the assumed given, or the imagined real; avoiding the question, in other words, of who establishes the idioms, and whose idioms they are that are established. Their attention to political process begins where the work of assuming and imagining ends, beyond what Étienne Balibar called the "threshold of irreversibility" (1991:88).

As a result, they have been curiously separated in the literature on nationalism. Neither endorses a simple binary division. Both, in these particular works and elsewhere, describe complex worlds in which there are multiple and distinct modes or styles of assuming and imagining. Yet now Geertz stands as an essentializer or reifier. His "assumed given" has been read as "given," and his allusion to the place of culture in the constitution of such norms overlooked. Anderson's work, by contrast, has been read as denying any such fixity. Whereas Geertz's Indonesians allegedly remain irremediably divided by emotions and stubbornly preserve what is rightfully theirs, Anderson's peripheries adopt a "modular" nationalism easily and, in the process, take on a new cultural form which has nothing to do with continuity and everything to do with novelty. The gulf between contingency and fate that all human societies seek to bridge, and that Anderson and Geertz sought to explain, now divides the two scholars, yawning wider than ever.

THE LURE OF THE REAL

Ultimately, it may be the fate of all those working on nationalism to find themselves categorized on one or the other side of this gulf of scholarship's making. In some respects, as this book has tried to demonstrate and others have argued, there is a deep affinity between the categorizing impulses of nationalists, philosophers, and social scientists in the Western tradition. Aristotle's principle of the excluded middle, for example, which holds that any statement is or is not true, appeals to those who define national cultures as sharply demarcated homogenous wholes (Handler 1988, 1993; Hayden 1993).

Yet locating anthropology in particular on that precarious middle ground of inquiry, where propositions are neither self-evidently true nor transparently false, seems preferable to any alternative. Only by envisaging our academic practice as a bridge can we apprehend how the gap is created, and how particular ideas and social forms traverse the gap. While some assert authenticity for their own culture, and deny any such quality to the culture of others, a richer understanding of culture is that it encompasses the means by which people identify processes in the present and past as genuine, God-given, or "real" as opposed to those they perceive as ideological, heretical, or "false." To trace these processes demands that we observe the traffic of symbols, institutions, and ideas from one side to the other, and recognize that much of what we say and do is similarly in transit.

A key inspiration for this understanding of academic practice is Evans-Pritchard's metaphor of the bridge in *The Nuer* (1940:94). In describing the means by which he, as ethnographer, will trace the connections between material environment and social structure, he also suggests that Nuer cosmology hovers at the same site, and therefore that "culture" can be understood as mediating this transition between different orders of reality. His purpose being to outline Nuer political structure, Evans-Pritchard never returned to the metaphor, yet he produced a work of outstanding clarity that Clifford Geertz memorably dubbed "that anthropological geometry book" (1988:67).

In the study of twentieth-century Macedonia which this book represents, what was most salient to me was the difficulty I had in locating for anthropological or historical study a position that was not embedded in the cultural politics of identity. For a key component of Macedonia's history is the role played by holders of the belief that cultures should have states, and therefore that cultural distinctiveness of groups is a key component of modern politics. This is common to much of the world. What distinguishes Macedonia is its procession of imposed or more voluntary population changes, and régimes with different unifying agendas which demanded that prior agendas be revised. In any particular present, observers can deny the "real" status of régime claims to cultural distinctiveness, in particular by invocation of a past when things were different. This is counteracted by nationalists who assert, of "their own" people, that things have always been the same.

Different approaches to history, then, are taken up and deployed as part of a nationalist agenda. Yet their potential contribution to the nationalist cause is in direct correlation to their identification as scientific and nonideological. Approaches that are cognate with the new "social history" are a particularly important resource. Their particular appeal, in societies where régimes sponsoring particular visions of history have come and gone, is their emphasis on the myriad unheard voices as representing the ground-swell of history. Marshall Sahlins describes those pursuing this approach as believing that "history is culturally constructed from the bottom up: as the precipitate, in social institutions and customs, of the prevailing inclinations of the people-in-general" (1985:33). Bernard Cohn, drawing humorously on medical terminology, has termed such "bottom-based" approaches to history "proctological"—considering them as the displacement of history to processes which are considered to make history "real" (1987:39–42).

Particularly significant is the notion that in this aggregate of voices there is a certain innocent quality. What appears to be celebrated, above all, is the presumed unselfconsciousness of these spokespeople for history, that lends their accounts an authority beyond the ideological manipulations of politicians or intellectuals who have their own agendas. This quality is described by Cohn in the following terms:

> The assumption behind the smallness of scale (temporal and/or spatial) of the research of contemporary historians is positivistic: that when we have studied the workers in enough industrializing English cities, we will have the building-blocks for a new and scientific history. (1987:41)

Yet without an authorial, editorial presence, such accounts yield only a chaotic jumble of impressions, a patternless whole. Should we term that history? While populists, and those who rehearse mantras of bringing unheard voices to light might consider so, Cohn points out the power politics inherent in their recording, selection, and arrangement.

It is precisely this dimension of the picture, whereby "everyman" is simultaneously celebrated by recall and spoken for by the historian that grants such versions of the past their new potential in the debates of nationalism. In this respect, the work of the French *Annales* school, from which much of the impetus to a new "social" history came, has at times come to serve the purposes of those in search of an enduring *volk*, which has survived the predations and prestations of any particular individuals or states from above. Perry Anderson, reviewing Braudel's *The Identity of France*, pointed to this quality in the work, whereby the *longue durée* of a people reaches ever backward in time (Anderson 1992:255):

> Fascination with prehistory is widespread today . . . [b]ut transposed into proto-national register, the distance to myth is short. Braudel's claim for five million neolithic farmers closes it . . . Here too the attributes of identity prove to be less specific than specious.

The political use of such a notion of the processes of history is apparent when one reads work on the break-up of Yugoslavia, such as the following:

> Yugoslavia passed its seventy years in accordance with Braudel's schema: on the political surface, seemingly turbulent in terms of events, with numerous splits and sudden changes; on the level of economic and social history there is the rhythm of gradual but persistent modernization; and as regards the collective

mentality, behavioral patterns and norms of value are caught in a cycle of lengthy duration. (Vodopiveć 1992:223)

The author's point here is that Slovene, Serb, and Croat communities were and are the enduring sites of "collective mentality." Yugoslavia, by contrast, is a mere epiphenomenon of history, irrelevant in the "long perspective." If Slovenes were not neolithic farmers in this vision, they were nonetheless there and knew they were there long before anybody thought to count them.

Such placement of "real" history in a realm which the state cannot touch is a characteristic noted by Partha Chatterjee in anti-colonial nationalisms. He argues that under those conditions nationalist discourse creates a hard distinction between a spiritual and a material domain. In the former, "its true and essential domain, the nation is already sovereign, even when the state is in the hands of the colonial power" (Chatterjee 1993:6). The maintenance and promotion of this impression of ineffable being, as Chatterjee points out, is a vital resource for those who cast themselves, temporarily at least, as the victims of history written by others. Orchestrated by hero-scholars, such iconoclastic alternative visions are made the property of the authentic and downtrodden people for whom they speak, and provide the material for new, deeper, and therefore, more true understandings of past and present.

REDISCOVERING THE MACEDONIAN PAST

In the anti-colonial struggles from which Chatterjee draws inspiration the lines between alien rulers and native resisters are often clearly marked. Individuals and groups elsewhere find themselves part of a political continuum where multiple positions and the invidious impact of invocations of spiritual solidarity can be more easily identified. As noted in previous chapters, some Macedonians have since 1991 publicly reclaimed certain figures from the past, alleging that they stand for the "true" Macedonian spirit which Tito's Yugoslavia sought to crush and replace with an ersatz, socialist version. In October 2000, a group of these champions of suppressed history commemorated Vlado Černozemski as a martyr for the Macedonian cause. Černozemski was responsible for the deaths of two leading Macedonian leftists in the 1920s, Naum Tomalevski and Dimo Hadži-Dimov, as well as the murder of King Alexander of Yugoslavia in 1934. His invocation as a national hero depends upon a vision of left-wing federalism as treachery, and of Serbia as the foremost historical enemy of Macedonian interests.

More disturbing than the revitalization of particular heroes from the past is the apparent rise of collective sentiments about national longevity and unique territorial ownership. Among Macedonians, these focus particularly around the topic of Macedonian-Albanian relations within the Republic, and the respective status of different groups. Ethnic Albanians constitute the largest single minority in Macedonia, accounting for 23 percent of the citizen body in the internationally supervised census of 1994. Albanian-speaking and mainly Muslim, they were throughout the Yugoslav period concentrated in rural areas and underrepresented in state employment. Their levels of education, especially among women, were generally lower than in the Macedonian community, and family sizes generally larger. Because the Yugoslav constitution and international opinion permitted only existing republics within the federation to secede, Yugoslav Albanians—mainly divided between western Macedonia, Kosovo, and Montenegro—were granted no right of self-determination. Albanians in Macedonia formed their own political parties in 1990 to challenge what they saw as Macedonian domination of the state and boycotted the referendum on independence in 1991. Among the demands they pursued against the new sovereign Macedonian Republic were constitutional change, university education in the Albanian language, and greater local autonomy. Some elements in the Albanian community consistently advocated the use of more radical forms of political action, and from 1992 onward Macedonia saw sporadic violence between ethnic Albanians and police—in Skopje's marketplace in 1992, Tetovo in 1994, Gostivar in 1997, and Arachinovo in 2000 (Brown 2000b).[4]

While Albanian politicians called for recognition of Albanians as equal partners in the state, most Macedonians steadfastly identified them as a minority, or *malcinstvo*. This insistence on the different ontological status of the Macedonian and Albanian communities in the Republic perpetuated the Yugoslav-era categorical distinction between narod and narodnost. Macedonians base their position on a range of arguments. Some indicate that Macedonia is home to other minorities, including Turks, Vlahs, Serbs, and Roms, and that such diversity demands commitment to a single official language, rather than descent into Babel. Others point out that the 1991 constitution guaranteed the individual rights of all citizens, and that Albanian activists are seeking collective rights, which run counter to the ideal of the civic state. Critics also point to the emphasis that is placed on Albanian *rights* and the absence of a discussion of civic *responsibilities*.

Some see the issue in developmental terms, arguing on the basis of stereotypes and half-truths about gender relations, household structures, and religious practices, that Albanians are backward. Again, there is some resonance with Marxist-Leninist ideas of historical progress that were widely taught in the Yugoslav period. An onus is placed on Albanians to transcend commitment to their cultural distinctiveness and adopt lifeways closer to those of the Macedonian majority. More prevalent, and gaining ground among Macedonians, is a belief that the cultural and civilizational difference between Macedonians and Albanians is insurmountable. A particular point of reference in statements which communicate this opinion is the idea of Europe, to which Orthodox Macedonians consider that they (and most of their former fellow-Yugoslavs) rightfully belong. Albanians, by contrast, are considered by many as part of an Islamic civilization, and therefore alien. Views of this kind strikingly recall the overall tenor of Samuel Huntington's controversial work on the "clash of civilizations," though Macedonians elide the potential fault line that he located between Eastern and Western Christian traditions (Huntington 1993).

The growing power of such beliefs is linked to socio-political developments. As part of Yugoslavia, Macedonians were citizens in a state with a population of around 24 million. In 1994, according to the census, there were almost half a million self-identified Albanians in the Republic: together with more than 1.5 million in Kosovo, where they constituted between 80 and 90 percent of the local population, Albanians made up around 9.5 percent of former Yugoslavia's population as a whole (Woodward 1994:32–33). Although there were fewer Macedonians than Albanians in the former Yugoslavia, Republican status and a certain Slavic solidarity embedded in the country's make-up afforded Macedonians a sense of security. After the country's fragmentation, those numbers acquired new significance. Although a majority within their own new state, Macedonians are outnumbered by the Albanians in the region. They are also acutely aware that many Albanians in Macedonia express a greater sense of solidarity with Albanians in Kosovo than with their Macedonian fellow-citizens.

For those who accept the ideology of the nation-state or of civilizational fault lines, the multi-cultural Republic of Macedonia created in the break-up of Yugoslavia was always a problem waiting to happen. Its borders do not enclose a homogenous population, and worse, in the north and west, they cut an ethnic community into separate parts. Elsewhere in Yugoslavia in the course of the 1990s, the same problem arose and was resolved either by bringing political boundaries into alignment with ethnic residential patterns, or vice versa. The logic of nationalism that both procedures encapsulate governed the initial fragmentation of Federal Yugoslavia, and drove subsequent violence, followed by mass displacement or murder of populations. In Croatia, Bosnia, and then Kosovo, a variety of local and international forces adopted different means to the same end: the creation of ethnically homogenous political units. Many Macedonians see their country's future in these terms, and especially fear the prospect of partition, which would confirm Albanian control and ownership of western Macedonia. Partly as a consequence, some voice the opinion that Slavic Macedonians are the true heirs to the autochthonous population of the territory now known as Macedonia, and that Albanians are more recent immigrants from the West: the implicit message is that Macedonia's problems would dissolve if its Albanian citizens would "go home."

In offering views of this kind, Macedonians are not spokespeople for a form of blinkered nationalism unique to the Balkans. As suggested, they share underlying principles with those of respected scholars in the United States. Besides the work of Samuel Huntington, they might also find common cause with those who have argued on empirical grounds that ethnic plurality is fatal to democracy (Roeder 1999). Their national thinking owes much to models of folk solidarity that emerged as part of the German national revival, and which made their way into contemporary German ideas of citizenship and, more generally, into social science.

Macedonia's lived reality, though, is particularly vulnerable to the violence of ideas. This was true at the beginning of the twentieth century when British officials discussed the possible merits of some form of international protectorate, or what they called a "Lebanon solution." By 1908 the concept had been rejected because "it would not satisfy sections of the population imbued with European ideas, and having the example before them of neighbouring states which have been emancipated" (*British Documents on Foreign Affairs* 1885–1908: vol 19:171). It remained the case in the 1940s, when Yugoslav authorities organized the wholesale slaughter of livestock to rebuild agriculture on a rational basis. At the beginning of the twenty-first century, the prospects for Macedonia's multicultural future are undermined by the seductive power that national thinking, in a rationalist guise, exerts over some of its inhabitants and many of its observers.

As this book has tried to illuminate, the history of national thinking in and about Macedonia is multi-faceted. European and American accounts of the region in the early twentieth century saw Macedonia as lacking an authentic character of its own, ripe for the nationalisms of its neighbors. At various points of the twentieth century Bulgaria, Greece, and Serbia have claimed Macedonia's Christian population as unredeemed brethren. Only since 1945 has an ethnic Macedonian identity received state sponsorship. The Yugoslav period saw a range of efforts to make visible a particular history of national struggle infused with socialist ideals. Macedonia's non-Slavic Muslims have at different times been categorized as complicit in Ottoman rule, sympathizers with brethren elsewhere, or the victims of Slavic majority rule.

Since Yugoslavia's fragmentation, the existential status of the Macedonian nation has been the subject of heated debate. The result has demonstrated the considerable power of the adversarial mode of thought which linguist Deborah Tannen called the argument culture (Tannen 1998). The complex and multiply inflected career of Macedonia and Macedonian identity has often been reduced to a discussion about truth and falsehood in past and present. When the anthropologist Anastasia Karakasidou documented the existence of a Slavic-speaking minority in northern Greece in 1993, she and her discipline were attacked in Greek media and in some academic circles as spreading dangerous fictions (Karakasidou 1993, 1994). Andrew Rossos's diligent work in making public the documentary traces of Macedonian political and cultural autonomism before 1944 has been criticized as "subjective revision" by those who see Macedonian history as the property of Bulgaria (Rossos 1994, 1995; Phillipov 1995a). The power of such adversarial framing is demonstrated also in Loring Danforth's discussion of the Macedonian conflict in Australia, where he lays out exaggerated forms of "Greek" and "Macedonian" versions of the past. Yet he, too, finds himself caught up in the overarching frame of truth and fiction, as he dismisses both "nationalist" versions and offers his own more authoritative account, explicitly counteracting the excesses of others (Danforth 1995a:26–78).

These discussions, as suggested in the introduction, are all responses to the commonsensical starting point of Hugh Poulton's 1995 book, *Who Are the Macedonians*? I have set out not to provide an answer, but to demonstrate the raft of contingencies that underlie that question. As Muriel Dimen-Schein pointed out a quarter of a century ago, writing about Vlahs in Northern Greece, "Ethnic identity, its meaning and importance vary in time and space" (1975:83). What it meant to be Macedonian (or Greek or Bulgarian) in 1903 was different from what it meant in 1944 and in 1991, whatever the efforts of particular interest groups to tie those meanings together. The meaning of being Macedonian in Kruševo, a town with Greek and Vlah dimensions to its past, has never marched in step with the meaning of being Macedonian in cities like Tetovo or Skopje, with their own different multi-ethnic histories. Pastoralist, bourgeois, and migratory modes of livelihood provided axes of solidarity and antagonism different from those highlighted in a focus on the narod as a unit composed of socialist workers tied to the soil of their native land. The chapters of this book have set out some of the struggles and negotiations over the meaning of Macedonian that attention to these dimensions reveals.

This book also constitutes a social history of twentieth-century Kruševo. As observed earlier, such history can serve the agenda of those who seek to invest their visions of national solidarity with longevity. However, it can also disrupt easy assumptions of inevitability, as Bernard Cohn points out:

> By focusing on conflict, repression and deprivation, I think unwittingly the proctological historians are bringing back as the problematic of social history not just history from the bottom up, but history from the top down as well. Their conclusions have directed us to the study of the structures and meanings involved in the creation of systems of solidarity and authority and to what appear to be the unconscious systems of control which mark most modern societies. (1987:40)

The role for the scholar that this suggests can be described as writing an account of the process by which various agents transform the contingent into the taken-for-granted. Central to this enterprise is not a chronological account of a nation's or a community's history, but rather an analysis of the ways in which histories come into contact and chronologies emerge.

In this sense, this book responds not to Hugh Poulton's question, but to that posed by the title of the opening chapter of Partha Chatterjee's (1993) *The Nation and its Fragments*: Whose imagined community? I have sought to communicate a sense of how well people in Kruševo apprehend the elusiveness of the past and the contingency of the present. They are not the Balkan zealots beloved of some observers, pursuing age-old grievances with passionate intensity. Nor are they chameleons who shift allegiance with the times for their own advantage. Their stance, instead, recalls that of scholars acutely conscious of the ways in which historical agents cast their own agendas as historic, and those of others as in need of correction.

Between 1900 and 2000, Kruševo's inhabitants and their predecessors made their way through a turbulent century, rebuilding their lives and fortunes as best they could after each new challenge or disaster. Doomsayers, or those who draw an essential dichotomy between forms of community, might argue that the solidarity they have conjured is an illusion, and that the town's fractious history of class, ethnic, and ideological hostilities will one day return. Through enduring memories that encompass not just those hostilities, but their destructive consequences, the people of Kruševo spent the twentieth century resisting the power of imagined inevitability. The stories they and their town can tell, and those told by others about them, remain open and fluid. They remind us, if we choose to listen, that there are other ways to negotiate the vagaries of the present than by accepting or rejecting master narratives of the past. They offer, instead, glimpses of a world of debate where passionate convictions, often so deadly, are tempered by knowledge of the uncertainties of nation.

Glossary and Acronyms

Alonia — (Greek) See *Gumenja*.

Aroumian — See *Vlah*.

bashi-bazouks — Turkish irregular auxiliaries, recruited from local Muslim population.

bey — Ottoman-era Turkish landholder.

Brsjak — Member of Slavic ethnic group, indigenous to the Krusevo region. Plural form *Brsjaci*. Bulgarian form *Brzjaci*.

četa — Armed band.

četnik — Member of a četa. During and after the Second World War, the term also described noncommunist Serbian forces, whether resisting Axis occupation or fighting against Tito's Partisans. In Yugoslavia, the term had a derogatory force. Plural form *četnici*.

čiflik — A large farm or estate owned by a landlord.

Cincar — (Serbian) See Vlah.

čirak — Junior apprentice of a *majstor*.

comitadji — See *komitadži*.

denar — Macedonian currency after 1992, replacing Yugoslav *dinar*.

dever — Groomsman or best man. Strictly, the groom's brother.

dolni — Term used especially between 1919 and 1944 in Kruševo to describe people living in the lower town who were mostly Vlah. See *gorni*.

domaćin — (Serb) Head of household. In Macedonian, *domakin*.

Éllines — Patriarchist Christians, usually loyal subjects of the Ottoman Empire, otherwise known as Greeks.

esnaf — Trade guild. Plural form *esnafi*.

ethnikótita — (Greek) Close in meaning to nationality or ethnicity.

Exarchists — Orthodox Christians who, in the Ottoman period, pledged allegiance to the Exarchate, created in 1870 and identified as Bulgarian. It was an alternative organization to the Patriarchate. See *Patriarchists*.

gastarbeiter — (German) Guest-worker or temporary migrant laborer.

gemidžii — Literally, boatmen. As a proper noun, the name of a group of VMRO activists who conducted dynamite attacks on a French steamship and public buildings in Thessaloniki during April 1903. Definite form *gemidžiite*.

Gheg — Dialect and tribe of northern Albania, Kosovo, and northwestern Republic of Macedonia around Tetovo. See also *Tosk*.

gorni — Term used especially between 1919 and 1944 in Kruševo to describe people living in the upper town who were mostly Slav. See *dolni*.

Grkoman — A member of a different linguistic or cultural group (for example Albanian, Vlah, Bulgarian) who is pro-Greek. Plural form *Grkomani*.

Gumenja — Hill at the northwestern edge of Kruševo. Derived from *gumno*.

gumno — A threshing-place.

imenden — Name day.

junak — Hero or champion.

kaimakam — Local administrator in Ottoman period.

kalfa — Senior apprentice or journeyman of a *majstor*.

kiradžija — Carting or transport trade.

komitadži — Member of Revolutionary Organization, which was organized into local and regional committees. Often used to describe armed activists of the Organization, and therefore overlapping in meaning with *četnik*. Plural form *komitadžii*. During the period 1941–44 and afterward, often used to refer to pro-Bulgarian paramilitaries.

konak — Ottoman-era local government office.

korzo — Social promenade.

kum — Godfather or wedding sponsor.

kumstvo — The relationship between two individuals or families, where one is *kum* to the other.

leva — Bulgarian currency.

maalo — Neighborhood or quarter. Derived from Arabic *mahalla*.

majstor — Master of a skilled trade, or *zanaet*, usually owning his own business.

malcinstvo — Minority.

Mijak — Member of a Slavic ethnic group indigenous to western Macedonia (around Galičnik). Plural *Mijaci*.

millet — Religious community recognized by Ottoman adminstration.

narod — Nation or people. Category assigned in Yugoslav period to "constituent peoples"—Serbs, Croats, Slovenes, Montenegrins, Macedonians and, after 1968, Muslims (Bosniaks).

narodnost — Close in meaning to nationality or ethnicity. In Yugoslav era, classificatory term for groups in Yugoslavia that had a kin-state outside Yugoslavia, such as Albanians and Hungarians.

opština — Municipality, or administrative region, in post-1945 Macedonia.

o.s. — Old Style—used to denote dates given in the older Julian calendar.

pastrma — Dried meat, a major product of Kruševo's pastoral economy.

Patriarchists — Orthodox Christians in Ottoman period who maintained their allegiance to the Patriarchate, the long-established religious authority, identified as Greek. See *Exarchists*.

pečalba — Temporary labor migration, undertaken by *pečalbari*.

poteklo — Descent.

pobratim — Groomsman or best man. Literally, a "fictive" brother, created by ritual rather than a blood relationship.

rabotnički narod — Working people. Term used in Yugoslav period, blurring class and ethnic loyalties.

redifs — Reservists in Ottoman army.

ruba — Household furnishings and clothes provided to the bride by her family as dowry.

Rum — Name of Orthodox Christian *millet* in Ottoman Empire until 1870, when its unity was challenged by the creation of the Exarchate.

spomenica — Commemorative medal given to veterans of Ilinden by Yugoslav Macedonian government.

spomenik — Monument.

Srbophil — Pro-Serb. In Yugoslav period, derogatory term suggesting allegiance to first Yugoslavia.

strojnici — Matchmakers.

Strunga — Southwest area of Kruševo, formerly location of sheepfolds.

svadba — Wedding.

terorist — Self-designation used by VMRO activists in 1903 period who carried out executions of spies, traitors, or other enemies condemned to death.

Tosk — Albanian dialect and tribal group of southern Albania and southwestern Republic of Macedonia, around Lake Prespa. See *Gheg*.

vilayet — Ottoman era administrative province.

Vlahs — Romance-speaking ethnic group in Macedonia, and major component of urban population of Kruševo.

vojvod — VMRO military leader.

vrski — Literally, connections. Instrumental relationships used to gain access to scarce resources.

v'rg'ri — (Vlah) Term used to describe Slavic population.

Wallachs — (Or *Wallachians*). See *Vlahs*.

zadruga — Collective household of more than one nuclear family.

zanaet — Skilled artisanal trade. Plural form *zanaeti*.

Acronyms

ASNOM — Anti-fascist Assembly for the National Liberation of Macedonia, held on 2 August (Ilinden) 1944.

AVNOJ — Anti-fascist Council for the National Liberation of Yugoslavia.

BCP — Bulgarian Communist Party.

CPY — Communist Party of Yugoslavia.

DA — Democratic Alternative. Political party committed to civic concept of nation, formed before Macedonian elections in 1998.

EC — European Community.

FYROM — Former Yugoslav Republic of Macedonia. Internationally accepted name for the Republic of Macedonia, in use after 1992.

JNA — Yugoslav National Army.

MPO — Macedonian Patriotic Organization. Diaspora organization in the United States and Canada, founded in 1921 under the name Macedonian Political Organization.

NATO — North Atlantic Treaty Organization.

NOB — National Liberation Struggle, conducted by partisan forces in Yugoslavia, 1941–44.

NOF — National Liberation Front. Macedonian resistance movement in Greece, founded April 1945.

NRM — People's Republic of Macedonia. Official Republic name 1944–48.

PDP — Party of Democratic Prosperity. Albanian political party formed before Macedonian elections in 1990.

SDSM — Social Democratic Alliance of Macedonia. Heir to Yugoslav-era communist party, formed after Macedonian elections in 1990.

SFRY — Socialist Federal Republic of Yugoslavia.

SRM — Socialist Republic of Macedonia. Official Republic name 1948–91.

SRZ — Agricultural cooperative instituted by Yugoslav state after World War II.

TMORO — Secret Macedonian and Adrianople Revolutionary Organization. Documented name of the revolutionary organization adopted in 1902.

VMRO — Internal Macedonian Revolutionary Organization. Paramilitary organization in existence, in different forms, from the 1890s to the 1930s.

VMRO-DPMNE — Internal Macedonian Revolutionary Organization–Democratic Party for Macedonian National Unity. Macedonian political party formed before Macedonian elections in 1990.

Notes

Chapter One

1. Macedonian historians give the dates of Samuil's reign as 976–1014. Reportedly, he died of grief when he saw his army returning from a defeat by Emperor Basil of Byzantium. Basil had blinded all save one man in a hundred, who was left with one eye, to guide the others home (Apostolski et al. 1979:40–44). The distinguished historian John Fine provides a similar narrative, but considers that Samuil was a Bulgarian king (Fine 1983:188–98).

2. The Bastille prison in Paris was stormed during the French revolution; Runnymede was the site of the signing of the Magna Carta in 1215, which gave barons and people legal protection against royal power. The Alamo was a fortress held to the death against a Mexican army by a small band of Texans during the war of 1836, which ended in Texan independence. Messolonghi was a Greek town besieged by the Turkish army during the Greek War of Independence, the inhabitants of which staged a break-out on 10 April 1826, which failed disastrously but is recalled gloriously. Serbian resistance to the advancing Ottoman Empire was weakened when Prince Lazar was defeated by the Sultan's army on Kosovo Field on 28 June (15 June in the old calendar) 1389. At Masada, in A.D., 73 AD, Jewish rebels killed themselves rather than fall into Roman hands. The Alamo, Kosovo Field, and Masada have been taken by anthropologists as starting points for discussions of power, memory, and forms of narration (Trouillot 1995; Flores 2002; Duijzings 2000; Bruner and Gorfain 1984).

3. Historically, Janissaries were soldiers of the Ottoman army, recruited as children from Christian populations and converted to Islam. They were eliminated by the Sultan in 1826 (Stavrianos 1958:300–4). Here the term seems to be used to denote Christian traitors, in a sense similar to that recorded by Danforth in Australia in the 1990s (1995:227).

4. This interpretation of identities in the town is based upon that given by Nikola Kirov-Majski, and discussed in chapter 4.

Chapter Two

1. Vukovar was a town on the Danube River on the Croatian-Serbian border that was shelled into rubble by the Yugoslav National Army in 1991. After the town fell in November, many of its Croatian defenders were rounded up and executed, including at least 200 wounded soldiers. Sarajevo spent three years besieged by surrounding Bosnian Serb forces, and artillery and snipers regularly killed civilians on the streets. Srebrenica, a UN-protected safe haven in Bosnia, was the site of a massacre of Bosnian Muslim men by Bosnian Serb forces on 11–12 July 1995.

2. In the British Parliament, on 14 December 1992, Prime Minister John Major called Macedonia "the tinder-box with the greatest risk of involving other countries." In a statement before the Commission on Security and Cooperation in Europe, in Washington, D.C., on 21 July 1993, U.S. State Department official Stephen A. Oxman

stated, "The Balkans are still the powderkeg of Europe. If the present conflict were to spread to Kosovo, or to Macedonia, or elsewhere, the entire region could be destabilized" (*US Department of State Dispatch*, volume 4, number 32: 9 August 1993).

3. It should be stressed that the pejorative implication of "nationalism" is a recent phenomenon. The positive associations of the nation have a lengthy heritage, being traceable to Herder, and certainly apparent in Renan's oft-cited statement of the late nineteenth century, "Qu'est-ce qu'une nation?" (Renan 1990). Hans Kohn (1962) and Carlton Hayes (1927) both worked to explicate this tradition, more recently explored by Greenfeld (1992). But the notion of nationalism as disease permeates the metaphors with which journalists have described the break-up of Yugoslavia. On 3 February 1992 the *New York Times* included an article with the title "A fear that Macedonia might metastasize." Other examples of the idiom of uncontrollable epidemic are recorded by Franklin Lytle (1992). In the Macedonian case, Danforth notes repeated cases of imagery from medical pathology (1995a:110n:225).

4. Anthropologists aligned themselves differently in this discussion. Some, like Tone Bringa, drew on intimate knowledge acquired through extended fieldwork to argue against popular ideas of "ancient hatreds." Bringa traced the patterns of coexistence in her ethnography of a mixed Catholic-Muslim village in central Bosnia (Bringa 1995), and played a key role in the Granada documentary film, *We Are All Neighbours* (1993) that stressed the novelty and external origin of violence in the village. Other ethnographers have found hierarchies of civilization and barbarism popular in local explanations of violence and argued that analysis should be sensitive to the existence of cultural dispositions to "perform manhood," that may deliberately foster images of wildness and violence (Van Der Port 1998; Živković 2001; see also Herzfeld 1985).

5. The Internal Macedonian Revolutionary Organization-Democratic Party for Macedonian National Unity. VMRO was the name of the revolutionary organization behind the Ilinden Uprising.

6. Another Macedonian soldier, Dragoslav Petrovski, was killed at Vukovar in late August 1991, when he reportedly had just eighteen days left to serve (*Nova Makedonija*, 31 August 1991).

7. The referendum was carefully worded to include the possibility of Macedonia remaining a part of a looser confederation. The text given in *Nova Makedonija*, 31 August 1991 was "*Dali ste za suverena I samostojna republika Makedonija so pravo da stapi vo eden sojuz na suvereni državi na Jugoslavija?*" (Are you for a sovereign and independent Republic of Macedonia with a right to enter an association of sovereign states of Yugoslavia?) The referendum was boycotted by the Albanian population of Macedonia. Relations between the two groups are discussed further in chapter 10.

8. For an account of UN deployment in Macedonia, see Williams (2000).

9. Zarobeni devizi could also be used to pay for weddings, funerals, and foreign study.

10. Around one-quarter of Macedonia's Roms live in a suburb of Skopje, called Šuto Orizari, or Šutka. There are also communities in Kumanovo and Štip. As well as the Vlahs of Kruševo, there are also Vlah communities in eastern Macedonia. Some former Roms classify themselves as Egyptians, a process of self-ascription explored by Duijzings (1997).

11. As explored in the Macedonian case by Victor Friedman (1996) and more generally by David Kertzer and Dominique Arel (2001), censuses have their own politics. In 1991 Macedonia's Albanian population boycotted the census, and their leadership made similar threats ahead of the 1994 census, which was internationally administered. The Albanian numbers were accordingly calculated by projection from the previous census. The high number of Turks counted in 1953 may have been bolstered by Albanians declaring themselves as Turkish, at a time when Tito's government pressured Turks to emigrate permanently to Turkey (Akan 2000). The category of Other has routinely included small numbers of Greeks and Bulgarians. In 1981 and 1991 it included between 30,000 and 40,000 Muslims, and around 15,000 Yugoslavs. In 1994 the number of Muslims had diminished to around 15,000, and there were reportedly only 595 Yugoslavs (Friedman 1996:90).

12. Tensions have continued to simmer between different sections of Macedonia's population, and have erupted into violence over issues of cultural rights and their threat to public order. See Brown 2000b, 2001.

13. A former Norwegian officer, with whom I spoke in 1999 stated that the Norwegians held an inquiry and found no basis for the accusations.

14. Other scholars have highlighted the existence of the Macedonian minority (see for example Danforth 1993), but the venom of nationalist organizations in Greece was concentrated against Karakasidou. Several prominent scholars rallied to her cause, and the book was published by the University of Chicago Press instead. (Karakasidou 1997a). As tensions over the issue receded, the town of Florina continued to attract the attention of anthropologists, becoming what Giorgos Agelopoulos wryly called an "ethnographic boomtown" (Agelopoulos n.d.).

15. I have largely followed conventions set by British consuls of the time, using a mixture of Turkish and Europeanized forms of names. Salonika (or Salonica) could also be called Selanik. Greek and Slavic-speakers disagreed over some names, including Kastoria, which in the local Slavic language was Kostur. For information on other naming variations, see the Glossary.

16. Greece's definition of Macedonia was different from those of Bulgaria and Serbia, excluding the Uskub vilayet entirely. Greek scholars justified this on historical grounds, but it had the pragmatic advantage of allowing statistics of schools and churches to show a higher proportion of Greeks in Macedonia (Friedman 1996:85; Christides 1949).

17. To make clear the diversity of groups competing to represent the Christian population, Perry uses the acronym MRO rather than VMRO. Many pension applicants in the period between 1948 and 1953 referred simply to "the Organization" in the early part of the twentieth century. Some did name VMRO, however, and I have opted to use this more familiar term throughout this book.

18. There are also two small pockets of territory considered by some analysts as historically Macedonian within modern Albania, around the Prespa lakes and at Golo Brdo. The region known as Gora, in Kosovo, is also home to Macedonian-speakers.

19. For accounts of government policy toward the indigenous Slavic-speaking peasantry, often called Slavophones, see Karakasidou 1997b and 2000; and Carabott 1997. For accounts of aspects of the population transfers, see Agelopoulos 1997 and Voutira 1997. In an illuminating discussion of the Macedonian Question in the 1920s, Patrick Finney argues that the settlement of these refugees in northern Greece, while

serving in the long run to further cement Greek claims to the territory, in the short term was seen as weakening Greece's ability to defend against military attack from Yugoslavia. That prospect was not as remote in the period 1920–25 as it came to appear in retrospect (Finney 2003).

20. The MPO was later renamed the Macedonian Patriotic Organization, and is still active. Within the Republic of Macedonia during the Yugoslav period, the MPO was considered to be strongly pro-Bulgarian.

21. This brief account does not do justice to the political nuances of the immediate post-war period and the consequences of the Tito-Stalin split. More detail is provided in chapters 6 and 8, in Brown (2003a), and in accounts by Palmer and King (1971) and Banac (1988).

22. By thus conjuring Balkan ghosts—for which he uses a poetic Macedonian word, *seništa*—President Gligorov anticipated the title of Robert Kaplan's best-selling book, *Balkan Ghosts* (1993), by two years.

Chapter Three

1. The works that Kaplan cites were John Reed's *The War in Eastern Europe* and A. G. Hales' *Daily News* articles. Kaplan also draws on a wide range of secondary material, and a memoir by a resident of Salonika (Sciaky 1946). Hales also wrote a memoir, which reveals the career of a part-time "Balkan-fancier." It includes an account of his fighting in a Bulgarian band during 1903 as "one of the happiest periods of my life" (1918:207). During the First World War he wrote to Lord Kitchener, offering to return to the region to raise the "Macedonian mountaineers" to fight on the side of the Allies. The offer was not taken up (1918:316–19).

2. It is in part for this reason that the pastoral Sarakatsani of northern Greece, among whom John Campbell worked in the 1950s, were so often considered to be Vlahs, and it is for this reason that Campbell devotes a portion of his introduction to disclaiming the connection (Campbell 1964).

3. The meaning of millet and the extent to which the Ottoman Empire relied upon a millet-system for indirect rule are discussed in Braude (1982). Intervention by the state in the workings of the Orthodox church in the nineteenth century was not new: in 1767, Greek-speaking élites in Constantinople, known as the Phanariots, had persuaded the Sultan to close down a rival center of ecclesiastical authority operating in Ohrid. The year 1767 was to prove significant in Yugoslav-sponsored church reorganization two hundred years later, as discussed in chapter 7.

4. Heathcote to Blunt, Salonika, 8 April 1898: FO 195/2029/305. McGregor to Graves, Monastir, 30 September 1903: FO 195/2157/580, 31 October 1903: FO 195/2157/731. Biliotti to Whitehead, Salonika, 26 January 1903: FO 195/2156/76; Graves to O'Conor, Salonika, 29 February 1904: FO 195/2182/120; 8 April 1904: FO 195/2182/286.

5. Biliotti to Whitehead, Salonika, 26 January 1903: FO 195/2156/76; McGregor to Biliotti, 19 April 1903: FO 195/2156/454, which lists a sixteen-year-old murder victim in Monastir as being "of Kutso-Vlach nationality." Graves to O'Conor, Salonica, 25 July 1904: FO 195/2183/74. A term not used in the foreign office correspondence is Tzintzar, or *Cincar*, an alternative, derogatory form to describe the Vlah population. The term is used by Irby and McKenzie (1877).

6. An example of the effect of translation can be seen in Upward when he notices that his interpreter translated *makedonski* as Bulgarian (1908:204)—a phenomenon that for all we know, was encountered all-unknowing by many other travelers. I am indebted to Victor Friedman for this source. The Ottoman authorities provided escorts ostensibly for protection. Booth and Moore, traveling together in 1904, did escape their escort for a short while, but the subsequent passage reveals that they could achieve very little without one. No guide would accompany a journalist breaking the rules, and they met no one during their hours of freedom, so that all they could write about in this episode was the landscape, each other, and their cleverness in escaping.

7. Malaria was still widespread in the region, especially in the lowland areas which are now fertile farmland in northern Greece, but were in the Ottoman period low-lying marshes. Certain cities were also unhealthy; it was proposed in August 1902 that Skopje, then known as Uskub, be classified by the British Foreign Office as an unhealthy post for purposes of leave allowance, "owing to the prevalence of malarial and rheumatic fevers in the town" (Biliotti to O'Conor, Salonica, 7 August 1902 FO 195/2133/295). Edith Durham reports a doctor calling the water in Ohrid "dysentery soup" and notes that the death rate was four times that of London (1905:166).

8. Moore relates this event rather differently, highlighting not Saki's cleverness, but his ill-judged attempt to use Bulgarian to speak to their captors, and his further obliviousness to impression-management by pulling out pen and paper to write an epigram (Moore 1906:108–15). Saki's assumption was that recognition as a foreign European would be a safeguard rather than a danger, this view was also expressed to John Fraser, who retained a slouch felt hat throughout his travels, by an Armenian companion, who considered the hat better than an escort (1906:116).

9. Unlike Amery, Wyon received some sympathy and restrained respect from consular staff. In Monastir, where he was the subject of official Ottoman complaint to the British government for his "offensive articles" based on interviews with victims of Turkish violence in Kruševo and the villages of Biloshi and Armensko, the local consul, McGregor, defended the accuracy of Wyon's reporting (Wyon 1904:95–9; McGregor telegram, 17/18 September 1903: FO 195/2157/502).

10. The power to classify was, as in all state surveillance projects, contested. Wyon reports bribing an official in order to falsify his name and profession in his teskere; he believed that he was well known by the administration as a robust critic and only by assuming a different identity would he be able to travel at all (Wyon 1904:122). Members of the revolutionary organization who feared they were known by name often used borrowed or forged documents when they were forced to travel openly.

11. Reports from Kruševo fill the correspondence from Monastir and Salonika in the latter part of August (FO 195/2157/314–426). Moore's visit appears to have taken place between October 10 and 21: London's permission was sought for the vice-consul to accompany him, and his report was later cited in a despatch from Monastir (FO 195/2157/632; 195/2157/679). A further eyewitness account from a family letter is given in Routier 1903:169–75. The nine centers were named as Monastir, Resna, Ohrid, Klissura, Kastoria, Florina, Biglishta, Kyrchevo, and Krushevo. Today, these centers are Bitola, Resen, Ohrid, Klissura, Kastoria, Florina, Bilisht, Kičevo, and Kruševo. The first three and last two are in the Republic of Macedonia, while Klis-

sura, Kastoria and Florina are in Greece and Bilisht is in Albania. H. N. Brailsford and Edith Durham were both involved in the distribution of aid. The operation in Kruševo was under the supervision of an American missionary from Salonica, Mr. Haskell (McGregor to Graves, Monastir, 9 December 1903: FO 195/2157/814). When efforts concluded six months later, according to British sources, 54,000 people from 132 burned and plundered villages had received 15,000 blankets, 7,000 wadded jackets, and a large quantity of other clothing, as well as food aid, at a cost to the fund of about £25,000 (Graves to O'Conor, Salonica, 26 March 1904: FO 195/2182/237).

12. Kruševo is about forty-five miles from Skopje as the crow flies. To get there, though, requires traveling through Prilep and then up a road with many switchbacks, which almost doubles the distance.

Chapter Four

1. A number of colleagues have questioned my use of the term "tipping point" especially in light of David Laitin's use of the notion of "tipping" or "cascading" to illuminate processes of identity change in the former Soviet Republic (Laitin 1998). I use the term in early-twentieth-century Kruševo to describe not just a "switch" made by individuals but a qualitative transformation in the way in which identity was conceived.

2. The autobiographies of pension applicants in the 1940s and 1950s make clear the central significance of oaths of loyalty for VMRO members. People pledged their loyalty to the organization, to the struggle, or to Macedonia, and often used the phrase "Until freedom or death." Swearing-in ceremonies were conducted by senior members of VMRO, and new members recited their *kletva* or the *zaklet*—words for curse as well as for oath—over a Bible, a revolver, and a dagger.

3. The 1935 text was published in standard Bulgarian; in his letters and some other writings, Kirov-Majski uses Kruševo dialect. He consistently called his hometown Krušovo, and I have preserved this spelling, as well as the Greek spelling of Krousovo, in this chapter.

4. Skopje National Archives, Kirov-Majski Fund, 1.976.2.19/70 and 1.976.2.81/132. The distinction made by Kirov-Majski was also recognized by Serbian ethnographer Jovan Cvijić, who referred to Mijaci and Brsjaci as tribal names (1907:19). Brsjaci, Cvijić says, were native to the Kičevo and Kruševo areas. Mijaci were native to the western Macedonian region of Mala Reka, close to modern Debar and including the villages of Galičnik and Lazaropole; they had migrated to other areas, including the region between Kičevo and Smilevo. Horace Lunt traces the etymology of the name to a linguistic usage; they used *mije* instead of *nije* for "we" (Lunt 1984:102n.). The Tomalevski family was also from Kruševo. The usual publication date for Georgi Tomalevski's novel is 1968, but the preface makes clear that an earlier version had been distributed and received critical commentary.

5. Throughout this chapter, I try to use the form of the town's name used by each author as that author is discussed—a conceit, perhaps, but intended to remind the reader of the multiple ways people thought of the town's name and identity.

6. Zbigniew Golab, who conducted linguistic fieldwork in Kruševo in the 1950s, recorded twelve regional origins in what he described as the town's Vlah community. Golab refutes Ballas's account of an origin-point near Naoussa, and pinpoints instead

the town of Nikolica in southern Albania. He makes no reference to a group called the Motslani (Golab 1984:19).

7. In translating *politismòs* as civilization, I follow Hart (1999). The tension she traces between "culture" and "civilization" on the Greek-Albanian border has certain resonances with the debate between Kirov-Majski and Ballas staged here.

8. This church, which was in the upper part of town and stands today, was St. Bogorodica, subsequently identified as the Bulgarian church. According to Matkovski's long account (1978:79–92), it was built at the initiative of the local Slavic-speaking community and against Greek opposition. It later came under the control of the Exarchate, and as a consequence, was then shut down by the dominant Patriarchist community.

9. The imagery is from Greek mythology: the hydra was a many-headed beast, and if any one head were cut off, two more would grow in its place. The secret to its defeat was to use sword and fire together, first cutting off a head and then scorching the neck so no more could grow. This would be the Greek method of destroying Bulgarian villages in the Second Balkan War.

10. For more on wedding practices in Kruševo and elsewhere, see chapter 5.

11. Ditsias's account thus agrees with Moore's composite version, given in chapter 1, indicating that some parts of the town were burned during the initial insurgent attack. This detail was also confirmed by oral histories recorded in Kruševo, in which one old man insisted that the town had begun to burn on Ilinden itself, the day of many weddings.

12. It is not clear who Givannof was, as the name is not recognizably the same as any of those widely commemorated as the Uprising's leaders. Frederick Moore, in the account given in chapter 1, referred to an Ivanoff. It is possible that the references are to one of two brothers, Kole and Alekso Ivanovski, who are given a small role in the taking of the town by modern Macedonian historians.

13. It is possible, given his presence at the Headquarters, that he is the Spyros H. Naskos listed by Ballas as treasurer of the first committee (1962:46).

14. As late as the 1940s, people in Macedonia used these terms interchangeably in describing the armed members of VMRO during the 1903 Uprising. Only in describing the Second World War did they acquire their ideological coloring, such that *četnik* meant Serb or pro-Serb, and *komitadži* Bulgarian or pro-Bulgarian.

15. The new victim was not only most likely unconnected with the perpetrators of the first act, but he may even have been opposed to them. Bulgarian schoolmasters had in other cases tried to reduce the polarization of society, and counseled others not to submit to the exactions demanded either by the Macedonian Revolutionary Organization or by bands associated with the Exarchate. They had sometimes paid for such positions with their lives, as occurred in a case reported on 25 February 1902 from Prilep (FO 195/2133/127).

16. In a replay of the post-mortem over the destruction of Kruševo, the authenticity of these letters became a major point of dispute, polarizing pro-Greek and pro-Bulgarian sides. One writer dismissed them as Bulgarian fabrications on several grounds; in one case the only Greek soldier whose name matched the signature had served on a different front, the combination of clear handwriting and poor spelling was suspicious, and the Bulgarians had a prior history of using forgeries (Cassavetti 1914:348–51). Another found convincing the weight of depositions from witnesses

testifying to Greek atrocities and attempts to shift blame to the Bulgarians—including, it was reported, dressing the disfigured body of "Dimitri Gheorgieff, the Bulgarian priest of Krushevo, cruelly killed by Greeks" in the vestments of an archbishop and claiming it to be that of a Greek victim of Bulgarian violence. In this context, the variety of addresses, types of paper, handwriting styles, and expressions of violence served as convincing proof of the letters' genuineness (Wallis 1914:513–23). In the wrangling over truth-status, the enormity of the human suffering gradually dropped out of view.

17. *The Other Balkan Wars* includes a description of Vlahs being ready to call themselves "brothers of the Servians." The description continues: "Their formula for the Bulgarian population, the most numerous, is as follows: 'Up to now you have been our masters and pillaged our goods; now it is our turn to pillage yours'" (in Kennan [ed.] 1993:145–46).

Chapter Five

1. Certain of these former Kruševans have interested themselves in professional history. These include Konstantine Vavouskos, mentioned in chapter 4, who headed the Center for Macedonian Studies in the early 1990s.

2. As noted earlier, both Ballas and Kirov-Majski offered short descriptions of the house and its destruction. Dančo Zografksi's description (1948:11) is taken from Popović (1937:294).

3. Kirov-Majski's letters from this period are in the National Archives in Skopje. Fund 1.976.2.

4. Ethnic groups from different locations specialized in certain trades. As noted earlier, the Mijaci from western Macedonia were skilled masons. Vlahs dominated the tailoring and metalworking trades. Nikolaos Ballas observed in 1905 that the village of Trstenik close to Kruševo, whose Vlah inhabitants had relocated to the town in the eighteenth century, had been mainly inhabited by tinsmiths (1962:21).

5. VMRO was revived by Todor Alexandrov in 1919, after the Versailles decision that ruled out an autonomous Macedonia. After Alexandrov's murder in a factional dispute in 1924, Ivan Mihailov took over. Under his leadership VMRO became more involved in criminal and terrorist activities, culminating in its participation in the assassination of King Alexander in 1934.

6. These rolls are called *ǵevreci* (singular: *ǵevrek*) and are still a staple snack.

7. Traces of Greek identity remained. One older man referred to Dr. Balabanov, a Kruševo physician with whom he worked in Tetovo in 1946, as Greek. I also met with an elderly man in a nursing home in Bitola who insisted that he was Greek—to the mild amusement of his younger relatives who had introduced us. Some individuals who married into Kruševo families from outside had no Vlah ancestry themselves; a friend's grandmother, for example, was from Constantinople and therefore qualified in the vernacular definition as *čista Grkinja*—a pure Greek.

8. Here ' signals schwa, the unstressed vowel sound.

9. Potential brides would be scrutinized for signs of physical robustness and child-bearing capacity. Another aspect of individuality that reportedly was significant was mental competence. From several sources, I heard the suggestion that insistence on marriage between families of equivalent station in the small community of Kruševo

had led to offspring with some form of mental handicap. Ekaterina reported using this commonly held belief in negotiations over her fate with her parents. See note 14.

10. Although formally clearly distinct, the terms dever and pobratim were sometimes used interchangeably to refer to the groomsman, or best man, irrespective of "real" kinship. Such blurring of meanings is recorded from other cases by Hammel (1968:96). Some Vlah speakers in Kruševo reckoned dever as a Serbian word, and pobratim as Macedonian.

11. The sequence of events described here closely follows that given by Olive Lodge, describing the village of Galičnik in western Macedonia, though the pacing differs. There, Lodge records a feast at the groom's home followed by one at the bride's home. Lodge documents other details that residents of Kruševo remembered from weddings in the town, including the ritual shaving of the groom. Although now almost deserted, Galičnik was once a populous and wealthy Mijak village, whose menfolk migrated seasonally to work as masons elsewhere. As in Kruševo, multiple weddings were thus conducted in a short season in the late summer, when most migrants returned home. The Galičnik wedding, conducted on St. Peter's Day, or *Petrovden*, in early July, was preserved as a piece of folklife spectacle in Yugoslav Macedonia, and has continued to be celebrated since independence in 1992. It generates particular excitement when a couple with family ties to the village elects to conduct their wedding according to this old practice. For more about Galičnik weddings in the 1990s, see Thiessen (1999).

12. This law, rigorously applied, could trump the distinction between the upper and lower town. I was told the story of Tome Naumovski, a Macedonian, by one of his sons. Naumovski was from the upper town, yet married a Vlah bride twenty years his junior in 1928. It was reportedly one of the very first marriages between the communities. Tome's extended absence from the town in the United States, where he had accumulated a respectable fortune, undoubtedly contributed to his ability to transcend the social demarcations of the town.

13. St. Erlich's correspondent suggests that children have warmer relations with both parents when the father spends time on pečalba. The pattern of consultation between husband and wife in Christian Macedonia represented an anomaly for St. Erlich's overall analysis, which generally mapped indicators of "modern" or "civilized" relations on a rising scale from Albanian Macedonia to the Adriatic littoral. Pečalba was one part of her explanation of what she saw as anomalously high levels of gender cooperation in Christian Macedonian marriages. St. Erlich also made reference to the custom of younger men marrying older wives, reported of the nineteenth century by some foreign visitors (Irby and Mackenzie 1877:129). Other authors have argued precisely counter to St. Erlich, and noted that pečalba can serve to maintain patriarchal structures. Hammel notes that in some cases, pečalba licensed sexual relations between the brothers and wives of absent men (1968:33). In her ethnography of Kosovo in the late 1980s, Reineck reports that wives left at home did not acquire greater responsibilities or freedoms, but were expected to maintain proper behavior (1991:129–32).

14. Beliefs persist in Kruševo that extended intermarriage among élites committed to endogamy has led over time to an increase in genetically based problems in offspring. See footnote 9.

15. For a discussion of the ongoing significance of imenden celebrations in Kruševo, see chapter 9.

16. Skerlić (1877–1914), a literary critic and advocate of federalism in Yugoslavia, helped found a citizen's club called The Slavonic South as early as 1907 (Batakovic [n.d.]). The founding of the Jovan Skerlić association in Kruševo is also recorded in Andonov-Poljanski et al. (eds.) (1983:43).

17. These details are taken from Risteski's autobiography. His activism is also attested in correspondence from Nikola Telesku to Nikola Kirov-Majski in September 1959 (AM 1.976.2.113/187ff). Telesku identifies Mile Bočvar, a cooper born in Kruševo in 1908, as another important member of the group, and confirms that the group was composed of people "from the two sides of the town." The Papakoča family were of Vlah descent, originally from Grammos.

18. The presence of this global commercial concern in the mountains of western Macedonia serves as a reminder that transnational capitalism's penetration into rural hinterlands is not new. The Singer Company had already been active for at least thirty years. In 1904 a British representative in Uskub (modern Skopje) reported that an agent of the American Singer Manufacturing Company had requested protection and assistance. At that time, the company had ". . . recently introduced a system by which women from certain villages are brought to Üsküb to learn a new method of sewing and embroidery which they will, on return to their villages, teach" (Satow to Graves, 2 July 1904, Uskub: FO 195/2182/520).

19. In his memoir, written before 1991, Risteski referred to the Yugoslavia of 1929–41 as "Former Yugoslavia," a term that has now come to refer to the country's 1945–91 incarnation.

20. The Bulgarian-Italian division of control is mapped in figure 6.

21. More details of Risteski's wartime career are given in chapter 8.

22. For an English-language account of the destruction of Macedonia's Jewish communities during the Bulgarian occupation, see Matkovski (1982).

23. Radical agricultural collectivization was not attempted until later. Yugoslav leaders recognized that it would risk losing the support of the peasants on which they ultimately relied. The effects of collectivization are discussed in chapter 6.

24. The communist campaign to eliminate the goat population of Yugoslavia was a case of the kind of "high modernist" reform programs described so vividly by James Scott (1998). The logic of the government was based on statistics that showed that, while a herdsman might apparently make clear profit by letting his animals graze highland forest, it would cost the government almost twice his profit to make good the damage to the environment. The "rational" response to such a situation was obvious: destroy the goats.

Chapter Six

1. Since this chapter was first drafted, a number of other scholars have conducted work with similar goals in northern Greece. Karakasidou (1997a) examined "passages to nationhood" in the town of Assiros, while Cowan (1997), Agelopoulos (1997), Van Boeschoten (2000), and Vereni (1998, 2000) offer sophisticated approaches to the meeting of individual, community, and national experiences of history in small communities in Greek Macedonia.

2. As noted in chapter 5, Kruševo provided the secretary of the Committee for

Ilinden Pensions, Tomo Kuturec, whose signature appears on decisions included in the Archive. The president of the Committee was Šakir, a veteran himself.

3. A copy of the decree is preserved in the State Archive of the Republic of Macedonia, in Box 42 of the Ilinden Dossier.

4. This in turn is followed by a list of the fringe benefits, which included free health care, subsidized transportation, and a free holiday every year. The government retained the right to withdraw the spomenica from those found unworthy of it; and also kept a clause that made explicit the restriction to participants and not their dependents or children, which made the pension into a personal and nontransferable asset.

5. Swire (1939) documents both the role played by the Macedonian lobby in Bulgarian politics, and the evolution of VMRO into a Bulgaria-based "state within a state" which controlled the border region until the early 1930s. He refutes some of Christowe's (1935) more partisan claims regarding the activities of VMRO leaders. A more critical account of VMRO's activities in Yugoslavia the early 1920s is given by Reiss (1924), who presents the Macedonian peasantry as their primary victims. The debate over the ethnological definition of the Slavs of Macedonia was already old in the 1930s. Cvijić's work (1918), inspired in part by a Serbian goal to distinguish Macedonians from Bulgarians so that the Wilsonian principle of self-determination might not wrench that part of the Serbian Kingdom away, claimed that they were of "unfixed national affiliation."

6. The flag and the other trappings of what came to be known as the *Ustaše* state have been brought out again in the newly independent Republic of Croatia. It is interesting to contrast again the Macedonian case, where following self-declared independence there ensued a long and painful discussion on the form that the symbols of modern nationhood—anthem, crest, flag—should take, when their ownership was disputed by neighboring states (Brown 1994).

7. The redrawing of boundaries in 1941, which erased Macedonia, is shown in figure 6.

8. In the case of Bitola, Phillipov (1995a:254) refers to archive film footage that shows the Bulgarian army being welcomed. Hallam Tennyson reported meeting a self-styled Macedonian who admitted that the people had greeted what he called Bulgarian "reoccupation" with "at least reserved enthusiasm" (1955:134).

9. Burks records that the district of Bitolj in Yugoslav Macedonia recorded a Communist vote of 51.1 percent in 1920, and was "the only electoral district in all of eastern Europe to give a straight majority to the Communists before 1945" (1961:79). Burks saw this as a demonstration of "Slavo-Macedonian separatism." Kirče Risteski's life history, though, cited in chapter 5, reveals the key role played by Vlahs in the communist-led struggle to overcome traditional and ethnic antipathies in the town (1983:4).

10. For a brief, clear overview of the machinations over communist leadership in Macedonia from 1941–43, see Palmer and King 1971:65–69. One of Tito's operatives, General Tempo, also wrote an account of the struggles of the period (Vukmanović 1990), while a defense of Šarlo's actions is given in Draguyčeva (1979:60ff.)

11. One of the first national crises that the new Yugoslavia faced was the confrontation over land-ownership between Macedonians and Serbs, seeking to return to their pre-war possessions (Shoup 1968:111–122; Žecević and Lekić 1991).

12. It should be stressed that only the Slavic-speaking Christian majority benefited from the Bulgarian régime. Besides outlawing the speaking of the Vlah language in Kruševo, the Bulgarian government treated other minority groups harshly. Barker (1950) suggests that it was Bulgarian oppression that led to the strong support for the partisan movement among Macedonian-speaking Muslims in Macedonia. This view is supported by the fact that *Nova Makedonija*, the newspaper of Yugoslav Macedonia, was first published in Gorno Vranovci, a village of Macedonian-speaking Muslims, or *Torbeši*, in the Veles region (Friedman 1993:165).

13. Although an obvious point, it should be noted that the period of 1941–44 is almost universally called the period of "Occupation" in the post-war Yugoslav pension requests.

14. His case may also have been weakened by the bad reputation of at least one of his witnesses. Petra Pare featured in Kirče Risteski's autobiography as an informer against partisans in Kruševo during the time of the Bulgarian régime.

15. Another pension applicant put a similar gloss on his membership in the Turkish gendarmerie after 1903. Božin Stefanov Ilievski of Bitola claimed that he obtained information and protected a četnik (13-I-36). Today, in Kruševo, the same mode of description can be seen in some accounts of the loyalty of Pitu Guli's son, Sterju Guli, during the Bulgarian occupation, discussed in chapter 8.

16. Illustrative examples of wariness are provided by the two petitioners from Boišta mentioned above, who had received pensions from Bulgaria. Both made a point of declaring their ignorance regarding the precise nature of VMRO. Between the wars, the organization bearing that name had fought a bitter war against a state bearing the same name as that in which Macedonia now found itself. Like others, they appear to have tried to hedge their bets and protect themselves against entrapment.

17. The unpopularity of the socialist zadruga is still evident today, both among supporters of the Yugoslav régime and opponents. One grandfather, an avid Titoist, admitted the error, saying "You can't work agriculture by the clock." Another, a supporter of the new anti-communist VMRO–DPMNE, recalled that his father was jailed for refusing to join the village zadruga, claiming that the members were all *aramii*—thieves, or bandits. Many farmers incurred loss on leaving the zadrugas, as legislation was passed in May 1953 that limited any individual's holding to ten hectares (Ferretjans 1963:75).

18. The coexistence of the zadruga with a governing, alien state in some sense mirrors the colonial organization of migrant labor in southern and eastern Africa, described by works from the Rhodes-Livingstone Institute between the 1930s and 1950s. These scholars drew attention to the organic and exploitative nature of colonial economies, which depended on the continued survival of apparently noncapitalist social collectivities outside the system to provide wage-labor. For a more explicitly Marxian analysis of exploitation of the domestic community, see Meillassoux (1981).

19. I follow standard practice and use the Serbian term for the male head. In Macedonian, he is a *domaḱin*.

20. Good descriptions of the zadruga system are given by Tomasevich (1955:178–89), Halpern (1958:134–64), and St. Erlich (1966:32–42).

21. A *dekar* is 1,000 square meters of land; a hectare is 10,000 square meters.

22. Women were also given the vote for the first time.

23. Sanders stresses these issues in post-war Bulgaria, where older women spoke

somewhat wistfully of the freedoms enjoyed by younger generations (1948:190) and where young-old tensions surfaced (1948:214). Halpern (1956) highlights similar cases in Serbia, as does Cowan (1990) in Greece. Bringa's ethnography of a Bosnian village makes clear the enduring burden of expectation for exemplary behavior for young brides (Bringa 1995), a point made also of early 1970s Belgrade by Simic (1973:142ff) and of early 1990s Skopje by Thiessen (1999).

24. Sanders does note the Bulgarian Fatherland Front's post-war attempts to represent the new system as an extension of an old ideal (1948:218).

25. St. Erlich (1966) documents the systematic differences in household structure that existed within pre-war Yugoslavia.

26. As noted earlier, St. Erlich's data suggested that the zadruga form persisted longest among Macedonia's Albanian Muslim population. Although the SRZ was introduced throughout rural Macedonia, the Ilinden pension program effectively excluded Macedonia's Albanian population. The Uprising in 1903 had involved mainly Slav-speaking Christians with the assistance of the Vlah population. Albanian villagers had largely found themselves either under threat from VMRO četas or recruited into the Ottoman effort to crush the Uprising. Albanians also had less disposition to engage with a new bureaucracy which operated through the medium of the newly codified Macedonian language.

27. This reading of the making of the post-war Macedonian state and the relations it created between government and people conforms largely with the model of "socialist-paternalism" advanced by Katherine Verdery (1994). It governed most closely relations between the ethnic Macedonian population and the Macedonian state. Other Christian groups that shared the Ilinden legacy—notably Vlahs—also entered the relationship; Turkish and Albanian communities, by and large, did not.

28. Friedman (1985) made the same point with respect to the newly codified and taught Macedonian language, in the speaking of which young correct old, who might use dialectal forms or words from Serbian or Bulgarian learned in previous school régimes.

29. In the 1990s, an echo could be seen in *Nova Makedonija*'s second section, which included a daily column, usually written by a professional historian, concerning some aspect of the national past. Since the end of Yugoslavia these have dealt still more with issues from the period 1903–08, as well as with previously denied versions of events after the Second World War.

Chapter Seven

1. A fuller account of this period and its effects on refugees from northern Greece is provided in Brown 2003a.

2. These gestures by the Bulgarian government took place in 1948. The remains of Goce Delčev had already been transferred to Skopje on 10 October 1946 and were reinterred in the courtyard of the church of Sveti Spas.

3. In these accounts, it should be noted, the claim to "Greekness" was more often than not framed in cultural terms. It is then taken that any person identifying himself in such a way would also logically aspire to be a citizen of the new Greek state. That this was not necessarily the case is demonstrated effectively by Stoianovich (1960) and also by Seton-Watson (1917).

4. This state of affairs continued into the 1980s and beyond. The first large-scale admission of Macedonian scholars to Bulgarian archives took place in 1992; relations at that time between the academies of Greece and FYR Macedonia remained virtually nonexistent, although the scholars of each state sniped at the other. Books were exchanged, but the flow was interrupted when Greece refused to recognize the new Macedonian Republic. For example, materials sent from the Institute for Balkan Studies in Thessaloniki to the Institute for National History in Skopje arrived and were read. But packages originating in Skopje and sent to Greece were returned by the Greek post office, with large red lines through any postage stamps which bore the constitutional name of the new country.

5. The Republic of Macedonia was home to a significant number of refugees from Greece who fled after the Greek Civil War; several historians were from that population. The reprint of Ballas's book was reviewed in the Institute for National History's journal, *Glasnik* vol. 8/1 (1964). In his history of Kruševo, Aleksander Matkovski does not really engage with Greek accounts of 1903. He dismisses the work of Ballas and of Konstantinos Vavouskos as tendentious and full of errors, but gives no basis for this claim (Matkovski 1978:254).

6. By drawing attention to 1767 when the Patriarchate engaged in politics against an Ohrid center of Orthodox belief, the Yugoslav state sought to silence those critics who denied the historical roots of Macedonian distinctiveness. The evocation of that history made the Macedonian church older than the Kingdom of Greece and its state-sponsored Orthodox church by more than fifty years. The recognition of the Macedonian church also served a domestic Yugoslav agenda, weakening the position of the Serbian Orthodox church. For more on the politics of religion in Yugoslavia, see Alexander (1979).

7. This movement, and the role and fate of its leader, Metodija Andonov-Čento, is discussed in chapter 9.

8. The hostility that Macedonians felt toward any "Yugoslav" state, in light of the nature of the interwar régime, is discussed in chapter 6.

9. The ideology of Republican voluntarism in the constitution of the Federal Yugoslavia proved vital in Slovenian and Croatian claims to the right to secede. For more information on the constitutional issues of Yugoslavia's break-up, see Hayden (1999).

10. Paul Shoup traces the Yugoslav authorization of this new take on Macedonian history to the publication by Lazar Koliševski, trusted Tito aide and leader of Macedonia, of a work entitled *The Macedonian National Question* in 1959 (Shoup 1968: 177–78).

11. Until the mid-1990s, there was still one room in the town's art gallery dedicated to this visit. On show were photographs taken by Tito himself and sent to the town.

12. Details given here are from the Grabul Archive in the National Archives of Macedonia in Skopje. It is a collection of unsorted clippings, notes, and drawings, donated after Jordan Grabul's death. All subsequent citations, unless otherwise indicated, are from this source.

13. In 1968 Stankovski's position was given was secretary of the Executive Committee of the Central Committee of the League of Communists of Macedonia (Arsov et al. [eds.] 1968). In 1974, when he spoke at the official opening of the monument, Stankovski was described by *Nova Makedonija* as the president of the Republican

Conference of the Socialist Association for the Working People of Macedonia (SSRNM). I was told he committed suicide in 1989 or 1990.

14. In 1968 Dragan Tozija was head of the Culture and Education Department of the Assembly of the Republic of Macedonia.

15. These representative roles had to be reconstructed from fragmentary sources; they are not given explicitly in one place in the Grabul archive. It is for this reason that the status of Mitevski, in particular, is not entirely clear. Veteran organizations were generally involved in the planning of monuments and other forms of commemoration.

16. Haralampiev's status at meetings of the commission is unclear. Nowhere is he listed as a member or a replacement for some other member. Most frequently absent from meetings was Ljuben Lape, the historian.

17. The particulars of this re-engineering are discussed in chapter 8.

18. The wall's mode is complicated by the inclusion of those Missing in Action— a factor which also plays a part in activities conducted around the memorial by veterans' organizations (Berdahl 1994).

19. The Vietnam Memorial differs in that it carries time in its form, giving names in the order of their deaths. It also excludes ranks, which English memorials sometimes did not. English memorials reveal other aspects of their societal context in the honorifics and different numbers of initials that names may carry, signifying class (Laqueur 1994).

20. Obolensky (1974) identified Samuil as ruling over Bulgars and Greeks, and opposing the Byzantine Empire. Kliment was a pupil of Kiril, who designed the Cyrillic alphabet to allow God's word to be communicated to the Slav-speaking peoples of the region. The Karpoš Uprising alone remains unclaimed by Greece and Bulgaria. However, even Macedonian accounts admit that it was a small-scale, opportunistic affair. Its center was around Kumanovo, and it coincided with an Austrian offensive against the Ottoman Empire that reached—and burned—Skopje on 25–26 October 1689 (Apostolski et al. [eds.] 1979:96–98).

21. The *Kale* is the old Ottoman fortress on a hill overlooking the old Stone Bridge across the River Vardar in downtown Skopje. The "Christmas Massacre on Skopje's *Kale*" was the subject of a sensationalist story in *Nova Makedonija* on 23 January 1991. Documents indicating that the incident in fact involved few deaths were published in 1997 (Simovski et al. [eds.] 1997).

22. Of Monastir vilayet's 11,708 square miles, 4,706 were ceded to Greece, 3,473 to Serbia, and 3,529 to the new Albania (Kennan [ed.] 1993:418).

23. Klisura and Neveska were both inhabited by Vlah populations with strong Hellenic ideologies. Neither were included in the first list. In a history of Neveska— now known as Nimfaio—eyewitness accounts of the occupation suggest that there was no local support (Loustas 1994:79ff.). This contradicts some claims reported in British Foreign Office documents of the period, which indicated that the population invited the insurgents into the town (FO 195/2157/510). A visitor to Klisura shortly after the Uprising reported the town to be still a "hotbed of revolution" (Comyn-Platt 1906:140). Neither town suffered in the same way as Kruševo during 1903, but Klisura was destroyed by German forces during World War II.

24. Kirov-Majski (1935:73), still one of the most reliable accounts, named forty-eight dead and six wounded. Only six of the dead, including Guli himself, were from

Kruševo, while fifteen were from the village of Bela Crkva and nine from Ostrilci. The significance of the difference between accounts of the fighting is discussed in chapter 8.

25. The same vision, in which Macedonians cast themselves as victims, is apparent in the cliché "Five hundred years under the Turks," which is a quick and sometimes humorous response to complaints about society or the order of things in modern Macedonia. The same phrase, with variations in the time spent under Ottoman rule, can be heard in Greece, Serbia, and Bulgaria. The notion of suffering is also, according to popular mythology, embedded in Macedonian surnames like Trpovski, derived in folk etymology from the verb *trpi*, to endure.

26. For more details on these figures, see Friedman (1975). A film version of "Bloody Macedonian Wedding" was made in Skopje in 1967, and the play was also a mainstay of Macedonian cultural activities in the 1930s (Danforth 1995a:185). Nikola Kirov-Majski, the ideologue and dramatist from Kruševo, was also included in the crypt.

Gone from the final list were the Miladinov brothers, whose legacy had been effectively claimed by Bulgaria. Included in both versions was Dimitrija Čupovski (57), an active exponent of Macedonian culture in Russia. Phillipov (1995a, 1995b) claims that Čupovski was condemned to death by VMRO for his willingness to collaborate with the Ottoman Empire in pursuit of Macedonian autonomy from Bulgarian influence. His remains were ceremonially returned from Russia to the Republic of Macedonia in 1989. The most overtly political figures included were Dimo Hadži-Dimov (1875–1924) and Dimitar Vlahov (1878–1953), both leftists involved in the bitter struggles between rival wings of the Macedonian Organization in the 1920s. Hadži-Dimov was an early victim of the assassin Vlado Černozemski who would go on to kill King Alexander of Yugoslavia. Vlahov survived to become a member of the postwar leadership of the new Macedonian Republic.

27. Their accession to this status was not always straightforward. Chapter 8 discusses the particular cases of Nikola Karev and Pitu Guli.

28. Post-war Macedonian historiography for many years emphasized the existence of TMORO over that of VMRO. The complex history of the evolution of the different, and sometimes competing, revolutionary movements is traced in Perry (1988). By the time of the Second World War, VMRO was a terrorist organization associated with Bulgaria (Christowe 1935; Swire 1939; West 1941).

29. Nožot was a battle between Macedonian revolutionaries and overwhelming Ottoman forces near the village of Rakle, in the Prilep region of Macedonia. Trapped on a sharp ridge, more than sixty members of VMRO were killed. The battle is remembered because the Ottoman commander was reportedly impressed by the courage of the revolutionaries, and ordered his men to pay respect to the fallen.

30. Sandanski was enshrined in the anthem of the Socialist Republic, along with Goce Delčev, Pitu Guli, and Dame Gruev. Sandanski was known in the period after Ilinden as the "Tsar of Pirin," but won his first fame for his central part in the kidnapping of Ellen Stone, an American missionary, in 1901. His exact agenda has come under renewed scrutiny since 1991; he has been claimed by some Vlahs as a conational, who sought some sort of limited autonomy for Macedonia in a deal with Ottoman Turkey. Mercia MacDermott, author of English-language accounts based on Bulgarian sources, saw Sandanski as a leftist and forward-thinking leader (MacDer-

mott 1988). He was killed in an ambush near Melnik on 10 April 1915, most likely by rivals in the Organization (Swire 1939:134).

The background to the murder is documented by Swire (1939:110). Panica was originally sent by Sarafov to kill Sandanski. Panica himself went on to become a prominent player in the upper echelons of VMRO, eventually falling victim to his own former lover, a woman from a Kruševo family named Menča or Melpomena Karničeva, who in turn went on to marry Ivan Mihailov, VMRO's leader after 1924. Different versions of this particular double-cross are told in Christowe (1935: 199–202) and Swire (1939:195–97).

31. The fate of non-Titoists like Venko Markovski and Pavel Šatev in Yugoslav Macedonia, discussed briefly in chapter 8, could be argued to derive in part from ongoing and mutating frictions within Macedonian political circles.

32. The qualifiers Slavic-speaking and Slavo- are used here to indicate that the people in question were not Yugoslav citizens, but members of a culturally distinctive and politically mobilized minority group indigenous to northern Greece.

Chapter Eight

1. Deca begalci is the Macedonian name given to people who as children during the Greek Civil War were taken from their villages in northern Greece and relocated in camps and homes across Eastern Europe. In 1988, various deca begalci associations from North America, Australia, and Europe organized a reunion in Skopje. For more on this and other forms of Macedonian diaspora activism, see Danforth 1995a and Brown 2002a.

2. Marko is another historical figure who encapsulates ambiguity. Celebrated in folksong in Serbia, Macedonia, and Bulgaria, he served as a vassal to the Ottoman Sultan. For more on his career see Brown (2003b).

3. This practice has been recorded throughout the region, but was not always recalled so fondly. A visitor to Bardovci describes the open space, or gumno, as a place to which peasants brought their crops to be taken by others: "So much for the Sultan's taxes, so much for the beg [landlord], and so much for the peasants themselves" (Edwards 1938:94–95).

4. The term "analogue" is used here to describe the attempt to highlight parallels with a discrete past event, rather than to place that event in historical process. For more on the notion of analogic thinking as a way to understand and mobilize the past, see Sutton 1998:119–47, 164–65.

5. Koliševski remained a powerful political figure in Macedonia after Tito's death. As Yugoslav vice-president at that time, he assumed Tito's place as head of state. In the mid-1990s, he lived in retirement in a wealthy section of Skopje on the hillside of Vodno where public access is limited. The area is now a favored residence for foreign diplomatic and aid industry personnel.

6. The order to abandon Kruševo has been generally attributed to Boris Sarafov, the member of the headquarters whose absence from the crypt and villainous reputation in modern Macedonian historiography was discussed in chapter 7.

7. Karev's socialism appears as a crucial component in the emphasis that Yugoslav historians lay on the distance between him and those figures whose connections with the Bulgarian state are acknowledged. The underhandedness and cunning of those

pro-Bulgarian elements is also a key trope that explains the failure of Karev and his colleagues, for all their energy and activism, to drive through their agenda for success. Thus Matkovski (1978:186) implies that Sarafov's machinations ensured that Karev, along with other leading opponents of a premature rising, was three days late for the Smilevo Congress, so that their ability to influence policy was weakened.

8. Matkovski (1978:175) gives a brief geneaology of the Karev family in Kruševo. A male ancestor, Miloš, moved from the village of Selce to Kruševo. He had two sons: Icko, who was father to Tirču and Taško, and Janaki, who was father to Petre (or Petruš), Nikola, and Gjorǵi. Tirču Karev was killed with Vele Markov, the Kruševo vojvod, in an engagement with Ottoman forces in the village of Rakitnica in June 1902 (Matkovski 1978:170; Kirov-Majski 1935:21–24). The participation of Taško and Janaki's three sons at the time of Ilinden is indicated by references in pension requests, including that of Donka Budžakoska cited in chapter 1, who refers to Tirču Kare as the standard bearer of Vele Markov's četa. Velika Nedanova Gaḱerkoska, a pension applicant from the village of Sveti Mitrani, recalled taking weapons to Petruš, Gjorǵi, and Nikola for repair, and carrying back letters, uniforms, and boots to the village (11-G-1).

9. Markovski was already a published poet. For more on the codification of the Macedonian language and his participation, see Friedman 1993.

10. A common counteraccusation, also used freely by Macedonian politicians, is that their opponents are either pro-Serbian or pro-communist.

11. Savo Klimovski continued his career in politics in post-Yugoslav Macedonia. A founder-member of Vasil Tupurkovski's Democratic Alternative (DA) in 1998, he was Parliament speaker until the governing coalition of VMRO-DPMNE and DA splintered in late 2000.

12. The Macedonian term *vnuk* can mean nephew or grandson, and can also be extended to refer to great-grandson or grandnephew. The female equivalent for a niece or grand-daughter is *vnuka*. When people use these terms in conversation, they usually clarify them with other information, specifying the people through which the blood relationship is transmitted. Thus, for example, *Vnuk od sestra mi*—literally, *vnuk* from my sister—refers to the speaker's sister's son. In the article reporting the interment of Nikola Karev's remains, no such qualification was provided. This suggests that these young relatives were removed from Nikola Karev by too many intermediate steps to be easily recounted.

13. This detail was reported by Frederick Moore, writing soon after the events of 1903. Ninety years later, the tale had grown more dramatic in Robert Kaplan's telling, so that forty insurgents did the same thing.

14. Different local sources attributed to Guli's aunt or sister the recovery of his remains. What was left was also disputed, but the consensus appeared to be his skull and two bones from limbs. These items are those required to make a skull and crossbones, which was to become the symbol of VMRO in later years. This may be coincidence, or some connection could be argued in one direction or the other. I did not raise the question with people in Kruševo.

15. Writing in 1937, Popović marked the Gule family in Kruševo as Vlahs from Gramoste, an area in modern Albania (Popović 1937:292n).

16. Mate Petrov Boškovski of Kruševo, a pension applicant mentioned in chapter 6, claimed that he had cared for Guli's children, who were left fatherless after 1903 (5-B-27).

17. The periodical was *Balkania*. It was consistently anti-Yugoslav and promoted the idea that Slavic Macedonians were really Bulgarians. Ivan Mihailov, the article's author, had headed the Bulgarian-based VMRO between 1924 and 1934, succeeding Todor Alexandrov, for whom he asserts Nikola Guli worked.

18. As noted earlier, some sources claimed that he was betrayed by Gjorǵi Karev. Risteski, however, attributes the betrayal to Menda Mladenoska and her son, Metodija, who worked as a clerk at the police station.

19. Stories like this fourth version crop up outside Kruševo, where they drive criticism of Guli. In the village of Bučin, for example, part of Kruševo's administrative region, I was told that Pitu Guli was generally reviled because of the story that he was drunk. In Skopje, Iskra Grabul reported that she had discussed Pitu Guli with his granddaughter, who had called him a *nevrotičen tip*—crazy. He had, she said, idled his time away in cafés, and then gone to face certain death with forty men against ten thousand. Such accounts also drive speculation that the defiance on Mečkin Kamen in some sense contributed to the subsequent disaster. This takes the interpretations one step further in Macedonian historiography. For example, Ljuben Lape wrote in 1973, "The General Staff of the Uprising for the whole revolutionary district of Bitola tried at all costs to get the rebels to withdraw from Kruševo to avoid endangering the civil population. Only Pitu Guli opposed this order." (Lape 1973: 130). It is sometimes suggested that negotiations had been successfully concluded and that the town would be spared if the insurgents withdrew peacefully. By opposing Ottoman forces, then, Guli did not just sacrifice himself and bring about the deaths of his men, he doomed Kruševo.

20. The distinction here is drawn from Gellner's work (1983). The particularly sharp distinction marked here between the quality of Greek and Albanian as identity categories is explored in a different geographical setting by Laurie Kain Hart (1999).

21. In the absence of hard evidence to support this claim, some interpreters of the past claim that in the parliament of sixty members, twenty places were reserved for delegates from nearby Muslim villages. Such readings of the past demonstrate the strength of present categorical oppositions between Muslim Albanians and Orthodox Macedonians in shaping how people interpret the past.

22. For Masada, Kosovo, and the Alamo, see footnote 2 to chapter 1. Verdun was held by the French army against the German army during the First World War despite intense pressure. Thermopylae is a pass in northern Greece where in 480 B.C.E. a small force led by Spartan King Leonidas held off a huge Persian army until the Spartans were betrayed, surrounded, and wiped out. Thermopylae's template was evoked in one description of the battles on Mečkin Kamen and on Sliva, which called the insurgents the Macedonian Spartans in an evocation of Greek ancient history that was not, it appears, perceived as signaling irredentist ambition (Dimovski, Tankovski, and Kočanovski 1979:109).

23. The most detailed account of Kruševo's history (Matkovski 1978) draws on Kirov-Majski's published work and unpublished memoirs, which in the 1970s were kept in the Historical Museum in Kruševo. I was unable to gain access to these materials.

24. Although Macedonian was not codified until 1944, Kirov-Majski wrote in the Kruševo dialect, reproduced in the 1968 version and clearly different from standard Bulgarian.

25. This translation is my own. The English translation in the 1968 publication is

less free, but I consider it loses some of the spirit of the original. It provides useful gloss for murtats as disloyal people of the Moslem religion but later translates such emotive terms in the language of class warfare, as feudalists.

26. Some people in Kruševo took the insistence by Skopje-based commentators on Karev's authorship as a sign of widespread ignorance of historical fact elsewhere in the Republic.

27. Karev, then, who in life espoused socialism, in death served as the vehicle by which the Macedonian church penetrated a national shrine and made it in part its own. In a letter to *Nova Makedonija* after the reburial, a Bitola resident suggested that Guli should receive similar recognition, and be reburied either along with Karev, in the monument, or at Mečkin Kamen. In either case, one could argue, the letter-writer reveals a nice sense of the ultimate logic of connection between the two strands in Kruševo's history.

28. The importance of written materials in various Macedonian evocations of the past was noted in chapter 3, in the discussion of textual communities. The inclusion of a book title in the crypt of the Ilinden monument is another indicator of the phenomenon.

Chapter Nine

1. The draft document that I was given was hazy with regard to whether this was a project by just the town or the municipality, or opština, of which it was the administrative center.

2. The term novljaci is, strictly speaking, Serbo-Croatian and not Macedonian. As in Skopje, people in Kruševo still frequently used such Serbisms in 1992–93 and not always consciously.

3. The term is also used more widely, and is for example used as a form of address by passengers to bus drivers.

4. Such labor migration to Western Europe was common in the years of socialist Yugoslavia, reaching a peak in the 1970s, but became more difficult in the 1980s (Zimmerman 1993). Such labor provided the means for house construction in otherwise undeveloped areas, including Bosnia and Kosovo (Bringa 1995:85–86; Reineck 1991:119–27). The young Kruševčanec did not refer to himself as a pečalbar, but used the German term instead, *gastarbeiter*. As of 2002 he had not taken up residence in the house, which was rented to international staff.

5. The celebration of St. Lazar's day is also noted in Zamfirovo in Bulgaria by Gerald Creed (1998:66). He notes there that the form of celebration was exploited during the collectivization of the village to induce householders to sign up in a spirit of community solidarity.

6. The photograph, taken by Polish ethnographer Joseph Obrebski, depicts a mother mourning her son six months after his death, and so there are no other grave-parties in the cematery.

7. For reflections on the revitalization of the ritual in Macedonia and in diaspora, see Schwartz (2000). In many locations the ceremony was practiced discreetly throughout the period of socialist rule.

8. The cover illustration depicts a community celebration of a slava, or saints' day. The photograph most likely represents a celebration on Petrovden, St. Peter's Day, near the village of Bitovo in western Macedonia. It was taken by Joseph Obrebski in

the 1930s, and is number 180 in the Obrebski collection at Special Collections and Archives at the W.E.B. Dubois Library at the University of Massachusetts Amherst, who kindly granted permission for its use here. I am grateful to Ljupčo Risteski for his detective work in interpreting the scene.

9. The Greek church moved the saints' days when they switched from the Julian to the Gregorian calendar, whereas the Slavic churches left the saint's days where they stood, which meant that their dates changed. For example, the name day of Antonio was on 17 January (o.s.), and is on 17 January (N.S.) in Greece; whereas in the Republic of Macedonia it is on 30 January (N.S.). St. Peter's Day is 29 June in Greece and 12 July in Macedonia. The case for former Greek influence is strengthened by the fact that people in Kruševo admit that Bitola, where a thriving Greek community also once lived, has somewhat similar practices.

10. In a breakdown of Kruševo's population by mother tongue in 1994, the number of Albanian-speakers in the town was given as two (1994 Census Data, vol. 2, p. 20). I am grateful to Victor Friedman for making these data available.

11. The shift in the balance of numbers claiming Turkish and Albanian identity is explored as a phenomenon elsewhere in the Republic of Macedonia by Burcu Akan (2000). The 1994 census was conducted under international supervision, and was followed in 1996 by the reorganization of administrative boundaries, which created a new municipality, Žitoše, from within the municipality of Kruševo. This had the effect of reducing the Kruševo's religious and linguistic diversity, as the majority of those included in the new municipality of Žitoše were Muslim Albanians.

12. The positive image presented to the Skopjean visitor in fact concealed tensions. In 1992, the eleven Albanian members of the forty-five-seat opština assembly were boycotting participation, awaiting resolution of their demand for their own vice-presidential post.

13. Denunciations as a part of the Ilinden Dossier described at length in chapter 6. See also Fitzpatrick and Gellately 1996.

14. One might imagine Greece as the most likely suspect. However, Greek scholars have not had easy access to archives in Istanbul for many reasons. Bulgarian scholars have a reputation in Macedonia and elsewhere for their willingness to falsify the documentary record (Lunt 1984:118–20; see also Cassavetti 1914:348–50), and so would likely be the villains of this piece.

15. The rule of the preservation of wealth in Macedonia laid out here was not ironclad. The early twentieth-century revolutionary movement in particular sought to liquidate the stored capital that was represented by the gold and silver hoarded and brought out only for display on ritual occasions. In 1905, reportedly as part of his progressive agenda, the vojvod Jane Sandanski forbade the wearing of jewelry at weddings (MacDermott 1988:189–90). A more pragmatic principle was perceived by a British consul in 1903, who wrote, "Bulgarian peasant women have been disposing of their coin-necklaces in order, it is said, that there may be a rifle in every cottage." McGregor to Biliotti, Monastir, 4 April 1903: FO 195/2156/363).

Chapter Ten

1. People reported, also, Yugoslav era visits to Greece where people would insist that the visitors were Yugoslavs, or Serbs, and call the language that they spoke Yugoslav. After a while, the visitors would go along with that definition. Macedon-

ians continued to be invisible outside Yugoslavia's borders. In 1993, when the new Macedonian Republic issued its own passports, many citizens preferred to keep their old Yugoslav passports; this was partly an economic decision, but partly because with Yugoslav passports they might be able to go to Greece. With the new Macedonian passports, they knew they would certainly not.

2. Irena's grandparents' own recollections of this time are described in chapter 5.

3. Kofos's analysis of the history of Greek nationalism also has a critical edge, drawing attention to its manipulative tactics. He writes, for example, that after the success of arms in the Balkan Wars, "the Greeks were *able to pose* not only as legitimate heirs to the heritage and name of the ancient Macedonians, but also as the legal possessors of their ancient land" (Kofos 1993:314; my italics). Elsewhere in the article he blurs the distinction that Danforth observes him making between Macedonian on one hand and Greek and Bulgarian on the other, by calling Yugoslav-sponsored Macedonian nationalism "a belated twentieth-century version of similar *visionary schemes concocted* by all Balkan peoples during their nineteenth-century national liberation struggles" (ibid.:317). The argument appears to be that the Macedonians of the Republic are not fundamentally different, but they have got off to a late start.

4. In early January 1991, the Republic of Macedonia experienced more widespread violence as the National Liberation Army, whose membership was mostly ethnic Albanian, seized territory in northwestern Macedonia, and staged a series of deadly ambushes against military and police forces seeking to restore government control. At least a hundred people died in the course of five months of crisis. The conflict was halted after international mediation, and in August 2001 Albanian and Macedonian political parties signed the "Ohrid agreement" which called for major constitutional change and greater fiscal and political decentralization. The agreement maintained the unitary character of the state, but gave greater power to any cultural or ethnic community that comprised over 20 percent of the country's total population. At the time of writing, implementation is still underway in a climate of lingering mistrust among Macedonia's citizens.

Bibliography

Abbott, G. F. 1903. *Tale of a Tour in Macedonia*. London: Edward Arnold.

Adanir, Fikret. 1979. *Die Makedonische Frage: Ihre Entstehung und Entwicklung bis 1908* (The Macedonian Question: Its Origin and Development Until 1908). Wiesbaden, Germany: Franz Steiner Verlag GMBH.

————. 1984–85. "The Macedonian Question: The socio-economic reality and problems of its historiographic interpretation." *International Journal of Turkish Studies* 3 (1):43–64.

Agelopoulos, Giorgos. 1997. "From Bulgarievo to Nea Krasia, from 'Two Settlements' to 'One Village': Community Formation, Collective Identities and the Role of the Individual." In *Ourselves and Others: The Development of a Greek Macedonian Cultural Identity Since 1912*. Edited by Peter Mackridge and Eleni Yannakakis, 133–151. Oxford: Berg.

————. n.d. "Three Years of Living in the Margins: Between Auto-ethnography and Fieldwork in Florina." Paper presented at the symposium "Negotiating Boundaries: The Past in the Present in South-Eastern Europe." University of Wales, Lampeter. September 1998.

Akan, Burcu. 2000. "Shadow Genealogies: Memory and Identity Among Urban Muslims in Macedonia." Ph.D. diss., School of International Service, American University.

————. n.d. "Invocation of Ottoman Shadows: The Impact of the Turkish Saatli Maarif Calendar on Diaspora Politics of Muslims in Macedonia." Unpublished paper.

Alexander, Nora. 1936. *Wanderings in Yugoslavia*. London: Skeffington.

Alexander, Stella. 1979. *Church and state in Yugoslavia since 1945*. Cambridge: Cambridge University Press.

Allcock, John B. 1992. "Rhetorics of Nationalism in Yugoslav Politics." In *Yugoslavia in Transition: Choices and Constraints*. Edited by J. B. Allcock, J. J. Horton, and M. Milivojevic, 276–96. New York: Berg.

Amery, Leo. 1980. *The Leo Amery Diaries*, Vol. 1 1896–1929. Edited by John Barnes and David Nicholson London: Hutchinson.

Anderson, Benedict. 1983. Reprinted 1991. *Imagined Communities: Reflections on the Origin and Spread of Nationalism*. London: Verso.

Anderson, Perry. 1992. "Fernand Braudel and National Identity." In *A Zone of Engagement*, 251–78. London: Verso.

Andonov-Poljanksi, Hristo, et al., eds. 1983. *Kruševo*. Skopje: Kl. Ohridski.

Apostolov, Aleksandar. 1962. *Kolonizacijata na Makedonija vo Stara Jugoslavija* (The Colonization of Macedonia in Old Yugoslavia). Skopje: Misla.

Apostolski, Mihailo, et al., eds. 1968. *Kruševskiot Manifest* (The Kruševo Manifesto). Skopje: Institut za Nacionalna Istorija.

————, et al. 1979. *A History of the Macedonian People*. Skopje: Macedonian Review Editions.

Appadurai, Arjun. 1990. "Disjuncture and Difference in the Global Economy." *Public Culture* 2:1–24.

———. 1993. "Patriotism and its Futures." *Public Culture* 5:411–29.

Appleby, Joyce, Lynn Hunt, and Margaret Jacob. 1994. *Telling the Truth about History*. New York: W. W. Norton.

Arsov, Ljupcho, et al., eds. 1968. *Celebration of the Sixty-fifth Anniversary of the Ilinden Uprising*. Skopje.

Atkinson, Paul. 1990. *The Ethnographic Imagination: Textual Constructions of Reality*. London: Routledge.

Bakic-Hayden M., and R. Hayden. 1992. "Orientalist Variations on the Theme 'Balkans': Symbolic Geography in Recent Yugoslav Cultural Politics." *Slavic Review* 51(1):1–15.

Balakrishnan, Gopal, ed. 1996. *Mapping the Nation*. London: Verso.

Balibar, Étienne. 1991. "The Nation Form: History and Ideology." In *Race, Nation, Class: Ambiguous Identities*. Edited by É. Balibar and I. Wallerstein. 86–106. London: Verso.

Ballas, Nikolaos. 1905. Reprinted 1962. *A History of Krousovo* (in Greek). Thessaloniki: Hidryma Meleton Hersonesou tou Haimou.

Banac, Ivo. 1988. *With Stalin against Tito: Cominformist splits in Yugoslav Communism*. Ithaca, NY: Cornell University Press.

Banfield, E. C. 1958. *The Moral Basis of a Backward Society*. Chicago, IL: The Free Press/Research Center in Economic Development and Cultural Change, The University of Chicago.

Barker, Elizabeth. 1950. *Macedonia: Its Place in Balkan Power Politics*. London: Royal Institute of International Affairs.

Barkley, Henry C. 1877. *Bulgaria before the War during Seven Years' Experience of European Turkey and Its Inhabitants*. London: John Murray.

Batakovic, Dusan T. n.d. *The Balkan Piedmont: Serbia and the Yugoslav Question*. Belgrade: Institute for Balkan Studies.

Bérard, Victor. 1897. *La Macédoine*. Paris: Calmann Lévy.

Berdahl, Daphne. 1994. "Voices at the Wall: Discourses of Self, History and National Identity at the Vietnam Veterans Memorial." *History and Memory*, 6 (2):88–124.

Berktay, Halil, and Suraiya Faroqhi, eds. 1992. *New Approaches to State and Peasant in Ottoman History*. London: Frank Cass.

Bokovoy, Melissa. 1998. *Peasants and Communists: Politics and Ideology in the Yugoslav Countryside, 1941–1953*. Pittsburgh, PA: University of Pittsburgh Press.

Booth, John L. C. 1905. *Trouble in the Balkans*. London: Hurst and Blackett.

Bourchier, J. D. 1917. Reprinted 1926. "The Final Settlement in the Balkans." In Lady Ellinora Flora B. Grogan, *The Life of J. D. Bourchier*. London: Hurst and Blackett.

Bourdieu, Pierre. 1973. "The Berber House." In *Rules and Meanings: The Anthropology of Everyday Knowledge*. Edited by Mary Douglas, 98–110. Harmondsworth, England: Penguin Education.

———. 1962. "Célibat et condition paysanne" ("Celibacy and the peasant condition"). *Etudes Rurales* 5–6:33–135.

———. 1977. *Outline of a Theory of Practice*. Cambridge: Cambridge University Press.

Bozhinov, V., and L. Panayotov, eds. 1978. *Macedonia: Documents and Material*. Sofia: Institute of History & Bulgarian Language Institute.

Brailsford, H. N. 1906. *Macedonia: Its Races and Their Future*. London: Methuen and Co.

Brashich, Ranko M. 1954. *Land Reform and Ownership in Yugoslavia 1919–1953*. New York: Mid-European Studies Center, Free Europe Committee.

Braude, B. 1982. "Foundation myths of the Millet system." In *Christians and Jews in the Ottoman Empire: The Functioning of a Plural Society*. Edited by B. Braude and B. Lewis, eds., 69–88. New York: Homes and Meier.

Breuilly, John. 1982. *Nationalism and the State*. Manchester: Manchester University Press.

Bringa, Tone. 1995. *Being Muslim the Bosnian Way: Identity and Community in a Central Bosnian Village*. Princeton, NJ: Princeton University Press.

———. n.d. Personal communication.

Brown, Edward. 1673. *A Brief Account of Some Travels in Hungaria, Servia, Bulgaria, Macedonia, Thessaly*. London: Printed by T. R. for Benj. Tooke.

Brown, K. S. 1994. "Seeing Stars: Character and Identity in the Landscapes of Modern Macedonia." *Antiquity* 68 (261):784–96.

———. 2000a. "A Rising to Count On: Ilinden Between Politics and History in Post-Yugoslav Macedonia." In *The Macedonian Question: Culture, Historiography, Politics*. Edited by Victor Roudometof, 143–72. Boulder, CO: East European Monographs.

———. 2000b. "In the Realm of the Double-Headed Eagle: Parapolitics in Macedonia 1994–9." In *Macedonia: The Politics of Identity and Difference*. Edited by Jane K. Cowan, 122–39. London: Pluto Press.

———. 2001. "Beyond Ethnicity: The Politics of Urban Nostalgia in Modern Macedonia." *Journal of Mediterranean Studies* 11 (2):417–42.

———. 2002a. Macedonia's *Child-Grandfathers: The Transnational Politics of Memory, Exile and Return, 1948–98*. Seattle, WA: University of Washington Press/ Donald W. Treadgold Papers.

———. 2002b. Forthcoming. "Villains and Symbolic Pollution in the Narratives of Nation: The Case of Boris Sarafov." In *National Identities and National Memories in the Balkans*. Edited by Maria Todorova. London: Hurst and Company.

Bruner, Edward, and Phyllis Gorfain. 1984. "Dialogic Narration and the Paradoxes of Masada." In *Text, Play and Story: The Construction and Reconstruction of Self and Society*. Edited by Edward M. Bruner, 56–79. Prospect Heights, IL: Waveland Press.

Burke, Kenneth. 1957. *The Philosophy of Literary Form*. New York: Vintage Books.

Burke, Peter. 1989. *The Historical Anthropology of Early Modern Italy: Essays in Perception and Communication*. Cambridge: Cambridge University Press.

Butterfield, Herbert. 1931. *The Whig Interpretation of History*. London: G. Bell.

Burks, R. V. 1961. *The Dynamics of Communism in Eastern Europe*. Princeton, NJ: Princeton University Press.

Campbell, John K. 1964. *Honour, Family and Patronage: A Study of Institutions and Moral Values in a Greek Mountain Community*. Oxford: Oxford University Press.

Carabott, Philip. 1997. "The Politics of Integration and Assimilation *vis-à-vis* the Slavo-Macedonian Minority of Inter-war Greece: From Parliamentary Inertia to

Metaxist Repression." In *Ourselves and Others: The Development of a Greek Macedonian Cultural Identity Since 1912*. Edited by Peter Mackridge and Eleni Yannakakis, 59–78. Oxford: Berg.

Cassavetti, D. J. 1914. *Hellas and the Balkan Wars*. London: Fisher Unwin.

Chatterjee, Partha. 1986. *Nationalist Thought and the Colonial World: A Derivative Discourse?* London: Zed Books.

———. 1993. *The Nation and its Fragments*. Princeton, NJ: Princeton University Press.

Chotziadis, Angelos A., et al., eds. 1993. *The Events of 1903 in Macedonia as Presented in European Diplomatic Correspondence*. Thessaloniki: The Friends of the Museum of the Macedonian Struggle.

Christides, Christopher. 1949. *The Macedonian Camouflage in the Light of Facts and Figures*. Athens: Hellenic Publishing Company.

Christowe, Stoyan. 1935. *Heroes and Assassins*. New York: Robert McBride & Co.

Cohn, Bernard S. 1987. *An Anthropologist among the Historians and Other Essays*. Delhi: Oxford University Press.

Collingwood, R. G. 1946. *The Idea of History*. Oxford: Oxford University Press.

Comaroff, Jean, and John L. Comaroff. 1992. *Ethnography and the Historical Imagination*. Boulder, CO: Westview Press.

Comyn-Platt, Sir Thomas. 1906. *The Turk in the Balkans*. London: Alston Rivers.

Corrigan, Philip, and Derek Sayer. 1985. *The Great Arch: English State Formation as Cultural Revolution*. Oxford: Basil Blackwell.

Cowan, Jane K. 1990. *Dance and the Body Politic in Northern Greece*. Princeton, NJ: Princeton University Press.

———. 1997. "Idioms of Belonging: Polyglot Articulations of Local Identity in a Greek Macedonian Town." In *Ourselves and Others: The Development of a Greek Macedonian Cultural Identity Since 1912*. Edited by Peter Mackridge and Eleni Yannakakis, 153–71. Oxford: Berg.

———, ed. 2000. *Macedonia: The Politics of Identity and Difference*. London: Pluto.

Creed, Gerald. 1998. *Domesticating Revolution: From Socialist Reform to Ambivalent Transition in a Bulgarian Village*. University Park, PA: Pennsylvania State University Press.

Čupeski,Vladimir. 1993. *A bre, Makedonče: Abecedar I Pamfleti za Naci-Bolševizmot 1982–1990* (A Primer on Nazi-Bolshevism, 1982–1990). Skopje: Mlad Borec.

Cvijić, Jovan. 1907. *Remarques sur L'Ethnographie de La Macédoine* (Remarks on the Ethnography of Macedonia). Paris: Roustan.

———. 1918. *La Péninsule Balkanique, Géographie Humaine* (A Human Geography of the Balkan Peninsula). Paris: A. Colin.

Dakin, Douglas. [1966] 1993. *The Greek Struggle in Macedonia 1897–1913*. Thessaloniki: Institute for Balkan Studies.

Danforth, Loring. 1993. "Claims to Macedonian Identity: The Macedonian Question and the Breakup of Yugoslavia." *Anthropology Today* 9 (4):3–10.

———. 1995a. *The Macedonian Conflict: Ethnic Nationalism in a Transnational World*. Princeton, NJ: Princeton University Press.

———. 1995b. "The Macedonian Minority of Northern Greece." *Cultural Survival Quarterly* 19 (2):64–70.

Denich, Bette. 1970. "Migration and Network Manipulation in Yugoslavia." In *Migration and Anthropology: Proceedings of the 1970 Annual Spring Meeting of the American Ethnological Society*. Edited by Robert Spencer, 133–45. Seattle, WA: University of Washington Press.

————. 1994. "Dismembering Yugoslavia: Nationalist Ideologies and the Symbolic Revival of Genocide." *American Ethnologist* 21:367–90.

Dimen-Schein, Muriel. 1975. "When is an Ethnic Group? Ecology and Class Structure in Northern Greece." *Ethnology* 14 (1):83–97.

————. 1977. *The Anthropological Imagination*. New York: McGraw-Hill.

Dimevski, Slavko. 1971. *Nikola Karev*. Skopje: Misla.

Dimovski, Ǵorǵi, Ǵorǵi Tankovski, and Jovan Kočanovski. 1979. *Ilinden I Ilindenskite Tradicii* (Ilinden and the Ilinden Traditions). Bitola, Macedonia: Razvitok.

Ditsias, G. N. 1904. *The Catastrophe of Krousovo: Outrages of Bulgarians and Ottomans against the Greeks*. (in Greek) Athens: S. Vlastos.

Draguycheva, Tsola. 1979. *Macedonia: Not a Cause of Discord but a Factor of Good Neighborliness and Co-operation*. Sofia: Sofia Press.

Du Boulay, Juliet. 1974. *Portrait of a Greek Mountain Village*. Oxford: Clarendon Press.

Duijzings, Ger. 1997. "The Making of Egyptians in Kosovo and Macedonia." In *The Politics of Ethnic Consciousness*. Edited by Cora Govers and Hans Vermeulen, 194–222. New York: St. Martin's Press.

————. 2000. *Religion and the Politics of Identity in Kosovo*. London: Hurst.

Dundes, Alan, ed. 1996. *The Walled-Up Wife: A Casebook*. Madison, WI: University of Wisconsin Press.

Durham, M. E. 1905. *Burden of the Balkans*. London: Thomas Nelson.

Edwards, Lovett Fielding. 1938. *Profane Pilgrimage: Wanderings through Yugoslavia*. London: Duckworth.

Eller, J. D., and R. M. Coughlan. 1993. "The Poverty of Primordialism: The Demystification of Ethnic Attachments." *Ethnic and Racial Studies* 16 (2):183–201.

Evans, Kristi S. 1992. "The Argument of Images: Historical Representation in Solidarity Underground Postage, 1981–87." *American Ethnologist* 19 (4):749–767.

Evans-Pritchard, E. E. 1940. *The Nuer: A Description of the Modes of Livelihood and Political Institutions of a Nilotic People*. New York: Oxford University Press.

Fermor, Patrick Leigh. 1966. *Roumeli: Travels in Northern Greece*. London: John Murray.

Fernandez, James W. 1986. *Persuasions and Performances: The Play of Tropes in Culture*. Bloomington, IN: Indiana University Press.

Ferretjans, Jean-Pierre. 1963. *Essai sur la Notion de Propriété Sociale: De la Propriété Privée à la Propriété Collective: L'Experience Yougoslave de Socialization de l'Agriculture* (An Essay on the Notion of Social Property, from Private to Collective Property: The Yugoslav Experience of the Socialisation of Agriculture). Paris: Pichon et Durand-Auzias.

Filipović, Milenko S. 1982. *Among the People: Native Yugoslav Ethnography. Selected Writing of Milenko S. Filipović*. Edited by Eugene Hammel, et al. Ann Arbor, MI: University of Michigan Press.

Fine, John V. A. 1983. *The Early Medieval Balkans*. Ann Arbor, MI: University of Michigan Press.

Finney, Patrick. 2003. Forthcoming. "The Macedonian Question in the 1920s and the Politics of History." In *The Usable Past: Greek Metahistories*. Edited by K. S. Brown and Yannis Hamilakis, 87–103. Lanham, MD: Lexington.

Fischer-Galati, Stephen. 1973. "The Internal Macedonian Revolutionary Organization: Its Significance in 'Wars of National Liberation.'" *East European Quarterly* 6 (4):454–72.

Fitzpatrick, Sheila. 1999. *Everyday Stalinism: Ordinary Life in Extraordinary Times: Soviet Russia in the 1930s*. Oxford: Oxford University Press.

Fitzpatrick, Sheila, and Robert Gellately. 1996. "Introduction to the Practices of Denunciation in Modern European History." *Journal of Modern History* 68:747–67.

Flores, Richard. 2002. *Remembering the Alamo: Memory, Modernity, and the Master Symbol*. Austin, TX: University of Texas Press.

Ford, George. 1982. "Networks, Ritual and 'Vrski': A Study of Urban Adjustment in Macedonia." Ph.D. diss., Arizona State University.

Foster, George. 1964. "Treasure tales, and the image of the static economy in a Mexican peasant community." *Journal of American Folklore* 77:39–44.

Fox, Richard, ed. 1990. *Nationalist Ideologies and the Production of National Cultures*. Washington, DC: American Ethnological Society Monograph Series.

Franklin Lytle, Paula. 1992. "U.S. Policy Toward the Demise of Yugoslavia: The 'Virus of Nationalism.'" *East European Politics and Societies* 6 (3):303–18.

Fraser, John Foster. 1906. *Pictures from the Balkans*. London: Cassell and Co.

Friedl, Ernestine. 1962. *Vasilika: A Village in Modern Greece*. New York: Holt, Rinehart and Winston.

Friedman, Victor. 1975. "Macedonian Language and Nationalism During the Nineteenth and Early Twentieth Centuries." *Balkanistica* 2:83–98.

―――. 1985. "The Sociolinguistics of Literary Macedonian." *International Journal of the Sociology of Language* 52:31–57.

―――. 1993. "The first philological conference for the establishment of the Macedonian alphabet and the Macedonian literary language: Its precedents and consequences." In *The Earliest Stage of Language Planning: The "First Congress" Phenomenon*. Edited by Joshua Fishman, 159–80. Berlin: Mouton de Gruyter.

―――. 1996. "Observing the Observers: Language, Ethnicity, and Power in the 1994 Macedonian Census and Beyond." In *Toward Comprehensive Peace in Southeast Europe: Conflict Prevention in the South Balkans*. Edited by Barnett R. Rubin, 81–105. New York: Twentieth Century Fund Press.

Fussell, Paul. 1980. *Abroad: British Literary Traveling Between the Wars*. New York: Oxford University Press.

Gal, Susan. 1991. "Bartok's Funeral: Representations of Europe in Hungarian Political Rhetoric." *American Ethnologist* 18 (3):440–58.

Gandolphe, Maurice. 1904. *La Crise Macédonienne* (The Macedonian Crisis). Paris: Perrin.

Garnett, Lucy M. J. 1904. *Turkish Life in Town and Country*. New York: G. P. Putnam's Sons.

Geertz, Clifford. 1963. Reprinted 1973a. "The Integrative Revolution: Primordial Sentiments and Civil Politics in the New States." In *The Interpretation of Cultures*. 255–310. New York: Basic Books.

———. 1963. Reprinted 1973b. Thick Description: Toward an Interpretive Theory of Culture." In *The Interpretation of Cultures.* 3–30. New York: Basic Books.

———. 1983. *Local Knowledge: Further Essays in Interpretive Anthropology.* New York: Basic Books.

———. 1988. *Works and Lives: The Anthropologist as Author.* Stanford, CA: Stanford University Press.

Gellner, Ernest. 1983. *Nations and Nationalism.* Ithaca, NY: Cornell University Press.

Gewehr, Wesley Marsh. 1931. Reprinted 1967. *The Rise of Nationalism in the Balkans, 1800–1930.* Hamden, CT: Archon Books.

Gillis, John, ed. 1994. *Commemorations: The Politics of National Identity.* Princeton, NJ: Princeton University Press.

Glenny, Misha. 1990. *The Rebirth of History: Eastern Europe in the Age of Democracy.* London: Penguin.

———. 1993. *The Fall of Yugoslavia: The Third Balkan War.* London: Penguin.

Gluckman, Max. 1958. *Analysis of a Social Situation in Modern Zululand.* Manchester: Manchester University Press/Rhodes–Livingstone Institute.

Golab, Zbigniew. 1984. *The Arumanian Dialect of Krusevo in SR Macedonia, SFR Yougoslavia.* Skopje: Macedonian Academy of Sciences and Arts, Section of Linguistics and Literary Sciences.

Gordy, Eric. 1999. *The Culture of Power in Serbia: Nationalism and the Destruction of Alternatives.* University Park, PA: Pennsylvania State Press.

Goulbourne, Harry. 1991. *Ethnicity and Nationalism in Post-imperial Britain.* Cambridge: Cambridge University Press.

Gounaris, Basil C. 1993. *Steam Over Macedonia 1870–1912: Socio-Economic Change and the Railway Factor.* New York: Columbia University Press.

Grant, Bruce. 1995. *In the Soviet House of Culture: A Century of Perestroikas.* Princeton, NJ: Princeton University Press.

Green, Peter. 1989. "The Macedonian Connection." In *Classical Bearings: Interpreting Ancient History and Culture.* 151–64. New York: Thames and Hudson.

Greenfeld, Liah. 1992. *Nationalism: Five Roads to Modernity.* Cambridge: Harvard University Press.

Hadži-Dimov, Dimo. 1986. *The Macedonian National Question.* Skopje: Macedonian Review Editions.

Hales, A. G. 1918. *My Life of Adventure.* London: Hodder and Stoughton.

Halpern, Joel M. 1958. *A Serbian Village.* New York: Columbia University Press.

Halpern, Joel M., and Barbara Kerewsky-Halpern. 1972. *A Serbian Village in Historical Perspective.* Prospect Heights, IL: Waveland Press.

Hammel, Eugene. 1968. *Alternative Social Structures and Ritual Relations in the Balkans.* Englewood Cliffs, NJ: Prentice-Hall, Inc.

———. 1972. "The Zadruga as Process." In *Household and Family in Past Time: Comparative Studies in the Size and Structure of the Domestic Group over the Last Three Centuries in England, France, Serbia, Japan, and Colonial North America, with Further Materials from Western Europe.* Edited by P. Laslett and R. Wall, 335–73. New York: Cambridge University Press.

Handler, Richard. 1988. *Nationalism and the Politics of Culture in Quebec.* Madison, WI: University of Wisconsin Press.

———. 1993. "Fieldwork in Quebec, Scholarly Reviews, and Anthropological Dialogues." In *When They Read What We Write: The Politics of Ethnography*. Edited by C. Brettell, 67–74. Westport, CT: Bergin & Garvey.

Hart, Laurie Kain. 1999. "Culture, Civilization and Demarcation at the Northwest Borders of Greece." *American Ethnologist* 26 (1):196–220.

Havel, Václav. 1985. "The Power of the Powerless." In *The Power of the Powerless: Citizens Against the State in Central-Eastern Europe* by Václav Havel, et al. Armonk, NY: M. E. Sharpe.

Hayden, Robert. 1993. "The Triumph of Chauvinistic Nationalisms in Yugoslavia: Bleak Implications for Anthropology." In *The Anthropology of Eastern Europe Review* 11 (1–2):72–78.

———. 1994. "Recounting the Dead: The Rediscovery and Redefinition of Wartime Massacres in Late- and Post-Communist Yugoslavia" In *Memory, History and Opposition Under State Socialism*, Edited by Rubie S. Watson, 167–84. Santa Fe, NM: School of American Research Press.

———. 1999. *Blueprints for a House Divided: The Constitutional Logic of the Yugoslav Conflicts*. Ann Arbor, MI: University of Michigan Press.

Hayes, Carlton J. H. 1927. "Contributions of Herder to the Doctrine of Nationalism." *American Historical Review* 32 (4):719–36.

Herzfeld, Michael. 1985. *The Poetics of Manhood. Contest and Identity in a Cretan Mountain Village*. Princeton, NJ: Princeton University Press.

———. 1986. *Ours Once More: Folklore, Ideology and the Making of Modern Greece*. New York: Pella.

———. 1991. *A Place in History: Social and Monumental Time in a Cretan Town*. Princeton, NJ: Princeton University Press.

———. 1992. *The Social Production of Indifference: Exploring the Symbolic Roots of Western Bureaucracy*. Chicago, IL: University of Chicago Press.

Hobsbawm, Eric J. 1959. *Primitive Rebels: Studies in Archaic Forms of Social Movement in the 19th and 20th Centuries*. New York: W. W. Norton.

Hobsbawm, Eric, and Terence Ranger, eds. 1983. *The Invention of Tradition*. New York: Cambridge University Press.

Holston, James. 1989. *The Modernist City*. Chicago: University of Chicago Press.

Holy, Ladislav. 1996. *The Little Czech and the Great Czech Nation. National Identity and the Post-communist Social Transformation*. London: Cambridge University Press.

Horvat, Branko. 1976. *The Yugoslav Economic System: The First Labor-Managed Economy in the Making*. Armonk, NY: M. E. Sharpe.

Huntington, Samuel P. 1993. "The Clash of Civilizations?" *Foreign Affairs* 73 (2):22–49.

———. 1996. *The Clash of Civilizations and the Remaking of World Order*. New York: Simon & Schuster.

Irby, G. M., and A. P. Mackenzie. 1877. *Travels in the Slavonic Provinces of Turkey-in-Europe*. London: Dalby, Isbister & Co.

Ivanovski, Orde. 1973. "Nikola Karev—Organizer of the Kruševo republic." In *The Epic of Ilinden*. Edited by Boris Vishinksi, 133–44. Skopje: Macedonia Review Editions.

Jelavich, Barbara. 1954–55. "The British Traveller in the Balkans: The Abuses of Ottoman Administration in the Slavonic Provinces." *Slavonic and East European Review* 33:396–413.

Jenkins, Romilly. 1961. *The Dilessi Murders*. London: Longmans.

Kapferer, Bruce. 1988. *Legends of People, Myths of State*. Washington, DC: Smithsonian Institute Press.

Kaplan, Robert. 1991. "History's Cauldron." *Atlantic Monthly* (June):93–104.

———. 1993. *Balkan Ghosts: A Journey through History*. New York: St. Martin's Press.

Karakasidou, Anastasia. 1993. "Politicizing Culture: Negating Ethnic Identity in Greek Macedonia." *Journal of Modern Greek Studies* 11 (1):1–28.

———. 1994. "National Ideologies, Histories and Popular Consciousness: A Response to Three Critics." *Balkan Studies* 35(1):113–46.

———. 1997a. *Fields of Wheat, Hills of Blood: Passages to Nationhood in Greek Macedonia 1870–1990*. Chicago: University of Chicago Press.

———. 1997b. "Women of the Familly, Women of the Nation: National Enculturation among Slav-speakers in North-west Greece." In *Ourselves and Others: The Development of a Greek Macedonian Cultural Identity Since 1912*. Edited by Peter Mackridge and Eleni Yannakakis, 91–110. Oxford: Berg.

———. 2000. "Transforming Identity, Constructing Consciousness: Coercion and Homogeneity in Northwestern Greece." In *The Macedonian Question: Culture, Historiography, Politics*. Edited by Victor Roudometof, 55–98. Boulder, CO: East European Monographs.

Kennan, George F. ed. 1914. Reprinted 1993. *The Other Balkan Wars: A 1913 Carnegie Endowment Inquiry in Retrospect with a New Introduction and Reflections on the Present Conflict*. Washington, DC: Carnegie Endowment for International Peace.

Kertzer, David I., and Dominique Arel. 2002. *Census and identity: the politics of race, ethnicity, and language in national censuses*. Cambridge and New York: Cambridge University Press.

Kirov-Majski, Nikola. 1924. *Ilinden* (in Bulgarian). Sofia.

———. 1935. Reprinted 1991. *Krušovo and the Struggles for its Freedom* (in Bulgarian). Sofia: Stopansko Razvitie.

———. 1994. *Stranici od Mojot život*. (Pages from My Life.) Skopje: Kultura.

Kofos, Evangelos. 1964. *Nationalism and Communism in Macedonia*. Thessaloniki: Institute for Balkan Studies.

———. 1984. "Attempts at Mending the Greek-Bulgarian Ecclesiastical Schism 1875–1902." *Balkan Studies* 25(2):347–68.

———. 1986a. "The Macedonian Question: The Politics of Mutation." *Balkan Studies* 27(1):157–72.

———. 1986b. "Patriarch Joachim III (1878–1884) and the Irredentist Policy of the Greek State." *Journal of Modern Greek Studies* 4 (2):107–120.

———. 1993. "National Heritage and National Identity in Nineteenth and Twentieth Century Macedonia." In *Nationalism & Communism in Macedonia: Civil Conflict, Politics of Mutation, National Identity* 305–30. New Rochelle, NY: Aristide D. Caratzas.

———. 1995. "The Impact of the Macedonian Question on Civil Conflict in Greece, 1943–1949." In *Greece at the Crossroads: The Civil War and its Legacy*. Edited by John O. Iatrides and Linda Wrigley. University Park, PA: University of Pennsylvania Press.

Kohl, Philip, and C. Fawcett, eds. 1995. *Nationalism, Politics and the Practice of Archaeology*. Cambridge: Cambridge University Press.

Kohn, Hans. 1962. *The Age of Nationalism.* New York: Harper and Row.

Kovačić, Olga. 1947. *Women of Yugoslavia.* Belgrade: Jugoslovenska Knjiga.

Kudžulovska, Galena. 1970. "Proslavuvanje na Ilinden vo Narodno-oslobitelnata borba vo periodot 1941–44 godina." (Commemorations of Ilinden during the National-Liberation Struggle in the period 1941–44.). In *Ilinden 1903.* Edited by Mihailo Apostolski, et al., 647–54. Skopje: Institut za Nacionala Istorija.

Kulić, Dimitrije. 1970. *Bugarska Okupacija 1941–44* (Bulgarian Occupation 1941–44). Niš, Yugoslavia: Prosveta.

Laitin, David. 1998. *Identity in Formation. The Russian-Speaking Populations in the Near Abroad.* Ithaca, NY: Cornell University Press.

Lange-Akhund, Nadine. 1998. *The Macedonian Question, 1893–1908 From Western Sources.* Boulder, CO: East European Monographs.

Langguth, A. J. 1981. *Saki: a life of Hector Hugh Munro.* New York: Simon and Schuster.

Lape, Ljuben. 1953. "Novi dokumenti za Ilindenskoto Vostanie" (New Documents on the Ilinden Uprising). In *Ilindenski Zbornik 1903–1953* (Ilinden Collection 1903–1953). Skopje: Institut za Nacionalna Istorija.

———. 1973. "The Republic of Krushevo." In *The Epic of Ilinden.* Edited by Boris Vishinski. 117–32. Skopje, Macedonia: Macedonian Review Editions.

———. 1983. "Commentary." In *Prilozi za Ilinden* V (Contributions on Ilinden Volume 5). Kruševo: Sovet "Deset Dena Kruševska Republika."

Laqueuer, Thomas W. 1994. "Memory and Naming in the Great War." In *Commemorations: The Politics of National Identity.* Edited by J. R. Gillis, 150–67. Princeton, NJ: Princeton University Press.

Lass, Andrew. 1988. "Romantic documents and political monuments: The meaning-fulfillment of history in 19th-century Czech nationalism." *American Ethnologist* 15 (3):456–71.

Lear, Edward. 1851. Reprinted 1988. *Journals of a Landscape Painter in Greece and Albania.* London: Century.

Lebrun, Fr. and I. Voinescu. 1911. *Macedonia.* Bucarest: Institut d'Arts Graphiques Charles Gobl.

Lewis, Oscar. 1953. *Tepotzlan Restudied: A Critique of the Folk-Urban Conceptualization of Social Change.* In *Anthropological Essays,* 35–52. New York: Random House.

Lodge, Olive. 1934–35. "St. Peter's Day in Galichnik." *The Slavonic Review* 13:650–73.

———. 1941. *Peasant Life in Yugoslavia.* London: Seeley, Service & Co.

Loggio, G. C. 1919. *Bulgaria: Problems and Politics.* London: Heinemann.

Loustas, Nikolaos A. 1994. *I Istoria tou Nimfaiou-Neveskas-Florinis* (The History of Nimfaio/Neveska, Florina). Thessaloniki: Ziti.

Lunt, Horace G. 1984. "Some Sociolinguistic Aspects of Macedonian and Bulgarian." In *Language and Literary Theory.* Edited by Benjamin A. Stolz, I. R. Titunik, and Lubomir Doležel, 83–132. Ann Arbor, MI: University of Michigan Press.

Lyon, James. 1996. "Yugoslavia's Hyperinflation 1993–1994: A Social History." *East European Politics and Societies* 10 (2):293–327.

MacDermott, Mercia. 1988. *For Freedom and Perfection: The Life of Yane Sandansky.* London: Journeyman.

Magaš, Branka. 1993. *The Destruction of Yugoslavia: Tracking the Break-Up 1980–92*. London: Verso.

Markovski, Venko. 1984. *Goli Otok: The Island of Death*. Boulder, CO: Social Science Monographs.

Martin Willis, P. L. 1906. *A Captive of the Bulgarian Brigand: An Englishman's Terrible Experiences in Macedonia*. London: Ede, Allum & Townsend.

Matkovski, Aleksandar. 1978. *Istorija na Kruševo i Kruševsko* (A History of Kruševo and its region). Kruševo: Sobranie na Opštinata i opštinski odbor na sojuzot na borcite od NOB—Kruševo.

———. 1982. *A History of the Jews in Macedonia*. Skopje: Macedonian Review Editions.

McClellan, W. D. 1964. *Svetozar Markovic and the Origins of Balkan Socialism*. Princeton, NJ: Princeton University Press.

Meillassoux, Claude. 1981. *Maidens, Meal and Money. Capitalism and the Domestic Community*. Cambridge: Cambridge University Press.

Meskell, Lynn, ed. 1998. *Archaeology Under Fire: Nationalism, politics and heritage in the Eastern Mediterranean and Middle East*. London: Routledge.

Mihailov, Ivan. 1967. "The Macedonian Rumanians." *Balkania* 1 (4):10–14.

Misirkov, Krste P. 1974. *On Macedonian Matters*. Skopje: Macedonian Review Editions.

Mitchell, Timothy. 1991. *Colonizing Egypt*. Berkeley, CA: University of California Press.

Moore, Frederick. 1906. *The Balkan Trail*. London: Smith, Elder and Co.

Mosley, Philip E. 1940. Reprinted 1976. "The Zadruga, or Communal Joint-family in the Balkans, and its Recent Evolution." In *Communal Families in the Balkans: The Zadruga. Essays by Philip E. Mosley and Essays in His Honor*. Edited by H. F. Byrnes, 19–30. Notre Dame, IN: University of Notre Dame Press.

Mosse, George. 1975. *The Nationalization of the Masses. Political Symbolism and Mass Movements in Germany from the Napoleonic Wars through the Third Reich*. Ithaca, NY: Cornell University Press.

Munro, H. H. 1919. *The Toys of Peace and Other Essays*. New York: John Lane.

Nairn, Tom. 1997. *Faces of Nationalism: Janus Revisited*. London: Verso.

Nora, Pierre. 1989. "Between Memory and History: Les Lieux de Mémoire." *Representations* 26:7–25.

Nora, Pierre, ed. 1997. *Realms of Memory: The Construction of the French Past: Traditions* Vol. 2. New York: Columbia University Press.

Obolensky, D. 1974. *The Byzantine Commonwealth: Eastern Europe 500–1453*. London: Weidenfeld & Nicolson.

Palmer, Stephen E., and Robert R. King. 1971. *Yugoslav Communism and the Macedonian Question*. Hamden, CT: Archon.

Pandevski, Manol. 1978. *Ilindenskoto Vostanie 1903* (The Ilinden Uprising 1903). Skopje: Institut za Nacionalna Istorija.

Perry, Duncan. 1986. "Ivan Garvanov, Architect of Ilinden." *East European Quarterly* 19 (4):403–16.

———. 1988. *The Politics of Terror: The Macedonian Revolutionary Movements, 1893–1903*. Durham, NC: Duke University Press.

Phillipov, G. 1995a. Letter to the Editor. *Slavic Review* 54 (1):253–54.

———. 1995b. "Macedonia then and now: A comment on Brown." *Antiquity* 69: 383–84.

Plamenatz, John. 1974. "Two Types of Nationalism." In *Nationalism: The Nature and Evolution of an Idea*. Edited by E. Kamenka, 22–37. Canberra: Australian University Press.

Popović, D. J. 1937. *O Cincarima* (Regarding the Vlahs). Belgrade: Drag

Poulton, Hugh. 1995. *Who Are the Macedonians?* Bloomington, IN: Indiana University Press.

Putnam, Robert. 1993. *Making Democracy Work: Civic Traditions in Modern Italy*. Princeton, NJ: Princeton University Press.

Radin, George. 1946. *Economic Reconstruction in Yugoslavia: A Practical Plan for the Balkans*. New York: King's Crown Press.

Ramet, Pedro. 1984. *Nationalism and Federalism in Yugoslavia, 1963–1983*. Bloomington, IN: Indiana University Press.

Rappaport, Joanne. 1990. *The Politics of Memory: Native Historical Interpretation in the Colombian Andes*. Cambridge: Cambridge University Press.

Redfield, Robert. 1956. Reprinted 1960. *Peasant Society and Culture* and *The Little Community*. Chicago, IL: University of Chicago Press.

Reed, John. 1916. Reprinted 1999. *The War in Eastern Europe: Travels through the Balkans in 1915*. London: Phoenix.

Reineck, Janet. 1991. "The Past as Refuge: Gender, Migration and Ideology Among the Kosova Albanians." Ph.D. diss., University of California, Berkeley.

Reiss, R. A. 1924. *The Comitadji Question in Southern Serbia*. London: Hazell, Watson & Viney.

Renan, Ernst. 1990. "What is a nation?" In *Nation and Narration*. Edited by Homi K. Bhabha, 8–22. London: Routledge.

Rheubottom, David B. 1976a. "The Saint's Feast and Skopska Crna Goran Social Structure." *Man* 11 (1):18–34.

———. 1976b. "Time and Form: Contemporary Macedonian Households and the Zadruga Controversy." In *Communal Families in the Balkans: The Zadruga. Essays by Philip E. Mosley and Essays in His Honor*. Edited by R. F. Byrnes, 215–31. Notre Dame, IN: University of Notre Dame Press.

———. 1980. "Dowry and Wedding Celebrations in Yugoslav Macedonia". In *The Meaning of Marriage Payments*. Edited by J. L. Comaroff, 221–49. London: Academic Press.

Risteski, Kirche Petrov. 1983. *Mojata Revolucionerna i partiska rabota pred i za vreme na NOB* (My Revolutionary and Party work before and during NOB). Unpublished manuscript. Kruševo.

Roeder, Philip. 1999. "Peoples and States after 1989: The Political Costs of Incomplete National Revolutions." *Slavic Review* 58 (4):854–82.

Rosaldo, Renato. 1993. *Culture and Truth: The Remaking of Social Analysis*. Boston: Beacon.

Rossos, A. 1994. "The British Foreign Office and Macedonian National Identity, 1918–1941." *Slavic Review* 53 (2):369–94.

———. 1995. "Reply to G. Phillipov." *Slavic Review* 54 (1):255.

Routier, Gaston. 1903. *La Question Macédonienne* (The Macedonian Question). Paris: H. Le Soudier.

Sahlins, Marshall. 1985. *Islands of History*. London and Chicago: University of Chicago Press.

Sahlins, Peter. 1989. *Boundaries: The Making of France and Spain in the Pyrenees.* Berkeley: University of California Press.

Said, Edward. 1978. *Orientalism.* New York: Pantheon Books.

Sanders, Irwin. 1948. *Balkan Village.* Lexington: University of Kentucky Press.

Šapardan. n.d. Spomeni na Kole Zdravev-Šapardan (Memoirs of Kole Zdravev-Šapardan). Unpublished typescript.

Schwartz, Jonathan. 2000. "Blessing the Water the Macedonian Way: Improvisations of Identity in Diaspora and in the Homeland." In *Macedonia: The Politics of Identity and Difference.* Edited by Jane K. Cowan, 104–21. London: Pluto.

Sciaky, Leon. 1946. *Farewell to Salonica: Portrait of an Era.* New York: A. A. Wyn.

Scott, James C. 1998. *Seeing Like a State: How Certain Schemes to Improve the Human Condition Have Failed.* New Haven, CT: Yale University Press.

Segalen, Martine. 1986. *The Historical Anthropology of the Family.* Translated by J. C. Whitehouse and Sarah Matthews. Cambridge: Cambridge University Press.

Sekulic, D., G. Massey and R. Hodson. 1994. "Who were the Yugoslavs? Failed sources of a common identity in the former Yugoslavia." *American Sociological Review* 59 (1):83–97.

Seremetakis, C. Nadia. 1994. "The Memory of the Senses, Part I: Marks of the Transitory." In *The Senses Still: Perception and Memory as Material Culture in Modernity.* Edited by C. Nadia Seremetakis, 1–18. Chicago, IL: University of Chicago Press.

Seton-Watson, Robert William. 1917. *The Rise of Nationality in the Balkans.* London: Constable & Co.

Shils, Edward. 1957. "Primordial, Personal, Sacred and Civil Ties: Some Particular Observations on the Relationships of Sociological Research and Theory." *British Journal of Sociology* 6 (2):130–45.

Shoup, Paul. 1968. *Communism and the Yugoslav National Question.* New York: Columbia University Press.

Sicard, Emile. 1976. "The Zadruga Community: A Phase in the Evolution of Property and Family in an Agrarian Milieu." In *Communal Families in the Balkans: The Zadruga. Essays by Philip E. Mosley and Essays in His Honor.* Edited by R. F. Byrnes, 252–67. Notre Dame, IN: University of Notre Dame Press.

Silber, Laura, and Allan Little. 1996. *Yugoslavia: Death of a Nation.* New York: TV Books.

Silberman, Neil A. 1989. *Between Past and Present: Archaeology, Ideology and Nationalism in the Modern Middle East.* New York: Henry Holt & Co.

Simic, Andrei. 1973. *The Peasant Urbanites: A Study of Rural-Urban Mobility in Serbia.* New York: Seminar Press.

Simovski, Todor, et al., eds. 1997. *Nastanite na Skopskoto Kale na 7 Januari 1945 godina: Dokumenti* (The Events on Skopje's citadel on 7 January 1945: Documents). Skopje: Archives of Macedonia, Institute for National History and Matica Makedonska.

Skendi, Stavro. 1967. *The Albanian National Awakening, 1878–1912.* Princeton, NJ: Princeton University Press.

Smith, Arthur D. Howden. 1908. *Fighting the Turk in the Balkans: An American's Adventures with the Macedonian Revolutionists.* New York: G. P. Putnam's Sons.

Smith, Anthony D. 1979. *Nationalism in the Twentieth Century.* New York: New York University Press.

Smollett, Eleanor W. 1989. "The economy of jars." *Ethnologia Europaea* 19 (2):125–40.

Sokolovsky, Joan. 1990. *Peasants and Power: State Autonomy and the Collectivization of Agriculture in Eastern Europe*. Boulder, CO: Westview Press.

Sonnischen, Albert. 1909. *Confessions of a Macedonian Bandit*. New York: Duffield and Company.

Stavrianos, L. S. 1958. *The Balkans Since 1453*. New York: Rinehart & Co.

St. Erlich, Vera. 1966. *Family in Transition: A Study of 300 Yugoslav Villages*. Princeton, NJ: Princeton University Press.

Stoianovich, Traian. 1960. "The Conquering Balkan Orthodox Merchant." *The Journal of Economic History* XX:234–313.

Stojčev, Vanče. 1996. *Bugarskiot Okupaciski Sistem vo Makedonija 1941–1944* (The Bulgarian System of Occupation in Macedonia 1941–1944). Skopje: Grigor Prličev.

Stoller, Paul. 1989. *The Taste of Ethnographic Things: The Senses in Anthropology*. Philadelphia: University of Pennsylvania Press.

Stone, Ellen. 1902. "Six Months Among Brigands." *McClure's Magazine* 19 (1):3–16; 19 (2):99–119; 19 (3):222–31; 19 (5):464–71; 19 (6):562–70.

Sudetic, Chuck. 1998. *Blood and Vengeance: One Family's Story of the War in Bosnia*. New York: W. W. Norton.

Sugarman, Jane. 1997. *Engendering Song: Singing and Subjectivity at Prespa Albanian Weddings*. Chicago, IL: University of Chicago Press.

Sutton, David E. 1997. "Local Names, Foreign Claims: Family Inheritance and National Heritage on a Greek Island." *American Ethnologist* 24(4):837–52.

———. 1998. *Memories Cast in Stone. The Relevance of the Past in Everyday Life*. Oxford: Berg.

Swire, Joseph. 1939. *Bulgarian Conspiracy*. London: Robert Hale.

Tanaskova, Fidanka, et al., eds. 1993. *Den na Razdelenite* (A Day for the Divided). Skopje: Nova Makedonija/Association of Macedonians from the Aegean Part of Macedonia.

Tannen, Deborah. 1998. *The Argument Culture: Moving from Debate to Dialogue*. New York: Random House.

Tennyson, Hallam. 1955. *Tito Lifts the Curtain: The Story of Yugoslavia Today*. London: Rider and Company.

Terzioski, Rastislav. 1974. *Denacionalizatorskata Dejnost na Bugarskite Kulturnoprosvetni Institucii vo Makedonija* (The De-Nationalizing Activities of Bulgarian Cultural-Educational Institutions in Macedonia). Skopje: Institut za Nacionala Istorija.

Thiessen, Ilka. 1999. "'T'ga za Jug—Waiting for Macedonia: The Changing World of Young Female Engineers in the Republic of Macedonia." Ph.D. diss., London School of Economics.

Thompson, Mark. 1992. *A Paper House: The Ending of Yugoslavia*. London: Vintage.

Tito, Josip Broz, ed. 1977. *Nikola Karev: Vreme i Delo* (Nikola Karev: His Life and Work). Skopje: Naša Kniga & Institut za Nacionalna Istorija.

Todorova, Maria. 1993. *Balkan Family Structure and the European Pattern: Demographic Developments in Ottoman Bulgaria*. Washington, DC: The American University Press.

———. 1994. "The Balkans: From Discovery to Invention." *Slavic Review* 53 (2):453–82.

————. 1997. *Imagining the Balkans*. Oxford: Oxford University Press.

Tomalevski, Georgi. 1968. *Krušovskata Republika* (The Kruševo Republic). Sofia: Bulgarski Pisatel.

Tomasevich, Jozo. 1955. *Peasants, Politics and Economic Change in Yugoslavia*. Stanford: Stanford University Press.

————. 1958. "Collectivization of Agriculture in Yugoslavia." In *Collectivization of Agriculture in Eastern Europe*. Edited by I. Sanders. 166–92. Lexington, KY: University of Kentucky Press.

————. 1969. "Yugoslavia During the Second World War." In *Contemporary Yugoslavia: Twenty Years of Socialist Experiment*. Edited by W. Vucinich. 59–118. Berkeley, CA: University of California Press.

Topuzoski, Krsto A. 1986. *The Battle of Mečkin Kamen Kruševo*. Bitola, Macedonia: Kiro Dandaro.

Torpey, John C. 2000. *The Invention of the Passport: Surveillance, Citizenship and the State*. Cambridge: Cambridge University Press.

Trajanovski, Aleksandar. 1983. "Učestvoto na Selanstvoto od Kruševsko vo Ilindenskoto Vostanie" (The participation of the village population from the Kruševo region in the Ilinden Uprising); *Prilozi za Ilinden* V (Contributions on Ilinden Volume 5), 325–44. Kruševo: Sovet "Deset Dena Kruševska Republika."

Trajkovski, Gjorgi. 1986. *Pregled na spomenicite i spomen-obeležjatat vo SR Makedonija* (Survey of Monuments and Memorial Objects in SR Macedonia). Skopje: Republički zavod za zaštita na spomenicite na kulturata.

Troebst, Stefan. 1997. "Yugoslav Macedonia, 1943–1953: Building the Party, the State, and the Nation. In *State-Society Relations in Yugoslavia, 1945–1992*. Edited by Melissa K. Bokovoy, Jill A. Irvine and Carol S. Lilly, 243–66. New York: St. Martin's Press.

Trouillot, Michel-Rolph. 1995. *Silencing the Past: Power and the Production of History*. Boston, MA: Beacon Press.

Trpkoski, Vangel J. 1986. Vlasite na Balkanot (The Vlahs in the Balkans). Skopje: Združenie prijateli na Vlasite od rodniot kraj "Pitu Guli."

Upward, Allen. 1908. *The East End of Europe: The Report of an Unofficial Mission to the European Provinces of Turkey on the Eve of the Revolution*. London: John Murray.

U.S. Department of State. 1954. "Macedonian Nationalism and the Communist Party of Yugoslavia." Typescript. Washington, DC.

Van Boeschoten, Riki. 2000. "When Difference Matters: Sociopolitical Dimensions of Ethnicity in the District of Florina." In *Macedonia: The Politics of Identity and Difference*. Edited by Jane K. Cowan, 28–46. London: Pluto Press.

Van der Port, Mattijs. 1998. *Gypsies, Wars & Other Instances of the Wild: Civilisation and Its Discontents in a Serbian Town*. Amsterdam: Amsterdam University Press.

Vasiliadis, Peter. 1989. *Whose Are You? Identity and Ethnicity Among the Toronto Macedonians*. New York: AMS Press, Inc.

Vavouskos, Konstantine. 1959. *I simvoli tou Ellinismou tis Pelagonias eis tin istorian tis neoteras Ellados* (The contributions of Hellenism in Pelagonia to the History of Modern Greece). Thessaloniki: Society for Macedonian Studies.

————. 1973. *Greek Macedonia's Struggle for Freedom*. Thessaloniki: Society for Macedonian Studies.

Verdery, Katherine. 1992. "Comment: Hobsbawm in the East." *Anthropology Today* 8/1: 8–10.

———. 1994. "From Parent-state to Family Patriarchs: Gender and Nation in Contemporary Eastern Europe." *East European Politics and Societies Special Issue: Gender and Nation.* 8 (2):225–55.

———. 1999. *The Political Lives of Dead Bodies.* New York: Columbia University Press.

Vereni, Pietro 1998. *Diaforentità: Il Duplice Confine Dell'Individuo e Dello Stato in Macedonia Occidentale Greca.* Difference: The Double Frontier of the Individual and the State in Western Greek Macedonia. (in Italian). Unpublished Ph.D. diss. Università "La Sapienza," Rome.

———. 2000. "Os Ellin Makedonas: Autobiography, Memory and National Identity in Western Greek Macedonia." In *Macedonia: The Politics of Identity and Difference.* Edited by Jane K. Cowan, 47–67. London: Pluto.

Vermeulen, Hans. 1984. "Greek Cultural Dominance Among the Orthodox Population of Macedonia During the Last Period of Ottoman Rule." In *Cultural Dominance in the Mediterranean Area.* Edited by Anton Blok and Henk Driessen, 225–55. Nijmegen, The Netherlands: Katholieke Universteit.

Vishinski, Boris. 1973. *Macedonian Vistas.* Belgrade: Yugoslav Review/Borba.

Vodopiveć, Peter. 1992. "Slovenes and Yugoslavia, 1918–1991." *East European Politics and Societies* 6 (3):220–41.

Voutira, Efi. 1997. "Population Transfers and Resettlement Policies in Inter-war Europe: The Case of Asia Minor Refugees in Macedonia from an International and National Perspective." In *Ourselves and Others: The Development of a Greek Macedonian Cultural Identity Since 1912.* Edited by Peter Mackridge and Eleni Yannakakis, 111–32. Oxford: Berg.

Vražinovski, Tanas. 1981. *Ilindenski Prozen Revolucioneren Folklor* (Ilinden Revolutionary Folklore in Prose). Skopje: Institut za Folklor "Marko K. Cepenkov."

Vucinich, Wayne S. 1969. *Contemporary Yugoslavia: Twenty Years of Socialist Experiment.* Berkeley, CA: University of California Press.

Vukmanović, Svetozar. 1990. *Struggle for the Balkans.* London: Merlin Press.

Wace, A.J.B., and M. S. Thompson. 1914. *The Nomads of the Balkans: An Account of Life and Customs among the Vlachs of Northern Pindus.* London: Methuen.

Wagner-Pacifici, Robin, and Barry Schwartz. 1991. "The Vietnam Veterans Memorial: Commemorating a Difficult Past." *American Journal of Sociology* 97 (2):376–420.

Wallerstein, Immanuel. 1991. "Social Conflict in Post-Independence Black Africa: The Concepts of Race and Status-Group Reconsidered." In *Race, Nation, Class: Ambiguous Identities.* Edited by É. Balibar and I. Wallerstein, 187–203. London: Verso.

Wallis, H. M. 1914. "The Devastation of Macedonia." *The Quarterly Review* 220: 506–23.

Walshe, Douglas. 1920. *With the Serbs in Macedonia.* London: John Lane & the Bodley Head.

Watson, Rubie S., ed. 1994. *Memory, History and Opposition Under State Socialism.* Santa Fe, NM: School of American Research Press.

Weller, Marc. 1992. "The International Response to the Dissolution of the Socialist

Federal Republic of Yugoslavia." *American Journal of International Law* 86:569–607.

West, Rebecca. 1941. *Black Lamb, Gray Falcon*. New York: Viking.

Wilkinson, H. R. 1951. *Maps and Politics: A Review of the Ethnographic Cartography of Macedonia*. Manchester: Manchester University Press.

Williams, Abiodun. 2000. *Preventing War: The United Nations and Macedonia*. London: Rowman & Littlefield.

Winnifrith, T. J. 1987. *The Vlachs: The History of a Balkan People*. New York: St. Martin's Press.

Wittgenstein, Ludwig. 1958. *Philosophical Investigations*. Oxford: Basil Blackwell.

Woodward, Susan L. 1994. *Balkan Tragedy: Chaos and Dissolution After the Cold War*. Washington, DC: The Brookings Institution.

Wright, Patrick. 1985. *On Living in an Old Country: The National Past in Contemporary Britain*. London: Verso.

Wright Mills, C. 1959. *The Sociological Imagination*. London: Oxford University Press.

Wyon, Reginald. 1904. *The Balkans From Within*. London: James Finch.

Young, George. 1915. *Nationalism and War in the Near East*. Oxford: Clarendon Press.

Young, James E. 1989. "The Biography of a Memorial Icon: Nathan Rapoport's Warsaw Ghetto Monument." *Representations* 26:69–106.

———. 1993. *The Texture of Memory: Holocaust Memorials and Meaning*. New Haven, CT: Yale University Press.

Ypomnima ton en Thessaloniki, Florina i Athenais Syndesmon Monastirioton (Memoirs of the League of Monastirotes in Thessaloniki, Florina and Athens). Thessaloniki: Papanesteros Press. 1920.

Žecević, Miodrag, and Bogdan Lekić. 1991. *Frontiers and Internal Territorial Division in Yugoslavia*. Belgrade: Ministry of Information of the Republic of Serbia.

Zimmerman, William. 1993. "Migration and Security in Yugoslavia." In *International Migration and Security*. Edited by Myron Weiner, Boulder, CO: Westview Press.

Živković, Marko Dušan. 2001. "Serbian Stories of Identity and Destiny in the 1980s and 1990s." Ph.D. diss., University of Chicago.

Zografski, Dančo. 1948. *Kruševskata Republika* (The Kruševo Republic). Skopje: Zemski Odbor na Narodniot Front.

Zonabend, Françoise. 1984. *The Enduring Memory: Time and History in a French Village*. Manchester: Manchester University Press.

Periodicals & Newspapers

Glasnik
Guardian
Makedoniki Zoi
MILS News
New York Times
Nova Makedonija
Service Newspaper of the Republic of Macedonia
Times (also referred to as London *Times*)
U.S. Department of State Dispatch

Archives

Archives du Ministère des Affaires Etrangères (AMAE/NS)
British Foreign Office Public Records (FO)
Grabul Archive, National Archives of Macedonia
Ilinden Dossier, National Archives of Macedonia
Nikola Kirov-Majski Archives, National Archives of Macedonia
British Documents on Foreign Affairs

Filmography

Republika na Plamen (Republic Ablaze) (dir. Ljubiša Georgievski, 1969).
Ulysses' Gaze (dir. Theo Angelopoulos, 1995).
We Are all Neighbours (dir. Debbie Christie and Tone Bringa, 1993).

Index

Page numbers in bold type indicate figures.